AF333136

FOR THE FRIENDS
OF NATURE AND ART

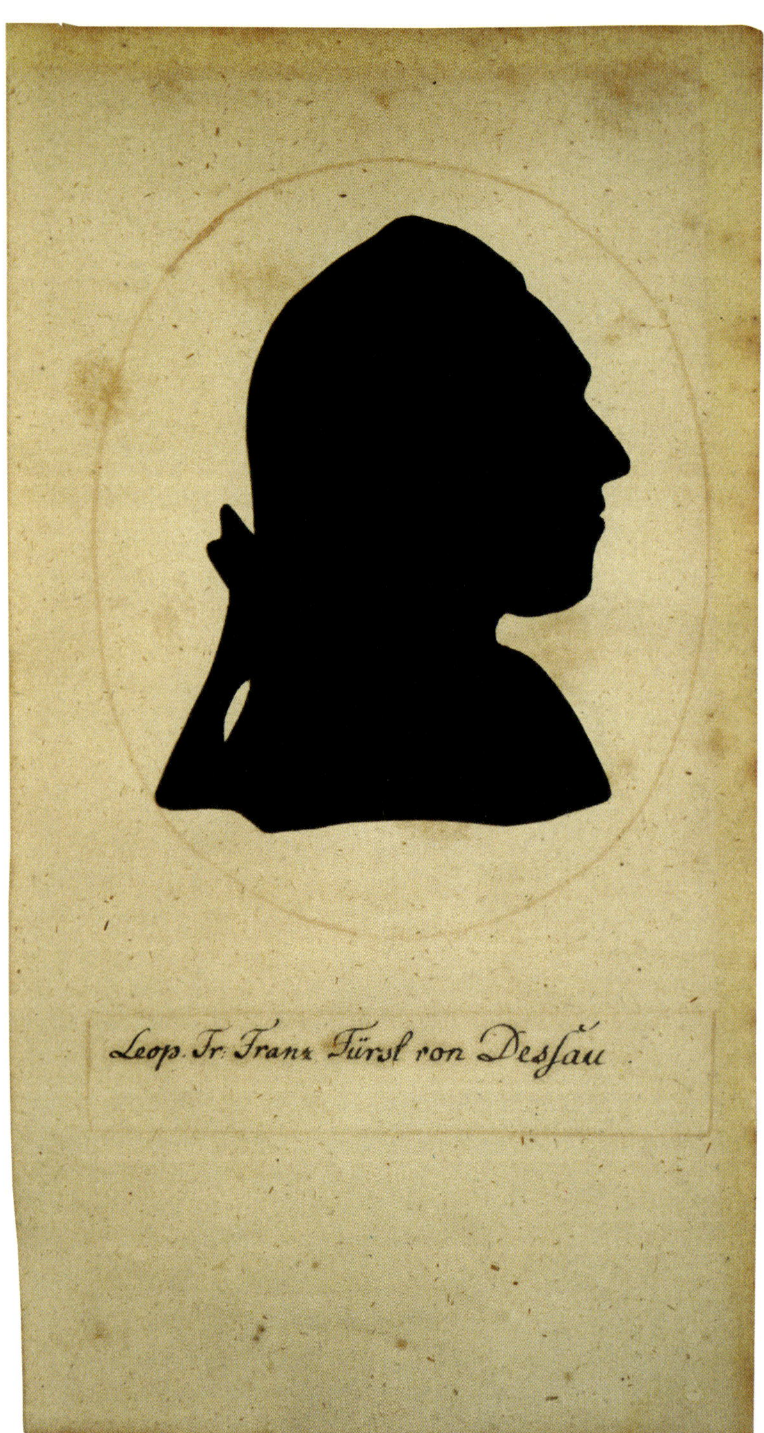

Leop. Fr: Franz Fürst von Dessau

FOR THE FRIENDS OF NATURE AND ART

The Garden Kingdom of
Prince Franz von Anhalt-Dessau
in Age of Enlightenment

Verlag Gerd Hatje

CONTENTS

This exhibition is devoted to the "garden kingdom" of Dessau-Wörlitz, as it is known today, an area encompassing some 300 square kilometres along the middle course of the Elbe and the lower Mulde Rivers. The exhibition and the catalogue are the products of a co-operative effort involving the Institut für Auslandsbeziehungen and the Kulturstiftung DessauWörlitz. The goal of this venture is to offer a broad public the opportunity to become acquainted with the exemplary life's vision of the Prince Leopold III. Friedrich Franz von Anhalt-Dessau during the Age of Enlightenment. The history of the region remains an object of fascination to this day. Despite its relatively small size, the fate of the principality was closely interwoven with the vagaries of European politics and caught up in the military conflicts involving the major powers. Although due in part to the particular personality of the Prince himself, his territory's role during this period is attributable as well to its geopolitical position between the kingdoms of Prussia and Saxony. The years of Prince Franz's rule changed Anhalt-Dessau in fundamental ways, although the pace of development was by no means uniform. The Prince's ideas took shape slowly at first, and the pioneering reforms came to an abrupt end with his death in 1817.

The title of the exhibition, "For the Friends of Nature and Art" alludes to the inscription above the portal of the pantheon built between 1795 and 1797 according to plans drawn by Friedrich Wilhelm von Erdmannsdorff under the Prince's commission. The pantheon was designed primarily to preserve and exhibit the royal collection of classical antiques. In keeping with Franz's principle of uniting beauty and utility, it was also used as a watchtower to observe the Elbe during periods of flooding. The interplay of nature and art emphasized in the garden kingdom was a topic of animated discussion in the age of Jean-Jacques Rousseau. And the subject is no less significant today – more than two hundred years after the inspired rule of Prince Franz von Anhalt-Dessau, a period that witnessed a multitude of reforms and a concerted effort to promote peace and toleration. Indeed, his principle of making economical use of resources is as germane in our time as it ever was. The fact that the garden kingdom, preserved as a historical monument, is an integral part of the "Mittlere Elbe-Steckby-Lödderitzer Forst", a biosphere established as a UNESCO protectorate, further underscores the significance of this cultural landscape.

The attempt to come to grips with a phenomenon as complex as the reform program of Prince Franz von Anhalt-Dessau, and in particular his ideas about landscape design, taxes the medium of the exhibition to its utmost limits. The selection of items for exhibition was based upon the significance of particular objects to the concepts upon which the entire complex was founded and to the history of public response to the garden kingdom. This goal has been achieved, thanks to the diverse efforts of many people, although it should be noted that matters of conservation always occupy the centre of attention in the case of an exhibition tour. The catalogue represents the fruitful work of many hands. The contributions of Michael Stürmer and Ursula Bode have enhanced its value immensely. They have succeeded with great sensitivity in sketching the Prince's reform policy during the latter half of the 19th century and in painting a personal portrait of Princess Luise, interpreted in light of previously unexamined aspects. The third major text is a recently discovered authentic source document which provides essential information about important events that occurred during the first journey of Prince Franz to England in 1763. Together with the illuminating commentaries, this primary source, illustrated with numerous scenes from the period, is now accessible to scholars interested in Wörlitz. It is hoped that all three texts will provide impulses for new avenues of thought and fresh insights. In the catalogue of works on exhibit Daniela Clare and Uwe Quilitzsch describe the nearly one hundred exhibited items. In deliberately brief explanatory sequence texts and object descriptions the authors have taken a didactic approach in an effort to provide general overviews and to establish patterns of relationship. Read within the context of the illustrations, many of which are published here for the first time, the texts offer even the layman access to the world of ideas embodied in the garden kingdom of Dessau-Wörlitz.

The Leipzig photographer Lutz Winkler, who has visited the garden kingdom with his camera at every season of the year for the past two decades, accompanies both the reader of the catalogue and the visitor to the exhibition on their personal journeys with his highly evocative black-and-white photographs. Particularly impressive are the panoramic views which correspond closely to famous pictorial renderings of garden scenes showing a dense network of vistas and views. The value of these fifteen photographs, however, is not confined to their documentary content alone but is also to be found in their imposing visual aesthetics.

The tasks of exhibition co-ordination and catalogue editing were entrusted to the capable hands of Bernd Burock at the Institut für Auslandsbeziehungen and to those of Uwe Quilitzsch at the Kulturstiftung DessauWörlitz. Karla Collmar and Michel Wetzel were responsible for the care and conservation of items donated on loan by the Kulturstiftung DessauWörlitz. Our sincerest thanks are due to them as well as to Ina Grünberg and Evelin Wagner, for their contribution to the manuscript.

We also owe a great debt of gratitude to the institutions which generously granted us photo and reproduction rights in the interest of our project: the National Maritime Picture Library, London, the Victoria & Albert Museum, London, the Bayerische Staatsgemäldesammlung, Munich, the Österreichische Nationalbibliothek, Vienna, and the Royal Collection, Her Majesty Queen Elizabeth II, Windsor Castle.

The Zentralbibliothek Zürich was similarly generous in providing assistance for our research. The still unpublished correspondence between Princess Luise and Johann Kaspar Lavater is held in the library's archives. The Landesamt für Denkmalpflege in Halle called our attention to previously unpublished maps, for which the Staatsbibliothek zu Berlin, Preußischer Kulturbesitz kindly granted approval for publication.

In a time characterised by increasing mobility, culture takes on greater significance with respect to national identity than ever before. Historical exhibitions held in conjunction with auxiliary events at the respective point of presentation play a particularly important role in fostering appreciation of our cultural heritage by providing an occasion for reflection upon particular points of view. We firmly believe that a careful analysis of the legacy of Prince Franz von Anhalt-Dessau and his garden kingdom, a program dedicated to peace and enlightenment, is especially pertinent in our time, as we approach the end of a millennium, and that it can be of help to us in efforts to come to grips with many of the challenges we face. This legacy can provide food for thought with regard to a productive approach to European and global interaction.

In conclusion we wish to express the hope that the exhibition and catalogue will motivate many people to visit the historical garden kingdom of Dessau-Wörlitz in order to experience the complex educational and cultural program of the enlightened Prince Franz von Anhalt-Dessau and his many assistants for themselves.

<table>
<tr><td>Ursula Zeller</td><td>Thomas Weiss</td></tr>
<tr><td>Institut für Auslandsbeziehungen</td><td>Kulturstiftung DessauWörlitz</td></tr>
</table>

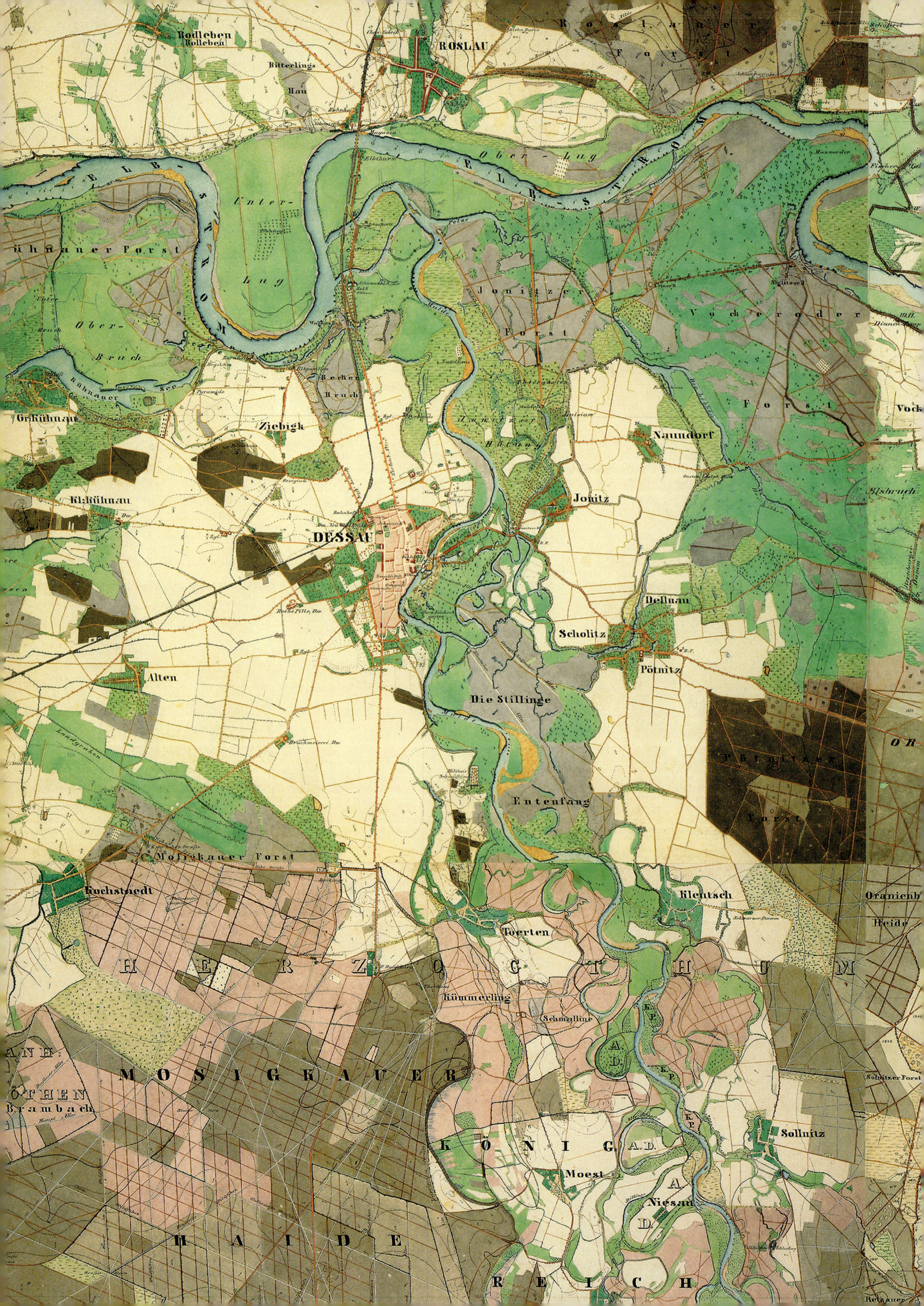

Rodleben
Rodleben
ROSLAU
Roslauer Forst
Büterlings
Hau
Bütterlings
ELB-STROM
ELB-STROM
Ober-Lug
Unter-
ühnauer Forst
Lug
Ober-
Bruch
Jonitzer
Forst
Vockeroder
Rähnauer See
Forst
Vock
Rechen Bruch
Gr.Kühnau
Ziebigk
Naundorf
Jonitz
Kl.Kühnau
DESSAU
Rothe Pütte, Vw.
Dellnau
Scholitz
Pötnitz
Alten
Die Stillinge
Entenfang
Forst
OR
Mosigkauer Forst
Kochstedt
 Silentsch
Oranienb.
Heide
Toerten
HERZOGTHUM
Kümmerling
Schmellne
A.D.
ANH:
MOSIGKAUER
KÖTHEN
Brambach
KÖNIG A.D.
Sollnitz
A.D.
Moest
HAIDE
Niesau
A.D.
REICH

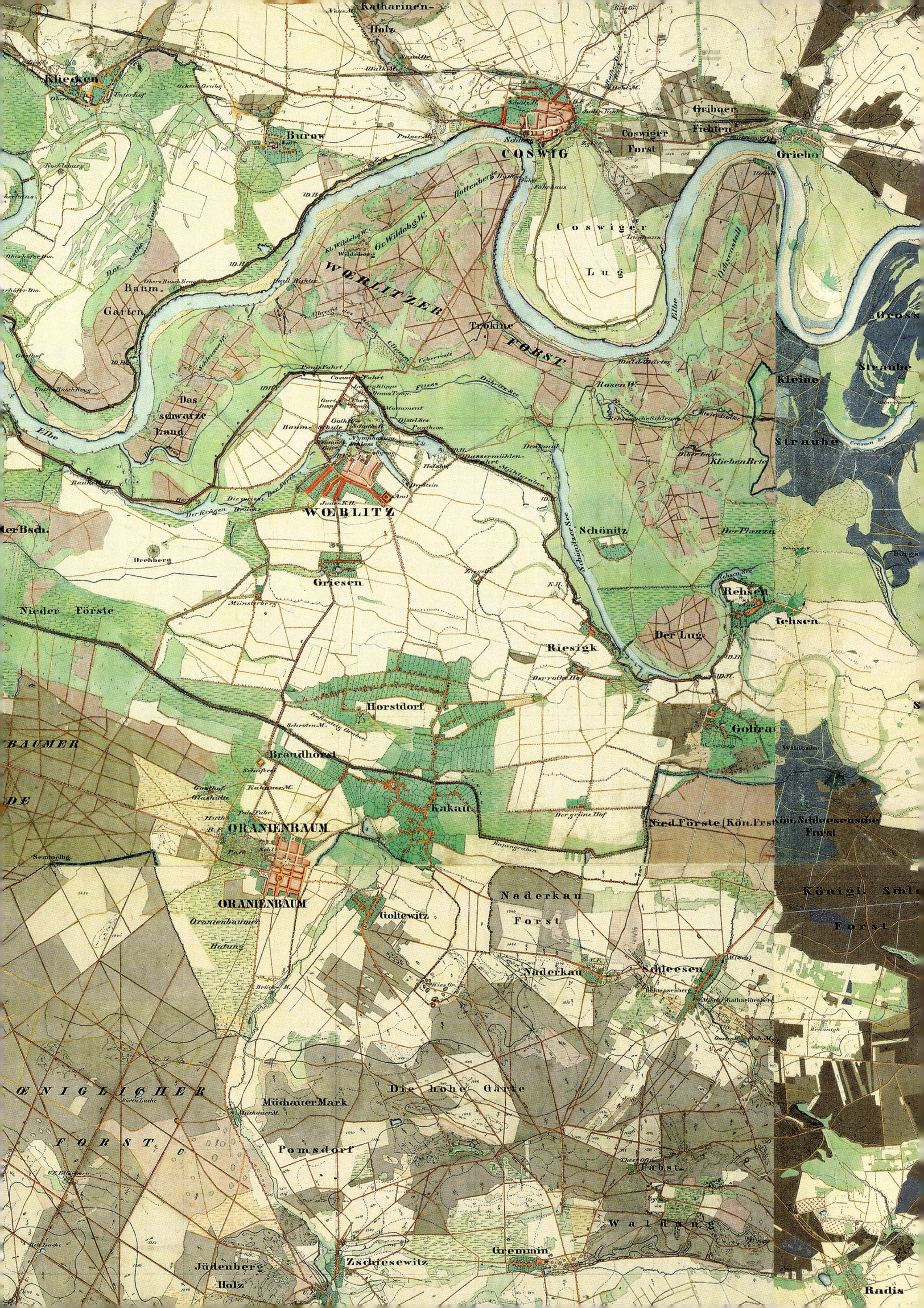

Katharinen-Holz
Klieken
Unterhof
Burow
COSWIG
Coswiger Forst
Griboer Fichten
Grieboe
Coswiger Lug
WÖRLITZER FORST
Trokine
Baum. Garten
Das schwarze Land
Elbe
Rosen W.
Kleine Strauhe
Gross Strauhe
WÖRLITZ
Schönitz
Der Plauza
Griesen
Rehsen
Nieder Förste
Der Lug
Fehsen
Riesigk
Horstdorf
Golbra
Brandhorst
BAUMER DE
Kakau
ORANIENBAUM
Nied.Förste (Kön.Frst.Kön.Schleesensche Forst
Goltewitz
Naderkau Forst
Königl. Schle Forst
ORANIENBAUM
Oranienbaumer Haltung
Naderkau
Schleesen
Müdhauer Mark
Die hohe Garue
KÖNIGLICHER
FORST
Pomsdorf
Pabst
Waldung
Jüdenberg Holz
Zschiesewitz
Gremmin
Radis

ARCADIA ON THE ELBE:
THE GARDEN KINGDOM OF WÖRLITZ

Michael Stürmer

"Once upon a time", as fairy tales begin … Once upon a time there was a garden
kingdom ruled by a wise prince. He was loved by all and looked upon as a father. He
needed no soldiers. His court, though small, attracted the best minds from near and
far and gained great renown for its culture and philanthropy. The prince promoted
literature and the arts, built schools for his subjects, preached brotherhood to Protestants, Catholics and Jews, fostered handicrafts and gave the farmers their liberty.
What reads like a fairy tale is a story that actually unfolded along the middle stretch of
the Elbe River in Germany some 200 years ago. Located midway between Weimar
and Berlin, the intellectual appeal of the little principality in the eyes of contemporaries was no less imposing than that of Weimar itself. The landscape scenes and architecture described in Goethe's *Wahlverwandtschaften* were inspired by much of what
the poet had seen in the expansive garden. Christoph Martin Wieland called the garden, which gave shape to the vision of Arcadia and enlightened reason for an entire
generation, the "ornament and epitome of the 18th century". "It is as if one were to
pass through a fairy tale…", remarked Goethe. The Austrian field marshall, diplomat
and writer Prince Charles Joseph Ligné concluded his famous work on the art of gardening with the words: "You gardeners, painters, poets, philosophers, go to Wörlitz."
Here, politics was transcended by utopia.
The garden kingdom offers "a true encyclopaedia of the cultural history of the 18th
century that has no equal" (Horst Möller). The allusions and architectural references
were much more readily comprehensible to educated people of the time than they
are to today's visitors. What they saw was shaped and structured nature. The subject of
the gable relief of the pantheon, designed by Friedrich-Wilhelm von Erdmannsdorff,
the Prince's friend and architect, was Athena's arbitration of the dispute between the
muses and the sirens. The one stood for nature, the other for art, which simply shows
that it was the intention of the Prince and his architect to achieve harmony between
nature and culture and bring them to a higher unity in the garden kingdom.
Harmony was much more difficult to find in the real world. Unlike Prussia, Wörlitz
was not an engine that drove Germany history. It would be more appropriate to say
that Wörlitz became the opposite, the counter-image of Prussia – an abundance of
mind and very little mass. The Dessau cultural circle grew around Prince Franz in
the decade following the Seven Years' War (1756–1763). As a young man, the Prince,
despite his status as a high-ranking officer, had cast off his loyalty to the Prussian flag
during the great war. He rebelled against the hard line of Frederician military despot-
ism and sought in the years that followed its intellectual opposite in Italy and its material equivalent in England. In England he studied the "new husbandry", intelligent
methods of land cultivation, observed parliamentary institutions with admiration and
recognised the separation of powers in the English system of government as a model
for social and political life. His desire was to see Dessau become the intellectual
contre-partie to Prussia: the small garden state versus the great military power.
Together with his court gardener Eyserbeck and the gentleman architect Erdmannsdorff, whose travel diaries contain a wealth of information, the young prince studied
gardening and architecture in England, became acquainted with the English version
of Palladianism, which had consistently influenced the design of country houses since
Inigo Jones and the early 17th century, and purchased furniture designed by Thomas

Chippendale for use as models and sources of inspiration for native craftsmen in his homeland. In 1769 he initiated the construction of the house and park in Wörlitz, located in the oak-wooded lowland region along the Elbe to the east of the old residential city of Dessau. The product of his efforts was the first and most beautiful Neoclassical *Gesamtkunstwerk* on the European continent. This Neoclassicism was inspired by the excavations at Pompeii, which Erdmannsdorff had studied on-site and which soon became familiar to educated European circles in engravings and source material. The austere style would soon replace rococo forms everywhere.

Prince Franz was one of the few figures of the past exuberance in whom even the historians of the former GDR found little to criticise, whom, in fact, they set apart as a shining example in contrast to the Frederician military state. Tour guides in Wörlitz were not known to make deprecating comments, and in 1985 a remarkable book appeared in honour of Wörlitz-style absolutism and the Prince who presided over it.[1] Goethe was often a guest there, and he praised the father and ruler of what he referred to as a "well-governed and at the same time outwardly beautified country". Together with Joseph II, the Emperor, and Frederick the Great, King of Prussia, Prince Franz, regardless of the relatively small size of his country, became one of the key figures representing the hope and illusion of reform from above in Germany. Prince Franz, had he possessed more power, ruled more people and wielded greater weight, was the kind of ruler the educated classes of the waning 18th century imagined when they thought of an enlightened prince. That had little to do with democracy, of course, and a great deal more with paternalism, with philanthropy, with a free market economy and with the belief that human beings, liberated from external constraints, would behave of their own volition in such a way – as the great Königsberg philosopher Immanuel Kant formulated his concept of the categorical imperative – that the maxims governing all of their actions could be taken as the foundation for generally applicable laws. Things were not quite so in Dessau-Wörlitz. The Prince was forced to intervene with corrective measures from time to time. His subjects were not saints, and some of his experiments, based upon trial and error, had to be broken off. Dessau became the centre of the imaginary "educational province" described by Goethe. And Dessau also epitomised the belief, prevalent in Germany, that the way to the future did not lie in bloody revolution but in forward-looking reform from above implemented by princely administration, without violence and without the need to cast off tradition. In both geographical and intellectual terms, Dessau was much closer to London and the ideas of liberty espoused by Edmund Burke than to the chaos of Paris and the rapidly burgeoning revolutionary expectations. It was a strange misunderstanding that prompted the Prince to dedicate a symbolic gravesite with a memorial on an island to Jean-Jacques Rousseau, the prophet of nature and dreamer of visions of ecological salvation. Rousseau had placed nature in irreconcilable opposition to culture, whereas concepts of synthesis, reconciliation and harmony dominated thought and action in Wörlitz. Yet just as the French Revolution took aesthetic and intellectual nourishment from the tensions of Neoclassicism, from *"nouveau gout"* and geometrical thinking during those decades, so, too, did enlightened absolutism and the idea of reform from above.

There was much to praise about the garden kingdom around Wörlitz with its population of 35,000. The historian Hirsch called it "ideologically the most potent creation of the Enlightenment". Particularly noteworthy was the educational optimism that embraced the Renaissance concept of the model prince and promoted it amongst the general public. It was thought that a well-educated and philanthropic prince would bring happiness to his country. In 1758 Johann Bernhard Basedow wrote essentially the same thing in his *Philosophie für alle Stände* (Philosophy for all Classes), as if announcing the reign of Prince Franz. And his treatise was indeed read and interpreted as a sign of things to come. In 1771 Basedow published his *Agathokrator oder von der Erziehung künftiger Regenten* (Agathokrator, or the Education of Future Rulers) which gained him his appointment in the small principality. There he was allowed to wield his pen on government pronouncements in which, in many cases, it was not readily apparent that they concerned a particular measure, since they sounded like philosophical discourses on the purpose of governments, the duties of rulers and the happiness of their subjects – fully in keeping with the dreams of intellectual Germany at the time: its feet far from the ground and its head well above the clouds. It was in this way that the mind of the global citizenry was to be educated. The world traveller Georg Forster remained sceptical, although he admitted that at least a "better progeny" might be expected. Enlightenment and sentimentality were closely intertwined. Both were encompassed by the central concept of "happiness". States found their purpose in creating the conditions for it; citizens found theirs in striving to achieve it. In Dessau-Wörlitz, everything was made subordinate to that idea, which promised mortals a bit of the magnificence of paradise in the here – and – now. It should be noted in this regard that the Virginia Bill of Rights of 1776 claimed the "right to the pursuit of happiness" for all citizens in sharp ideological defiance of the British motherland. It was in the very same year that the French reform minister Turgot sought to tear down and rebuild the whole rotting structure of French absolutism and its rigid guild system in the name of the right to the pursuit of happiness, to which every human being was entitled. We should also remember that Adam Smith, the Scottish economist and moral philosopher, published his epoch-making treatise on the origins of national wealth, *An Enquiry into the Causes of the Wealth of Nations* (1776) – the point of departure from which the entire body of modern liberal economic theory grew forth. What took shape between Wörlitz and Dessau was not merely a game played by a few intellectuals and a young prince in isolation; it was a point of departure for North American and European innovation. The concept of "happiness" does indeed incorporate the modern idea of liberty, for the inalienable right of all people to the pursuit of happiness means nothing other than that human beings are entitled, each in his own way – or in his own "fashion", as Frederick the Great expressed it – to attain happiness, and not in heaven, but here on earth. The right to determine oneself what happiness is, the right to claim the fruits of one's own labour; the right to be free from feudal constraints and to shape one's own life – all of this was encompassed by the concept of happiness, and it was the fabric from which the cloth of Dessau was woven. Goethe placed the pilgrimage to Dessau's Arcadia in sharp contrast to the allure of Berlin and Potsdam in speaking critically of the "magnificence of the royal cities, the noise of the world and the arms of war". Anhalt-Dessau's "shining prince" became more and more of a model, passing almost beyond reality.

Wörlitz's happiness was financed through income from the Prince's extensive lands in eastern Prussia, from the proceeds of agriculture, rationalised in accordance with the standards of contemporary experimental economists and focused upon export down the Elbe River, from orchards and from forestry. It was discovered, for example, that the precious mahogany from which the finest furniture of the period was made could be replaced by the wood of the native pear tree. A furniture industry was established which supplied many of the courts in the Protestant states of Germany. Favourable to the Prince's reform efforts was the fact that the landed nobility and feudal prerogatives had been abolished by the *"Alter Dessauer"*, Prussia's merciless field marshall under Friedrich Wilhelm I, who had alienated the nobility and acquired its land with money and through the exercise of power in order to convert it into lands within the princely domain. Thus there was no veto against reform measures to be expected from noble estates, a circumstance which permitted the grandson to initiate the process of modernisation in his principality which had been recommended with such urgency by all of the enlightened economists of old Europe. Sound finances, low taxes and the expansion of construction activity promoted by the Prince in the lean decades following the Seven Years' War made Dessau-Anhalt more an island of idealism coupled with wealth than a typical patch of German soil in the late phase of the Holy Roman Empire.

The list of reforms undertaken in Dessau reads like a catalogue of all of the measures tirelessly proposed and recommended, awarded prizes and given over-abundant words of praise by enlightenment thinkers in their journals: general public education, not merely on paper but as a practical reality; emancipation of the Jews, represented most notably in the state school and synagogue completed in 1799 – the latter, by the way, rescued from destruction at the hands of a Nazi mob in 1938 by a courageous civil servant; the liberation of farmers on princely lands, social security for labourers, middle-class culture, in which the Prince and Princess took part. Most important of all was the adoption of British approaches to modern agriculture in fruit cultivation, clover planting and sophisticated systems of crop alternation intended to renew the soil and replace the three-field system of traditional medieval agriculture that had become firmly entrenched in social and legal structures. Agricultural yields increased substantially. Systematic orchard husbandry and a reform economy benefited the wood exporting industry. Exemplary urban architecture was added to the overall picture, funded for the most part by the Prince who as a minimum provided financial support through the supply of wood for construction. Running water and modern toilets could be found not only in the *Schloß* but in the better houses in the city as well.

Anhalt-Dessau also witnessed the growth of a critical, reasoning public supported by a free publishing industry unhampered by censorship, which encouraged writers with inconvenient views. While this freedom of thought was born under the protection of the court, it took on an independent form of its own after 1781 in the *"Buchhandlung der Gelehrten"* (Scholars' Publishing House). This was an enterprise of European proportions and ambitions which sought to achieve what Alexander Pope in England, Voltaire in France and Leibnitz, Lessing and Kloppstock in Germany had been striving to achieve for some time: a republic of scholars with its own publishing house. The fruits of the mind were to be as free of the influence of commercial speculation as they were of the commandments of the Prince – and for a limited period Dessau enjoyed both liberties.

As an enterprise devoted to enlightenment, Reiche's *"Allgemeine Buchhandlung der Gelehrten und Künstler"* (General Publishing House for Scholars and Artists) was the second in significance only to the *Philantropin* education institution. There was hardly a literary figure in Germany during this period who was not associated, or as Goethe expressed it, "in close union" with the Dessau institute. Financing arrangements were structured in such a way that authors initially paid printing costs in advance, eventually receiving compensation from the proceeds of sales. This procedure eliminated the danger of market saturation with subsidised mediocre works. At the same time, the *"Verlagskasse"* (Publisher's Fund), established alongside the publishing house, served to promote young, unknown authors. The object of these undertakings was the development of a *res publica litterarum*, an educated public inclined to engage in political reasoning. Prince Franz was – *avant la lettre* – liberal enough not only to permit such developments to take place but to support them as well through the provision of property, capital and buildings and by offering a high degree of protection.

Beginning in 1782, a journal entitled *Literatur und Völkerkunde* (Literature and Ethnology) appeared in Dessau bearing the publisher's statement: "Published at the expense of the Publisher's Fund and available in the Scholar's Publishing House". The third volume contains a description of Dessau in the form, quite popular at the time, of a traveller's letter to a friend. Although the piece is abundant in its self-praise, it also reveals a great deal about the scenes being staged there during the period: "I found it nearly impossible to persuade myself that I was in the middle of Germany. Yes, my friend, this little, unnoticed part of the earth has so many distinctions to praise that I fear you will regard even the most authentic description of these matters as fictional invention." The writer compared the country to a garden; avenues, canals, bridges and attractive residential buildings, the homes of court officials, combined to form a work of art. "All of this forms the most delightful of painted landscapes; and added to it are happy citizens and a wise government." Most important of all, however, was the "freedom of thought and action…" that reigned there. "I make the claim that this treasured liberty prevails in no other monarchic state in Europe to the degree that it does here. The Prince was in England for a long time, where he himself experienced the advanced rights of mankind that he so generously promotes here." The article goes on to praise the *Philantropin*, the educational institution established in accordance with a "most favourite plan" of the Prince. According to the author, the Prince regarded the students of the *Philantropin* as members of his family. They were treated with love and kindness – by no means a foregone conclusion in light of the educational standards accepted at the time. Enlightened thinking and sentimentality were joined together. A description of the commencement celebration contains the following passage: "All was immersed in tears; there was not a single dry eye to be seen." The development of physical aptitudes and exercises in character building augmented the academic program in which students from many countries took part. The only point of criticism to be found in the midst of so much perfection: too much emphasis was placed, wrote the author, on the French language, and that in "a genuine German institute". There was no end to the commendations. They proceeded with a mention of the *"Verlagskasse für Gelehrte und Künstler"* and the *"Buchhandlung der Gelehrten"*, shifting into an unmistakable tone of unabashed self-praise: "The flourishing bloom of both institutions is fully in keeping with the well-conceived plans and their intelligent implementation." Where, if not in Dessau, had the Enlightenment found its home? Where, if not here, was liberty the work of absolutism? In this last decade before the French Revolution shook the foundations of the *ancien régime* it was a German dream that reform from above and universal human rights could be united under the banner of happiness – and that this would occur in Germany, just as it had already come to be in Dessau.[2]

But the axis upon which this world of ideas turned was not the "educational province" nor the politics of the periphery nor even the alliance of enlightenment and absolutism. It was to be found instead in the *Schloß* and park of Wörlitz. "Noble simplicity and tasteful arrangement" were united here, as the traveller from Dessau reports, in the first English park created in Germany, in the Palladian villa built for the Prince by Erdmannsdorff on the English model. Prince Franz himself was cited as the author of the dedication of the house: "Love and friendship have built it; peace and contentment shall live in it; and then domestic joys will not be lacking."

Such an architectural concept was worlds apart from the baroque pretension to power evident in the nearby *Schloß* in Oranienbaum, built eighty years before. And it was worlds apart as well from Schlüters' *Stadtschloß* in Berlin, indeed even from Knobelsdorff's noble *Sanssouci* in the Weinberg near Potsdam. And it is characteristic of Wörlitz as a historical architectural complex that it was begun just as the late baroque *Neues Palais* in the Potsdam park landscape, inspired by Vandenburgh's Castle Howard and begun before the outbreak of the Seven Years' War, was approaching completion. It represented a world of ideas very different from that of the baroque rulers. It was indeed the gentle revolution of the Enlightenment which found its expression in Wörlitz.

The park and *Schloß* in Wörlitz were regarded from the very beginning as the epitome of Enlightenment culture. In retrospect, the viewer also recognises the complex as the cradle of German Neoclassicism. The English Palladian style influenced the *Schloß*, with its Corinthian portico facing the city and the window façade with its eleven axes and a view of the park over a sloping lawn. The *Wörlitzer Schloßpark* thus became more European in design and more cosmopolitan in actual construction than any other architectural structure built in the style of German Neoclassicism. The English model was overpowering, and incorporated allusions to early Gothic architecture reflected in the surrounding buildings. Chairs, console tables, chests of drawers and cupboards everywhere in Wörlitz revealed English inspiration. They possessed more than an elegant simplicity in contrast to the magnificence and alluring qualities of French interior decoration. They also revealed the influence of an ideological program of political and economic reform: to be like the English isle, without the confining corset of the past, with parliamentary freedom and a market economy. For the people of the late 18th century, Wörlitz became a place of pilgrimage. But was Wörlitz's influence upon Neoclassical furniture design, architecture and horticulture predestined to have no appreciable effect upon the politics of reform from above? Was everything accomplished in Dessau nothing but empty gesture, played out on the stage of the tiny state and noticed only in passing by those who occupied the best boxes in the great political theatre? It was, and then again it was not. For although Wörlitz was indeed the goal of an aesthetic and philosophical pilgrimage for educated people in the waning 18th century, the little state in the shadow of powerful Prussia had no chance to affect change in the logic and grammar of European politics. Yet Dessau-Wörlitz did produce more than erudite theory. It seemed possible here to purify and reform German monarchic rule through the spirit of the English constitution. It was here that an enlightened prince proved that the idea of human happiness was more than a hollow promise for contemplation during idle hours. Here one might hope that reform from above would preempt the need for revolution from below. Who could know then that the royal road of enlightened absolutism would lead Germans a century later to a divergent path of opposition to the West?

Until the mid-18th century it had been France, with its fashionable metropolis of Paris, its material culture and its luxury industry, arts of war and national economy, that set the standards for what was deemed right, and indeed absolute, by people in Germany. The turn towards England came about in the third quarter of the 18th century. Germans looked to England for their inspiration after the great famine and economic crisis around 1770, which raised the spectre of civil war over France, and even more intently following the appearance of Adam Smith's Enquiry into the Nature and Causes of the Wealth of Nations (1776). The universities in Göttingen and Königsberg became harbours receiving imports of everything that was English, and therefore of exemplary character. Nowhere was this process of change more evident than in Dessau-Wörlitz. Nowhere was the German hope for the achievement of unity between state reason and civil liberty more eloquently expressed than in the garden kingdom on the banks of the Elbe. And nowhere was the illusion – in the form of the Neoclassical *Gesamtkunstwerk* – created with such perfection as it was in Wörlitz.

1　E. Hirsch, *Dessau-Wörlitz. Zierde und Inbegriff des 18. Jahrhunderts*, Leipzig and Munich, 1985.

2　*Litteratur und Völkerkunde. Ein periodisches Werk*, Vol. 3, Dessau, 1783, pp. 127–131; see also the correspondence in which England and the "enviable happiness" of its inhabitants is idealised, *ibid.*, pp. 273–295.

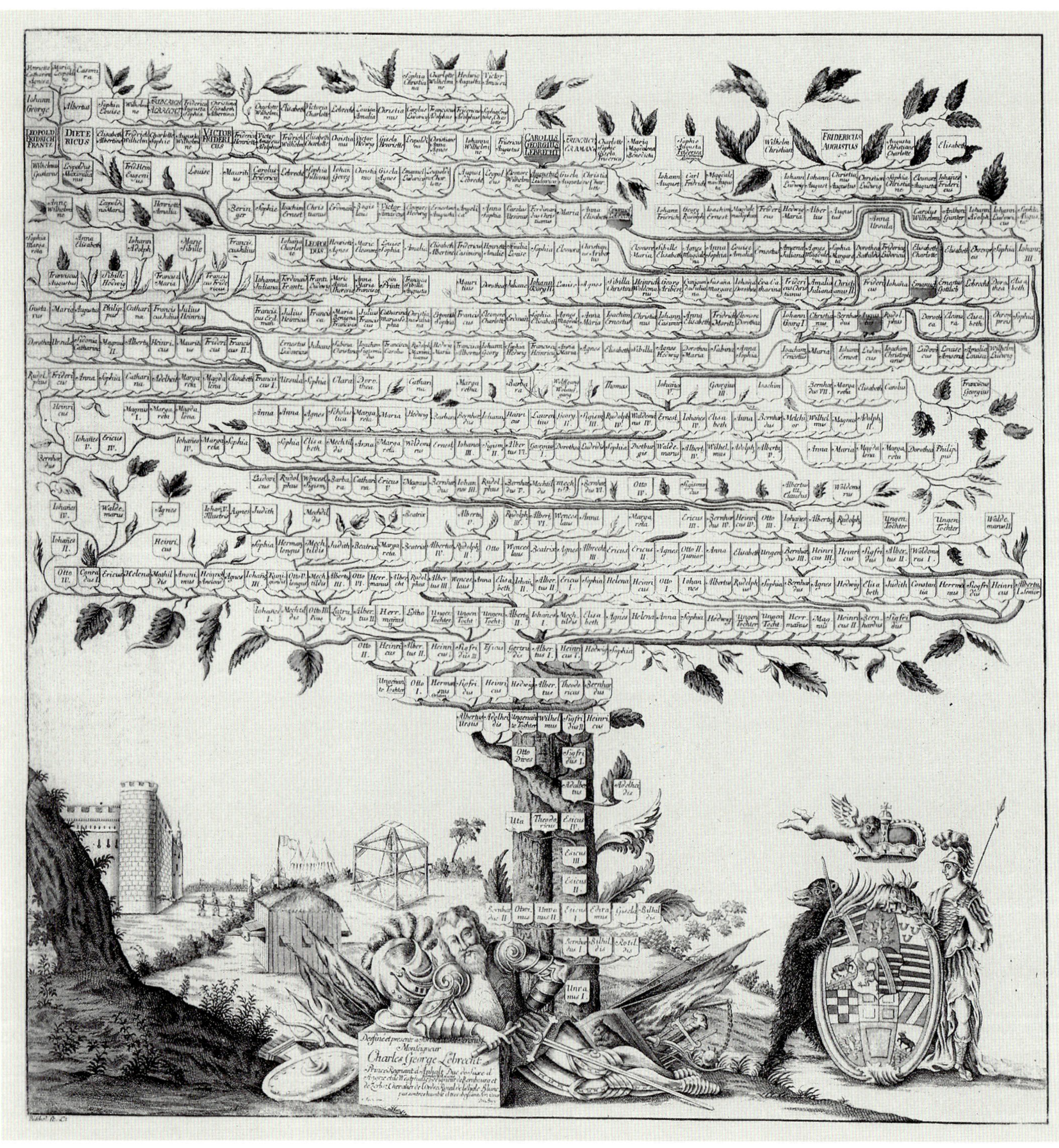

Genealogy of the House of Anhalt-Dessau (cat. no. 4)

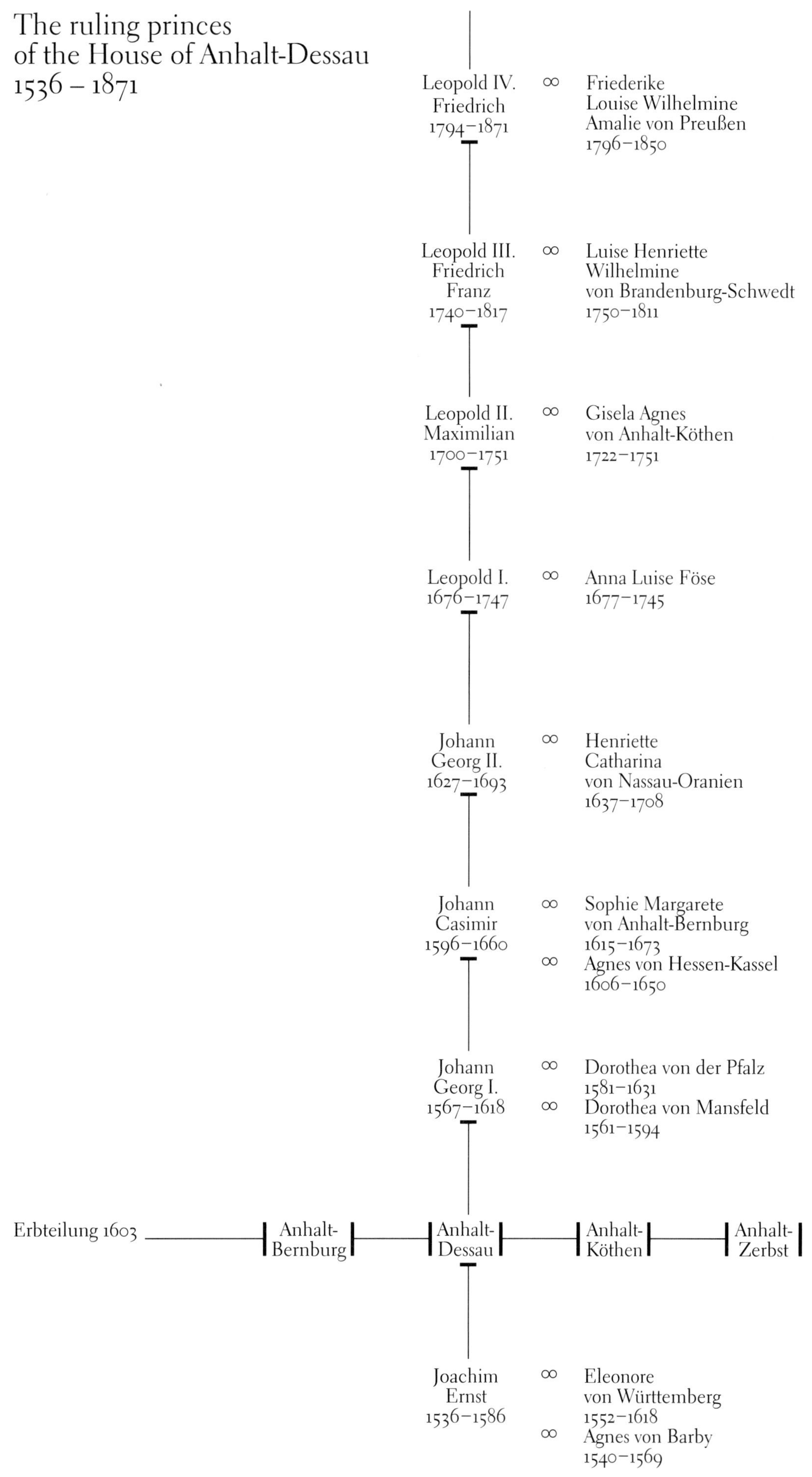

The ruling princes
of the House of Anhalt-Dessau
1536 – 1871

Leopold IV.
Friedrich
1794–1871
∞ Friederike
Louise Wilhelmine
Amalie von Preußen
1796–1850

Leopold III.
Friedrich
Franz
1740–1817
∞ Luise Henriette
Wilhelmine
von Brandenburg-Schwedt
1750–1811

Leopold II.
Maximilian
1700–1751
∞ Gisela Agnes
von Anhalt-Köthen
1722–1751

Leopold I.
1676–1747
∞ Anna Luise Föse
1677–1745

Johann
Georg II.
1627–1693
∞ Henriette
Catharina
von Nassau-Oranien
1637–1708

Johann
Casimir
1596–1660
∞ Sophie Margarete
von Anhalt-Bernburg
1615–1673
∞ Agnes von Hessen-Kassel
1606–1650

Johann
Georg I.
1567–1618
∞ Dorothea von der Pfalz
1581–1631
∞ Dorothea von Mansfeld
1561–1594

Erbteilung 1603 — Anhalt-Bernburg — Anhalt-Dessau — Anhalt-Köthen — Anhalt-Zerbst

Joachim
Ernst
1536–1586
∞ Eleonore
von Württemberg
1552–1618
∞ Agnes von Barby
1540–1569

"THE BENEFITS OF SOLITUDE"
THE LIFE OF PRINCESS LUISE VON ANHALT-DESSAU

Ursula Bode

"I shall come whenever you wish, and the Luisium project pleases me greatly…" It is
not entirely clear what Karoline von Berg actually meant in her letter to Luise von
Anhalt-Dessau of March 7th, 1797. The Countess, Herder's "clever confidante" and a
woman regarded by Jean Paul as an "intellectual Amazon", reminded the Princess in
her letter of their first meeting seventeen years before, recalling their original euphoric
affection and affirming that "I shall always come back to you, like one returning to
her homeland". The letter is a heartfelt affirmation of friendship, full of tenderness
and buoyant feeling. Yet like much of what is recorded of the exchanges of feeling
between intimate friends of Luise, and like many of her own statements, a great deal
of what Countess Karoline wrote defies interpretation today.

It is impossible to say whether the reference to the "Luisium project" was an allusion
to a planned visit or to an architectural renovation, a gardening program involving the
country house and park, the retreat between Wörlitz and Dessau that bore the name
of the Princess. Luise was 47 years old when she received Countess Berg's letter, and
the Luisium had been in her possession for some 20 years. She had long since grown
accustomed to regarding the little palace, built by the court architect Erdmannsdorff
beginning in 1775 and completed, with respect to its interior furnishings, in the 1780's,
as a refuge in which she could enjoy "room to breathe" and the "benefits of solitude".
It was a summer residence, a guest house for those close to her heart. And it was a
place of retreat and escape from the droves of visitors who came to visit the *Wörlitzer
Schloß* as a tourist attraction in keeping with the express wishes of Prince Franz. The
Princess had specified as early as 1780 that the grounds of the Luisium were to be
open to visitors only on Monday and Friday afternoons. Yet even this arrangement was
not without its threatening aspects, as an entry in the Princess' diary made in 1795
clearly suggests: "After dinner, as it was the day all of the people were permitted to
visit my garden, I remained in my room and worked at the table… I could not go
down again at eight, once the people had left the garden, because the dew was falling
already and the air was very cold. So I ate downstairs in the dining hall in the moonlight – Oh God, God, how I felt there!"

The dining hall was designed for festive occasions – and actually used accordingly at
first. Now it gave the Princess as little pleasure as the moonlight, the spacious park
and the silence of her surroundings, all characterised by a beauty still in evidence
today; a sense of solitude that has been perpetuated in the Luisium like the "quiet
dream image passing by" experienced by Goethe on his first visit to Wörlitz. It is a
landscape of tamed nature, which at that time was much less a setting for refined conversation, reminiscences of travels to antiquity and stimulating encounters with the
past than the Wörlitz portion of the "garden kingdom".

In the silent green of the Luisium – once a bird sanctuary at the edge of the royal
game reserve – one's sensibilities were left to their own devices: an inclination typical
of the period to immerse oneself in the pleasures and agonies of self-reflection and
intercourse with nature to which the Princess was particularly susceptible. The journey of a sensitive soul in quest of itself – it could be undertaken at the Luisium in the
shade of oaks already ancient in her time; or amidst the decorations of the Palladian
country house; or amongst the English-style "follies" placed sparingly and with
deliberate care within the park. Thus was the answer of the "ornamental farm" of the

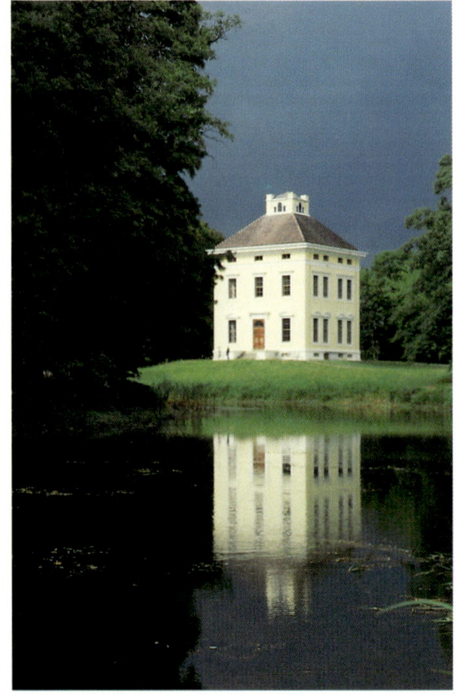

1
Dessau, Schloß Luisium
Built from 1774–1778

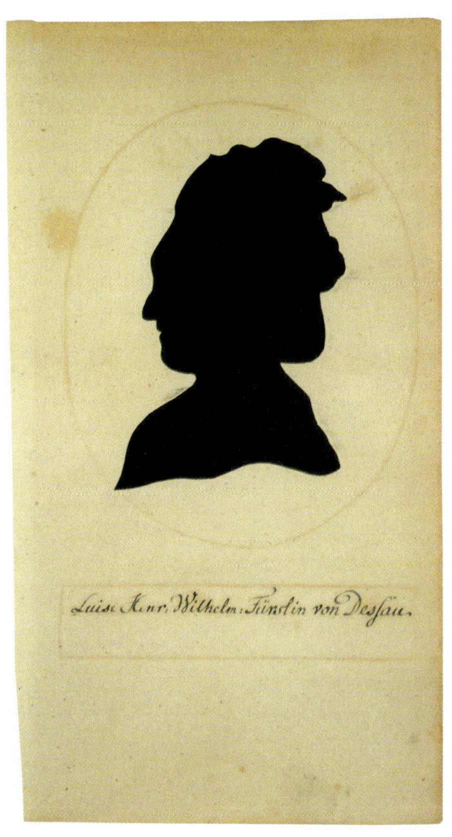

2
Artist Unknown
Silhouette of Princess Luise von
Anhalt-Dessau,
Scissors cut-out
Circa 1780
Kulturstiftung DessauWörlitz

otherwise utilitarian late Gothic stable building to the Neoclassical shape of the *Schloß*. The no less picturesque replica of the ruins of a triumphal arch directs the gaze towards a life-sized sculpture of a veiled female figure. What the general populace soon came to refer to as the *Nonnentor* (Nun's Gate) and simply the *Nonne* (Nun) and alluded perhaps to the life of relative solitude led by the noble resident of the Luisium was something much like a stage scene beneath the trees – a setting of magnificent ruin for the statue of the Goddess of Sais, a symbol of nature's victory over death.

The proximity of the rough-hewn hermit's grotto (including an outlook platform) and the Neoclassical pavilion (in front of the site of Luise's flower garden) appears to betray a more modest conception. It is reasonable to assume that the nearby tower of the *Schlangenhaus* (Snake House), named for the ornamental shape of his rain guttering, once catered to guests as a setting for pleasant summer chats. Shadowed by trees, with the remains of an orchard meadow as a parterre, the late Gothic structure – its appealing brickwork still visible today – stands on a grassy knowl as an invitation to partake in conversation.

We know that there were guests, visitors who knew and trusted one another: several female friends, a very few court officials, sometimes the Prince himself on a visit. Left largely to herself, however, Luise von Anhalt-Dessau sought at the Luisium the stimulus and refreshment she found "so necessary and salubrious" with an both unconcealed sense of melancholy and an unmistakable understanding of the possibilities open to her. Thus she wrote in 1799, at nearly fifty years of age: "As I wandered alone through the garden of the Luisium in years gone by, my melancholy enveloped me more sweetly yet whispered feelings to me which, translated into words, were such as I then wrote down forthwith: my enjoyment of people and my pleasure in being human is mostly gone, never to return again like the ever-returning spring."

Those who study the "Weltbild Wörlitz" (the Wörlitz view of the world), the cultivated landscape around Dessau that is one of the most imposing documents of the Enlightenment in Germany, soon form an impression of the personality of Prince Leopold Friedrich Franz von Anhalt-Dessau (1740–1817). It is to him and his friend Erdmannsdorff that we owe the existence of the "garden kingdom" and its aura of enchantment, which continues to evoke delight and pleasure today, whereas most of his epoch-making economic and educational undertakings belong to the past.

Prince Franz must have been a man of winning ways: erudite and energetic, intent upon the present and the necessities it presented yet full of devotion to the lessons and accomplishments of antiquity. He was "Good Father Franz" in the eyes of his subjects. In keeping with the customs of his English contemporaries, everything he undertook was devoted in equal measure to "utility" and "beauty". With the self-assurance that permitted him to oppose the Emperor Napoleon he secured significant protection for his little principality from the victor of the battle of Jena and Auerstadt and became Duke with the blessing of the Empire in 1807.

He was a man of action, but at the same time a "great and beautiful nature" – as Goethe remarked – and a person who tolerated neither "artificial conceits" nor the "geniuses" and their cult of devotees at the neighbouring court of Weimar.

In contrast, our picture of the Princess Henriette Luise Wilhelmine, the woman who became his wife in 1767, remains vague. Compared to the popular image of her spouse as the epitome of vitality, the picture drawn of the Princess tends to be dull and uninspiring. The negative attributes assigned to her by the Wörlitz Provost Friedrich Reil in his 1845 biography of Prince Franz von Anhalt-Dessau ("…the moody sentimentality of the Princess") suggested the way in which Luise's shadow-existence was to be interpreted in the memory of posterity: as that of a failed life, despite the

somewhat self-righteous respect paid to her "great talents of mind and spirit". For, as
the biographer Reil has interpreted it, "her life was pervaded by an almost never-
ending lament, by a virtually uninterrupted wail of agony and pain. She suffered from
the sickness of sentimental dreaminess that was so prevalent in her times, sought
ideals the world did not have to offer and experienced one disappointment after the
other… and thus through fruitless self-torture cast the rich magnificence which life
spread about her in dark shadow."

A portrayal that certainly would encourage no one to find anything in the life of the
Princess beyond its disturbing, at best pitiable aspects. The silence of Luise's few true
friends, her own discretion and her misanthropic view, conditioned not least of all by
a history of chronic illness, have all done their part to diminish the perceived importance of her role in the culture of Dessau-Wörlitz. One may be tempted in our day to
reduce the complex figure of the Princess to the stereotyped image of the unfortunate
victim of an unhappy marriage. That a domineering husband and womaniser could
cause serious emotional injury to a sensitive young woman is an entirely plausible
explanation. There is no question that Luise's permanent susceptibility to allergic skin
disorders, her hearing loss and eventually her severe hearing impairment are inter-
pretable in the light of current knowledge as psychosomatic illnesses. Yet the attempt
to read between the lines of letters and available statements of those close to the life of
the court simply reveals what is already evident: that the actual circumstances in that
era of princely rule and sentimentality were much more complicated than the black-
and-white image of the vigorous husband and the frigid wife seeking refuge in her illness would suggest. Luise's life was not, as various passages from correspondence permit us to conclude, totally without its joys. It is also obvious that respect and affection
continued to characterise relations between the marriage partners – and that to a
greater degree than convention demanded.

The "separation without divorce" in the 1780s and the Prince's unblessed relationship
with Luise Schoch, daughter of the Wörlitz gardener, led at least to a clarification of
the situation and prevented the endless repetition of the "marital scenes" which
Franz, unfortunately as indiscreet as he was naive, would describe to his biographer
much later: "[I found] her self-centredness, which turned to outright stubbornness at
times, impossible to bear. She did not always grant me what I was entitled to demand.
If I wished to sleep, she would not stop playing the piano… I did not care for her relations with certain scholars and artists and the manner in which she dealt with them.
I saw in that a certain affront to my own person."

Visitors to the "garden kingdom" today encounter Luise von Anhalt-Dessau, daughter
of the Margrave of Brandenburg-Schwedt, a niece of Friedrich II of Prussia and a
cousin of Prince Franz through her mother's side of the family, in two full-figure portraits. A copy based on the conventional painting by the court painter Lisiewski hangs
in the dining hall of the *Wörlitzer Schloß*. The portrait done by Johann F. A. Tischbein in 1799 is shown in the Anhaltinian Gallery of Paintings at *Schloß Georgium* in
Dessau. Despite the vivacity she is said to have exhibited in the company of those she
knew and trusted, the Luise portrayed in these paintings is not a vigorous, vivacious
beauty, nor was she that in life. Yet it is evident that the fashionably dressed lady in
the Tischbein portrait in particular, shown in the sentimental-pensive pose favoured
by the artist, enjoyed a reputation as a woman of cultivated intelligence.

The poet Friedrich von Matthison regarded her as one of the "wisest and most erudite
of her sex". He considered himself fortunate to have been engaged by Luise as "her
reader and travel director" for her trip to Italy in the mid–1790s ("…and I consider
this event the most favourable of my entire life"). The Princess, as Matthison
remarked to his Swiss friend Bonstetten in January of 1795, "was the only one among

3
Christian Friedrich Reinhold
Lisiewsky
Portrait der Fürstin Luise von
Anhalt-Dessau
Portrait of Princess Luise von
Anhalt-Dessau
Oil on canvas
Circa 1769
Kulturstiftung DessauWörlitz

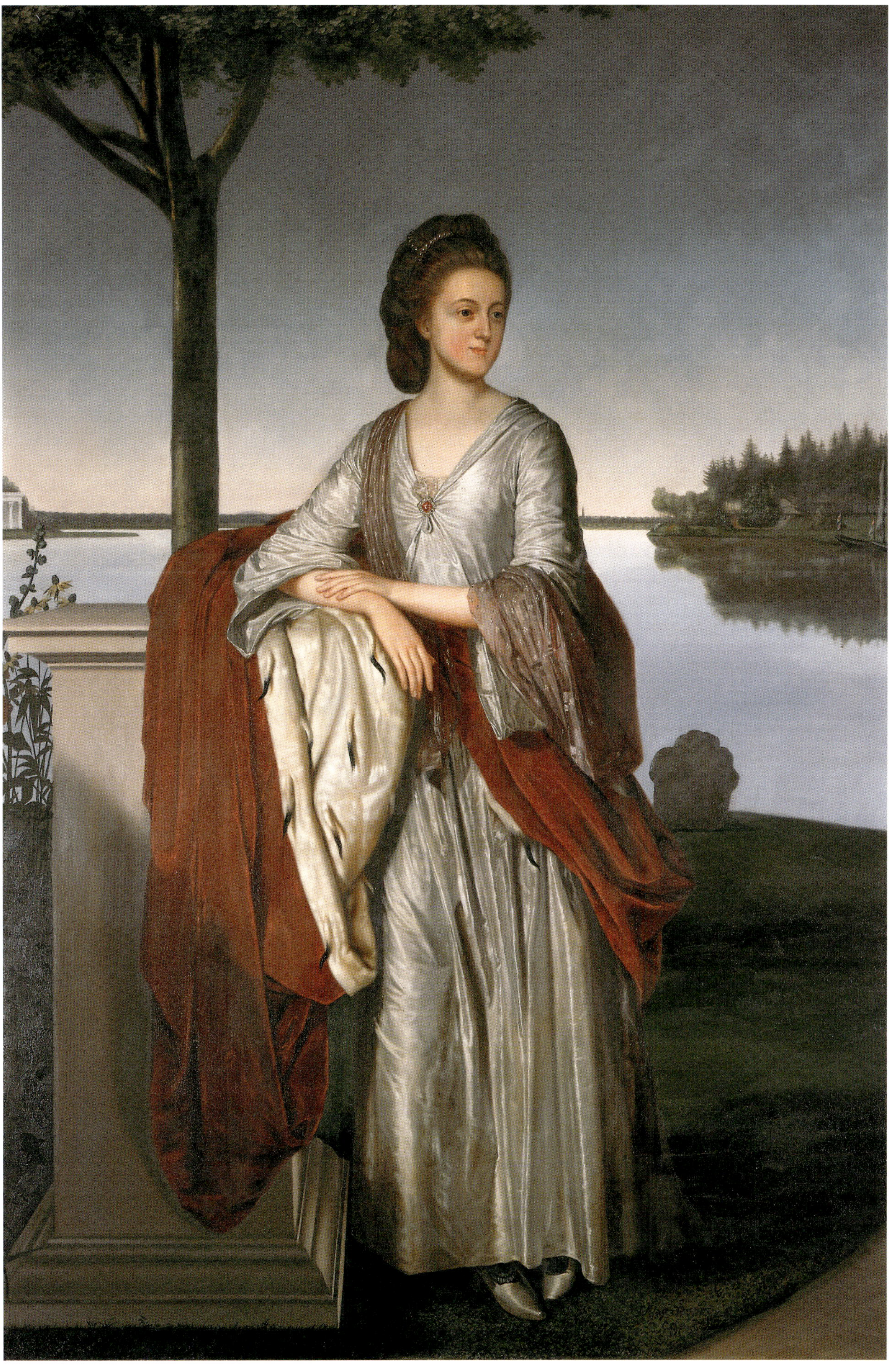

the princesses of the House of Prussia who honoured Frederick the Great with an unmistakable resemblance… The eyes of the Princess of Dessau are much like those of Frederick, and in her entire physiognomy the original features of her old Prussian ancestry can be found, line for line."

The Prussian king – and this, too, is of relevance to the unhappy marriage drama – was the very person from whom Franz von Anhalt-Dessau was intent upon distancing himself both politically and personally. Yet it was Friedrich II who designated his 15-year-old niece as the wife-to-be of Prince Franz, a man ten years older than she. The wedding took place in Charlottenburg two years later. Thus it was that, in accordance with the will of the Prussian king, the House of Anhalt-Dessau was spared the embarrassment of seeing the young regent Franz leave the country to live, according to his own wishes, the life of a privateer in England in the company of his first mistress, a commoner, and their son (who later became Count Waldersee).

The royal couple named their son, the Crown Prince, born in 1769, after Frederick the Great. Luise had previously suffered a miscarriage and the death of a daughter only hours after birth. That she later surrounded herself with "step-daughters"; that she was forced to accept her husband's interruption of their dinner upon receipt of news that Luise Schoch had given birth to his daughter in the "Gothic House"; that three daughters were raised there – all of these facts were recorded by the Princess with stoical brevity in her diary.

The more "the Princess' [hearing difficulty] … turned her predestined isolation into an urgent necessity" (Matthison), the stronger her tendency towards self-observation grew. Most of her diary entries have been preserved, some of them in different versions – in German and French translations and in copies and summaries prepared by Matthison or by Luise herself. The only partially transcribed autobiography preserved in the Anhalt State Archives in Oranienbaum has yet to be examined in its entirety and edited for publication.

It was not reticent Luise but one of the "woman writers" – a new species that appeared on the 18th-century literary scene – who left behind unambiguous remarks about life in Wörlitz and Dessau: notes written by Elisa von der Recke in her diary during her visit in January 1795, sighs of woe from a sensitive writer who nevertheless gave vehement expression to her thoughts. She felt sorry for her friend the Princess, concealing her feelings in silence but later recording her critical thoughts in her own diary.

"Dessau, Jan. 29th, 1795. Two more days of our lives wasted – not a trace of our existence left behind by these days … what depresses me unspeakably … here … is that I recognise that my noble Princess and I have become a burden to the good-natured Prince, to the Crown Prince and thus to the entire court. We are making the hours bitter for one another."

Nevertheless, Elisa von der Recke's stay seems not to have been totally devoid of its pleasures. Two months later she was still in the company of the Princess in Wörlitz: "How wonderful life would be here amongst one's chosen friends, if only the owner of this beautiful estate could appreciate the joys of companionship and a Socratic enjoyment of life… I was saddened during my walk today, for I was depressed by the thought that two people, such a fundamentally good couple as the Prince and Princess, should make life difficult for each other for lack of mutual understanding…"

Only in the midst of the "cultivated middle-class", as the noble writer commented, "could one find true happiness and wise, cheerful appreciation of life" – an insight obviously shared by Luise von Anhalt, who maintained ties of friendship with diverse physicians, among them the intelligent and empathetic Hanover court physician Zimmermann, and who placed her trust in Johann Kaspar Haefeli, the Swiss preacher

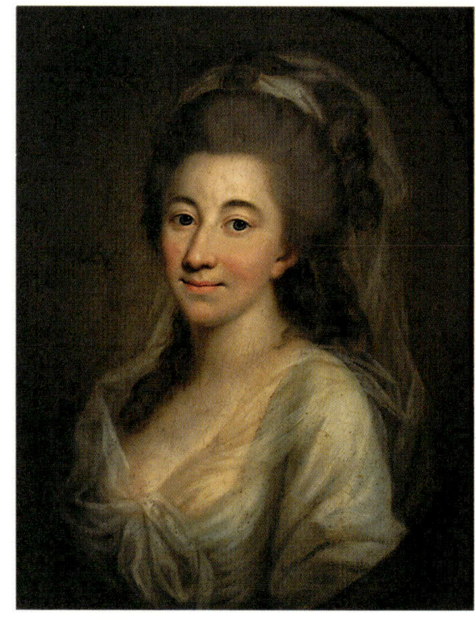

4
Joseph Friedrich Darbes
Portrait der Elisa von der Recke
Portrait of Elisa von der Recke
Oil on canvas
1785
Gleimhaus, Halberstadt

and student of Lavater and a man nearly her own age, who served as pastor at the church in Wörlitz during the 1780s upon the recommendation of his mentor. Luise, the melancholy model of female sentimentality, had a well-developed sense of appreciation for "alliances of the soul" – a talent that irritated her husband and motivated close friends including the ladies von der Recke, and von Berg or Jenny Möser, who took the married name von Voigts, to reflect upon the constitution of their "worshipped Princess". "You should finally get to know Lavater. I beseech God to grant you this devoutly heartfelt wish", Jenny von Voigts wrote in a letter to the Princess, giving expression to a desire that many women would happily have seen fulfilled. Johann Kaspar Lavater (1741–1801), the Zurich preacher befriended with Herder and Goethe during the *Sturm-und-Drang* period, was also the author of *Physiognomische Fragmente zu Beförderung der Menschenkenntnis und Menschenliebe* (Fragments on Physiognomy Dedicated to the Increase of Knowledge and Love of Humankind), published between 1775 and 1778, a work received with great enthusiasm not only in the young literary public but among many groups of educated women.

In the autumn of 1783, on the occasion of a visit by the Prince and Princess, who still enjoyed travelling together, Franz and Luise met the famous preacher, to whom Goethe was the first to attribute "an unequalled grace". Months later, Karoline von Berg would remark in jubilation that she had "known in advance what an impression Lavater would make upon Luise". "May God reward the Prince for bringing you to him, for not merely showing him off as one of the rarities of our century but allowing you to be with him in peaceful circumstances."

Luise lived with Lavater and his family. She met their friends. She enjoyed the nature around her. She was content. And while Lavater, the multi-talented Swiss Pietist, would be of service to the Prince as an expert on medieval art and a buyer of Swiss glass paintings (which found their place in the "Gothic House") in the years that followed, he was also to serve the Princess as an advisor and provider of comfort – a "dear" and "most precious soul", as she addressed him in the most intimate of her letters and notes.

A "l'ange conducteur and maître de plaisir", as Wilhelm Hosäus, Privy Councillor at the Ducal Court of Anhalt, remarked with severity in a treatise on Lavater's relations with the royal couple published in 1888: "Yet the Princess' choice cannot be regarded as a happy one." The churchman, according to Hosäus, "often failed to exhibit the reserve appropriate to a man of his calling … in particular in his relations with women." Moreover, as the Ducal Councillor commented, "faith and philosophical rationality" had allied itself in Lavater's writings with "far-fetched fantasy".

Be that as it may, there was great harmony. Luise thrived. The Prince called upon Lavater for advice in marital matters: "…It would contribute greatly to my sense of moral contentment if my dear Luise were satisfied with the improvement in her health and if I could make some contribution to her satisfaction." And he also indicated quite pragmatically to his "dearly beloved" friend: "What I discovered yesterday upon unpacking the case … is indeed too much, especially as you, my dear friend, refuse to accept anything from me. – The things are all so beautiful that the sight of them is cause for joy."

According to Elisa von der Recke, Lavater counselled his friend the Princess to the extent of his empathetic capacities. He instructed her to "undertake [daily] an examination of her heart and to record her feelings, moods and thoughts precisely in her diary, and then to send reports of such to him and accept his comments, warnings and encouragements relating to them" (Hosäus). We would regard this today as a totally reasonable form of therapy, and the prescription did not differ very much from the approach taken by her personal physician Zimmermann, who urgently questioned his

5
Wörlitz, Labyrinth, Rondell mit
der Büste Johann Kaspar Lavaters
Wörlitz, Labyrinth and circular
path with the bust of Johann
Kaspar Lavater
Built in 1784

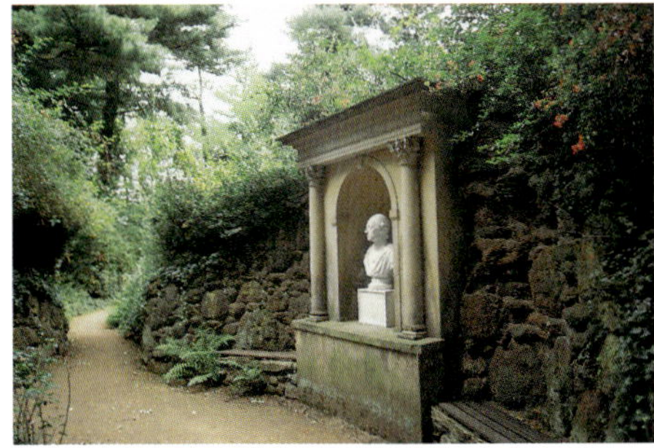

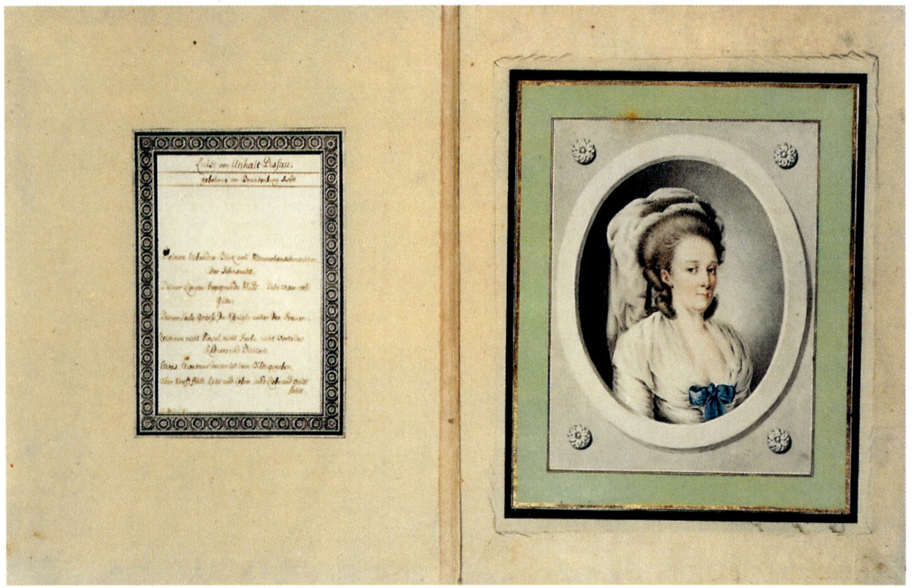

patient with regard to details of her mental and physical condition. The relationship between the philosophising preacher and his blossoming female friend may have been more than purely platonic. One exchange of letters began with great politeness and a touch of over-eagerness. "Dear Lavater", wrote Luise, "I cannot describe the joy your dear little note caused me … oh, I have not been so happy for a long time, and this new proof of your benevolent thoughtfulness, which I could hardly have dared hope for, makes me all the happier…" In Lavater's response to Luise, dated September 7th, 1784, we read: "What am I to write to the nearest and farthest of my loves? Oh, were I strong enough for myself? Loving enough to you to promise to write no more, not a syllable more, until I can write a single word . . . but so strong and so loving I am not." In April 1785 Lavater wrote to Luise again: "Dear soul! I am writing now in the room where your picture hangs opposite that of my wife and looks down at me from the left on a cold, last morning in April."

Luise answered her friend's now serious, now trifling tone with consistent animation. At first, under the influence of her status as a guest, she addressed the slightly older husband and wife Lavater "Mama" and "Papa", later returning to "dear soul" and relating details of everyday life: "This noon the Prince of Coethen dined with us, arriving quite unexpectedly … half a head taller than my F., and twice as fat and strong."

The Princess signed her personal notes with an energetic "L." – her handwriting characteristically much livelier, more animated and flowing, though unfortunately also more difficult to decipher in such communications as it was in the elegant official messages written in a courtly style.

As an advisor to both Luise and Franz, Lavater, probably the most influential figure among those close to the royal couple for a number of years, most likely played a significant role in bringing about their amiable separation. His influence was for the most part supportive. He encouraged Luise's literary interests, giving her on one occasion a personal copy of Goethe's *Iphegenia*. He was never at a loss for grand words or poor verses – in his poems on the occasion of Luise's birthday on September 24th, for example: "Blessed be the joyous day / On which all rejoiceth may…"

Sometime in 1796, however, this complex alliance, which no one was inclined to investigate thoroughly or able to comprehend completely, was shaken when Lavater committed "that horrid indiscretion involving the most sacred matters of friendship" (Karoline von Berg), an event that put an abrupt end to the liaison between Luise and

Lavater – a relationship Franz "so much desired to see continue". Hosäus makes no mention of the affair but later cites two strange messages dedicated to the Princess as legacies of Lavater, who died of wounds inflicted by an assassin in 1801: "The good purple winter coat that Luise von Dessau gave me in 1783, which I wore through every winter and which is now so worn that Mama and Luise [his daughter] will no longer put up with it, I was forced to give away yesterday." Thus the text of one note to Luise. The other reads: "Full of complete love [she] wishes to possess a wholeness, as she gives wholeness as well; she is incapable of accepting circumstances that permit only one-sided enjoyment."

Since Luise and Franz von Anhalt-Dessau – probably in accordance with the Princess' wishes – returned Lavater's letters to him after 1786, many of the written items – though not the complete body of correspondence – have been preserved in the Lavater Archives of the Zurich Central Library, where the originals can be examined today. They have not been edited, however, nor has the entire "Princess chapter". Therefore the quotations provided here are also intended as encouragement to further research on this subject.

This sketch of the life of the Princess of Anhalt-Dessau could be pursued to its end as the history of the illness of a woman disappointed in life. She suffered at her own hand and under the influence of her environment, not to mention the numerous maladies typical of her time – tooth problems, febrile infections, injuries incurred in coach accidents. Apart from such factors, she presumably consulted too many doctors and underwent too many curative treatments at health spas – a consequence of her particular social status. Yet aside from the ineffective cures in Carlsbad, her more cheerful journeys to Switzerland and her stays at the home of the artist Hartmann and his family in Stuttgart, Luise enjoyed at least one long year of happiness. This was in 1795/96, when she journeyed to Italy in the company of a small following (of which Friedrich Matthison was also a member) joined as well by the poet Friederike von Brun and her children. Luise's "deep and refined appreciation of art" would "now receive the ultimate blessing of the gods in Rome through the antiquities and Rafael", as Matthison reported to his friend Bonstetten.

In his memoirs, published in 1814, the poet had praised the Princess' "richly endowed mind" and her "abundance of beauteous spirit", citing her approach to the reading of literature as well: "It is very interesting, from both an aesthetic and a psychological standpoint, to peruse a book that has been read by the Princess, for she never reads without a pen or pencil in her hand… Kloppstock's odes are hardly more than lines… But Göthe boasts the most double underlinings, especially in 'Iphegenia in Taurus' and in 'Torquato Tasso'." Matthison notes, however, that only French works were read in the evening hours, for "French is much more audible to her than German. Ordinarily, she prefers travel accounts and works of natural history. On occasion she reads a tragedy by Corneille, Racine or Voltaire, in which the Princess then customarily speaks one of the roles herself."

Rousseau's writings had long since gained attention within Luise's circle of friends. The Prince and Princess, who had stopped in Paris on their return journey from England in 1775 and made an incognito visit to Jean-Jacques Rousseau on October 16th, dedicated the memorial island in Wörlitz, modelled on the original in the park at Ermenonville, to the admired philosopher four years after his death in 1778. The revealing text of Luise's diary entry can be found in the 1996 Frankfurt catalogue for "Weltbild Wörlitz". As she wrote at the end of the visit with Rousseau, the Princess, 25 years of age at the time, was reluctant to part with the philosopher, "because I was compelled to fear that I would never see him again, and because I had now seen for myself that people's judgement of him, based upon his humour, was wrong, and so I

7
Ferdinand Hartmann
Portrait des Friedrich von
Matthisson
Portrait of Friedrich von
Matthisson
Oil on canvas
1794
Gleimhaus, Halberstadt

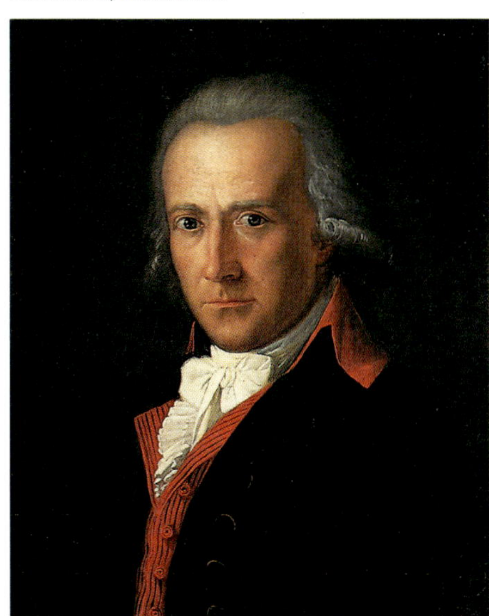

believe as well that he has been treated unfairly in many things and am convinced that this man, if people only knew how to respond to him, would be very pleasant company and of great benefit to reason."

Twenty years later and in the midst of the confusion of war that enveloped central Europe, Luise von Anhalt-Dessau departed on her "grand tour" of Italy – and found, aside from medical advice and new experiences of ancient historical sites and the art of antiquity, the very "pleasant company" she had missed at home. Her grape treatment at Lake Lugano, the expertise of physicians in Switzerland and Pavia – what were they in comparison to her encounter with the "greatest bridle path in Europe", the Gotthard Pass, which she negotiated on horseback with her entourage. And what could be more pleasurable than wandering through Rome, accompanied by the "erudite and considerate expert on classical antiquity" Aloys Ludwig Hirt, upon whose "truly romantic banquet on the Palatina" amidst garlands of ivy and an atmosphere of good cheer Matthison heaped lavish praise in his memoirs. A woman able to ride on horseback over the mountains, cross rivers on unsafe ferry barges and pass through the Alban mountains on the back of a mule "on an enchantingly beautiful day", a woman who had the strength to celebrate a "feast of friendship and nature" amidst a "world in bloom" could not really be so ill after all.

Matthison describes only the Princess' pleasant experiences, such as the encounter with Angelika Kaufmann in the latter's flat near the Trinita di Monte. Luise had met the painter during a stay in London in 1775. Now in Rome, she renewed her acquaintance with this "quiet woman with qualities of a vestal virgin". And she recalled in her own inimitable lively manner whatever "might be interesting and important, while her rediscovered friend continued to paint at her easel."

The poet and travelling companion also mentions the purchase of a work of art: "A…large painting, in which Cupid wipes away the dew of a tear of sadness from the grieving eye of Psyche with a lock of his rich, golden mane of hair, was purchased for three hundred Zechins, and indeed, among brothers, this excellent painting is worth that sum. The superior quality of the painting is fully commensurate with the setting chosen for it. I mean the Luisium, the Princess' house near Dessau…"

Angelika Kauffmann also painted a portrait of Luise, and Matthison expressed regret that the likeness of his friend the Princess, "the accustomed harmony and vitality of her colour" was unfortunately not rendered "in the main point", with sufficient similarity: "The head appears much too idealised and recalls only too weakly the characteristic features of the original."

Luise was guided on an excursion to Naples by Philipp Hackert, the landscape painter – "a Prussian in body and soul" and a master of the culinary arts. "He presented the Princess with noonday banquets … in which magnificence, taste and abundance were united in harmony. Even the angora cat Marchesina, the artist's darling, dined from silver."

In Naples Luise refused, "pleading all manner of trifling excuses", an invitation to visit Lady Hamilton, a woman notorious for her liberal ways. "As if by a magical power … and … genuine worth", however, Luise was attracted to her spouse, Sir William. At the first opportunity she returned to Rome, where she made excursions into the surrounding countryside and pursued her "sentimental affection for the old city on the Tiber". Nowhere else, neither in Paris, nor London nor "at any other place on this earth" had Luise felt so "complete and so very much at home".

"I would like to have the autumn of life pass by quietly and unrecognised in that villa", she is said to have declared in view of the Cestius Pyramid in Rome's Protestant cemetery. "There life would fade to its end without clouds, and here a simple stone would mark the grave of the worthy German recluse."

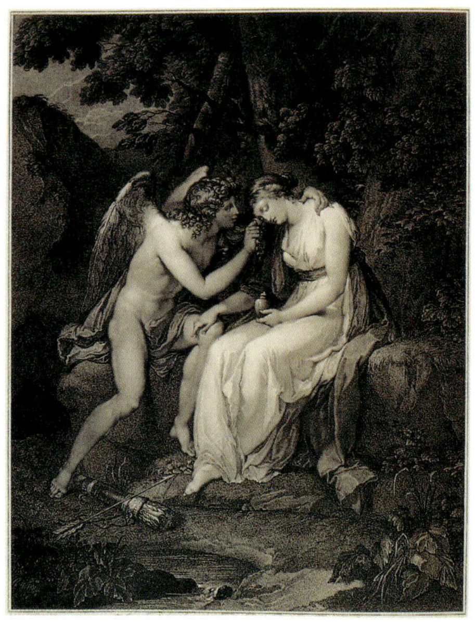

8
Karl Ludwig Buchhorn
after Angelika Kauffmann,
Amor und Psyche
Cupid and Psyche
Drypoint engraving,
1804
Private collection

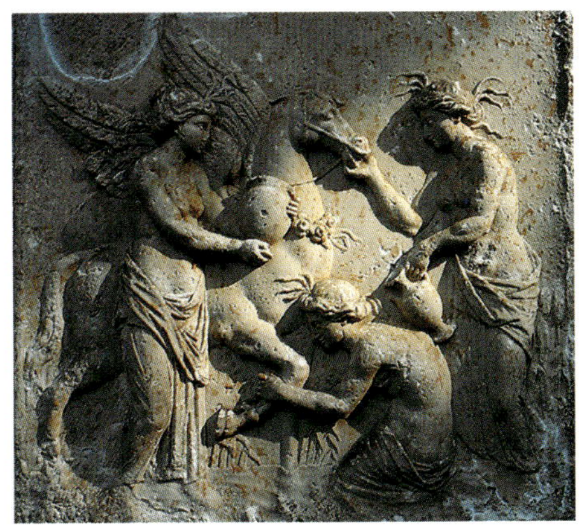

9
Dessau, Luisium, Pegasusbrunnen
(Pegasus Fountain)
Detail
1781-1782

The life of the Princess went on in accustomed stillness after her return. She lived in the Luisium or in the "Grey House", the Neogothic structure built as a commoner's residence adjacent to the church in Wörlitz. She undertook further treatments at health spas and journeys to Switzerland. Her maladies took charge of her life. Her deafness grew worse, and her eye and skin infections became more threatening as time passed.

No further mention is made of the *Wörlitzer Schloß* or the quarters of the Princess, the rooms so masterfully designed by Erdmannsdorff and preserved to this day. As a young woman Luise had greatly enjoyed taking part in the work of decorating her surroundings; she herself planted hundreds of Lombard poplar seedlings in the park. Now all of that was over.

It is difficult to imagine, however, that the elegance and quality of her surroundings in the "suburban villa" of the Luisium did not give the Princess a certain sense of comfort. "There can be no greater degree of comfort, convenience and good taste in such a confined space [than is to be found here]", wrote August Rode in 1801. The Dessau court advisor, writer and author of the first tourist guide to Wörlitz left out Luise's private home in his first descriptions. And it surely would never have occurred to him to mention her influence upon its appearance.

The country house is currently undergoing restoration – the great hall with its painted allegories of the womanly virtues and the stimulating marble-stucco pilasters, the salons with their high windows facing the park, the "Pompeiian Room" and the room in which the painting *Cupid and Psyche* once hung… The little *Schloß* is to be reopened in 1998, on the anniversary of Luise's birth. Even now, in its unfinished state, one senses that the Princess must have been closely involved in the decoration process. In view of all we know from her own statements this must have been so. Yet documentary evidence is nowhere to be found. As is true of so much of her life.

Luise von Anhalt-Dessau died on December 21st, 1811 at the home of Caroline von Hills, the widow of her brother-in-law, in Dessau. Buried at first in the residential city, she found her final resting place in 1822 at the side of her husband Franz von Anhalt-Dessau, who died in 1817, in the obelisk-crowned tower of the village church in Waldersee. The church and the tower, both in a lamentable state of ruin, are also being restored at this time. And so the gravesite remains hidden from view for the time being – yet another reason to turn one's attention to the life of Luise von Anhalt-Dessau.

Carte des Postes d'Allemagne et de Pays Voisins, 1790 (cat. no. 1)

Bounderies of the Whole Roman Empire, circa 1790 (approximate)

Bounderies of principality of Anhalt-Dessau, circa 1790 (approximate)

Landholdings of Anhalt-Dessau in the Kingdom of Prussia (East Prussia)

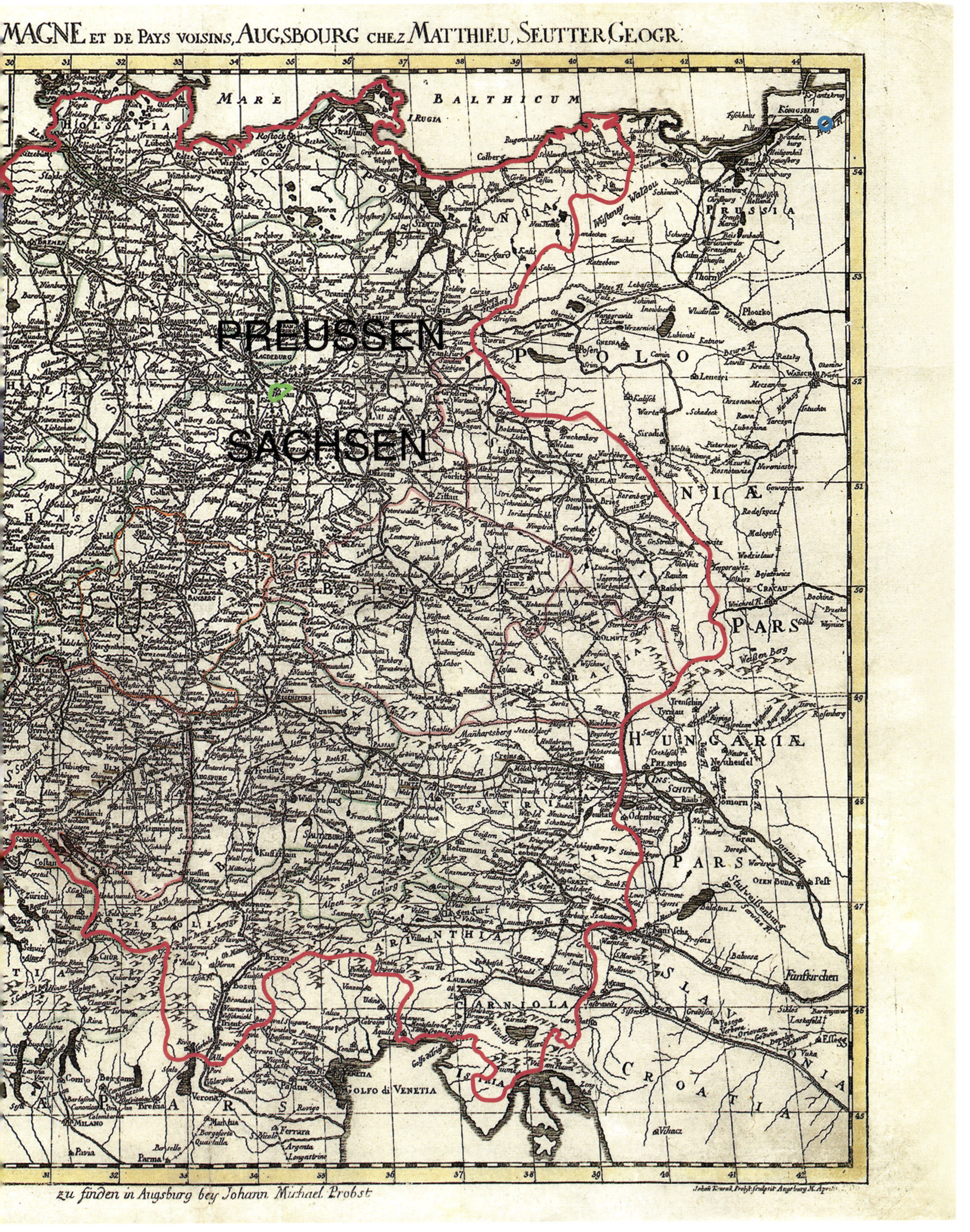
MAGNE ET DE PAYS VOISINS, AUGSBOURG CHEZ MATTHIEU SEUTTER GEOGR.
MARE BALTHICUM
I. RUGIA
HOLSATIA
PRUSSIA
POLONIA
POLO
PREUSSEN
SACHSEN
BOHEMIA
MORAVIA
PARS
HUNGARIÆ
PARS
CARINTHIA
CARNIOLA
ISTRIA
CROATIA
SLAVONIA
GOLFO di VENETIA
KÖNIGSBERG
zu finden in Augsburg bey Johann Michael Probst

"J'EUS LE BONHEUR DE VOUS ACCOMPAGNEZ…"
TRAVEL NOTES OF FRIEDRICH WILHELM
VON ERDMANNSDORFF FROM THE YEAR 1764

Thomas Weiss

> *"Where order in variety we see,*
> *And where, tho' all things differ all agree".*
> Alexander Pope, 'Windsor Forest'

Introduction

The travels of Prince Leopold III Friedrich Franz of Anhalt-Dessau (1740–1817) and his attendants through various countries in Europe during the second half of the eighteenth century and the host of impressions that he gained were without doubt the most important sources of inspiration for the design of the park now known as the Dessau-Wörlitzer Gartenreich. So far, this cultivated area of land which ranks at European level has sacrificed none of its unique aura of authenticity (at least with regard to the core areas) as an integral part of the "Central Elbe Biosphere Reservation". As the legacy of its princely founder (and many of his assistants), the park is in many respects an incomparable representative of the Age of Enlightenment in Germany.

Friedrich Wilhelm of Erdmannsdorff (1736–1800) was the lifelong friend and master builder for Prince Friedrich Franz, who was four years his junior. Erdmannsdorff was almost entirely self-taught and took full advantage of his participation in several study tours. They made him into the creative architect who with his truly illuminating ideas established the early classical building style – as exemplified by Wörlitz mansion – in Germany.

In addition to studying the objects themselves, any available written source material – particularly travel reports – must be read to understand the complex origin and reasons for such extraordinary, multi-faceted achievements, particularly in the fields of architecture and landscaping, as well as agricultural science and social and educational systems. Unfortunately, these often very individualistic accounts of the time are quite rare, so that in the past extraordinary emphasis has been placed on the two travel reports prepared in French by Friedrich Wilhelm von Erdmannsdorff[1] and Georg Heinrich von Berenhorst[2], which are in the collection of the Anhaltische Landesbibliothek in Dessau. We owe most of our current knowledge of the facts to their extensive diaries about the educational grand tour made from 1765 to 1767 by the nobility from Dessau. It is astonishing that a complete transcription of the manuscripts and an annotation of those contemporary witnesses have not yet been published. However, they still provide concrete information about the influences on and models for many practical and intellectual ideas about reform in the *Gartenreich* or Garden Province. Unfortunately, until now almost nothing has been known about the first official trip by Prince Franz of Anhalt-Dessau in 1763–1764, with England as his destination. It was certainly one of his most important initiatives at the beginning of his attempted reforms, including the exemplary land beautification project (which began in Wörlitz in 1764). A few letters[3] and the remarkable publications by August (von) Rode[4] and Friedrich Reil,[5] both of whom had close personal ties to their sovereign, provided a few vague indications about the approximate route of that first journey. However, in addition to the length of the journey, which lasted about a year, only general statements could be gleaned about its interest due to the "grandiose buildings, the splendid parks, the farming and livestock husbandry, the cultivation of meadows and the horticulture"[6] in England. Many later authors, such as E. P. Riesenfeld[7] and numerous others,[8] used them as a basis for speculations on the itinerary.

Today we can only guess why Prince Franz did not follow the lead of most highly cultivated men of his rank and first head south to Italy, but instead made England his first destination. It is particularly astonishing that he chose the British Isles at such an early date, if Erdmannsdorff indeed returned to the Court in Dessau from his three-year journey to Italy in April 1763, shortly before the Prince's planned departure, filled with splendid impressions which he would have certainly described to his sovereign. Perhaps the reason is that the Prince intended to stop at several places in Holland during his long journey to England, in order to trace the roots of his origins in the House of Orange, with its rich traditions. It is generally acknowledged that the minor state of Anhalt-Dessau in the seventeenth century primarily owed its important economic and cultural tendencies to his great-grandmother Henrietta-Catharina, a Princess of Nassau-Orange by birth. The House of Anhalt also had a tradition of travelling through the Netherlands to England. The Prince's forefather Prince Louis of Anhalt-Köthen travelled through those countries in 1596 and also recorded his experiences "in German verse"[9].

The decision to travel to the British Isles may also have reflected the Prince's wish for physical contact with the places where the major English landscape designers and architects were working. It is likely that he hoped for major sources of inspiration for his own wish to transform the desolate area on the Elbe and Mulde Rivers.

Great Britain, the cradle of the Enlightenment, had also been portrayed in contemporary literature as an ideal country; it was a century in advance of the Continent and best fit to Franz's own liberal notions. He saw his personal ideals embodied in the English body politic, literature, and individual freedoms, and hoped that he could gain experiences there with regard to charitable societies. In addition, England had been a leader in artistic matters and questions of taste since the 1760s. In his almost fanatical enthusiasm for all things English, Prince Franz of Anhalt-Dessau later liked to call England his second homeland.

A look at the group of people whom Prince Franz deliberately sought out or fortuitously encountered during his first journey will show that some of them took an anti-Prussian position. That means that another possible reason for the journey might have been to quietly seek allies against Prussian predominance and in favour of the unification of several minor states, which he himself favoured.

For the reasons mentioned above, it was a piece of extraordinary luck to discover in private ownership at least a fragment of the report penned by Erdmannsdorff about the first journey in 1763/1764 and to be able to publish it here for the first time with annotations (Figure 1).

What struck Erdmannsdorff during his journey; what does he mention? Perusal of the French-language manuscript, which is reproduced in its entirety below (with a modern translation) gives us a very direct impression of his personal view of all of the places of interest that he visited during the tireless sightseeing on his journey. The value of his writings lies primarily in the high potential for arousing interest and providing greater detail about what is already known. At the same time, this report offers new perspectives for the reader in evaluating an important phase in the lives of both protagonists in the cultural circle in Dessau, who at that time were laying the foundation for their exquisite taste in buildings, gardens, and the fine arts in general. In addition, at each stop we experience Erdmannsdorff's surprisingly frank appraisals of important people, while at the same time recognising through certain episodes the roots of his affection for the Anglo-Saxon world, which he and the Prince both cultivated.

1 Page 27 of F. W. von Erdmannsdorff's manuscript describing stops at "Stow" and "Newmarket" in the first week of October 1763. Private owner (Detail).

The extraordinarily strong effect that a first trip abroad generally has, as well as the specific case of the young Prince's journey to the British Isles, immediately comes into focus against the background of the political and economic conditions in the German minor state of Anhalt-Dessau. A few years previously, Franz, impressed by the pedantic military strength of his grandfather and Field Marshal (Prince Leopold I of Anhalt-Dessau, the *"Alter Dessauer"*) and having spent his youth without his parents (his father Leopold II Maximilian and his mother Gisela Agnes, a Princess of Anhalt-Köthen by birth, died when he was 11), set the stage for his own future development. In 1758, when he was just 18, he took over the reins of government from his uncle, Prince Dietrich, who had ruled since 1751 as guardian responsible for his upbringing. In addition, on 6 October 1757, under very difficult circumstances, he wrote to his uncle, recalling his war experience as Commandant of his father's former regiment from Halle before Prague and asking for permission to resign from the Prussian Army[10]. His uncle sent a friendly reply from Dessau on 7 October 1757[11], and Prince Franz of Anhalt-Dessau left the Prussian army two weeks later.

Directly after taking over the regency on 20 October 1758, he declared with surprising resoluteness to Frederick II the Great of Prussia that his principality would be neutral in the Seven Years' War (1756–1763). Prussia's resulting demands to Anhalt-Dessau for contributions of soldiers, money, and food lasted until the end of the Seven Years' War. The results of the long years of war were catastrophic for the small sovereign state and its devastated population. They forced the Prince to be exceedingly thrifty in his budget, and his secret wish for socio-economic reforms to eliminate the deplorable state of affairs became increasingly evident.

However, it was not until after the Treaty of Hubertusburg was signed on 15 February 1763 that living conditions began to change in the Principality of Anhalt-Dessau, thereby allowing the 22-year-old Prince to seek new stability on the basis of reasonable rules for social and political life that were intended to influence both individual morality and the relationship of states among themselves. To solve problems fundamentally and over the long term, it seemed to him that the only feasible approach was to study conditions in other countries that were considered to be models, so the Prince made increasingly concrete plans for his first long study tour, although he did not yet plan an exact itinerary.

Because Prussian demands still had to be satisfied even after the peace treaty was signed, he continued to delay his journey, and it was not until 8 July 1763, six days before his definitive departure, that he could decide to prepare the final chamber instruction with a total of 12 paragraphs in his own hand and sign it himself[12]. This was primarily to get conditions in his impoverished state into proper order in accordance with his thinking before he left for several months. In addition, Franz no doubt also wanted to relieve his conscience somewhat for leaving his state on its own during such a difficult economic situation. Deeply concerned about the future, he did not forget to say specifically in his instruction that "what was best for him and his state should never be separated"[13].

A list attached to the instruction showing the income and expenditures of the treasury includes at the end "38,573 taler surplus… which I wish to retain at my free disposal"[14]. That appears to indicate that the Prince had also financed his pending journey to England from that amount.

However, it was not only the domestic political background in his state that caused serious difficulties for the young Prince. In his private life, he no doubt had to clarify matters related to his liaison with his first love, Sophie (?) Eleonore Hoffmeier of Dessau (born on 12 November 1739), before he left Dessau. This close relationship with the daughter of a middle-class family, who was one year his senior and not of his rank, is known to have produced children. Her first son, Johann Franz Georg, later Count von Waldersee, was born on 5 September 1763, in the Prince's absence. To avoid being directly confronted with the joys of fatherhood and any resulting familial problems (he was not married as befitted his rank to Luise Henriette Wilhelmine von Brandenburg-Schwedt (1750–1811) until pressured to do so by Frederick the Great in 1767), it was more diplomatic to hear about the birth of his first illegitimate son while abroad.

Eleonore Hoffmeier, who two years later bore the Prince a daughter named Luise Eleonore Friederike[15], married Adolf Heinrich von Neitschütz (Neidschütz) (1730–1722) on 12 November 1765, which was no doubt deliberately arranged by the Prince himself, who also had an imposing house built for her in Dessau (now destroyed). As equerry of the princely court in Dessau (beginning on 20 October 1756), Neitschütz was one of the select participants of the first journey to England in 1763, and the Prince therefore considered him to be particularly suitable for assuming the responsible role of father in his place.

Even if young Prince Franz's main reasons for making the journey were the diverse impressions that could be gained and the anticipation of new experiences with the objective of self-improvement, it is also understandable, given the difficult conditions in his own state, that he simply planned to break out of his everyday routine and flee his official, social, and personal obligations, at least for a limited time.

Comments on the manuscript

In autumn of 1764, in other words several months after the return to Dessau, at the Prince's specific request, Erdmannsdorff prepared his description of the events of the journey and the remarkable sights in the countries they had visited. On 13 September 1764, in a letter from Dessau to his sovereign, who was staying at his East Prussian latifundia at Insterburg in Bubene (now Bubainen), he mentioned the travel journal that was currently occupying his time: "(…) parce/qu'il me paroit que je ne puit vivre ici quand/Vous n'y etes point, que pour travailler avec/plus de loisir au journal de Votre voyage d'An-/gleterre…"[16].

He primarily based his report – as he specifically states in the fragment – on his "little diary" (which has unfortunately never been found), which provided an important basis and support for his memory of individual experiences, thoughts and feelings. Naturally, he also relied on his memory, which was – as he apologetically wrote in courteous humility to the Prince on the first page of the fragment – hampered by "my lack of attention and the speed with which we viewed everything". That remark by the author is important for our evaluation of his report, because Erdmannsdorff recapitulated the voyage after some time had passed. That was a very common approach to preparing travel reports at that time. He described his experiences critically and reflectively, which means that the assumed freshness of the spontaneous entry of experiences in the present has now yielded to rather rational, cool reporting. The various dates in the margins of the entries were briefly noted in retrospect and not consistently set down each day. Erdmannsdorff felt that only certain eventful passages in the text, usually when changing location, required the abbreviated names of the months and the date to make the text more understandable to the reader. Similarly, the time of day is only sporadically indicated. That is done directly in the text, for example, when he states that the journey continued "in the morning" or "at midday". Surprisingly, not all stops on the itinerary had been set by the date of departure from Dessau on 14 July 1763. Instead, given Prince Franz's lack of experience, they were not decided until later in the trip. Given the "speed" of the journey that Erdmannsdorff mentions at certain places in the manuscript, today's reader must wonder at the choice of route. The travellers did not proceed directly to the English Channel, but instead took a zig-zag course across the continent to their destination in England. They headed north-west from Dessau, and then left Hannover for Frankfurt-am-Main. From there they proceeded north up the Rhine to Dusseldorf, but then headed south to Liege. Their path then led to Amsterdam and along the coast via Rotterdam, Gent, Antwerp, Brussels, Menin, and Dunkirk toward Calais. So far, there has been no explanation of the route they took.

One particularly important advisor in their choice of route was Count Daniel Christoph von der Schulenburg (1716–1772), Prince Franz's host at his first stop in Lucklum (Figure 2). This highly educated man was familiar with England and had already seen many of the noteworthy places on the way to it. At Spa, the Belgian watering place, the travellers from Dessau later quite coincidentally made the acquaintance of Sir John Clavering (1722–1777), an English man of the world (Figure 3). He had his own estate near Southampton, and at Prince Franz's specific request acted as the group's "Cicerone" during their entire sojourn in England. Erdmannsdorff mentions his "excellent advice that you [Prince Franz, editor's note] have never ceased praising". Georg Heinrich von Berenhorst mentions John Clavering later in his "Travel Journal" of the second journey to England as a man "whom I esteem above all others with whom I became acquainted in England".

The fragmentary remains of the report provide no other information about preparations for the journey, and they do not mention the members of the group by name (or function) or describe the carriages in which the group rode. In addition to the Prince himself and his closest confidant Erdmannsdorff, it can be assumed that the gardener Johann Friedrich Eyserbeck (1734–1818) was one of the group, since he prepared the earliest plan for the gardens in Wörlitz (1764), and that the afore mentioned Adolf Heinrich von Neitschütz came along in his function as equerry[17]. The group also included several court servants, such as menservants, a hairdresser, and a cook. With regard to the travel conveyances, we may be able to assume that on this journey in 1763 the Prince did as he would do on his trip to Italy two years later and also used two of his own coaches (even if it was more expensive than to use a hackney carriage or mail coach): "The two princes [Prince Franz and his brother John George, editor's note], Herr von Erdmannsdorff and I were in the first, the brand new but exceedingly heavy 'Vessau de Guerre' (as we jokingly called it); the second was an open chaise in the form that used to be called a *chaise de landau*"[18].

The pages of this illuminating discovery are written on both the front and reverse sides, with about two-thirds of each page characteristically covered with text and the resulting margin reserved for references about dates and a few additions to the text. A comparison of the handwriting with the diary of the grand tour that was written about three years later shows that Erdmannsdorff also personally drafted this first description of a journey in clear, legible handwriting that reveals meticulousness, a sense of aesthetics, and resoluteness. Here, too, he obviously enjoyed using the French language throughout. Perhaps he was guided by the same consideration that Georg Heinrich von Berenhorst later mentioned on the first page of his own travel journal on 19 April 1775: "I have written in French, certainly not in the erroneous conviction that I can express myself better in a foreign language than in my own (I am convinced that in spite of all possible knowledge, one can always best use one's own mother tongue), but instead from the necessity of myself once also using that language, which is understood by all of Europe"[19]. Erdmannsdorff later much enjoyed using English in his confidential letters to his future wife Wilhelmine (Willi) von Ahlimb – also in an

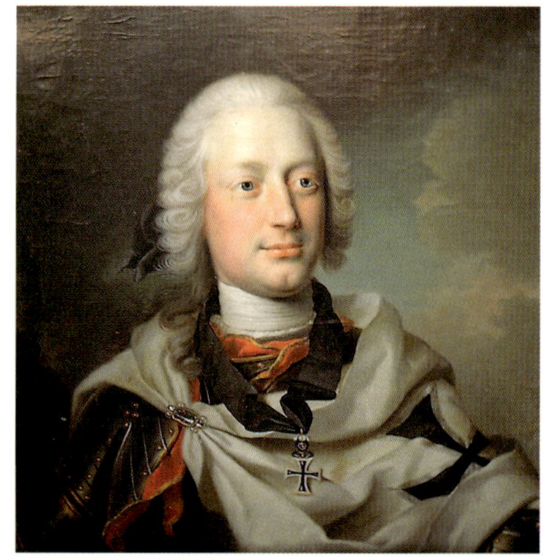

2 Unknown artist, Daniel Christoph Graf von der Schulenburg (1716–1772), (Detail), oil on canvas, dated 1746. Private owner.

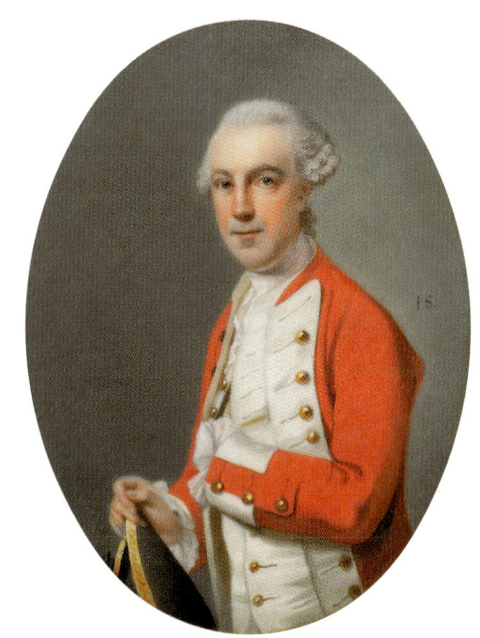

3 Unknown artist, Sir John Clavering (1722–1777), ivory miniature, Victoria & Albert Museum, London.

attempt to teach her the language. However, he had not yet mastered the English language during his first stay in London in September 1763, which caused severe difficulties for him because he was limited to perceiving everything visually. When weighing everything that appeared noteworthy about the journey, the budding architect always placed greater emphasis on sights related to culture and art history. Only in exceptional cases does he mention important people or occasionally describe social occasions. The fact that his notes concentrate on what was important to him is entirely in keeping with his rather sober temperament. It is also understandable that in this first travel report he tells us almost nothing about the dendrologic particularities of English parks, although Prince Franz must already have had a great deal of interest in them. That is particularly regrettable when one compares the types of trees that were most popular in English landscape gardens beginning in the mid-eighteenth century with those in the Wörlitz gardens and realises that some species must have come from the British Isles.

The 31 vertical-format pages (34.5 x 20.5 cm) are thread-stitched and have no page numbers. The manuscript fragment covers the period from 14 July until about 20 October 1763; to date, it has generally been assumed that the entire journey lasted until spring of the following year. To summarise, this document tells us about all of the stops on the way through Germany, Holland, and Belgium, but unfortunately about only a two-month period spent in southern England and the Midlands. We can only continue to speculate about the rest of the voyage. Nonetheless, in spite of the continuing uncertainty about the further itinerary in England and the date the journey ended, Erdmannsdorff's first travel notes significantly flesh out the history of Dessau's cultural circle. For example, it is now quite clear that in addition to the Palladian buildings and antiquities in general that Erdmannsdorff studied in Italy, classical architecture in the Netherlands also had a significant influence on his earliest architectural work[20]. While previous suspicions about the exemplary role played by certain specific buildings in England and English landscape gardens in the creation of the gardens in Wörlitz have been confirmed, other knowledge considered to be a certainty by researchers will have to be revised in the future.

For their thorough archival research, which is particularly vital for understanding the content of this primary source, and for much other valuable information, I would like to thank the museologist Ms. Daniela Clare of Wörlitz and, in the Kulturstiftung DessauWörlitz, Mr. Uwe Quilitzsch, section head and Dipl. Ing. Ludwig Trauzettel. Messrs. Thomas Grosse of Brussels and Bernard Korzus of Munster also kindly helped me in my research. I am indebted to Ms. Ingrid Seeger-Helmberger, M.A. of Munich for her constructive criticism of the text. Finally, I am most grateful to Ms. Ina Grünberg of Wörlitz for having rendered the manuscript in a proper form.

1 Friedrich Wilhelm von Erdmannsdorff, Reise-Tagebuch der zweiten Italien-Reise 1765 bis 1766. Anhalt Provincial State Library, Dessau, classification no. HS 10012.

2 Georg Heinrich von Berenhorst, Journal de voyage des princes Léopold Frédéric Francois et Jean Georg d'Anhalt du 18. Octobre 1765 jusqu'au 3. mars 1768, conduit par de Berenhorst le 19. Avril 1775. Dessau, ce 19. d'Avril 1775. Copy of a copy from 1932. Anhalt Provincial State Library, Dessau, classification no. HB 8089.

3 For example, F. Siebigk, Aus dem brieflichen Verkehre des Fürsten Leopold Friedrich Franz von Dessau mit Friedrich Wilhelm von Erdmannsdorff, in: Mitteilungen des Vereins für Anhaltische Landesgeschichte, Volume II, Dessau 1880, p. 117 ff. (These 107 letters extend over a period from 1760 to 1790.)

4 August Rode, Leben des Herrn Friedrich Wilhelm von Erdmannsdorff, Dessau 1801, Reprint Wörlitz 1994, pp. 8–9.

5 Friedrich Reil, Leopold Friedrich Franz, Herzog und Fürst von Anhalt-Dessau, „ältestregierender Fürst in Anhalt, nach Seinem Wirken und Wesen, Dessau 1845, reprint Wörlitz 1995, pp. 12–15.

6 Ibid., p. 14.

7 E. P. Riesenfeld, Erdmannsdorff – Der Baumeister des Herzogs Leopold Friedrich Franz von Anhalt-
   Dessau, Berlin 1913, pp. 15–16.

8 Most recently Michael Rüffer, Grand Tour – Die Reisen Leopolds III. Friedrich Franz von Anhalt-
   Dessau und Friedrich Wilhelm von Erdmannsdorff, in: exhibition catalogue: Weltbild Wörlitz –
   Entwurf einer Kulturlandschaft, published by Frank-Andreas Bechtoldt and Thomas Weiss, Wörlitz
   1996, pp. 117–130.

9 Fürst Ludwigs zu Anhalt Köthen, Reise-Beschreibung von ihm selbst in Deutsche Verse gebracht, in:
   Johann Christoff Beckmann, Accessiones Historiae Anhaltinae, Zerbst 1716, pp. 165–292.

10 Oranienbaum Provincial State Archive, classification no. Abt. Dessau, A 9b VII 2 II fol. 286.

11 Ibid., fol. 288.

12 Ibid., Abt. Dessau, C 5c, No. 10a, 16, 2–4.

13 Ibid., Introduction to Chamber Instruction of 8 July 1763; see also the first supplement to the Anhal-
   tischer Staatsanzeiger no. 150 for the year 1883.

14 Ulla Jablonowski, Bausteine zu einer Geschichte der Stadt Dessau, 9. Neuanfang nach dem
   siebenjährigen Kriege, in: Dessauer Kalender, Volume 41, pp. 60–69, here p. 68.

15 Ibid., p. 69, note 45.

16 "(…), then it appeared to me that, as long as you are absent, I can live here only in order to devote more
   leisure time to the diary of your journey to England (…)" Oranienbaum Provincial State Archive, classification no. Abt. Dessau, A 10, 1759–1768, No. 187, p. 81.

17 Like note 14, here p. 69, note 32.

18 Like note 2, here first part.

19 Ibid.

20 See also Thomas Weiss, Den Freunden der Natur und Kunst. Das Gartenreich Dessau-Wörlitz und
   Andrea Palladio, in: Bauen nach der Natur – Palladio. Die Erben Palladios in Nordeuropa, Ostfildern-
   Ruit 1997, pp. 181–199, esp. p. 183.

De touts tems Monseigneur je comtoi
Vos ordres, (Monseigneur furent de touts
ordre) mes devoirs les plus sacrés. Si mes forces
n'ont pû toutjours y sufire, mon empres-
sement au moins de les exécuter selon
ma capacité. Vous s›en‹ont les garans de
mon zéle inaltérable & du plus sincére
attâchement. Außi les bontés, les géné
rosités & j'ose dire les amitiés dont V.
a.S. daigne me combler me donnent tout
lieu de me flater qu' Elle en est entiére
ment persuadée. >Tant qu'< elle (veut) >voudra< bien me les
conserver, mon bonheur sera parfait,
rien ne me restera à désirer si non de
pouvoir les mériter en quelque manière
Des (le) >Votre< retour (de Vos voyages) >Monseigneur<, Vous me
chargeates, (Monseigneur), de recueillir
avec un peu plus d'ordre ce que j'avois man
qué dans mon petit journal ou ce que ma
mémoire me fourniroit de plus remarquable, dans Votre tour en Angleterre où
j' eus le bonheur de Vous accompagnez.
J'aurais obei plus promtement, si l'aßiduité avec laquelle Vous me permettez d'être
autour de Votre personne n'eut employé
bien>3< agréablement>4< mon>1< tems>2<. Aprésent que
(Elle) Vous étes absent, je m'éfforcerai de
satisfaire à Vos commandemens, et pen-
dant que >je ne puis< faire que des voeux pour Votre
heureux retour, je Vous consacrerai quelque semaines de loisir & de retraite.
Je sens aßés, que mon peu d'attention
et la rapidité avec laquelle nous avons
tout vu, pourront m'avoir fait oublier
une quantité de choses ou m'avoir (fait
tomber) >entrainé< dans bien des erreurs sur d'autres.
Mais je connois aßés Votre indulgence
envers moi, Monseigneur, et je sais
combien Vous étes capable de supléer
à mon inadvertence et de corriger mes
incongruités. Puißai-je au moins Vous
rapeller avec plaisir les (faits) d'un voyage
où Vous avez (employé Votre tems) su
acquerir des conoißances qui joints à
Votre excellent caractére et à la nóbleße
de Vos sentimens forment en Vous un aßem-
(End of page 1)

blage de qualités >personelles< qui Vous élévent encore au
deßus de la grandeur de Votre illustre nais-
sance.
Ce fut le 14. de Juillet que Vous partites
de Deßau. Vous ne Vous arretates qu'à
Lucklum², maison apartenante à l'ordre Theu-
tonique et demeure ordinaire du C.ᵗᵉ de
Schulemburg homme de beaucoup de conois-
sances et qui >pendant quelques jours que V. y futes< Vous aida à
   former

Your Excellency, I have always considered your
orders to be among my most sacred duties. If
my strength has not always been sufficient,
my effort has nonetheless been to carry them
out to the best of my ability. You are the guar-
antor of my unceasing zeal and most sincere
attachment. Moreover, the kindness, the generosity, & I dare to say the friendship that
Your Grace has condescended to show to me
give me every reason to flatter myself that you
are entirely convinced of this. As long as you
wish me to retain them, my happiness will be
complete and I will have nothing else to wish
for except to be worthy of them in some manner. Excellency, since you returned you have
charged me with collecting together with
somewhat greater order what I noted in my
little diary, or the most remarkable things furnished to me by my memory, about your tour
in England, where I had the good fortune to
accompany you. I would have obeyed more
promptly, if the regularity with which you
allow me to be around your person did not
employ my time so agreeably. Now that you
are absent, I will do my utmost to fulfil your
commands and while I can only wish for your
happy return, I will devote several weeks of
leisure & retirement to you. I know full well
that my lack of attention and the speed with
which we viewed everything may have caused
me to forget a good deal of things or led me
to make many errors on others. However, I
know your indulgence to me, Your Excellency, and I know the extent to which you are
capable of remedying my inattentions and
correcting my incongruities. I hope that I will
at least recall for you with pleasure a journey
during which you were able to make acquaintances which, combined with your excellent
character and the nobility of your feelings,
form in you a combination of
(End of page 1)

>personal< qualities that further raise you
above the grandeur of your illustrious birth.
It was on 14 July that you left Dessau. You
first stopped in Lucklum², a house belonging
to the Teutonic Order and usually the
residence of Count von der Schulemburg, a
man of great knowledge who, >during the
several days that you were there<, helped you
to prepare the plan for your journey. He
accompanied you to Saltzdalen³ to visit the

*Translation*¹

*Juillet
le 14.
le 15.*

*July
14th
15th*

le plan de Votre voyage. Il Vous accompagna à Saltzdalen[3] pour faire une visi- *le 16.*
te au Duc de Brunswic >qui y paßait la saison<. Toute la Sept.bre
maison y étoit raßemblée excepté le
Prince Ferdinand et le Prince Héréditai-
re qui étaient aux bains d'Aix la Chapelle.
Sans m'arreter à parler de la Maison de
Saltzdalen & du jardin que le mauvais
tems nous empécha de voir, je me bor-
nerai de dire deux mots de la galerie des
tableaux où Vous Vous amusates une
couple d'heures. Il me semble qu'elle est
composée d'un nombre de bons tableaux
qui (est) sont placés parmi une quantité
de bien médiocres. N'est ce pas domage
qu'un Prince ne préfére un cabinet de
piéces choisies à un amas de peintures
auquel on tâche de donner le titre de
Galerie. Il m'a encore paru que la lu-
miére n'est pas avantageuse dans la
Galerie de Saltzdalen. Vous continuates *le 18.*
Votre chemin à Hanovre, d'où Vous allates
donner un coup d'oeil au jardin de
Herrenhausen[4], qui est beau dans le gout
des jardins d'Allemagne pour la largeur
des (ses) allées et la hauteur des hayes. Aureste il a l'avantage ne pas etre enfer-
mé par une muraille. De Hanovre nous
arrivame a Caßel, où (vous) nous ne (Vous) de *le 23.*
meurames que pour voir quelque cu-
riosités comme le Landgrave n'y étoit
point. Le Kunst=Haus et le Model=Haus[5] ne
laissent pas de mériter quelque attention.
Le grand modéle de Winter-Halter & du
Weißenstein nous présentent peut-étre
une des idées les plus vastes qu'on ai eu dans
(End of page 2)

nos siécles modernes. Le Landgrave *Juillet*
qui en projetta le deßein >&< en commenca l'éxé-
cution prouva au moins que son imagina
tion surpaßait son pouvoir. Il est
a croire que s'il avoit été poßible de la
terminer, avec la situation >naturelle< de la montagne cela auroit fait un superbe coup
d'oeuil. La galerie des tableaux est fort
belle est particuliérement>1< en>11< tableaux>12<
de>13< Rembrandt>14< je>2< ne>3< crois>4< pas>5< qu'il>6< y
ait>7<
de>8< ses>9< pareilles>10<. Les environs de Caßel
rendent encore aßéz témoignage des
dégats que la derniére guerre à cau-
sé dans ces pays. Nou continuames *le 25.*
notre route d'une traite jusqu'à Franc- *le 27.*
fort sur le Main où Vous allates, Monseigneur, pour faire visite à M.me Votre
Tante[6] une des plus estimables et respe-
ctables Princeßes. Il y a deux peintres
à Francfort qui ont quelques mérite l'un
est Schutz[7] peintre de paysages et l'autre
Seekatz qui traite en petit des sujets
de conversations. L'aimable M.r de Wreeck
qui était venu Vous faire sa cour à
Francfort, nous accompagna par eau sur
le Main à Mayence. Le jardin de l'Ele- *le 30.*
cteur qu'on nomme La Favorite[8] ne dedit

Duke of Brunswick, >who was spending the *16th*
season there<.
Throughout September, the house was gathered there, with the exception of Prince Ferdinand and the Hereditary Prince, who was
taking the waters at Aachen. Without dwelling on the House of Saltzdalen & the garden,
which bad weather prevented us from seeing,
I will limit myself to two words about the gallery of paintings that amused you for a couple
of hours. It appears to me that it includes a
number of good paintings that are placed
amongst a quantity of rather mediocre ones.
Is it not a pity that a Prince does not prefer a
cabinet of selected pieces rather than an
accumulation of paintings to which one tries
to give the title of gallery. It also appeared to
me that the light was not advantageous in the
Saltzdalen Gallery. You continued on your *the 18th*
way to Hanover, from whence you went to
have a look at the garden of Herrenhausen,[4]
which is beautiful in the style of German
gardens for the width of its avenues and the
height of the hedges. Moreover, it has the
advantage of not being enclosed by a wall.
From Hanover we proceeded to Kassel, *23rd*
where we lingered only to view a few curiosities, as the Landgrave was not there. The
Kunsthaus and the Modellhaus[5] were not
worthy of attention. The large models of
Winter-Halter & Weissenstein give us perhaps
one of the most grandiose ideas that anyone
has had
(End of page 2)

in our modern centuries. The Landgrave, *July*
who prepared the design and began its execu-
tion, showed at least that his imagination
surpassed his ability. It can be believed that, if
it had been possible to complete it, the view
would have been superb with the natural
situation of the mountains. The gallery of
paintings is very beautiful and I believe that
the paintings by Rembrandt are peerless. The
countryside surrounding Kassel still bears
sufficient witness to the damage caused by
the last war in these lands. We continued
our journey along a route that led us to Frank- *25th*
furt am Main, where Your Excellency paid *27th*
a visit to your noble aunt[6], one of the most
highly-esteemed and respectable Princesses.
There are two painters of some merit in
Frankfurt; one of them is the landscape
painter Schutz,[7] and the other is Seekatz,
who paints subjects of conversation in small
format. The amiable Herr de Wreeck, who
came to Frankfurt to pay his respects to you,
accompanied us to Mainz by ship on the
Main. The Elector's garden, which is known
as La Favorite,[8] does not disavow the cheap *30th*
taste which still all too frequently prevails in
Germany. In addition to several beautiful
churches, there are two houses with beautiful

pas le gout colifichet qui ne régne encore
que trop en Allemagne. Autre quelques
belles églises il y a deux maisons à Mayence qui ont de belles facades. L'une est
la maison de Dalberg qui est pourtant
un peu trop chargée & placée peu favorablement dans une rue un peu étroite,
la seconde la maison apartenante à l'ordre Theutonique⁹ qui à mon avis est préférable à la précédente et bien située
sur les bord du Main. Le Landgrave de
Heße Caßel se trouvant à Schlangen-
bad¹⁰, nous allames y faire un tour. La
situation en est charmante et les promenades qui Vous (font monter) >ménent< à douce pente le
    long de la cote de la
la montagne sont tres bien ménagées.
(End of page 3)

Nous nous rembarquames à Mayence sur le
Rhin et nous fimes jus qu'à Cologne le voyage le plus doux et le plus agréable du
monde. Les bords du Rhin tantot aßez unis
pour Vous ouvrir une vue libre dans les
campagnes fertiles et les prés fleuris cou-
vert de coteaux & de maisons de campagne,
tantôt bordés de rochers escarpés sur le
sommet desquels Vous voyés les ruines de
quelque chateau (inhabité) >abandonné< depuis plus d'un
siécle, où quelqué superbe couvent entour
de vignes qui soutient l'oisiveté
(la bonne humeurs) >l'embonpoint< de ses paisibles habitans
Vous ofrent partout une varieté de
tableaux qui devroient continuellement
exercer le pinceau de nos paysagistes
allemands. Jusques vers Bonn on Vous
nomme de touts cotés les noms fameux
de ces vins auxquels on fait l'honneur
de les laisser vieiller dans les caves
des Princes & des Chanoines. Trois fois
heureux pays qui étes comblés des plus
riches dons de Bacchus, on den devroit
Vous aproches sans une espéce d'ado-
ration. Le jus que Vous produisez fut
quelquefois notre vainqueur, mais
quelle Philosophie sans lui seroit capable (de) >de nous faire< surmonter nos malheurs et
de charmer nos ennuis. Aureste
Vous trouvés tout le long des bords de
ce fleuve superbe un nombre de
magnifiques chateaux et plusieurs
villes trés-bien baties. Coblence, residence
de l'Electeur de Treves est belle et bien
située. Bonn, où l'Electeur de Cologne
fait sa demeure a un aßéz grand palais
Nous descendimes pour le voir de même
que Popelsdorf qui en est a une petite
distance. Cologne est une très-grande
ville, nous ne nous y arrétames que
pour faire une course à Bruhl¹¹ où
feu l'Electeur séjournait très-souvent.
C'est un endroit charmant où l'on
reconoit partout le bon gout & la magni
(End of page 4)

le 31.

Aout
le 1.

le 2.

le 3.

facades in Mainz. One of them is the Dalberg house, which is, however, rather over-
ornate and located somewhat unfortunately
in a rather narrow street. The other is the
house belonging to the Teutonic Order⁹,
which in my view is preferable to the first and
well situated on the banks of the Main. The
Landgrave of Hessen-Kassel was in Schlangenbad,¹⁰ so we went to have a look at it.
Its location is charming and the promenades
which lead to the gentle slope along the
mountainside are very well maintained.
(End of page 3)

We re-embarked on the Rhine in Mainz and
the trip to Cologne was the most gentle and
agreeable in the world. The banks of the
Rhine are at times quite uniform, revealing a
clear view of fertile countryside and flower-
filled meadows with hillsides & country
houses and at times are lined with rocky cliffs
on the summit of which you can sometimes
see ruins of castles that were abandoned more
than a century ago, or a superb monastery
surrounded by vineyards, which support the
carefreenes >the corpulence< of its peaceful
inhabitants, everywhere offering you a variety
of images that should continually exercise the
brushes of our German landscape painters.
All the way to Bonn, on every side, people tell
you the names of the famous wines that have
been given the honour of aging in the cellars
of the Princes & Canons. Thrice-blessed
country, showered with all of the rich gifts of
Bacchus, one should not approach you without a certain admiration. The juice that you
produce at times vanquished us, but without
it what philosophy would be able >to make<
us surmount our problems and charm our -
difficulties. Moreover, you will see along the
banks of this superb river a number of magnificent castles and several very well built
cities. Koblenz, residence of the Elector of
Trier, is beautiful and well situated. Bonn,
where the Elector of Cologne resides, has a
rather large castle. We disembarked to see it,
as well as Popelsdorf, which is a short distance
away. Cologne is a very large city; we stopped
there only to go to Brühl¹¹, where the late
Elector often stayed. It is a charming spot and
everywhere can be seen the good taste and
splendour
(End of page 4)

31st

August
1st

2nd

3rd

ficence d'un Prince qui avoit de l'esprit *Aout*
qui n' épargnoit rien pour ses plaisirs &
qui s'empressoit à les faire partager à
sa cour & à touts les étrangers qui l'a-
prochoient. La maison >l'a< meublé (dans le
dernier gout) >très-riche<, & le jardin et le Parc sont
très vastes. Nous partimes encore le mème
jour pour Dußeldorf.[12] Le gout que
Vous avez pour les beaux arts>tel surtout pour la peinture< Vous y
attira, Monseigneur. Les Tableaux de
la Galerie n' avoient été raporté que
depuis peu de Manheim où l'Electeur de
Cologne les avoit fait transporter pendant la derniére guerre. Nous employa- *le 4.*
mes toute la journée à admirer les
chefs d'oeuvre de Rubens, de VanDyck,
de Van der Werff, dont cette nombreuse
collection est enrichie, (et duquels) >& dans lesquels elle
    surpasse les galleries des touts les autres Souverains<
on a destiné une piece à part. >à chacun a ces trois grands
    maitres<. Il
y a encore une sale pour les tableaux
Italiens où il y en a quelques uns de très
beaux. Au reste il ne me paroit pas qu'on
puisse comparer la Galerie de Dußeldorf
à celle de Dresde ni pour le choix ni pour
le nombre de tableaux (quant aux) >dans les< diférentes écoles d'Italie aussi bien que de celles
de Flandres et de Hollande. Nous quitames
Dußeldorf pour prendre notre chemin par
Aix la Chapelle à Spa où la saison ras- *le 6. le 8.*
sembloit une quantité prodigieuse d'
étrangers et particuliérement d'Anglois.
Vous y fites la conoissance du Colonel
Clavering[13] qui Vous accompagna depuis
en Angleterre & des bons conseils duquel
Vous n'avez ceßé de Vous louer. Les promenades et les bals, amusemens ordinai-
res de en fortes d'endroite et un nombre
infini. de nouvelles conaißances nous
y firent employer très-agréablement
quelques jours. De Spa nous fimes tou- *le 11.*
te diligence pour la Hollande. Nous
paßames par Liege, une grande ville
fort peuplée, connue par ses manufactures d'armes et son négoce. Les habitans
(End of page 5)

y étoient encore dans de grandes inquiétudes *Aout*
pour l'éléction de l'Evéque, protestant
le plus vivement contre celle du
Prince Clement de Saxe qu'on leur destinoit
et à quoi ils se font néaumoins confor-
mé depuis. Nous passames Mastri(cht)[14] *le 12.*
sans avoir le tems de donner un coup
d'oeuil à la fortereße. Nous ne nous arrétames pas nonplus à Bois le duc et quel- *le 13.*
ques heures seulement à Utrecht. Il me
faut avouer qu'à mon entrée en Hollande
je fus enchanté de la beauté des campagnes et de la netteté avec laquelle on entretient les maisons tant dans les villes
que dans les villages. La propreté, cette
vertu qui sait aßaisoner les mets les plus
simples et faire des plus humbles cabanes
des habitations charmantes, y est por-

of a Prince who had the spirit to spare nothing *August*
for his own pleasures and was sedulous in
sharing them with his court and all of the
outsiders who approached him. The house
>is< >very richly< furnished & the garden
and park are very vast. We then left for
Dusseldorf[12] the same day. Your Excellency's
taste for the fine arts, >particularly painting<,
led you there. The paintings in the gallery
had only recently been brought back from
Mannheim, where the Elector of Cologne
had them transported during the last war. We *4th*
spent the journey admiring the masterpieces
of Rubens, Van Dyck and Van der Werff with
which this comprehensive collection is
enriched >& in which it surpasses the galler-
ies of all other sovereigns<. A separate room
has been reserved >for each of these great
masters<. There is also a room for the Italian
paintings, including some very beautiful
ones. For the rest, it does not appear to me
that the gallery in Dusseldorf can be compared with the one in Dresden, either as
regards the choice or the number of paintings
>of the< various schools in Italy, as well as
Flanders and Holland. We left Dusseldorf, *6th 8th*
proceeding by way of Aachen to Spa, where
the season had gathered together a prodigious
quantity of foreigners, particularly the English. There you met Colonel Clavering,[13] who
then accompanied you to England and
whose excellent advice you have never ceased
praising. We spent several very agreeable days
with promenades and balls, ordinary amuse-
ments in this type of location and an infinite
number of new acquaintances. From Spa we
hastened toward Holland. We passed through *11th*
Liege, a large, very populous city, known for
its weapons manufacturing and its trade. The
inhabitants
(End of page 5)

there were still in great disquietude about *August*
the election of the Bishop, protesting most
vigorously against that of Prince Clement of
Saxony, who had been chosen for them and
with whom they nonetheless are now in
agreement. We passed through Maastricht,[14] *12th*
without having time to have a look at the fortress. We did not stop at 's-Hertogenbosch, *13th*
either, and spent only a few hours at Utrecht.
I must confess that when I entered Holland I
was enchanted by the beauty of the countryside and the neatness with which the houses
are kept in both the cities and in the villages.
The cleanliness, that virtue that can season
the simplest dishes and make the humblest
cottages into charming habitations there, is
taken to excess, if I may dare to use that term.
I was particularly struck by it because we had

tée à l'excés si j'ose me servir ici de ce
terme. J'en fus d'autant plus éblouï que
nous venions de parcourir une partie
de l'Allemagne où l'on soufre bien du
contraire. Le chemin d'Utrecht à Amsterdam est connu de touts les voyageurs
par sa beaute et la belle saison nous le
montra le plus favorablement que possible. Qu'on le faße par eau sur les
canaux qui y conduisent ou qu'on le
faße par terre, on paße continuelle
ment par (entre) une suite de jardins entre lesquels il n'y a que de tems en tems
de grandes espaces qui Vous montrent
les plus riches paturages couverts
de troupeaux de toute espéce de betail.
Je me souviens qu'étant en Italie des
Hollandois voulurent me faire la description du Chemin d'Utrecht à Amsterdam
et me le comparant à celui qui conduit de Venise à Padoue le long de la
Brenta, donnérent même beaucoup
la préférence à leur patrie. Je ne puis
me conformer tout-à-fait à leur sentiment.
Outre qu'un (les) grand nombre de palais
situés sur la Brenta sont batis sur les
(End of page 6)

just traversed a part of Germany that suffers
from quite the contrary. Every traveller knows
the beauty of the route from Utrecht to
Amsterdam and the beautiful season showed
it to us in its most favourable light. Whether
by boat on the canals that lead there or by
land, one continually passes a succession of
gardens between which there are only occa-
sional large spaces to show you the richest
pastures covered with herds of all kinds of
livestock. I remember that when I was in
Italy, Dutchmen wanted to describe to me
the route from Utrecht to Amsterdam and
compared it to the one from Venice to Padua
that runs along the Brenta, even giving much
preference to their own country. I cannot
completely concur with their sentiments.
Besides the fact that a large number of castles
located on the Brenta have been
(End of page 6)

Aout

deßeins des plus célébres architectes d'Italie
la situation naturelle du pays me paroit
infiniment plus variée & plus riante.
Peut-étre außi que la quantité de gens de
la premiére qualité>nobleße< et la gayeté qui
règne en Italie dans touts les états m'a
inspiré des idées plus avantageuses que
l'air pesant et großier des bons marchands
Hollandois. Au reste les jardins de Hollande m'ont paru pour la plupart plus
beaux par le dehors qu'en dedans. Vous en-
trez ordinairement par une belle allée
d'arbres fort hauts qui Vous promet quelque chose >de plus< élégant quand Vous n'y trou-
vez que des parterres de fleurs des grotes
où Vous plaignez les dépenses >du maitre< et la patien-
ce de l'artiste, des hayes taillées gothique
ment et des statues du plus bas grotesque.
Notre séjour à Amsterdam[15] ne fut que de
trois jours que nous tachames d'employer
le mieux que poßible. Nous vimes d'abord
le port, le Magasin de l'Amirauté et la
Maison de ville. La bourse étoit plus remplie que d'ordinaire et il y regnoit un
trouble qu'on pouvoit lire (dans) >sur< touts les
visages. La banqueroute des Neuvilles >qui s'était déclaré
     depuis peu de jours< cau-
soit cette consternation générale. Elle
faisoit trembler >tout< ce qu'il y avoit de plus
riches négocians en Hollande & menaçoit
la ruine au comerce de toutes les villes
marchandes de l'Allemagne. Le peu de
tems ne nous permit de voir que de deux
cabinets de tableaux, bien qu'il y en ait
un bon nombre dans cette grande ville
où l'on a beaucoup le gout des tableaux
flamans. Le premier fut celui de Bramkan[16], qui est un des plus renomés. Il est

*depuis le 14.
jusqu'au 18.*

August

built according to the plans of the most celebrated architects in Italy, the natural situation
of that country appears to me to be infinitely
more varied and pleasant. Perhaps, too, the
number of people of top rank >nobility< and
the gaiety that reigns in all conditions in Italy
inspired me with more advantageous ideas
than the heavy, coarse air of the good Dutch
merchants. For the rest, most of the gardens
in Holland appeared more beautiful to me
from the outside than from the inside. You
normally enter by a beautiful avenue of very
tall trees that promises you something more
elegant but you find only flower beds and
grottoes that make you pity the money spent
>by the master< and the patience of the art-
ist, Gothically-pruned hedges and statues of
the lowest grotesqueness. Our sojourn in
Amsterdam[15] lasted only three days, during
which we did our utmost to see as much as
possible. We first saw the harbour, the Magazine of the Admiralty and the Town Hall.
The Stock Exchange was more crowded than
usual and disquiet could be read >on< every
face. The bankruptcy of the Neuvilles,
>which had been declared a few days ago<,
caused the general consternation. It caused
>all< of the richest tradesmen of Holland to
tremble and threatened to ruin business in all
of the merchant cities of Germany. There was
little time, so we could see only two cabinets
of paintings, although there is a goodly number of them in this large city, where people
set great store by the Flemish paintings. The
first of them was that of Bramkan,[16] one of the
most famous. It is comprehensive, well chosen and worthy of the attention of any art
lover. One reproach could be that it is nor-

*from the 14th
to the 18th*

nombreux, très-choisi et digne de l'attention
de tout amateur. Ce qu'on pourroit y trouver
à redire c'est qu'il y a ordinairement quelque dificulté à parvenir à le voir, (et) >ou< que le
maitre Vous acorde enfin cette grace avec
tout l'insuportable orgueil d'un marchand
qui n'a d'attention que pour ses richeßes.
Cela me parut bien le contraire des autres
(End of page 7)

pays, où toutes les personnes qui poßédent
des cabinets sont bien flatés de les montres
aux étrangers et surtout aux (conoyseurs) >amateurs<
et d'y étaler leur conoißances. On nous
fit voir encore le cabinet (d'un au) de Lubelink, moins nombreux à la verité que
le premier, mais qui dans ce gout poßède
de très beaux tableaux, surtout de Berghem,
de Guillaume et d'Adrien van de Velde, et
de Honder Koter. L'arrangement que Vous
avies pris pour vos voyages ne Vous
permit que de donner un jour à voir
La Hage. Le Baron de Larez s'empreßa
à Vous le faire paßer agréablement. Il
Vous accompagna au chateau du Stathoudre, à La Maison du Bois[17], au cabinet de
curiosités du Prince d'Orange[18], à Schevelingen et à Sorgfliet[19], jardin apparte-
nant au Cte de Bentheim, qui est trés
bien entretenu et qui nous donna le
premiér l'idée des jardins anglois.
Comme ni le Prince de Brunsvic ni
le jeune Prince d'Orange n'étaient pres-
sents à la Hage, Vous ne crutes pas de
voir Vous y arréter plus longtems et
Vous continuates Votre route par Rotterdam et Bergopzoom[20], où Vous employates
quelques heures à voir la fortification et
les souterains. Les ouvrages y sont très
bien entretenus et ont été reparés sur le
même plan qu'ils étoit du tems du dernier
siége. De là Vous paßates par Anvers
>et Malines< à Bruxelles. Le Braband & la partie de
la Flandre qui reste encore à la maison
d'Autriche, sont des pays extrémement
fertiles & bien cultivés, remplis de belles
et grandes villes. On sait aßés le grand
(negoce) >comerce< que la ville d'Anvers avoit dans
les Siécles paßés, sans la ruine duquel
celui d'Amsterdam ne seroit jamais mon-
té au degré où il est aujourd'hui. Il paroit néaumoins que la cour de Vienne
néglige extrémement les Pays Bas. Livrés
(End of page 8)

à l'arbitre d'un ministére, qui ne cherche
qu'à en tirer tout le profit poßible ils
languißent sous un joug que touts les habitans semblent haïr. Les fortereßes même
n'y sont pas entretenus avec le soin né-
ceßaires, quand celles que la France a
sur ses frontiéres sont dans le meilleur
état du monde. Bruxelles est un grande
ville bien batie. Le Prince Charles[21] qui
>Son Palais, ses curiosités & les
apartemens à la Chinoise<

Aout

le 19.

le 20.
le 21.

le 22.

mally rather difficult to get to see it; >when<
the master finally grants you that honour, it is
with all of the unbearable pride of a merchant
who is interested only in his treasures. That
appeared to me to be the opposite of the
other
(End of page 7)

countries, where everyone who possesses cabinets is
very flattered to show them to foreigners and
particularly to >art lovers< and to display
their knowledge on that occasion. We were
also shown the cabinet of Lubelink, truly less
comprehensive than the first, but which in
this style does possess very beautiful paintings, particularly by Berghem, Guillaume
and Adrien van de Velde and Honder Koter.
The arrangements that you had made for
your voyages allowed you to devote only one
day to visiting The Hague. Baron von Larez
did his utmost to have you spend it agreeably.
He accompanied you to Stathoudre castle, to
the Maison du Bois,[17] to the Prince of
Orange's cabinet of curiosities,[18] to Schevelingen and to Sorgfliet,[19] a garden belonging
to Count de Bentheim, which is very well
maintained and gave us our first idea of English gardens. Because neither the Prince of
Brunswick nor the young Prince of Orange
were present in The Hague, you did not think
it necessary to spend any more time there and
you continued on your way through Rotterdam and Bergopzoom,[20] where you spent
several hours viewing the fortification and the
underground passages. The buildings there
are very well maintained and have been re-
paired according to the same plan that existed
at the time of the last siege. From there you
proceeded via Antwerp >and Mechelen< to
Brussels. Brabant & the part of Flanders still
belonging to the House of Austria are extremely fertile and well-cultivated lands full
of beautiful and large towns. It is known that
major >trade< flourished in the city of Antwerp in past centuries, without the ruin of
which Amsterdam would never have risen to
the degree that it has today. Nonetheless, it
appears that the Viennese Court neglects the
Low Countries exceedingly. Subject to the
control
(End of page 8)

of a ministry that seeks only to make every
possible profit there, they are languishing
under a yoke that all of the inhabitants
appear to hate. Even the fortresses are not
maintained with the necessary care, while
those that France has on its borders are in the
best condition in the world. Brussels is a
large, well-built city. Prince Charles[21], who
resides there with >his castle, his curiosities
and his apartments in Chinese style<, >holds
the title< of Governor of the Low Countries,

August

19th

20th
21th

22th

y fait sa residence (est) >a le titre<Gouverneur des
Pays bas, (mais) >quoique< c'est proprement le Cte de
Cobenzel²² qui dirige tout, même jusqu'au
militaire. (Au reste) Le Prince est rempli
de conoißance en toute sorte de choses,
extrémement poli evers tout le monde
et aime de touts ceux qui l'entourent.
Il est d'une conversation agréable, il
aime à discourir sur le metier de la guerre
il en parle avec savoir, avec expérien-
ce et avec modestie. Quoique la fortune
ne l'ait guere accompagné dans ses
campagnes, il est néaumoins estimé
des plus grand Généraux de notre siécle,
Le Cte de Cobenzel, est un homme qui ne
manque pas d'esprit, mais gonflé de la
fierté qui regne encore à la Cour imperia-
le. Son épouse, fille du Feldmarechal
Palfi, surpaße tout ce qu'il me souvient
d'avoir jamais vu de vain orgueil & de
fatuité dans und femme. Quoique notre
séjour ne fut que (très) de quatre ou cinq
jours, Vous avez toutjours paru, Monseigneur, en étre infiniment content et
surtout des amitiés que le Prince Charles Vous temoigna. Nous allames encore
voir la maison de ville, où il y a de super-
bes tapißeries en haute-liße, et on nous
en montra encore à la fabrique où on
les travaille de très belles et de toute sorte
de sujets. Le Colonel Clavering²³ qui Vous
avoit promis de Vous rejoindre à Bruxelles, y arriva le même jour que Vous et nous
repartimes avec lui pour prendre le chemin de Calais   *le 27.*
(End of page 9)

Nous repaßames encore par Anvers où nous   *Aout*
nous arretames un jour pour donner quel-   *le 28.*
que attention (aux) à quelques uns des plus
fameux tableaux des maitres de l'école fla-
mande. On y voit encore l'academie de
Rubens où Vandyk, Jaques Jordans et un
grand nombre d'autre célébres artistes
firent leurs études. D'Anvers nous passames par Gant, Courtrai, Menin et Ypres
à Dunkerque. Ce port qui a eu >plusieurs fois< le fort d'être
ruine et racomodé tour à tour, venoit d'étre
mis hors d'étât de servir pour des vaißeaux
de guerre et on en avoit rempli la Cuvette
conformément aux articles de la derniére
paix. Nous y vimes encore une vingtai-
ne de ces vaißeaux plats que les françois
construisirent jusque vers trois cent pour
faire une descente en Angleterre pendant
la derniére guerre. Ils n'ont pourtant
pas jugé devoir les employer et ils >les< ont
(été) depuis vendus quasi touts aux mar-   *Septembre*
chands, ou destiné à d' outres usages.
Nous arrivames le même jour à Calais,   *le 1. er*
et le>4< lendemain>5< nous>1< nous>2< embarquames>3<.   *le 2.*
Le tems étoit extrémement serain et à peine
fumes nous sortis du port que nous pumes
découvrir les rochers qui bordent les cotes
de Dover et qui sont d'une couleur blanche
comme de la Craye. Nous fimes le trajet
en six heures et nous eumes un vent doux

>although< it is actually the Count de
Cobenzel²² who directs everything, including
the military. The prince is full of knowledge
about all types of things, extremely polite to
everyone and loved by everyone around him.
He is agreeable in conversation and he loves
to discourse on the military profession, about
which he speaks with knowledge, experience
and modesty. Although fortune has hardly
accompanied him on his campaigns, he is
still considered to be one of the greatest gen-
erals of our century. The Count de Cobenzel
is a man not lacking in spirit, but swollen
with the pride that still rules at the Imperial
Court. His wife, the daughter of Field Marshall Palfi, exceeds all that I can remember
ever having seen of vain pride and self-con-
ceit in a woman. Although our sojourn lasted
only (very) four or five days, you, Your Excellency, always had the appearance of being
infinitely content, particularly with regard to
the kindnesses that Prince Charles showed to
you. We also visited the Town Hall, where
there were superb high-warp tapestries and
we were also shown the factory where they
are worked in beautiful subjects of all sorts.
Colonel Clavering,²³ who had promised to
join you at Brussels, arrived on the same day
you did and we left with him on the road to
Calais.   *27th*
(End of page 9)

We went through Antwerp again, where we   *August*
stopped for one day to devote some attention to   *28th*
several of the most famous paintings by mas-
ters of the Flemish school. You can still see
the academy of Rubens, where Van Dyk,
Jaques Jordans and many other famous artists
studied. From Antwerp we proceeded by
Ghent, Courtrai, Menin and Ypres to Dunkirk. This port, which has been alternately
ruined and rebuilt >several times<, had just
been put out of service for war ships and the
basin had been filled in compliance with the
most recent peace treaty. We still saw about
twenty of the 300 flat vessels that the French
built to invade England during the last war.
However, they never found it necessary to use
them and since that time they have sold
almost all >of them< to merchants or used   *September*
them for other purposes. We arrived in Calais   *1st*
on the same day and we embarked on the   *2nd*
next day. The weather was very calm and we
had hardly left the port when we could dis-
cern the cliffs that line the Dover coast and
that are as white as chalk. We made the crossing in six hours and had a gentle wind and
tranquil sea until a short distance from the
port of Dover, when it suddenly began to agi-
tate with some violence. Because it was low
tide and a vessel then cannot enter the port of
Dover, we got into one of those boats that are

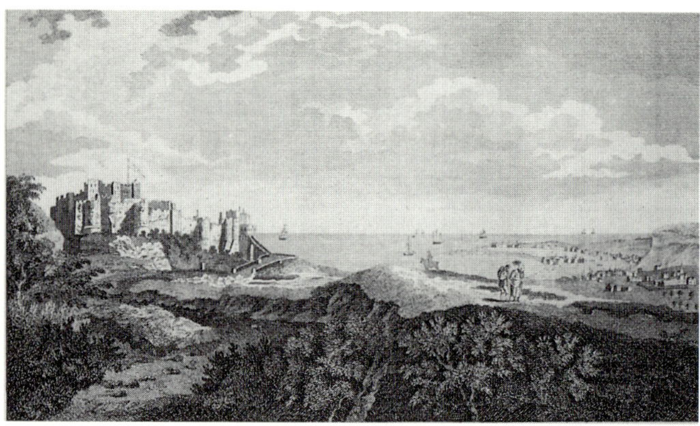

4 View of Dover Fortress and part of the town in the county of Kent, copper-plate from: Ch. Burlington, D. L. Rees u. A. Murray, The Modern Universal British Traveller; A New, Complete and Accurate Tour Through England, Wales, Scotland and the Neighbouring Islands, London 1779. Private owner.

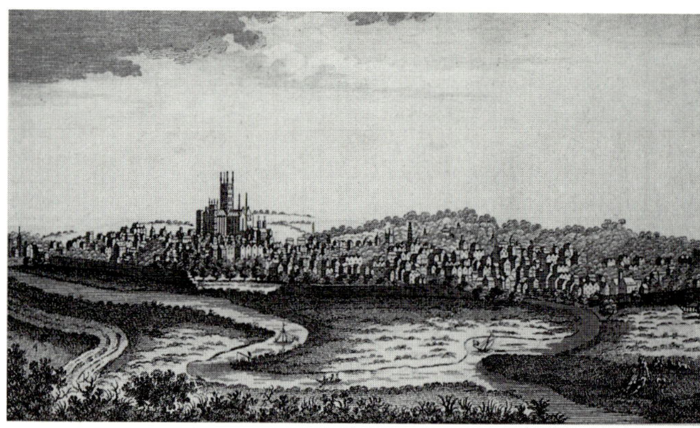

5 View of the city of Canterbury with cathedral in the county of Kent, copperplate from: The Modern Universal British Traveller, London 1779 (cf. ill. 4). Private owner.

et la mer tranquile jusque à peu de distance du port de Dover, qu'elle commenca
tout d'un coup à s'agiter avec aßes de violence. Comme la marée étoit basse & qu`
on ne pourroit alors entrer dans le port
de Dover avec un vaißeau, nous nous mi-
mes dans une de ces barques que l'on trouve toutjours à l'avenue du port, & qui
nous y conduisit. La ville de Dover s'étend
le long de la cote au bas des rochers desquels
elle est entourée. Il y a un chateau ou
une espéce de fort sur le sommet d'un
des plus hauts de ces rochers, pour garder
(End of page 10)

le port. Nous allames encore le me soir
jusqu'à Canterbury. C'est ville aßés
mal batie, qui n'est guere digne d'attention.
La Cathedrale nous donna une idée des
la simplicité des églises angloises qui
en cela montre bien la (diférence) >contraire< de la
magnificence et des trésors des eglises
catholiques, quoique pour la facon du
culte (et les cérémonies) on y ait beaucoup retenu des cérémonies de l'égli-
se Romaine. Cette cathedrale est un
batiment fort vaste dans le gout gothique, sans les moindres ornemens
ni tableaux. On travaille beaucoup en
étofes de foye à Canterbury et ce (fut par) furent
les protestans qui allérent chercher un azile
en Angleterre, qui y aporterent les premiers
ces manufactures. Nous continuames
notre route par Rochester >ancienne< ville aßés
mal batie ne consistant >quasi< que d'une rue
fort longue qui aboutit à un très beau
pont où l'on paße (la Riviére) la Medway,
>sur la quelle un peu plus bas
Vous trouvés Chatham<
(à l'autre coté de laquelle est Chatham)
Chatham[24] est un des meilleurs chantiers
du Royaume pour y construire toute forte
ce vaißeaux de guerre fondé par la Reine
Elisabeth, et on le tient aujourdhui pour

*Septembre
le 3.*

always found at the entrance to the harbour
& which took us there. The town of Dover
extends along the coast at the bottom of the
cliffs that surround it. There is a castle or a
sort of fort on the top of one of the highest of
those cliffs, to guard
(End of page 10)

the port. We continued to Canterbury the
same night. The town is rather poorly built
and is hardly worthy of note. The Cathedral
gave us an idea of the simplicity of English
churches which, in that respect, clearly show
the >contrast< of the splendour and treasures
of the Catholic church, although with regard
to the worship (and the ceremonies) much of
the ceremonies from the Roman church have
been maintained. The cathedral is a very vast
building in the Gothic style, without the
slightest ornaments or paintings. A great deal
of silk cloth is manufactured in Canterbury
and it was the Protestants who sought asylum
in England who brought the first of the factories there. We continued on our way through
Rochester, >an old<, rather poorly built town
that consists practically of one very long street
that leads to a very beautiful bridge crossing
the (River) Medway, >on which you will find
Chatham a short distance downstream<.
Chatham[24] is one of the best dockyards in the
Kingdom for building war ships. It was
founded by Queen Elizabeth and today it is
considered to be one of the most complete
naval arsenals. The buildings used to build
and maintain the ships are enormous and the
houses where the officers are lodged are well
built. We climbed onto a ship that was being

*September
3rd*

des Arsenaux de Marine les plus complets.
Les batimens qui servent pour la construction
des vaißeaux et pour y garder les matenain
sont très vastes et les maisons où les
oficiers sont logés, sont bien batis. Nous
montames sur un navire auquel on
travailloit, qui sera de cent piéces de
Canons et auquel on donnera le nom de
la Victoire. Cette importante place est
gardée par deux forts, Upnor, qui est
vis à vis du chantier de l'autre coté de la
Medway et Gillingham un peu plus bas
qui defend l'entrée de la rivière. (Nous)>En<
continuant notre chemin nous nous arré-
tames sur>11< les>12< bords>13< de>14< la>15< Támise>16<
    à>1< Inn Grays²⁵>2<   (cf. ill. 22)
où>3< il>4< y>5< a>6< un>7< très>8< joli>9< jardin>10<.
    La situa-
tion en est charmante et l'arrangement du
jardin, le premier que nous vimes en Angleterre nous frappa infiniment. La partie
(End of page 11)

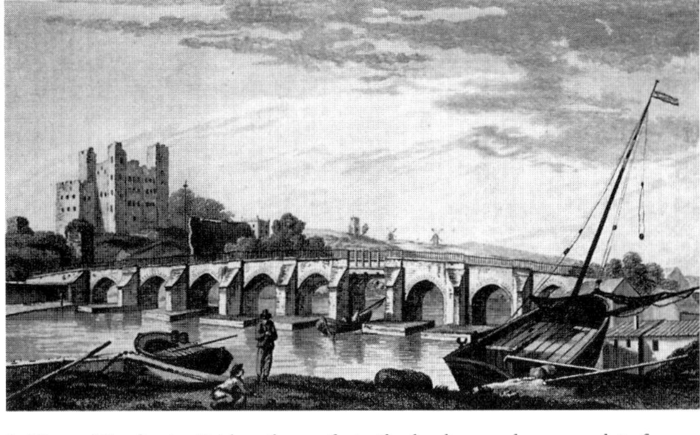

6 View of Rochester Bridge, the castle in the background, copperplate from:
The Modern Universal British Traveller, London 1779 (cf. ill. 4). Private
owner.

worked on, which will have 100 cannon and
will be called the Victory. This important
location is protected by two forts, Upnor,
which is opposite the dockyard on the other
side of the Medway and Gillingham, a little
further downstream, which defends the
entrance to the river. >In< continuation of
our voyage, we stopped on the banks of the
Thames at Inn Grays,²⁵ where there is a very
pretty garden. The location is charming and   (cf. ill. 22)
the arrangement of the garden, the first that
we saw in England, astonished us infinitely.
The most elevated part
(End of page 11)

la plus élévée Vous ofre (une) la vue et   *Septembre*
d'une riviére très large, surtout quand
la marée est haute qui est trés navigable. Tout à l'entour vous ne voyes qu'un
pays cultivé semé partout d'habitations.
Quand Vous descendes au (bas) pied de la
montagne, la belle verdure des bouquets
de lauriers, un temple (au fond) le sommet
vous présentent un table digne du
pinceau d'un Claude Lorrain. Vous croiries
que les nymphes vont y danser, où que des
Bergers y célébreront leurs fétes. Ce jardin
est orne trés-élégamment de quelque statues et de quantités de marbres, et de bas
reliefs aportés d'Italie. Il apartient apre
sent à un nommé Mr. Calkrat²⁶, un des Comis-
saires qui amaßa ses richesses à l'armé
en Allemagne pendant la derniére guerre.
Nous employames le lendemain matin à
Greenwich²⁷. Le fameux Hopital des Invali-   *le 4*
des de la marine est un des plus beaux
édifices qui soit en Angleterre, et (rend) est
(aßes) un témoignage >autentique< comment cette nation
fait recompenser les merites et les services qu'on lui rend. Il est vrai que l'Hotel
les Invalides à Paris entretient un plus
grand nombre de personnes, mais pour
la beauté des Batimens celui de Greenwich
ne lui en cede en rien, & il me paroit infiniment préférable pour l'arrangement
et surtout pour l'extréme propreté qui

offers you the view of a river that is very broad,   *September*
particularly when the tide is high, and which
is very navigable. All around you, you see
only cultivated land with houses scattered
everywhere. When you descend to the foot of
the mountain, the beautiful greenery of the
groups of laurels, a temple, the summit
present you with a picture worthy of the
brush of a Claude Lorrain. You would think
that the nymphs are going to dance there, or
that the shepherds will do their merrymaking
there. The garden is very elegantly decorated
with several statues and quantities of marble,
as well as bas reliefs brought from Italy. It
currently belongs to a certain Mr. Calkrat,²⁶
one of the commissioners who amassed his
wealth in the army in Germany during the
last war. We spent the next morning in
Greenwich.²⁷ The famous Royal Naval Hospi-   *4th*
tal is one of the most beautiful buildings in
England and bears >authentic< witness to
the way this nation rewards the merits and
services rendered to it. It is true that the Hotel
des Invalides in Paris can hold more people,
but for the beauty of the buildings, Greenwich in no way occupies second place, & it
appears to me infinitely preferable for its
arrangement and particularly with regard to
the extreme cleanliness that prevails there. In
the past this place was a royal palace, where
Henry VII and particularly Henry VIII, >who

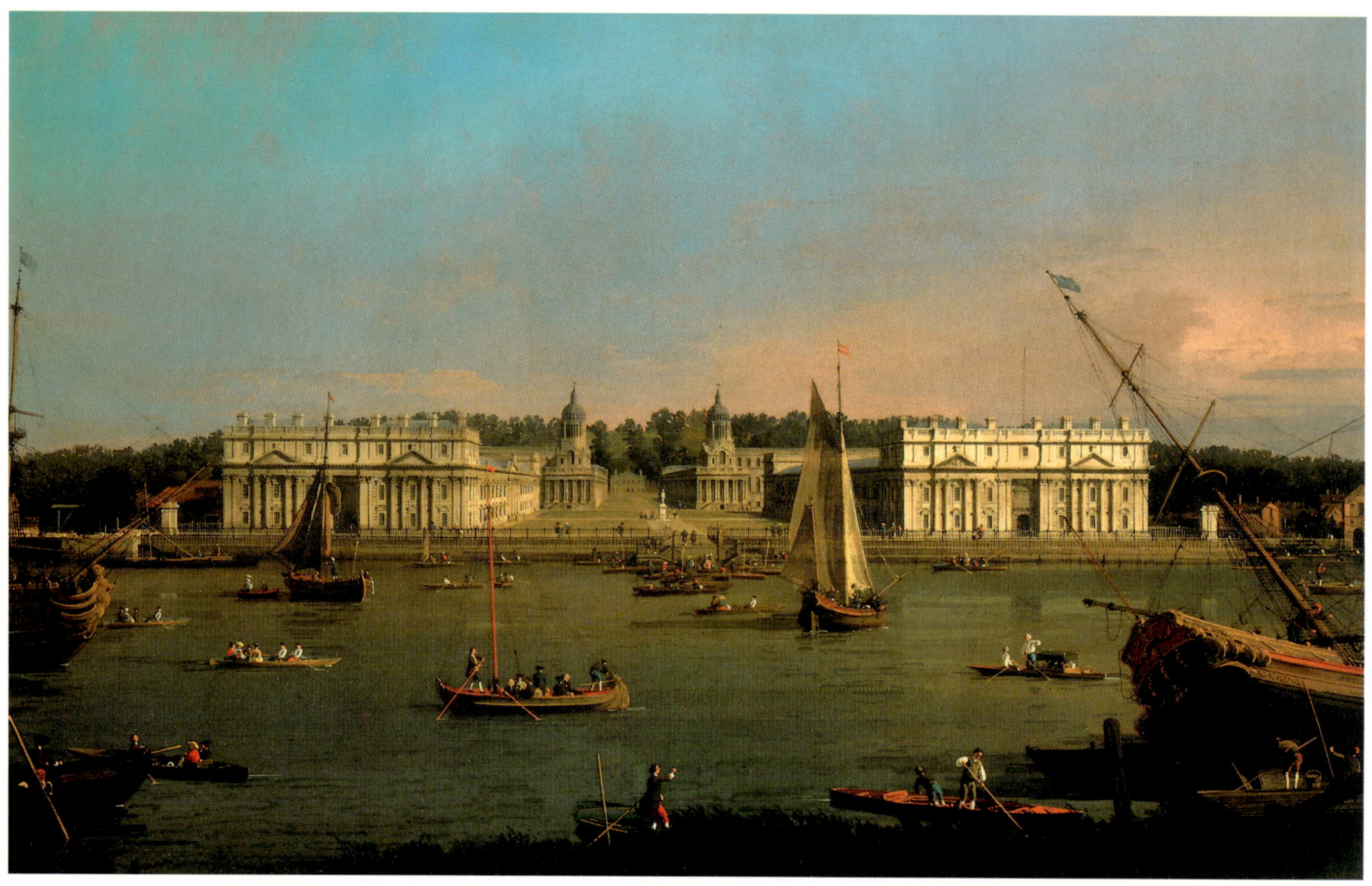

7 Antonio Canal (Canaletto), 1697–1768, Greenwich Hospital from the north
bank of the Thames, National Maritime Museum, London.

y régne. Cette place étoit dans le tems
paßé un palais Royal où Henri VII. et
surtout Henri VIII. >qui l'acheve< y faisoient souvent
quelque séjour. Les Reines Marie & Elisabeth y (naquirent) puivent leur naißance. Ce palais ayant été négligé dans la suite Charles second le fit abattre pour en eriger
un nouveau. On acheva pendant son regne
l'aile gauche tel qu'il est aprèsent, auquel
il employa £ 36000. (L'anné)>En 1694< Le Roi Guillaume III.
cherchant à encourager le comerce & la
navigation, destina ce batiment en même
tems qu'un grand espace de terrain pour
finir l'edifice, pour servir d'Hopital pour
gerecevoir ceux >à< qui leur age ou leur infirme
(End of page 12)

tes ne permettoient plus de servir, de même qu'aux veuves et aux enfans de ceux
qui auroient perdu la vie au service de la
couronne. L'aile droite fut commence sous
son regne et continué sous celui de ses
succeßeurs et tout l'ouvragne ne fut
achevé que par le Roi George II. (Un) Plusieurs particuliers zelés firent des dons
gratuits très considérables pour une si
noble fondations, et le table suspendue
à l'entrée de la grande Sale les fait mon
ter jusqu' à la somme de £ 58209. Enfin
touts les biens de Cte de Derwentwater[28]
qui alloient à £ 6000. de revenus, qui avoit

completed it<, often resided. Queens Mary &
Elizabeth were born there. The palace was
afterwards neglected and Charles II then had
it razed and built a new one. During his reign
the left wing, on which he spent £ 36,000,
was completed as it now stands. In (the year)
>1694<, King William III, in an effort to
encourage trade and navigation, dedicated
the building, as well as a large parcel of land
for its completion, to be used as a hospital to
receive those who could no longer serve due
to their age or infirmities,
(End of page 12)

as well as widows and children of those who
lost their lives in service of the crown. The
right wing was begun under his reign and
continued under those of his successors and
the entire project was completed by King
George II. Several zealous private parties
made very considerable donations to such a
noble foundation and the table suspended in
the entry of the great room caused them to
rise to the sum of £ 58,209. Finally, all of the
assets, amounting to income of £ 6,000, of
the Earl of Derwentwater,[28] who played an
>important< role in the last rebellion, were
given to the Hospital in >1732< by an act of

en (beaucoup) >principalement< part à la derniére rebel-
lion, furent donnés en (1715.) >1732.< à l'hopital
par un acte du parlement. Les façades
des deux ailes sont sur les bords de la
Tamise, et c'est la que logent les Gouver-
neur et les Officiers. Les logemens des
mariniers >invalides< sont dans de grandes sales
ou il y a des deux cotés une suite de
petites chambres. Chaque homme a sa
chambre à part où il y a un lit une table
& des chaises le tout entretenu avec la
derniere netteté. La chapelle est comme
le restes d'une belle architecture et la
grande sale est peinte par Thornhill.
La grande place est ouverte du coté de la
Tamise, & le batiment qui est dans le
fond et fait face à la riviére forme une
colonnade &.ou espéce de portique pour
s'y proméner dans le mauvais tems.
Ces colonnades de tout l'édifice sont de
l'ordre Corinthien. Il y a présentement
près de deux mille invalides à Greenwich,
et une centaine d'enfans de mariniers
qui y sont élevés. Autre cela il y a encore
un nombre de femmes qui servent pour
avoir soin de tenir la maison propre et
qui sont de meme femmes ou veuves de
mariniers. Les pensionaires sont habillés
de bleu, et on leur fournit encore des sou-
tiers, des bas et du linge. Ils sont nourris
très-abondamment et autre cela ils ont encore chacun un shelling par semaine en monnoye
(End of page 13)

Parliament. The facades of the two wings are
on the banks of the Thames and that is where
the Governor and the officers are housed.
The >disabled< sailors are in the large rooms,
where there is a row of small chambers on
each side. Every man has his own chamber
where he has a bed, a table, & chairs, all
maintained with the utmost cleanliness. Like
the rest, the chapel is a beautiful work of
architecture and the large room is painted by
Thornhill. The large square is open toward
the Thames and the building that is in the
background and faces the river forms a colonnade or a sort of portico for walking when the
weather is bad. All of the colonnades on the
building are in the Corinthian style. There
are currently about 2,000 disabled sailors at
Greenwich and about 100 children of sailors
are being brought up there. In addition, there
are a number of women who keep house;
they are also wives or widows of sailors. The
pensioners are dressed in blue and they are
also given linens, stockings and undergar-
ments. They are very generously fed and each
of them also receives a shilling in cash every
week
(End of page 13)

pour les petites dépenses. Il y a encore
à Greenwich un très-beau parc apartenant
au Roi, d'où L'on a une très belle vue du
cours de la Tamise et de Londres. Comme
le jour étoit extremement serain nous eumes
l'avantage de voir très-distinchement cette
Capitale et ses environs, ce qui n'est pas
ordinaire à cause du brouillard et de la
fumée qui epaißit (ordre) communément
l'air de la Cité. Sur la partie la plus éléve
du parc est un observatoire fondé par
Charles II. pour les observations astrono-
miques et fourni des instruments neceßai-
res. En quittant la province de Kent je
dois ajouter encore que c'est une des mieux
cultivérs et des plus fertiles tant en productions de bled, que particulierment en
fruit de toute espéce. On voit partout des
vergers et des plantations de cerisiers de
pomiers et autres arbres fruitiers. Quand
on descend des montagnes vers Rochester
on a une des plus belles vues qu'il y ait
en Angleterre. Sur la droite vous voyés la
Medway et plus loin la Tamise à laquelle cette riviere se joins. >…ment
…t,…de jetter dans la mer. L'embou
chure de ces deux riviére est toutjours couverte de vaißeaux.< De l'autre
coté la vue se perd dans les riches campagnes ornées d'une quantité infinie de
belles maisons de campagne et de jardins.
Nous allames diner chés Mylord Tyrawly[29]

as pocket money. In Greenwich there is also
a very beautiful park belonging to the king,
from which there is a very beautiful view of
the course of the Thames and London.
Because the day was extremely fine, we had
the advantage of seeing the capital and its
environs very distinctly, which is not ordinarily the case because of the fog and the smoke
that commonly thicken the air of the city. In
the most elevated part of the park there is an
observatory founded by Charles II for astro-
nomic observations and furnished with the
necessary instruments. On leaving the county
of Kent, I must add that it is one of the best
cultivated and most fertile in production of
both wheat and particularly all types of fruits.
Orchards and plantations of cherry, apples
and other fruit trees can be seen everywhere.
When descending from the mountains
toward Rochester, there is one of the most
beautiful views in England. On the right you
see the Medway and, more distant, the
Thames, which that river joins, >after which
they flow into the sea. The mouth of the two
rivers is always covered with vessels.< On the
other side, one's view is lost in the rich countryside ornamented with an infinite quantity
of beautiful country houses and gardens. We
dined with Lord Tyrawly,[29] who resides very
close to the Greenwich park in a little country house built in the Gothic style by Sir Vanbrugh. He is third field marshall >and was

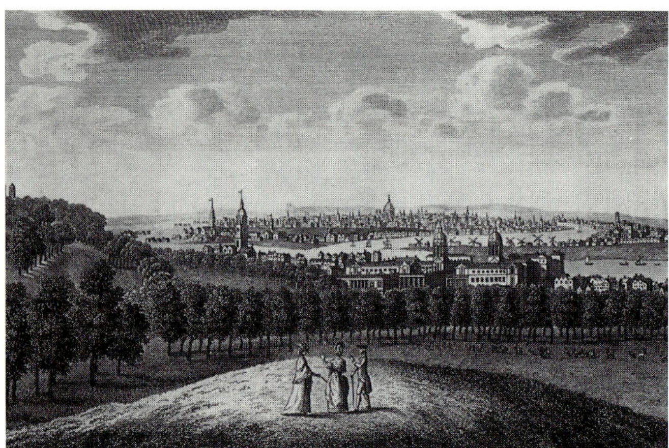

8 View of London from "One Tree Hill" in Greenwich Park, copperplate from: The Modern Universal British Traveller, London 1779 (cf. ill. 4). Private owner.

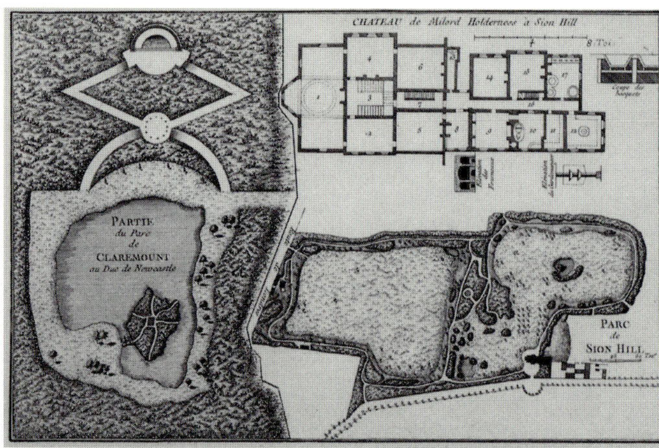

9 Floor plan of Sion-Hill country house and plan of the park belonging to Lord Holderness, copperplate from: Georges-Louis Le Rouge, Détails des nouveaux Jardins … la Mode; Jardins anglo-chinois … la Mode, 21 issues, Paris 1776–87, here issue 2, plate 8. Kulturstiftung DessauWörlitz.

qui demeure tout pres du parc de Greenwich
dans une petite maison de campagne batie
dans le gout gothique par le Chevalier
(Vanbrock) Vanbrugh. Il est le troisiéme Feldmarechal,
>et fut aide de camp du Duc de Marle-
borough à la bataille de Blendheim<
C'est un vieillard qui a blanchi dans les
service, mais qui malgré son age et ses
infirmités, garde encore la gayeté & l'hu
meur d'un jeune homme. Il paße le reste
de sa vie dans cette retraite dans la compa-
gnie d'une fille & de deux ou trois fils qui
a de diférentes maitreßes, auquels il cherche à faire autant de bien qu'il peut pendant
sa vie parcequ'il ne pourra guere leur en
laißer après sa mort. Nous arrivames enfin
se soir à Londres. Je ne pourrai guere, Mon
seigneur, Vous rendre comte des des premiers
jours que nous passames dans ce grande
ville. La quantité de nouveaux objets qui se
(End of page 14)

the aide-de-camp of the Duke of Marlborough at the Battle of Blenheim.< He is an
old man whose hair turned white during his
service, but in spite of his age and infirmity
he still retains the gaiety and humour of a
young man. He is spending the rest of his life
in this retreat in the company of one daughter and two or three sons from different mis-
tresses and he is trying to do as much good as
he can for them during his life because he
can hardly leave anything to them after his
death. We finally arrived in London this evening. Your Excellency, I can hardly report to
you on the first days that we spent in this
great city. The quantity of new things that
(End of page 14)

présentérent à mes yeux, la confusion avec la
quelle je ne peu que les voir surtout par l'im
poßibilité de pouvoir m'en informes par
l'ignorance de la langue, ne put me donner
que des idées très imparfaites, que je ne
pourrois qu'à peine me rapeller. Cequi à
mon avis, doit fraper tout étranger qui
arrive en Angleterre de quelque pays qu'il
soit, c'est de voir l'abondance qui y regne
dans touts les états, l'aßiduité au travail
dont elle est le fruit >la beaute des chemins< laisance avec
    laquelle
on voyage, la propreté et la promtitude
avec laquelle on est servi dans toutes les
auberges, et enfin cet air d'assurance et de
male fierté que l'idée de la liberté fait
empreindre sur tout les visages & que l'on
ne trouve point dans les pays somis à un
gouvernement despotique. Je pense encore
qu'il seroit inutile, mon Prince, de Vous
rapeller les cérémonies dont on Vous acca-

Septembre

were presented to my eyes, the confusion with
which I could only view them, particularly
due to the impossibility of being able to
inform myself because of my ignorance of the
language, could only give me very imperfect
ideas, which I can only recall with difficulty.
What in my view must strike any foreigner
who arrives in England from any country
whatsoever, is to see the abundance that
prevails in all conditions, the industriousness
of which it is the fruit, >the beauty of the
paths,< the ease with which one travels, the
cleanliness and punctuality with which one is
served in every inn and finally that air of
assurance and pride that the idea of liberty
imprints on every face and which is not
found in countries subject to a despotic government. I also think that it would be useless,
my Prince, to remind you of the ceremonies
with which you were overwhelmed at the
audience that you afterwards had with the

September

bla à l'audience que Vous eutes auprès
du Roi, quoique vraiment Vous futes très
content de l'accueil gracieux que Sa majesté
Vous fit. Il est vrai que ne pouvant Vous
dispenser de faire d'abord (…) cour à la famille royale, Vous vous arretates pour la
premiere fois à Londres d'avantage que Vous
n'en aviés en deßein, surtout dans une saison où cette ville est quasi abandonnée et
où toutes (la nobleße est) >les personnes de qualité sont<
    encore >suposées< présumée
davior étre (en) >à la< campagne[30]. Vous aviez decidé
de faire un voyage pour Vous instruire et
Vous amuses utilement. Vous aviez dès lors aßéz
de conoißance >du monde< pour étre persuadé que ce n'est
pas absolument dans la capitale qui l'on peut
aprendre à juger du commerce et des qualités
d'un pays (…) ni étudies les moeurs d'une
nation. Principaliment en Angleterre (tous)>chaque<
(les) ville(s) (sont) >en< (re)marquable par >des< diférentes
manufactures, chaque port sur les diféren-
tes cotes à son négose particuliers. Enfin
un grand nombres de maisons de campagne
dans les diférentes provinces méritent d'étre
pour la beauté de leur architecture
ou de leurs tableaux. La cultivation même des
terres, une étude que tout Prince quelque grand
qu'il fut ne (…) devroit jamois négligen
(End of page 15)

King, although you were truly very content
with the gracious welcome that his majesty
gave you. It is true that since you were not
able to refrain from first waiting on the royal
family, you stopped in London for the first
time longer than you intended, particularly
during a season when the city is nearly abandoned and all >persons of quality< >are
assumed< to be still in the country.[30] You had
decided to make a journey to instruct and
amuse yourself usefully. Therefore, you had
sufficient knowledge >of the world< to be
persuaded that it is not absolutely in the capital where one can learn to judge the commerce and qualities of a country, or to study
the customs of a nation. In principle, every
city in England is remarkable for its different
factories and every port on the different
coasts, for its own particular trade. Finally, a
large number of country houses in the various
provinces are distinguished by the beauty of
their architecture or their paintings. Even the
cultivation of the land, a subject that no
prince, no matter how important he may be,
should ever neglect,
(End of page 15)

le 9.
9th

n'est pas en Angleterre la chose la moins
digne d'attention. Je ne suis pas nonplus
persuadé que c'est dans la capitale que
l'on aprenue à connoïtre les coutumes
& la maniére de penser d'un peuple.
Je ne suis pas la deßus du sentiment
de M.ʳ Muralt[31] & je (era) soupçonnerees
que ce préjugé l'a emprétré plus d'une
fois à s'eclercir, à fond sur bien des choses
qu'il a avancées. Deplus en Angleterre
la nobleße en général n'est pas établie
à Londres, elle n'y vient que pour y paßer
l'hiver ou pour aßister au parlement et
soit les occupations qui empéchent les
uns, soit les plaisiers qui dißipent les
autres, les mêmes personnes ne vous pa-
roißent plus à la ville ce qu'ils Vous sem-
bloiret à la campagne. Toutes ces raisons
Vous avoient fait prendre la resolution
de faire quelque grand tour dans le pays
avant l'arrivée de l'hiver. Pendant les
tems que les visites que Vous pensies
de faire à la maison royale vous arre-
tois>en< encore à Londres. Vous vous conten-
tates de l'employer à voir quelques endroits
aux environs de cette ville. Un des pre-
mier(e)s fut Sion-hill[32], maison apartenan
te à Mylord Holderneß. Il n'y a pas longtems qu'elle est batie et le jardin qui n'
est planté que depuis peu d'années montre qu'il era beau dans quelque tems, et
nous donna une idée de la maniére dont
on commence à arranger les jardins en
Angleterre. La maison n'est pas grande com
me si proche de Londres n'étant pas destinée
à y demeurer, mais elle est meublée trés-

is not the thing least worthy of attention in
England. I am also not convinced that the
capital is the place to get to know the customs
& mentality of a country. I concord with the
feeling of Mr. Muralt[31]; I would imagine that
more than once this prejudice has prevented
him from thoroughly clarifying many of the
things which he promotes. Furthermore, the
English nobility have not established their
homes in London; they merely come there to
spend the winter or to sit in parliament and,
whether it is in the activities that hinder some
or the pleasures that distract others, these persons seem to you to be no longer the same
people they were in the country. All these
reasons led you to resolve to undertake a
great tour of the country before winter set in.
During the time that you thought of visiting
the Royal household you were still in London. You contented yourself with visiting a
number of places near this city. One of the
first was Sion Hill,[32] a house belonging to
Lord Holderness. It was built not long ago
and one can see that the garden that was
planted only a few years ago will be beautiful
in a short time; it also gave us an idea of how
the English begin to lay out their gardens.
The house is not large and so close to London that is not designed for long sojourns, but
it is very elegantly furnished and surprisingly
clean. Lady Holderness is Dutch and tries to
surpass the cleanliness that one finds generally everywhere in England. Sion Hill is near
Sion House,[33] a >very fine< house belonging
to Lord Northumberland situated on the
Thames in the county of Surrey a little above

le 10
10th

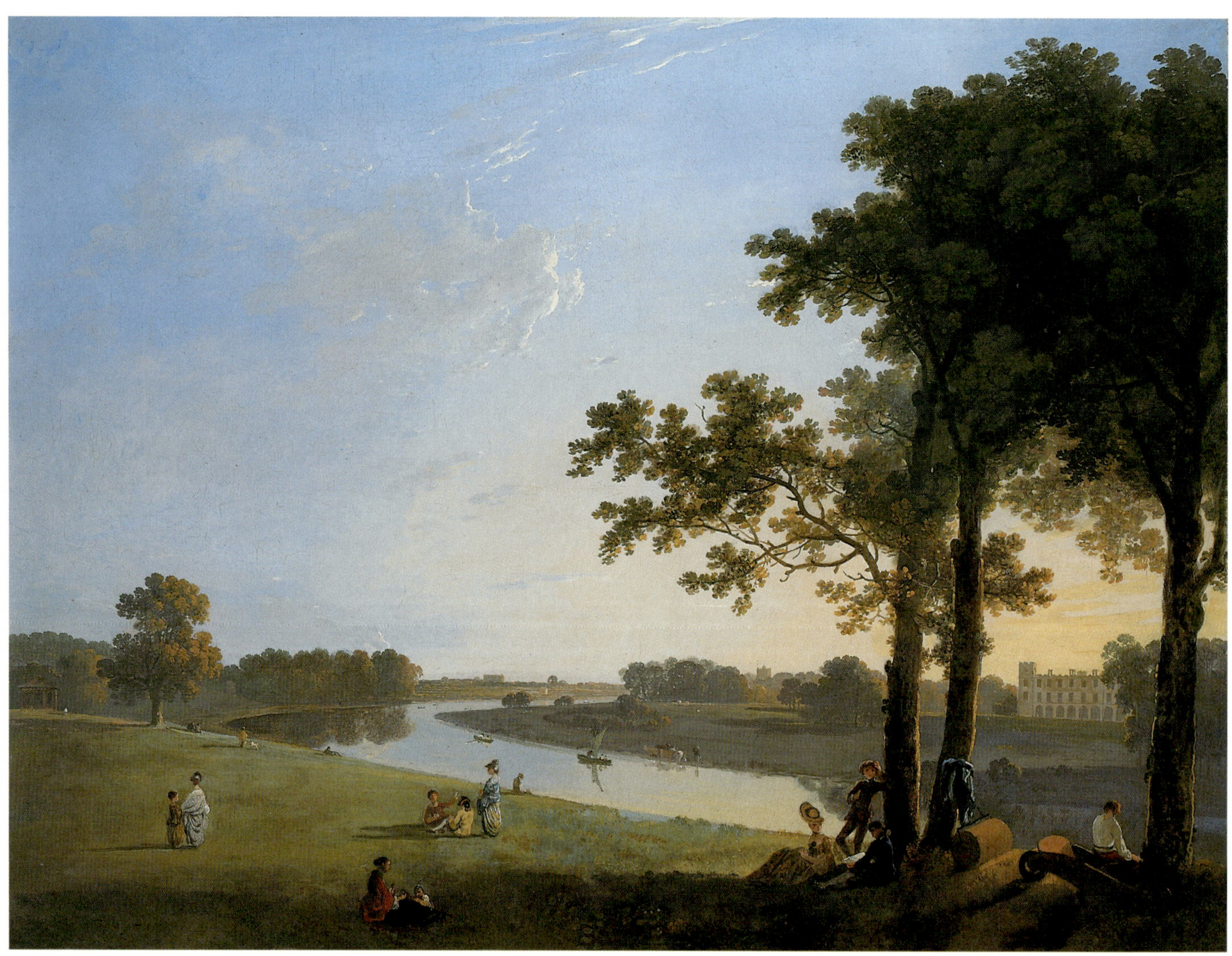

10 Richard Wilson, 1714–1782, view across the Thames at Kew Gardens to Syon-House, oil on canvas, circa 1760/1770, Bayerische Staatsgemäldesammlungen, Munich.

élégamment et d'une propreté surprenan-
te. Mylady Holderneß qui est Hollandoise
à cherche à renchérir encore sur la nette
té que l'on trouve généralement partout
en Angleterre. Sion-hill est tout proche
de Sion-house33, >très belle< maison apartenante à
Milord Northumberland située sur les
bords de la tamise dans le province de
Surrey un peu au deßus de Richmond.
Nous repaßames la Tamise pour voir (Hamp)
>la maison Royale de< Hampton court.34 Ce palais fut bati
    par le fameux
(End of page 16)

Cardinal Wolsey, qui en fit présent à Henri VIII. *Sept^{bre}*
son maitre. Le Roi Charles I. y fut >dans la suite< priso-
nier pendant quelque tems. Mais ce fut
le Roi Guillaume III. & la Reine Marie
qui y ajoutérent la plus grande partie
et y demeurérent très souvent. La Tamise
forme un demi circle au tour du jardin
est forme une très agréable situation.
Au reste le jardin en soi même est dans
le gout Hollandois. Le palais de Hampton

Richmond. We crossed the Thames in order
to visit >the royal palace of< Hampton
Court.34 This palace was built by the famous
(End of page 16)

Cardinal Wolsey, who gave it to his sovereign, *September*
Henry VIII. >Subsequently< King William
III & Queen Mary had most of the additions
built and spent a great deal of time living
there. The Thames forms a semi-circle around
the garden, creating a very pleasant situation.
Incidentally, the garden itself is laid out in
the Dutch style. Hampton Court Palace is
very extensive, it has (several) >three<
>adjoining< square courtyards, >the first two

court est très-vaste, il a (plusieurs) >trois< cours
>quarrees qui se suivent
l'une l'autre dont les deux
premiéres sont gothiques. La
troisiéme et (…) la façade du
coté du jardin avec l'autre du
coté gauche sont baties sous le
Roi Guillaume sur le plan de
Christophe Wren fameux architecte dans ce tems.<
(diférentes. La façade du coté du jardin
est grande belle). Le grand escalier qui
conduit à la Sale d'armes est peine par
un Italien nommé Verio. Les apartemens
sont d'une belle suite quoique meublés,
un peu à l'antique. Ils sont ornés d'un
bon nombre de peintures surtout de portraits par Van Dyk, Kneller[35] & Thornhill[36]
Ce qu'il y a de plus beau dans ce palais
c'est la gallerie des Cartons de Raphael.[37]
De douze qu'il y en avoient, il n'en reste
plus que sept. Ce sont des Cartons que
ce celebre peintre avoit fait pour servir de modeles à des tapißeries et qu'il
avoit colorie pour cette raison. Des sept
qui y restent, le premier représente la
péche miraculeuse, le second notre Seigneur qui donne les clefs de l'eglise à
St. Pierre, le troisieme l'estropié gueri à
la porte du temple, le quatrieme la mort
d'Aeneias, le cinqieme Elymas le sorcier
frappé d'aveuglement, le sisciéme le sacrifice que les peuples de Lycaonie vaulurent
faire à St. Paul & St. Barnabas et le septieme
St. Paul qui préche aux Atheniens.
Deux jours après nous allames faire un au-
tre tour en Surrey. La première place >qui nous vimes< fut
Wooburn Farm[38] qui apartenoit a M.r Southcot
mort depuis quelque tems. La(e) (jardin) plus grande beauté de ce jardin consiste dans l'art
avec lequel on a su ménager partout les
vues les plus charmantes. D'abord en entrant
nous paßames par une allée qui tourne
le long d'une grande piéce d'eau à l'autre coté
de laquelle il y a une jolie maison. En mon-
tant à gauche vers la partie la plus élévé
(End of page 17)

le 12

du jardin nous parvinmes aux ruines d'un
espéce de temple gothique entouré de cipres
et de saules pendants, qui font une idée très
singuliere. De là une allée principale (con)
aboutit à un pavillon. Mais de touts cotés
il y a de petites allées irregulieres, qui ofre
a la vue les plus jolis paysages du monde.
Sur le coté droit le pont de Walton, sur
la gauche le pont de Cheiseg, le Chateau
de Windsor & Windsor Lodge vous présentent partout de diferents tableau. Arri-
vé au pavillon, l'oeuil est plus libre et
se perd dans le objets varie du pays le
plus riant. Au(bas) >pied< de la coline sur laquelle le pavillon est situé serpente un ruißeau
qui descend de la foret de Windsor et qui
fait les bornes du jardin de ce coté là. De
la nous descendimes par une douce pente

Sept.^{bre}

of which are Gothic. The third one and the
facade on the garden side, along with the one
on the left side, were built under King William to plans by the famous architect of the
time, Christopher Wren.< The large staircase
which leads to the armoury was decorated by
an Italian called Verio. The living apartments
are in a lovely sequence, although their furnishings are somewhat old-fashioned. They
are decorated with a good number of paintings, particularly portraits by Van Dyck,
Kneller[35] & Thornhill.[36] The most beautiful
thing in this palace is the Gallery of Cartoons
by Raphael.[37] Of the dozen that existed
originally, only seven remain. They are the
cartoons that this famous painter created in
preparation for the wall hangings and which
he coloured for that reason. Of the seven
remaining, the first depicts the Miraculous
Draught of Fishes, the second Our Lord
giving the keys of the Church to St. Peter, the
third the lame man healed at the doors of the
temple, the fourth the death of Aeneas, the
fifth the sacrifice the Lycaonians wanted to
make to St. Paul and St. Barnabas, the sixth
the sorcerer Elymas who was struck blind and
the seventh St. Paul preaching to the Atheni-
ans. Two days later we undertook a further
trip in Surrey. The first place >we visited<
was Wooburn Farm,[38] which belonged to Mr.
Southcot who passed away recently. The
great beauty of this garden lies in the way the
most charming views have been created
everywhere. On first entering the garden we
walked along an avenue running along a
large expanse of water, on the other side of
which a pretty house stands. Climbing up to
the left towards the highest part
(End of page 17)

12th

of the garden we arrived at the ruins of a
kind of Gothic temple surrounded by
cypresses and weeping willows which made a
very curious impression. From there a main
avenue leads to a pavilion. But on all sides
there are small, irregular avenues affording
views of the prettiest countryside in the
world. To the right Walton Bridge, to the left
Cheiseg Bridge; different views of Windsor
Castle & Windsor Lodge appear everywhere.
On arriving at the pavilion the eye can wan-
der more freely and lose itself in the most
amusing features of the country. At the
>foot< of the hill on which the pavilion is
situated, a stream comes winding from the
Forest of Windsor and forms the border of the
garden on that side. From there we went
down a gentle slope to another part of the

September

dans une autre partie du jardin qui est
plus baße mais qui n'en est pas moins
agréablement située. Un autre ruißeau,
qui vient de Guilford la parcourt irre-
gulierement & y forme plusieurs petits baßins d'eau. Les allées qui y sont
pratiquées sans ordre simetriques nous
raménérent insensiblement à l'endroit
pas lequel nous étions entrés a peu de
distance de Wooburn. Milord Portmore
à une maison de campagne à Weybridge
>nomée Ham-Farm<,³⁹ (qui est) dont le jardin est plus
ancien que le précédent & paroit être un des premiers
qui ont été fait >en Angleterre< dans le gout moderne
par la hauteur d'une quantite d'arbres
étrangers qui en font une des principales beautés. Devant la maison vous
voyes un grand bowling-green ou tapis
verd au bout duquel une belle allée vous
conduit à un baßin d'eau, formé par le
ruißeau de Guilford qui vient s'y jetter
par un arc ou espece de grotte (de rocailles)
bordé de faules pendans & d'un toufe d'arbres qui forment une idée très-pitoresque.
En continuant notre chemin nous trouvames au dela de cette piece d'eau un canal
navigable qui traverse le jardin. On le
paße sur un pont de bois aßés curieux, que
l'on tourne sur un piveau pour laißer le
(End of page 18)

garden that is in a lower position but none
the less pleasant. Another stream, which
comes from Guilford, takes an irregular
course through it & makes a number of small
pools. The avenues, which are laid out there
without symmetry, took us, without our notic-
ing, to the place where we had entered, not
far from Wooburn. Lord Protmore has a
country house in Weyridge, >called Ham
Farm<,³⁹ the garden of which is older than
the previous one & appears to be one of the
first to be laid out >in England< in the modern style, which is indicated by the great
number of foreign trees that are one of its
most beautiful features. In front of the house
you can see a large lawn [French says bowling green], a green carpet, at the end of
which a lovely avenue leads to a pool formed
by the Guilford stream which flows there
through an arch or a kind of grotto (of shells)
and is lined by weeping willows & a copse of
trees creating a very picturesque impression.
Further along our way we found a navigable
canal flowing through the garden behind this
pool. A rather strange bridge crosses it, which
can be swivelled on a pivot to
(End of page 18)

chemin libre aux bateau. (que) De l'autre coté
du canal le jardin continue jusqu'aux
bords de la Tamise, ou il y a une belle
terraße. Le lendemain matin nous allames
à Oatland⁴⁰ (aß) tout proche de Weybridge. Ce
jardin apartient à Milord Lincoln. On y e-
tre par une terraße au milieu de laquelle
est une très-belle maison. La vue en est
(très-belle) des plus agreables. Tout le jardin est situe presque sur la pente d'une
montagne au pied de laquelle Vous voyez
serpenter un petite riviére, qui paroit
naturelle mais qui neaumoins est faite
par l'art. De la nous allames à Walton
voir de plus près le pont⁴¹ que (l'on) nous a-
vions vu de loin dans touts ces environs
et qui est d'une beauté singuliére. Ce pont
n'est que de trois arches, qui peposent
sur quatre pilliers de pierre, et tout le
reste n'est que de bois. >la voute de< L'arche du milieu
est d'une (est d'une hauteur prodigieuse) >espace prodigieuse<
et la charpente en est jointe d'une manié-
re singuliére. Nous mésurames environ
soixante pas >entre les deux piliers< d'un pilier a l'autre qui
soutiennent cette arche. Ce fut M.ʳ Sa-
muel Decker qui fit batir ce pont avec la
permißion du parlement. Il l'achiva en
1750. Ce pont n'est pas moins utile (par)
aux deux provinces de Middlesex et de Surrey qu'il joint par le grand chemin qui
y paße et il sert en même tems d'orne-
ment à touts ces environs. Nous ne paßames
pas Waltonbridge mais nous restames dans
la province de Surrey pour prendre notre
chemin vers Cobham qui est situe tout près

allow ships to pass. On the other side of the
canal the garden continues to the banks of
the Thames where there is a lovely terrace.
The next morning we went to Oatland⁴⁰ by
Weybridge. This garden belongs to Lord Lincoln. It is entered from a terrace in the middle of which is a very beautiful house. The
view there is extremely pleasant. Almost the
entire garden is situated on a hillside, at the
foot of which a small river meanders; it looks
natural but is in fact artificial. From there we
proceeded to Walton to look more closely at
the bridge,⁴¹ which we had seen from a distance wherever we were in this area and
which is of unique beauty. This bridge consists of just three arches, resting on four stone
piers, and everything else is entirely of wood.
>The vault< of the central arch is astonish-
ingly wide and the beam is fixed in a peculiar
manner. We measured some sixty paces
>between the two piers< from one of the
piers carrying this arch to the next. It was Mr.
Samuel Decker who had this bridge built
with the approval of parliament. It was completed in 1750. This bridge is of equal useful-
ness to the counties of Middlesex and Surrey,
which it links via the large road running over
it, and at the same time it is of decorative
value for the entire area. We did not cross
Walton Bridge but remained in the county of
Surrey in order to continue on our way to
Cobham which is very close to the London to
Guilford road. In Cobham⁴² there is a garden
belonging to Mr. Hamilton which has been
embellished over the last few years. He con-

du chemin de Londres à Guilford. Il y a à Cobham[42]
un jardin qui apartient à M.ʳ Hamilton qui
va beaucoup embelli depuis quelques années
et qui travaille encore continuellement à
y ajouter quelque chose. Comme il n'y a point
de maison qui mérite quelque attention on
nous conduisit d'abord au jardin qui est très spa-
cieux et qui consiste en plusieurs collines sur
le sommet desquels on a posé diferents bati
mens qui servent de point de vue et forment partout de très agréables perspectives. Une partie
de ces collines sont faites avec la terre que l'on
(End of page 19)

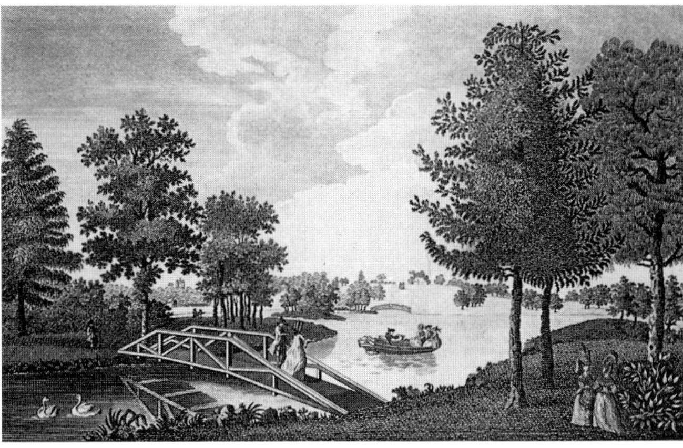

11 View from the west of Mr. Hamilton's landscape garden near Cobham
(now Painshill), copperplate from: The Modern Universal British Traveller,
London 1779 (cf. ill. 4), Private owner.

tinues the work of adding to it. As there is no
house worthy of note there, we were taken
first to the gardens which are extensive and
include several hills, on the tops of which
various buildings have been placed which
serve as outlooks and create very pleasant
perspectives everywhere. Some of these hills
have been made from the earth that
(End of page 19)

y a (…) creusé pour faire le canal qui parcourt tout le (terrain) jardin. D'abord nous
arrivames à un espéce de temple gothique
ouvert de touts cotés qui Vous presente (tout
le jardin) une variation d'objet admirable.
Au pied de la (montagne) >coline< sur laquelle le pavillon est situé Vous voyez une grande piece
d'eau où le canal >qui sort entre les rochers d'une
montagne qui< vient terminer sa course
irreguliére. Au milieu vous voyéz une Ile
avec une grote qui n'étoit pas encore toute
achevée. Les ruines d'un arc orné de quelques
antiques se presentent de l'autre coté du
canal entre les (arbres) pins et les lauriers.
Tout le >reste du< jardin Vous paroit une foret et comme
il est rempli d'une quantité de diferents arbres
étrangers il >vous montre un paysage< a d'une variation de teintes
    mer-
veilleuse. Sur la main gauche un petit hermitage décoré très rustiquement semble pendre
sur le précipice d'une coline. Une autre coline à main droite mais plus loignée Vous
montre un très-beau temple de Bacchus, &
plus dans le lointain encore une grande
tente ou pavillon >à la<turque. Plus au milieu &
sur la coline la plus éminente une tour s'
élève, sur laquelle nous montames après avoir
fait la tour du jardin. Je dois ajouter encore
que la petite riviére nommé le Mole qui
paße tout proche du jardin y fournit (…)
l'eau neceßaire. Mais comme le lit de
cette riviére est bien plus bas on fait monter l'eau par une machine qui ne consi-
ste que dans une roue & qui (conduit l'eau) la fait entrer
par le milieu de la montagne d'où le canal

Sept.ᵇʳᵉ

was excavated to build the canal which
runs through the garden. First of all we
arrived at a kind of Gothic temple which is
open on all sides and offers a number of
wondrous things. At the foot of the >hill< on
which the pavilion stands you see a large
expanse of water where the canal, which
comes out between the rocks of a mountain,
ends its irregular course. In the middle you
see an island with a grotto that was not quite
finished. The ruins of an arch decorated with
antique figures could be seen on the other
side of the canal between pine and laurel
trees. All the >rest of the< garden looked to
you like a forest and since it has a large number of different foreign trees >it reveals to you
a landscape< with a wonderful variety of
colours. On the left a small, very rustically
decorated, hermitage seems to hang over the
precipice of a hill. Another hill on the right,
but further away, shows you a very beautiful
temple to Bacchus and further away still a
large marquee or Turkish-style pavilion. More
in the centre & on the most prominent hill a
tower rises up which we climbed after completing our tour of the garden. I must add
here that the small river, called the Mole,
which flows close to the garden, provides the
water required for it. But, since the river bed
is much lower, the water is drawn up by a
machine which consists of only one wheel &
which channels the river into the mountain
from where it seems to feed the canal. This
machine, like everything else, is the invention of the master himself. Esher[43] is another

September

semble tirer sa source. Cette machine et
comme tout le reste de l'invention du
maitre même. Esher[43] est un autre fort
jolie endroit, qui a apartenu à Mr Pelham.
La maison est batie dans un gout gothique,
mais le jardin quoique simple, ne laiße
pas d'etre très agréable. Claremont[44] maison
du Duc de Newcastle fut bati par Mr John
Vanbrugh, connu en Angleterre par son gout
singulier pour l'architecture gothique tout
contraire au bonnes regles, mais qu'il a su
menager de façon à rendre neaumoins ses
maisons très logeables. (Cette) La maison de Claremont a une façade aßés longue, mais elle
n'est pas haute. Une fort grande place d'un
beau gazon devant la maison, la coline qui s'élé-
(End of page 20)

ve derriere couverte d'arbres qui aboutèrent   *Sept.[bre]*
au deux ailes du batiment et bordent ce
bowling-green feroient croire qu'elle est
placée à l'entrée d'un bois. Tout au haut
de la montagne a presque une mille der-
riere la maison vous voyer une tour >ou précisément un pavillon<
de la quelle on a la plus belle vue du mon-
de à Londres, à Windsor, à Hamptoncourt
& dans touts les environs. Tout le jardin
est d'un trèsbel arrangement. Le lendemain   *le 14*
nous allames à Richmond[45], où le Roi a un
très-grand jardin où il m'a paru que la
nature a plus de droit d'étre admiré que
l'art. La terraße qui conduit tout le long
des bords de la Tamise, les bois, les allées
irregulieres, l'hermitage en font les principaux ornemens. Dans les siècles paßés
beaucoup des souverains d'Angleterre ont
demeuré a Richmond. Le Roi George I. aimait
beaucoup ce jardin et y fit beaucoup de
changements. Le Roi qui regne aujourd'hui
y vient regulièrement plusieurs fois la
semaine. Nous rentrames à midi à Londres
et le même soir Vous aßistates à la cérémonie du Batéme du Prince Frédéric[46]. Ce fut
l'Archevéque de Canterbury qui en fit la
fonction dans les apartemens de la Reine
où toute la famille Royale étoit aßemblée.
La Reine étoit couchée dans un lit très magnifique. Les Pairs du Royaume y aßistèrent,
außi bien que ce qu'il y avoit de la première
nobleße de même que les ministres du cours
étrangères. Vous employates les jours sui-
vans à visiter quelques artistes dont je
me reserve de parler plus bas, et à pas courir
cette grande ville où toutes les boutiques
sont remplies des choses dignes de curiosité.
Un matin nous allames voir Chiswick[47]   *le 17*
en Middlesex, >où il y a une maison< qui apartient à présent
au fils du Duc de Devonshire, mais qui fut batie
par feu Milord Burlington. Elle paße pour
une des plus belles piéces d'architecture en
Angleterre, et elle est veritablement dans
le gout de l'anciennne Gréce. Une allée de
cédres extrémement hauts qui aboutit a
la belle façade de la maison Vous présente
une entrée des plus majestueuses et semble
Vous conduire dans un temple. Un très-bel esca-

---

very pretty place which belongs to Mr. Pelham. The house is built in the Gothic style
but the garden, although simple, is nevertheless very pleasant. Claremont,[44] the house of
the Duke of Newcastle, was built by Mr. John
Vanbrugh, famous in England for his singular
taste for Gothic architecture which is quite
contrary to all good rules but which he has a
way of using so that his houses are nevertheless very pleasant to live in. Claremont House
has quite a long facade but is not high. A
lovely, very large lawn in front of the house,
the hill behind
(End of page 20)

with trees which lead to the two wings of the   *September*
building and form a border with the lawn
[French says bowling green] create an impression of being at the entrance to a wood.
Right on top of the mountain, almost a mile
behind the house, you can see a tower, or to
be more precise a pavilion, from where you
have the most magnificent view of London,
Windsor, Hamptoncourt and the entire
environs. The whole garden is beautifully
designed. The next day we went to Richmond,[45]   *14th*
where the King has a very large garden and
where it seemed to me that it was nature
rather than art that merited admiration. The
terrace running along the bank of the Thames,
the woods, the irregular avenues, the hermitage are the main ornamental elements there.
In previous centuries many of the rulers of
England lived in Richmond. King George I
loved this garden and made many changes
there. The present king comes there several
times a week. We returned to London at midday and on the same evening you took part in
the baptism ceremony of Prince Frederick.[46]
The Archbishop of Canterbury conducted
the ceremony in the King's apartments where
the entire Royal Family was gathered. The
Queen lay in a magnificent bed. The peers of
the realm were present, as were the entire
high aristocracy and the envoys of foreign
courts. You used the subsequent days to visit
some artists, about whom I shall report below,
and to visit rather hurriedly this large city
where all the shops are filled with things that
arouse curiosity. One morning we paid a
visit to Chiswick[47] in Middlesex where there   *17th*
is a house that currently belongs to the son of
the Duke of Devonshire, but was built by the
late Lord Burlington. It is considered to be
one of the finest pieces of architecture in
England and is in fact built in the style of
Ancient Greece. An avenue of extremely high
cedars leads to the most beautiful facade of
the house and presents to you a most majestic
entrance that appears to lead into a temple. A
very beautiful staircase and a portico in the
Corinthian style in front of the
(End of page 21)

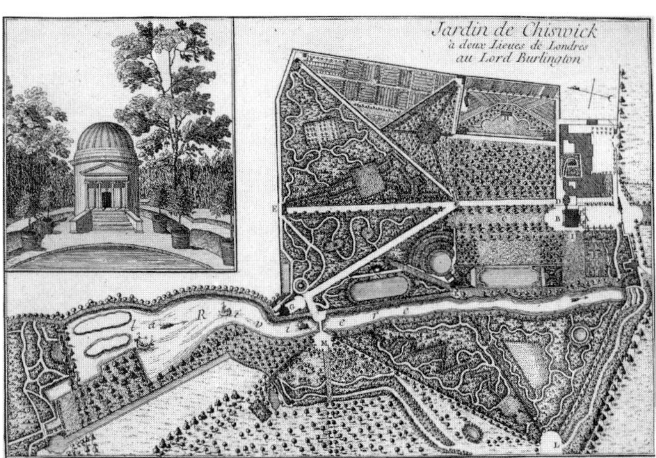

12 Chiswick, plan of garden and view of the temple in the Orangerie Garden, copperplate from: G.-L. Le Rouge, Détails des nouveaux Jardins à la mode, 21 issues, Paris 1776–87, here issue 1, plate 22. Kulturstiftung DessauWörlitz.

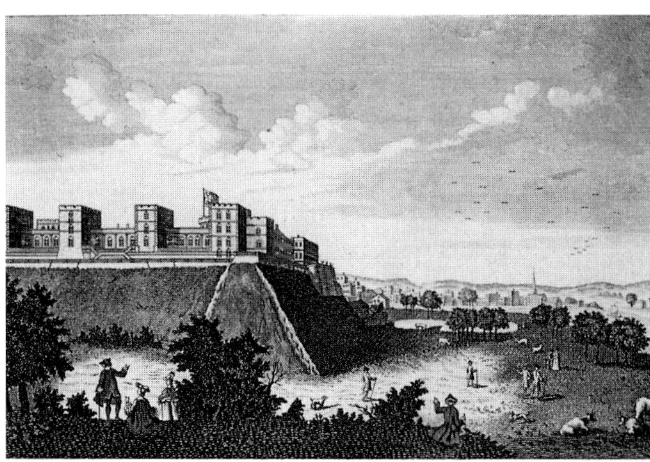

13 View of the castle or royal palace at Windsor in Berkshire, copperplate from: The Modern Universal British Traveller, London 1779 (cf. ill. 4). Private owner.

lier & un portique dans l'ordre corinthien devant
(End of page 21)

l'entrée forment la façade principale. Dans le
dedans il y a une sale en forme de octogone
qui termine en dome par lequel la lumière
y tombe. Cette sale außi bien que les autres
apartemens sont ornés de marbres, de bronzes,
& d'un bon nombre de beaux tableaux.
La belle proportion et la noble simplicité
tant dans le dedans que dans le dehors de
cette maison (sont) méritent l'admiration
de tout le monde. On pourroit souhaiter
qu'une architecture si elégante eut été
employée pour un batiment plus vaste.
Il m'a encore paru que les apartemens
ne sont pas aßés clairs, ce qui n'est pas
à l'avantage des tableaux. Le jardin est
aßés grand et bien ordonné. Mais tant d'é-
difices, d'obelisques, de statues et de vases
qu'on y trouve partout me font penser
qu'on a travaillé à y étaler les productions
de l'art plus qu'a y erichir les beautés de la
nature. De Chiswick nous allames encore
faire un tour à Grove[48] maison de M.ʳ Eliot
très elégante avec un fort joli jardin, et
de là à Wimbleton[49] en Surrey. Cette maison
qui apartient à Milord Spencer est très bien
batie et ornée de beaux tableaux >parmi lesquels< entre
autres il y en a deux qui sont gravés par
Strange, l'un du Guide representant la modestie & la liberalité, l'autre d'André Sacchi
representant le merite récompensé. On
travailloit à aplanir une coline ou terras-
se du coté du Sud pour procurer une vue
plus libre à la maison. Milord Spencer a
encore une belle ménagerie à Wimbleton
remplie d'oiseaux étrangers. En reprenant
notre chemin à Londres nous >vîmes< en paßants encore devant une petite maison aparté-
nante à M.ᵐᵉ Pitt qui est très jolie pour son
ameublement & pour le parti qu'on a su
tirer d'un si petit terrain. Quelques jours
après, Monseigneur, quand Vous eutes fini

Sept.^{bre}

entrance constitute the main facade. Behind
it there is an octagonal room with a dome
letting daylight into the room. This room,
like all the other apartments, is decorated
with art objects of marble and bronze and a
good number of fine paintings. The beautiful
proportions and noble simplicity of the house,
both its interior and exterior, deserve general
admiration. One could wish that such elegant
architecture had been used on a much larger
building. I also had the impression that the
apartments did not have enough light, which
is not advantageous for the paintings. The
garden is large enough and well ordered. But
all the buildings, obelisks, statues and vases
that are to be found all over the garden made
me think that much work had gone into
exhibiting works of art rather than enhancing
the beauty of nature. From Chiswick we
made another trip to Grove,[48] the elegant
house with its very pretty garden belonging to
Mr. Eliot, and from there we continued to
Wimbleton[49] in Surrey. This house, which
belongs to Lord Spencer, is very well built
and decorated with fine paintings including
two engravings by Strange, one of Guide representing modesty and generosity, the other
of André Sacchi representing rewarded
merits. On the south side they are attempting
to create a hill or terrace to permit a clearer
view of the house. Lord Spencer also has a
fine menagerie in Wimbleton, full of exotic
birds. We set off once more for London and
on our way paid a brief visit to a small house
belonging to Madame Pitt which is very
pretty due to its furnishing and due to the way
such clever use has been made of such a
small plot of land. A few days later, when you,
Excellency, had completed all your first cere-
monial visits, we left London for our first tour
of the country which we began with Windsor

September

toutes Vos premières visites de cérémonie, nous
partîmes de Londres pour aller faire notre premier tour, que començames par Windsor >en Berkshire<.
On nomme »Windsor Lodge«[50] le palais où le Duc
de Cumberland fait sa demeure ordinaire. La
maison n'en est aucunement magnifique mais
on y arrive par un très-beau chemin qui paße
par le grand parc. Ce parc a 14. miles de circonférence, & le Duc a fait beaucoup de depenses
pour l'embellir, a quoi la belle situation lui a
(End of page 22)

fourni touts les avantages. Les grandes pièces
d'eau, le beau pont d'un arche sur lequel on
paße une petite rivière, le pavillon à
la Chinoise bati et meublé le plus élégament
qu'il est poßible dans le gout, la grote avec
la cascade font les principaux ornemens (de
cet). Il y a encore un autre grand pavillon sur
(le haut) une coline des plus hautes nomée Shrub's
Hill, d'où l'on a une très-belle vue nonseule-
ment du parc, mais de touts les environs.
Quoique le Duc ne se trouvat pas ce matin à
sa maison, il >avoit< eut neaumoins l'attention d'y
laißer le General Hotson pour Vous y recevoir
et d'ordoner des voitures pour la comodité de
parcourir un endroit si spacieuse. Ce grand
parc est contigu à la foret de Windsor, qui
embraße une grande partie de Berkshire. Cette
foret est célebre par Mr. Pope qui y naquit
a Binfield et qui tira à jamais de l'oubli
le nom de la contrée ou il prit sa naißance.
Son poeme Windsor-forest[51] est une des plus
belles descriptions qu'on ait dans ce gout
& comme ce grand homme demeuroit sur
le lieu même dans le tems qu'il le composa,
on peut dire que c'est un tableau fait d'après
nature. Le chateau de Windsor[52] est situé sur
le haut d'une montagne et la terraße, qui en
entoure une grande partie est fameuse pour
ses belles vues. Guillaume le conquerant après
s'étre emparé de la couronne, batit (le chateau) >Windsor Castle<
et les Rois ses succeßeurs y resident. Mais
ce fut Edouard III. qui le changea tout à fait
et y érigea le (chateau) >palais< qui y subsiste encore.
Enfin Charles II. l'acheva et il y paßait
ordinairement l'été. La statue equestre de
ce prince est au millieu de la Cour du palais.
Les apartemens de ce palais sont grands, meublés un peu à l'antique; et on y voit une
quantité de tableaux gatés pour la pluspart.
Il y a un apartement qu'on nomme la sale
des Beautes, the room of Beauties, ou sont les
portraits des plus fameuses beautés sous le
regne de Charles II. >peintus par Lely<. Ce sont celles dont
    les mé-
moires du Chevalier de Grammont fournißent
les anecdotes les plus amusantes. Le chateau
de Windsor est encore fameux pour l'institution de l'ordre de la jarretière. Cet ordre fut
fondé l'an 1349 par le Roi Edouard III. comme une
recompense de service militaire. La jarretiè-
re fut (prise) >choisee< (comme le) en signe du lieu d'amitié
qui doit joindre l'honneur & la valeur >le courage<. Le Roi
(End of page 23)

in Berkshire. "Windsor Lodge"[50] is the name
given to the palace where the Duke of Cumberland normally resides. The house is in no
way splendid but one arrives there by a very
beautiful path through the great park. This
park has a circumference of 14 miles; the Duke
has spent a lot of money to embellish it, in
which enterprise the beautiful location has
(End of page 22)

given him every possible advantage. The large
expanses of water, the lovely arch of a bridge
on which one crosses a small river, the Chinese pavilion, which has been so elegantly
built and furnished as this style allows, the
grotto with its waterfall, form the main decoration. There is another large pavilion on one
of the highest hills, known as Shrub's Hill,
from where there is a magnificent view not
only of the park but of the whole area.
Although the Duke was not at home on that
morning he was nevertheless so attentive as to
have General Hotson receive you and ordered
carriages to enable you to drive in comfort
through such a vast estate. This great park
borders on the Forest of Windsor which
covers a large part of Berkshire. This forest
gained fame through Mr. Pope who was born
there in Binfield and who ensured that the
name of the place of his birth will never fall
into oblivion. His poem Windsor Forest[51] is
one of the loveliest descriptions in this style
and, since this great man lived in the place
itself during the time he composed the poem,
one can say it is a picture painted from nature.
Windsor Castle[52] is on top of a hill and the
terrace surrounding a large part of it is famous
for its splendid views. William the Conqueror
built Windsor Castle after he seized the crown
and his successors had their residence there.
However, it was Edward I who had it completely re-designed and who built the palace
in its present form. Finally, Charles II completed the building and usually spent the
summer there. The equestrian statue of this
prince is in the middle of the palace court-
yard. The apartments of the castle are large
and furnished in a rather antique style and
there are a number of paintings, most of them
damaged. There is one apartment, called the
Room of Beauties, which houses the portraits
painted by Lely of the most famous beauties
during the reign of Charles II. The memoirs
of the Chevalier de Grammont contain the
most amusing anecdotes about them. Windsor Castle is also famous for the Order of the
Garter. The order was founded in 1349 by
King Edward III as reward for service in the
military. The garter was chosen as a symbol
for the bond of friendship which should link
honour and bravery >courage<. King
(End of page 23)

le 23.

Sept.^{bre}

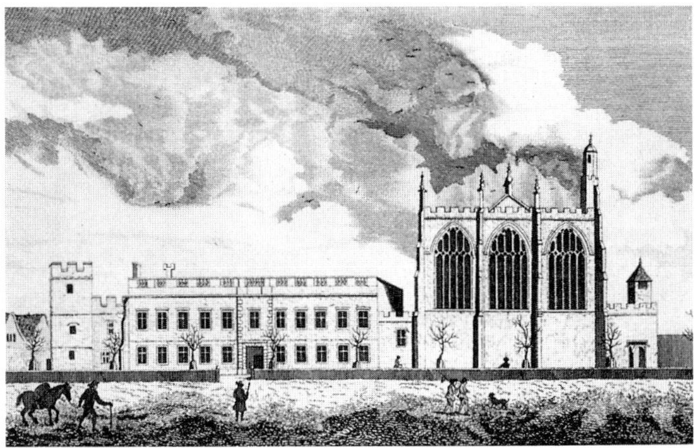

14 View of "Eaton-College" in the county of Buckinghamshire, copperplate from: The Modern Universal British Traveller, London 1779 (cf. ill. 4). Private owner.

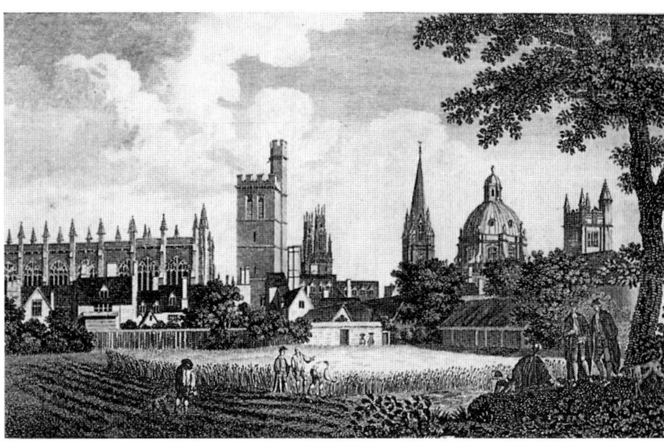

15 View of the city of Oxford with the College Church, the tower of St. Mary's Church, the dome of the Radcliffe Library and the tower of the school building, copperplate from: The Modern Universal British Traveller, London 1779 (cf. ill. 4). Private owner.

Edouard qui étoit alors en guerre avec la France *Sept.*^{bre} en prit l'ocasion pour la devise, Honi soit qui
mal y pense. Le conte qu'on a inventé de la
 jarretière de la Comteße de Salisbury a été
refuté depuis longtems. Cet ordre consiste
>outre le Souverain en< vingte cinq chevalier companions.
    Il y a encore 18. autres qu'on nomme les pauvres Cheva-
liers, qui ont une petite pension, mais que
ne portent point de marque. Le chevalier
s'aßemblent touts les ans à Windsor le jour
de St. George, patron d'Angleterre, en l'hommage
duquel cet ordre fut institué. La ceremonie
d'investir les Chevaliers se fait dans la chapelle de St. George et après la fonction le Roi
& les Chevaliers dinent dans la sale de St. George.
Cette sale est aßés pien peinte par Verrio[53].
Il y a représente le triomphe du fameux
Prince Noir, qui y >a en< méne les rois de France
& d'Ecoße ses prisoniers au Roi Edouard III.
son père. On nous aßura que le Roi Charles I. fut enseveli dans la Chapelle de St. George
par Ordre du Protecteur, & on nous y montra
son tombeau. Vis a vis du chateau de Windsor
mais au delà de la Tamise en Buckinghamshire est le College d'Eton[54] qui fut fondé par
Henri VI. dont la statue en bronze est encore
au milieu de la grande Cour. Ce college est
institué pour soixante et dix écoliers qui y sont
eléves ou depend du Roi, ou plustôt du college.
Outre ceux-ci la plus grande partie des jeunes
gens de qualité font leurs premières études à
Eton, où ils sont en pension chès les profeßeurs.
Il y en avoient jusqu'à 600 dans les tems que
nous y fumes. Le batiment au reste n'est pas
beau, (mais) >mais très logeable< et le college a une belle
    Bibliothèque
& £ 5000 de revénus. Le lendemain nous continuames notre chemin à Oxford, et nous ne nous
arrètames que quelques momens pour voir
la maison de Milord Harcourt à Newnham[55] >entre Dorchester &
    Oxford<.
Oxford est situé sur les bords de la Tamis à
miles de Londres. C'est une des plus grandes villes de l'angleterre & les batimens qui

Edward, who at the time was at war in France, *September* took the opportunity to coin the motto
"Shamed be he who thinks evil of it". The
story that was invented about the garter of the
Countess of Salisbury has long since been
refuted. Apart from the sovereign, some 25
knights belong to the order as companions.
Another 18 belong to it with the designation
Poor Knights; they draw a small pension but
do not wear any mark of recognition. The
knights assemble each year at Windsor on the
feast day of St. George, the patron saint of
England, in whose honour the order was
founded. The investiture of the knights takes
place in St. George's Chapel and after the
official ceremony the King & knights dine in
St. George's Hall. This hall has fine wall
paintings by Verrio.[53] They depict the triumph
of the famous Black Prince who took the kings
of France and Scotland prisoner and handed
them over to his father, King Edward III. We
were assured that King Charles I was buried
in St. George's Chapel on the orders of the
Protector and were shown his tomb. Opposite
Windsor Castle, on the other side of the
Thames in Buckinghamshire, is Eton College[54] which was founded by Henry IV. His
bronze statue still stands in the middle of the
great quadrangle. 70 scholars form the core of
the pupils and are supported either by the
King or more frequently by the college. Apart
from these pupils, most of the young people
of standing pursue their first studies in Eton
where they board in the teachers houses. At
the time we were there there were 600 of
these pupils. The building is not particularly
beautiful but perfectly comfortable and the
college has a splendid library and an income
of £ 5000. On the next day we continued on
our journey to Oxford stopping only briefly to
visit the house of Lord Harcourt in Newnham[55] between Dorchester and Oxford.
Oxford lies on the Thames, 56 miles from
London. It is one of the largest cities in Eng-

apartiennent à l'université, & qui font
près de deux tiers de la ville, sont en partie
de très-beaux édifices. L'université consiste
en vingt Collèges, dont nous ne vimes >les dedans< que trois,
le Collège de l'Université, le College de la Trinité & celui de la Reine, qui est un très-beau batiment. Chacun de ces Collèges a ses profeßeurs
àpart, mais letout ensemble ne forme qu'un
corps d'universités qui a ses propres magistrats
à la tête desquels est un chancelier, qui est élu
par l'Université et qui garde sa charge pendant
(End of page 24)

toute sa vie. C'est ordinairement un des Pairs
du Royaume ou au moins de la première nobleße;
il doit avoir soin de maintenir les anciennes
loix de l'Université. On comte à peu près trois-
mille personnes qui forment toute l'université, dont mille sont entretenus aux fraix des
diférens Colleges. Outre ces vingt Colleges il y
a encore cinq batimens qu'on nomme Halls
où il y a außi des profeßeurs & des étudians,
mais les étudians y vivent à leurs propres frais.
Le Profeßeurs außi bien que les étudians portent une espèce de robe pardeßus de leurs habits
et une berette au lieu de chapeau pour leur
distinction. Nous allames voir encore quelques
autres édifices publics, comme le Theatre où l'on
tient les harangues publiques, le Museum, la
galerie des peintures, et la fameuse Imprimerie
de Clarendon[56], qui a une belle façade. Nous quitames
Oxford le lendemain pour aller à Woodstock, petite ville renomée pour le beau travail en
acier que l'on y fait. Nous allames descendre
chez quelques ouvriers, qui nous firent voir
des chaînes pour les montre et quantités d'autres petites bagatelles admirablement bien tra-
vaillés >et poliés< mais d'une chereté exceßive. Sous
le regne de la Reine Anne la Seigneurie de Woodstock fut donnée par un acte du parlement
au celèbre Duc de Marlborough en recompense
(pour) des services qu'il avait rendu à l'état.
De plus le parlement fit bâtir a une (bien) mile
de Woodstock le chateau de Blenheim[57] en mémoire de la Bataille que ce >grand< capitaine gagna
contre les François et le Bavarois. (le Palais) >Blenheim house<
(qui) sera à jamais fameux & par la mémoi-
re des actions éclatantes de ce grandhomme
& par celle des bienfaits d'une nation qui
ne menage rien quand il s'agit d'elever le
mérite. Ce palais est très-vaste & magnifique
mais d'une architecture trop lourde, du Chevalier Vanbrugh. Toutefois les apartemens
sont superbement meublés de tapißeries de
haute liße qui representent les principales
victoires que le Duc remporta, et d'un bon nombre de beaux tableaux. La Bibliotheque est très
nombreuse et la sale où elle est, est très élégamment arrangée. À l'entrée du chateau
feu la Ducheße à fait ériger un arc de Triomphe où la memoire du Duc, de même qu'un obe-
lisque sur la principale avenue du parc avec
une inscription qui contient un raconti les
(princip) actions les plus remarquables. Le
Parc est très-vaste mais le jardin n'est pas en-
(End of page 25)

land; some of the buildings which belong to
the university and account for almost two-
thirds of the town are very beautiful. The university consists of twenty colleges, only three
of which we saw from the inside: University
College, Trinity College & Queen's College,
a very fine building. Each of these colleges
has its own tutors but together they form a
single university corpus with its own wardens
headed by a chancellor who is elected by the
university and retains his office
(End of page 24)

for life. Usually he is one of the peers of the
kingdom realm or at least one of the high
aristocracy. His task is to ensure that the ancient laws of the university are upheld. Almost
three thousand persons belong to the university, one thousand of whom are supported at
the expense of the different colleges. Apart
from these twenty colleges there are also five
buildings, known as halls, where there are
both students & tutors but the students live
there at their own expense. Both the tutors
and the students wear a kind of robe over
their clothes and a mortar-board instead of a
hat so that they are distinguishable. We also
visited some other public buildings, such as
the theatre where public addresses are held,
the museum, the art gallery and the famous
Clarendon Press[56] which has a beautiful
facade. We left Oxford the next day to go to
Woodstock, a small town, renowned for its
excellent steelwork. We visited several work-
ers who showed us watch-chains and other
remarkably well made trinkets which were,
however, excessively expensive. Under the
reign of Queen Anne, a parliamentary resolution made the famous Duke of Marlborough
Lord of the manor of Woodstock in recognition of his services to the state. Furthermore,
parliament had Blenheim Palace built one
mile from Woodstock in memory of the battle
which this great captain had won against the
French and Bavarians. Blenheim Palace[57] will
always remain famous both owing to the
memory of the outstanding deeds of this great
man & to the memory of the goodness of a
nation that spares no effort when it comes to
honouring merit. This palace is very spacious
& magnificent but its architecture, the work
of Sir Vanbrugh, is too heavy. Nevertheless,
the apartments are superbly furnished with
tapestries woven in the high-warp technique,
depicting the most important victories won
by the Duke, and a good number of fine
paintings. The library is very extensive and
the room housing it is very elegantly furnished. At the entrance to the castle the late
Duchess had a triumphal arch built in memory of the Duke; an obelisk on the principal
avenue through the park with an inscription
also recounts his remarkable deeds. The park
is vast but the garden is not yet
(End of page 25)

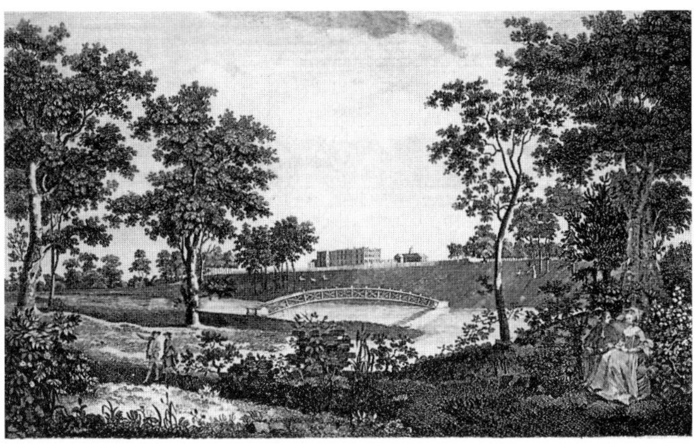

16 Ditchley, the country seat of the Earl of Lichfield near Woodstock in Oxfordshire, copperplate from: The Modern Universal British Traveller, London 1779 (cf. ill. 4). Private owner.

core achevé. Le descendans du Duc sont obligés de présenter tout les ans le 2. d'Août jour anniversaire de la victoire de Blenheim, un étendant au Roi en signe d'homage pour la seigneurie de Woodstock. Cet étendant se conserve dans un des apartemens à Windsor. A quelques miles de Blenheim nous nous arretames à Ditchley[58] maison de Milord Litchfield. Elle est bien batie élégament meublée et sa situation me paroit préférable à celle de Blenheim. Milord Shrewsbury a encore une belle maison dans ces environs à Haythorps[59] dont la façade est très magnifique. Elle consiste dans une belle colonnade. Le parc en est fort beau. Nous arrivames le lendemain à Birmingham* ville remarquable par ses manufactures. On y travaille extrémement bien en fer & en acier. On y fait une très grande quantité d'armes à feu, qui ne sont pas tout à-fait bonnes mais il en va un gran nombre en Amerique pour les sauvages. Nous allames voir un nomme M.ʳ Taylor qui a une fabrique de boutons de métal où il employe un grand nombre d'hommes, de femme & d'enfans. Il fait encore travailler toute sorte d'autres bagatelles en émail, en argent, en pinsbeem. Ce M.ʳ Taylor a amaßé par ce trafic plus de cent mille livres sterlings outre ce qu'il a dans son négoce, & il fait subsister quelques centaines d'habitans. On fait außi à Birmingham toute sorte de petits meubles de fer blanc vernißé et peint le plus joliment du monde. L'imprimerie de Basquevill à Birmingham est en reputation pour la beauté de ses caractères, quoiqu'on aßure qu'on n'y imprime pas trop correctement. Le chevalier Cottrel qui Vous avoit accompagné dans ce petit voyage, Vous avoit invité, mon Prince, de paßer quelques jours à sa maison sur Votre retour à Londres. Sa campagne est à quatre miles de Woodstock, on la nome Rowsham[60]. Quoique ni la maison ni le jardin ne soyent grand, la belle situation en fait un endroit très agréable. Le jardin est située sur la pente d'une coline,

finished. The duke's descendants are obliged to present a standard to the king on 2nd August each year by way of paying homage for having received the manorial rights to Woodstock. This standard is kept in one of the rooms at Windsor. A few miles from Blenheim we stopped at Ditchley House[58] which belongs to Lord Litchfield. It is well constructed and elegantly furnished and I found its position more agreeable than that of Blenheim. Lord Shrewsbury of Haythorp[59] has a lovely house with a very fine facade in the same area. The facade consists of a splendid colonnade. The park is very beautiful. The next day we arrived in Birmingham* a town notable for its manufacturing. Exceedingly good iron and steel products are made there. Large quantities of firearms are also manufactured there. They are not of particularly good quality but are shipped in great quantities to the savages in America. We visited a certain Mr. Taylor who has a metal button factory employing a large number of men, women & children. He also manufactures all manner of other things made of enamel and silver. With this commerce Mr. Taylor has accumulated one hundred thousand pounds sterling, not counting the value of his business; he provides a livelihood for several hundred inhabitants. They also make small pieces of furniture from tin-plate in Birmingham, which are painted in different colours in the prettiest way imaginable. The printers at Basquevill in Birmingham are also famous for the beauty of their letters although it is said that their printing is not overly precise. Lord Cottrel, who accompanied you during this brief visit, has invited you, my lord, to spend a few days in his house when you return to London. His estate, which is situated four miles from Woodstock, is called Rowsham[60]. Neither the house nor the gardens are large but it is a very pleasant place on account of its lovely position. The garden is on the side of a hill at the foot of which a small stream runs, forming the boundary of his land. There is a beautiful view across to a large waterfall on a hill opposite. The house is nicely furnished and has a few good paintings. We had three very pleasant days hunting at Rowsham. Finally we continued our journey to London
(End of Page 26)

au pied de laquelle coule une petite rivière qui
en fait les limites. Une grande chute d'eau sur
une coline oposée forme un beau coup d'oeil.
La maison est jolliment meublée & il y a quelques
bons tableaux. Nous paßames trois jours à Rowsham très-agréablement à courir la chaße. Nous
reprimes enfin notre chemin pour Londres par
(End of page 26)

Stow[61] maison de campagne de Milord Temple près   *Octobre*
de Buckingham à 60. miles de Londres. C'est un jar-   *1.*
din très-vaste qui a cinq miles de circonférence.
Il est si rempli de temples, de pavillons, d'obelisques, de piramides et de toute sorte de monumens, qu'il faudroit une brochure entière pour
en donner la description. Quoique quelquesuns
de ces monumens soyent érigés au plus grands
hommes d'Angleterre, & que dans la plus part
on puiße reconnoitre le genie plus >encore< que le bon
gout de (...) Milord Cobham qui arrangea >ordonna< ce jardin,
    le tout ensemble me paroit neaumoins une
chose beaucoup trop surchargée. Il y a neaumoins quelques grandes parties dans le jardin
aßés belles. La maison est fort vaste, bien
meublée, mais l'architecture n'y est pas de plus
élégantes. Nous returnames le lendemain à   *2.*
Londres, mais nous ne nous y arrètames qu'une
couple de jours. Les courses d'automne qui alloient   *5.*
commencer à Newmarket[62]* Vous engagèrent de   *à 60. miles*
prendre Votre tour vers ce coté. La ville en soi-   *de Londres dans*
même ne mérite pas d'attention elle est située   *Cambridgeshire*
justement sur les frontières de Cambridgeshire
& de Suffolk. La ville ne consiste presque que dans
une rue de maisons mal baties. (Le Roi) Il y a une
maison Royale, où les Rois logeoient autrefois
pour voir les courses, mais a présent c'est le Duc
de Cumberland[63] qui l'habite pendant cette saison.
Il y encore deux ou troix autres maison paßab-
les qui apartiennent (aux) >à quelques< seigneurs. Les
courses des chevaux sont un spectacle que l'on ne voit
qu'en Angelterre avec cet ordre, & ceux de Newmarket sont les plus fameuses de tout le pays.
C'est une chose qu'un etranger >ne laiße pas de mérites< y faße
    quoi-
que attention, non seulement pour la nouveauté
du spectacle, mais principalement pour voir
avec quelle paßion les personnes du premier
rang et même le peuple s'y abandonnent. Comme on la traite si sérieusement, le parlement
a jugé devoir s'en meler, & en a constitué les
loix par un acte exprès sous le regne de George II.
Il est étonnant de voir les Ducs et Pairs et les premiers
seigneurs du Royaume non seulement risquer
leur biens dans les paris, mais (...) donner
avec une aplication infatigable à l'entretien
de leurs chevaux. Ce ne sont plus les mêmes hommes
qu'on les voit ou à Londres où à leurs maisons
de campagne. Il ne font que courir d'une écurie
à l'autre et méditer de nouvelles subtilités &
bien souvent de nouveaux moyens pour se tromper
les uns les autres. Au reste il ne faut regarder
ces courses que comme une sorte de jeu de hazard
(End of page 27)

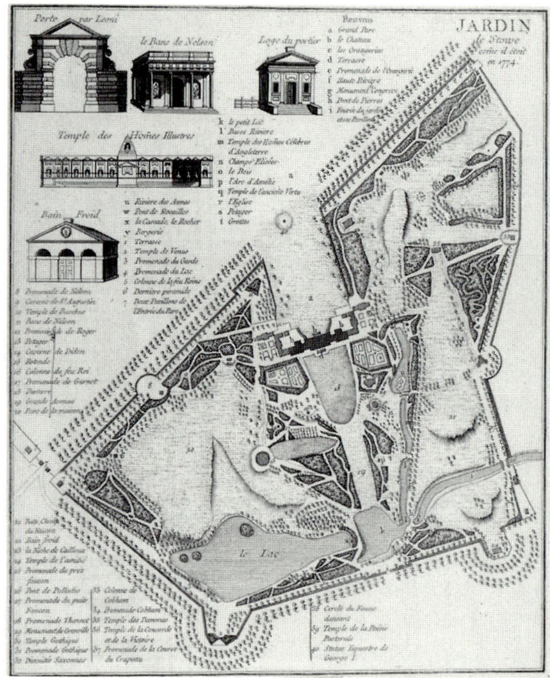

17 Plan of the garden at Stowe in 1774 with some examples of the park architecture, copperplate from: G.-L. Le Rouge, Détails des nouveaux Jardins…
la mode, 21 issues, Paris 1776–87, here issue 4, plate 18. Kulturstiftung Dessau
Wörlitz.

passing Stow House[61] which is near Bucking-   *October*
ham, 60 kilometres from London, and belongs
to Lord Temple. The gardens there are very
extensive, having a circumference of five
miles. They are full of temples, pavilions,
obelisks, pyramids and all kinds of monuments that would require an entire brochure
to describe. Although some of these monuments were erected in honour of the great
men of England & bear witness more to the
spirit than to the good taste of Lord Cobham,
who >designed these gardens< ordered these
gardens, nevertheless the ensemble as a
whole seemed over-ornate to me. The house
is very spacious and well furnished. We
returned the next day to London but stayed   *2nd*
there only a few days. The imminent autumn
races at Newmarket[62]* led you to continue   *5th*
your tour in this direction. The town itself   *60 miles*
does not make a notable place. It is situated   *from London in*
on the border between Cambridgeshire &   *Cambridgeshire*
Suffolk. The town consists almost entirely of
one street with badly built houses. There is a
royal house where the kings used to lodge
when they came for the races but at present it
is the Duke of Cumberland[63] who lives there
in this season. There are two or three other
reasonable houses which belong to men of
standing. The races are a spectacle such as can
only be seen in England and the Newmarket
Races are the most renowned in the whole
country. They are something which a foreigner
will not want to miss, not just because of the
novelty of the spectacle but principally in order
to see with what passion persons of highest rank

and even the ordinary people let themselves
go there. So seriously do they take the races
that parliament considered itself obliged to intervene & enacted a law about them under the
reign of George II. It is astonishing to see the
dukes and peers and the highest lords of the
kingdom not only risking their worldly goods
on betting but also dedicating themselves with
unwavering devotion to looking after their horses. They are no longer the same men one sees
in London or in their country houses. They
are preoccupied with running from one stable
to the next to think up some new hair-splitting
notion and often new ways to trick each other.
Moreover, these races can be seen as nothing
other than a kind of game of chance.
(End of Page 27)

*même et pendant même que les chevaux sont déjà
à courir c'est un vacarme continuel de gens qui
offrent de nouveaux paris, qui vont quelquefois
jusqu'à cent contre vingt, contre dix contre
cinq. Il est impoßible d'entrer d'abord dans le
secret de cet espèce de jeu de hazard, et eux mêmes n'y parviennent qu'au dêpend de bien des
sommes & par une longue étude non seulement
de la conaißance des races & de l'entretien des
chevaux, mais encore plus des artifices qui
s'y employent, malgré le dehors d'honetété &
de franchise qui y paroit à un etranger.
Outre cela, il y a un langage exprès pour ce
metier qu'un Anglois même qui n'en est pas
instruit ne sauroit comprendre. On sort
ordinairement pour voir les courses a une
heure après midi. Après les courses on va à
la coline qui est l'endroit où l'on monte tous
les matins & touts les soirs les chevaux pour
les tenir en exercice. Il y en a quelquefois 150
à deux cent sur la place. Il y sont toutjours
couverts, les chevaux de chaque seigneur vont
ensemble se suivant l'un l'autre. Ceci fait
véritablement un très-joli spectacle. Le Duc
de Cumberland est un des plus fermes soutiens
de ces courses. Il y a perdu des sommes immen-
ses pendant bien des années, mais il gagna con-
siderablement quand nous y fumes. On craint
même qu'après sa mort on se relachera beaucoup de l'exactitude & du zéle avec lequel on
y aßiste actuellement. Au reste c'est un Prince fort aimé pour sa manière d'agir et sa
politeße envers tout le monde. Il sacha de
Vous témoigner toutes les attentions poßibles
pendant le tems que nous fumes à Newmarket.
La ville de Cambridge⁶⁴ n'est qu'a 13. miles de Newmarket et à 52. de Londres La ville en soi est mal
batie et n'est connus que par l'Université,
qui est arrangée à peu près sur le même ordre
que celle d'Oxford, quoiqu'elle ne soit pas si
nombreuse. Elle à ses magistrats et son Chancelier qui pourroit être élu touts les trois ans,
mais qui par un consentiment la cite garde
sa charge pendant toute sa vie. Toute l'Université consiste en seize colleges. Nous rencontrames
M.ʳ Broket profeßeur pensionné du Roi au College
de la Trinité. Il sacha de nous montrer ce qu'il y
avoit de plus remarquable. Le College de la Trini-*

Even when the horses are already
racing, in fact especially then, there is a con-
tinual din with people shouting new odds,
sometimes of 100 to 20, 10 or 5. At first it is
impossible to penetrate the secret of this kind
of game of chance and those who do manage
it only by spending large sums of money &
studying at length not only the horses breeding and care but even more the tricks that are
common here. They pay no heed to the fact
that a stranger is left with the impression that
honesty & integrity have no place here. Furthermore, this domain has a language of its
own that even an Englishman would not
understand without special instruction.
Usually everyone goes out to watch the races
at one o'clock in the afternoon. After the
races people go to the hill, the place where
the horses are ridden mornings and evenings
to keep them in training. Sometimes there
are 150 to 200 horses out there. They are
always bridled, the horses of each owner keep
together, following one behind the other. It is
truly a very pretty sight to behold. The Duke
of Cumberland is one of the most ardent sup-
porters of these races. Many a year he has lost
immense sums of money but when we were
there his winnings were considerable. People
even fear that after his death the precision &
enthusiasm with which proceedings are run
there will be sorely missed. Incidentally, he is
a prince who is very popular due to his behaviour and courtesy to everyone. During our
stay in Newmarket he paid you every possible
attention. The town of Cambridge⁶⁴ is only
13 miles from Newmarket and is famous only
for its university which is organised like that
in Oxford, although it is not as large. It has its
wardens and its chancellor who could be
elected every three years but who by agreement retains his office for life. The university
consists of sixteen colleges in all. We met Mr.
Broket, a professor with a pension from the
King at Trinity College. He was able to show
us the things of greatest interest there. Trinity
College is famous for several eminent scholars who studied there including Chancellor
(End of page 28)

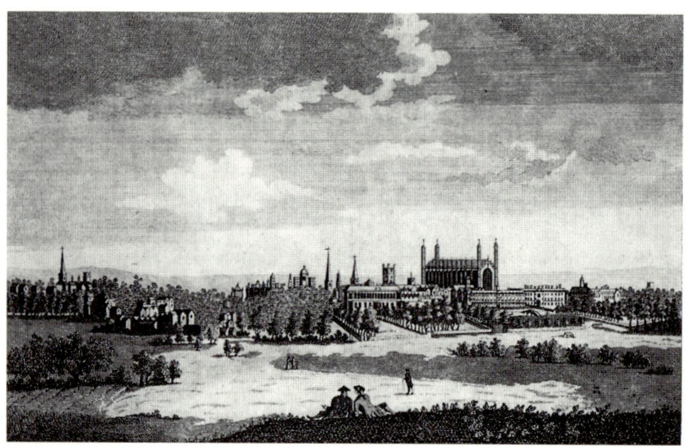

18 View from the west of Cambridge, copperplate from: The Modern Universal British Traveller, London 1779 (cf. ill. 4). Private owner.

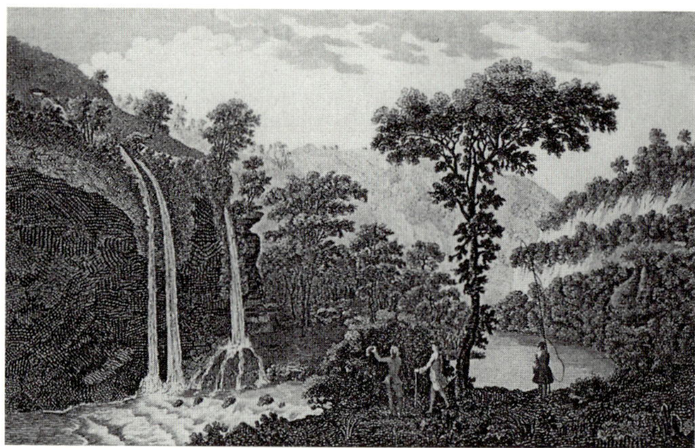

19 View of the waterfall near Matlock Spa in Derbyshire, copperplate from: The Modern Universal British Traveller, London 1779 (cf. ill. 4). Private owner.

té et fameux par plusieurs des premiers savans
qui y ont fait leurs études entre autres le Chancelier
(End of page 28)

Bacon & le célébre Newton. On a erigé >depuis peu d'années<
   à ce dernier
une aßes belle statue dans la Chapelle de la Tri-   *Oct.*^{bre}
nité. Ce grand Philosophe y est representé avec
un prisme à la main dans le moment qu'il de-
couvrit les regles de la refraction des rayons
du soleil. Cette statue est du ciseau de Roubiliac.
La bibliotheque de ce collège est nombreux &
d'une belle architecture. La chapelle du Collège royal est fort belle et quoique grande il n'y
a aucun pilier et, toute la voute se soutient par
soi-même. Nous allames encore voir le Theatre
où l'on tient les cerermonies et les harangent
à l'ecole publique pour les lectures publiques
fournie d'une belle bibliothèque. Nous continuames notre de Cambridge sans guère nous
arrèter jusqu'à Derby⁶⁵. Cette ville est à cent vingt   *11.*
et deux miles de Londres située sur la rivière
Derwent. Ce qu'il y a de plus remarquable est une
grande machine pour filer la soye (qui) >dont l'idée< a été
(aporte) prise en Italie. On ne la fait pas voir
ordinairement & nous fumes même obligés
de quiter Derby cette fois-ci sans pouvoir y
parvenir. Mais comme depuis nous y fumes
une seconde fois & que nous avions munis d'un
billet du maitre, nous eumes le loisir de la voir
tout à notre aise. Ce fut un nommé Sir Thomas
Lombe qui trouva moyen de s'introduire à Ancone dans (la) une maison oú il y a une semblable machine & d'en faire secrètement un modèle, que
l'on (nous y) conserve encore >à Derby< en pièces détachées.
Il aporta ce modele en Angleterre & commen-
ça à (faire) >construire< cette grande machine à Derby. Le
Parlement lui donna le privilege d'en avoir
lui seul la proprieté & l'usage pendent quatorze
ans, & après qu'elle furent écoulés, il lui (…)
donna encore une recompense de quatorze mille
livres sterling à condition qu'il permettroit
qu'on copiat un parfait modèle, de peur que
cette invention ne perit un jour après sa mort

Bacon & the famous Newton. A rather fine   *October*
statue was erected to the latter a few years ago
in Trinity Chapel. This great philosopher is
depicted holding a prism in his hand to illus-
trate the moment he discovered the refraction
of the sun's rays. The statue was sculpted by
Roubiliac. This college has an extensive
library; it is also a fine piece of architecture.
The chapel of the royal college is very beautiful and despite its size has no columns, the
vaulting is entirely self-supporting. We also
visited the theatre where lectures and ceremonies are held & the public school for public lectures which has a fine library. We continued our [journey – translator's addition]
from Cambridge, hardly stopping until we
reached Derby.⁶⁵ This town is on the River   *11th*
Derwent, two hundred and twenty miles from
London. The most remarkable thing there is
a large machine for spinning silk, the idea for
which originated in Italy. Viewing is not normally permitted & we were obliged to leave
Derby on this occasion without having managed to go there. But as we were there a
second time & had equipped ourselves with a
ticket from the master we were able to visit at
our leisure. A certain Sir Thomas Lombe had
found an opportunity to gain entrance to a
building in Ancone where there was a similar
machine & to secretly make a model of it; the
dismantled parts have been kept in Derby. He
brought this model to England and began to
build the large machine in Derby. Parliament
granted him the privilege of sole ownership
and sole right to use the machine for forty
years, after which he would receive forty
thousand pounds sterling on the condition
that he would allow a perfect replica to be
copied, to ensure that the invention would
not be lost one day after his death or due to

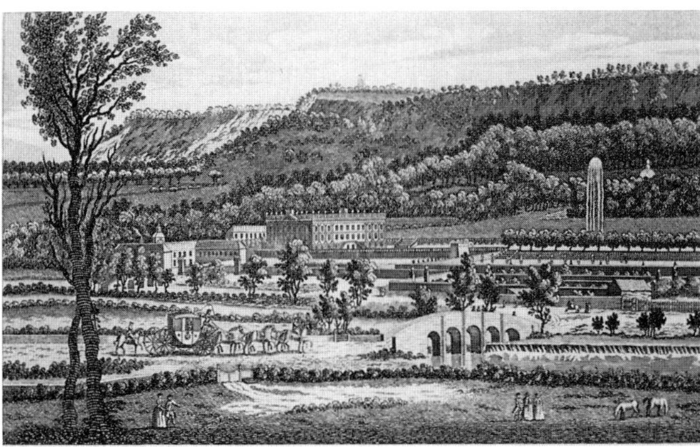

20 View of Chatsworth House and Park in the county of Derbyshire, country seat of the Duke of Devonshire, copperplate from: The Modern Universal British Traveller, London 1779 (cf. ill. 4). Private owner.

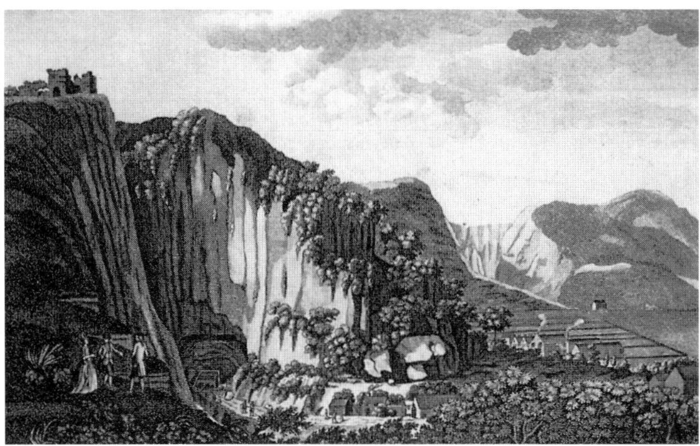

21 View of the mountains and caves near Castleton, "Devil's Arse" in the "Peak District" of Derbyshire, copperplate from: The Modern Universal British Traveller, London 1779 (cf. ill. 4). Private owner.

ou par quelque accident. Ce modèle fut achevé et on le conserve dans la Tour à Londres. Cette machine sert à filer la soye dans une quantité prodigieuse avec l'aide de peu de personnes, et avant qu'elle fut construite les Anglois étoient obligés d'acheter toute la soye filée en Italie. Le batiment qui y est employé est tres-vaste, il est situé sur le bord de la Derwent et parle moyen d'une seule roüe que cette rivière fait tourner elle fait aller trois machines qui forment le tout ensemble. Elle a 26586. petites
(End of page 29)

roües & 97746. mouvements produits par la grande *Oct.^{bre}* roüe qui tourne trois fois en une minute & à chaque tour de laquelle toute la machine file 73726. yards de soye. Un avantage encore est que l'on peut arreter chaque petite roue à part sans empécher les autres. On a encore (trouve) inventé une machine à feu par laquelle touts ces grands apartemens sont chaufés également à la fois. Il y a encore une autre machine pour filer la soye à Derby que l'on montre ordinairement à tout le monde et qui est pareille à celle qu'on ce à Utrecht en Hollande mais il n'y a point de comparaison avec l'autre. La partie occidentale de Derbyshire est extremement montagneuse. On la nomme communément the Peak & comme elle est remplie de rochers le pays est >désert< & peu fertile. Il y a pourtant de bons paturages pour les brebis dont on y trouve de (grand) >nombreux< troupeaux. Outre cela il y a des mines de plomb & de fer et des carrières de marbre. On raconte ordinairement des choses aßes singulieres des curiosités de Peak. Vous ne crutes pas devoir negliger d'y aller faire un tour, comme nous en étions si proches. Nous allames donc monter le long des bords de la Derwent et nous nous arrètames quelques momens à Matlock à 10. miles de Derby. Il y a dans cet endroit des bains chauds (dont) >et l'on se sert ces eaux même intérieurement<. La situation en est agréable, il y a une maison aßés comode et des promenades & de

an accident be lost. A model was made and kept in the Tower of London. The machine requires only a few people to spin large quantities of silk. Before it was built the English were obliged to buy all their spun silk in Italy. The building used for this is very spacious; it is situated on the banks of the River Derwent. One single wheel driven by this river powers the three machines which make up the whole ensemble. It has 26,586 small
(End of page 29)

wheels & 97,746 movements are produced *October* by the large wheel which turns three times per minute & at each revolution the machine spins 73,726 yards of silk. A further advantage is that it is possible to stop each small wheel separately without impeding the others. A fire-machine has also been invented which makes it possible to heat all the large rooms evenly at the same time. In Derby there is another machine for spinning silk which is usually shown to everyone and which is similar to the one in Utrecht in Holland but there is no comparison between this machine and the other one. The western part of Derbyshire is extremely mountainous. It is generally known as the Peak [District – English translator's addition] & being very rocky the area is quite desolate and barren. There is, however, good grazing land for sheep of which there are many flocks. There are also lead & iron mines and marble quarries. People usually say quite strange things about the peculiarities of the Peak District. You felt we should not miss the opportunity of touring there since we were so close. So we began to climb along the banks of the Derwent and we stopped briefly in Matlock, ten miles from Derby. There are hot baths there and people take the waters there, even internally. The situation is pleasant, there is a comfortable house and promenades with beautiful views

très belles vues sur une montagne vis à vis des
bains de l'autre coté de la rivière. Nous arrivames le soir à Chatsworth[66] où le Duc de
Devonshire a une aßés belle maison. Elle a
quatre façades diférentes & elle est plûtôt arrangée dans le gout François qu'Anglois. Le jardin n'est extrèmement grand mais sa
situation & les environs d'un pays sauvage
lui donne un air singulier. Il y a une quantité de jets d'eau ce qui n'est pas commune
en Angleterre et une cascade (…)
qui fait un bel effet. Cette maison
est batie des pierres dont ces environt fournißent de bonne carrières & même les marbres
qu'on >y< a empoyés sont touts pris sur le lieu
même et sont aßés beaux. Avant que celle ci
fut batie il y en avoit une autre sur la même
place, où l'infortunée Reine Marie d'Ecoße
fut tenue prisonière pendant 17. ans sous la
garde de la Comteße de Shrewsbury. De là nous
(End of page 30)

allames a Buxton[67] ou il y a encore des eaux minérales & un bain chaud avec une maison aßés bien
batie. Cet endroit est aßés fréquenté (…).
Non loin de là est une caverne qu'on apelle Pool's
hole qui ne mérite pas grande attention quoiqu'
on en faße toute sorte de coutes qui nous engagèrent d'y entrer. A 7. ou 8. miles de la il y a une autre espèce de caverne (…)
qu'on nomme Eden hole qui est aßés
singulière. C'est une grande ouverture plus
longe que large sur le sommet d'un rocher,
qui est d'une si prodigieuse profondeur qu'on
n'en a jamais pu trouver le fond avec la sonde.
Nous y jettames de großes pierres et le bruit qui
dura aßés long tems se perdit peu à peu sans que
nous pumes entendre qu'elle (…) arrivat
au fond. La plus grande de ces Cavernes du Peak
est près d'une petite ville nommée Castleton
à laquelle on donne communément le nom de
Devil's arse[68]. L'entrée en est très-spacieuse &
(…) on y voit dans le dedans plusieurs
cabanes habitées de pauvres gens, qui travaillent
à filer avec de grandes roues. Les feux qu'ils
y font et la lueur qui s'en éclairait >(…)end
sur ces fondres habitations et dans< une partie
de cette caverne au reste fort (sombre) >obscure< forme
une idée si pitoresque ou poetique, que l'on
croiroit descendre dans le Tartare.(…)
Ce pouvre peuple, qui vit principalement des
largeßes des étrangers que la curiosité y attire,
nous eut à peine aperçus, qu'ils vinrent
touts s'atrouper autour de nous, pour nous
conduire dans ce souterrain. Le chemin est
si incomode que nous fumes obligés de nous
laißer soutenir par quelques uns de ces gens
pour marcher plus surement, tandis que le
reste femmes & enfans nous éclairoient d'une
cinquantaine de lumières & faisaient reten-
tir les echos de leurs airs rustiques. Et de cette
façon nous nous enfonçames quatre ou cinq cent
pas dans cette caverne. Nous trouvames quelques
fois le paßage si étroit que nous fumes quasi
obligés de ramper sur le ventre. Mais en plusieurs endroits les voutes sont tres vastes.

of the mountain opposite the baths on the
other side of the river. In the evening we
arrived at Chatsworth,[66] where the Duke of
Devonshire has a quite beautiful house. It has
four different facades & is designed more in
the French than in the English style. The gardens are not extremely large but their position & the wild countryside surrounding
them give it an unusual atmosphere. There
are a great number of fountains, which is not
common in England, and a waterfall which
creates a lovely effect. The house is built of
stone from the good local quarries & even the
marble used there comes from these environs
and is quite beautiful. Before this house was
built, there was another house on the same
spot where the unfortunate Mary Queen of
Scots was kept prisoner for 17 years, guarded
by the Countess of Shrewsbury. From there
we went
(End of page 30)

to Buxton[67] which also
has mineral waters & thermal baths with a
quite well constructed house. This place is
quite frequented. Not far from there is a cave,
called Pool's Hole, but it deserves little attention, despite the fact that all manner of antics
were used to tempt us in. 7 or 8 miles from
there is a different kind of cave, called Eden
Hole, which is quite strange. It is a large
opening, longer than it is wide, on top of a
rock which is so deep that they have never
managed to plumb its depth. We threw large
stones into it and the sound, which sustained
for quite a long time, gradually died out without our hearing that the stone had hit the bottom. The largest cave in the Peak District is
near a small town called Castleton. It is generally known as the Devil's Arse.[68] The
entrance is very spacious & inside it you can
see several huts inhabited by poor people,
spinning at large wheels. The fire they make
and the light they radiate >these dwellings
and< in a part of this cave which is otherwise
very dark, creates such a picturesque or
poetic impression that one could imagine
one was descending into Tartarus. These poor
people, who live mainly on the generosity of
visitors who are attracted through curiosity,
hardly noticed us but then came and surrounded us wanting to take us down beneath
the ground. The path is so uncomfortable
that we were obliged to let some of these people support us so that we could walk more
safely, while the women & children lit our
way with some fifty lights whilst their rustic
songs echoed around us. And in this way we
came four or five hundred paces into the
cave. A few times the the passage was so
cramped that we were obliged to crawl on our
stomachs. But in many places the vaults were
vast. We crossed two streams, one of them,
which was quite wide, we crossed on a kind
of small ferry. The rock out of which this cave
is formed is of fine marble[69] and different kinds

(…) Nous paßames deux ruisseaux, l'un desquels étant aßés
large on en fait le trajet dans une espèce de
petit bac. Le rocher qui forme cette caverne
est d'un beau marbre et de diférentes sortes de
pierres minérales. On y trouve encore cette espèce
de matière petrifiée qui reßemble tout-à-fait
à un bel albatre et dont on travaille de jolies choses.[69]
(End of page 31)

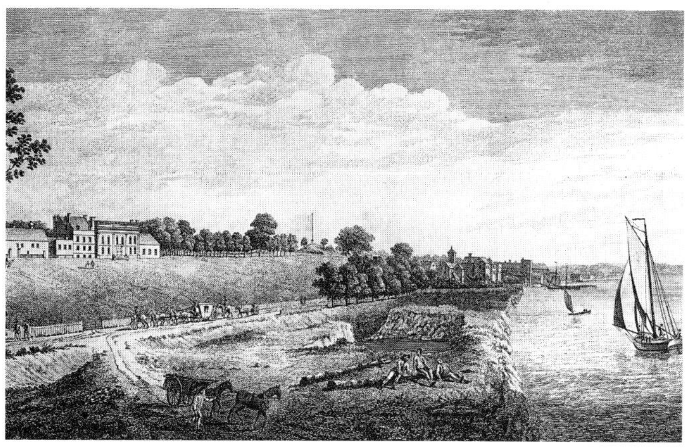

22 The Greenhite Garden (Ingress), 1752. Copper engraving from: John
Boydell, A collection of Views, Vol. III, London, 1770; plate 19. The Royal
Collection® Her Majesty The Queen Elizabeth II. Ingress was the first of the
gardens Prince Franz visited in England. (See p. 45.)

of minerals. All kinds of petrified matter can
be found there; it resembles fine alabaster
and is made into nice things.[69]
(End of page 31)

1 This edition reproduces the complete wording, spelling, and punctuation of the original text throughout. Word-for-word appreciation of the peculiarities of the original was the guiding principle. In spite of the author's clear handwriting, some words in Erdmannsdorff's Latin handwriting were difficult to decipher. That is because he wrote on both sides of every page and the handwriting bled through in some places. Those gaps are indicated in the transcription with parentheses (…), while short forms at the end of words are spelled out. The handwritten additions that Erdmannsdorff made between the lines or in the margin are indicated by angle brackets >…< and deletions are marked with square brackets […]. The "?" was retained. Spellings such as "etoit" or "pourroit" were also retained instead of using the modern spelling "etait or "pourrait". His French is somewhat faulty in many respects, but the linguistic rough patches have been smoothed out in the translations when necessary for better understanding. Spelling errors are corrected in the notes. They occurred quite frequently in place names and personal names, because Erdmannsdorff often transcribed them as he heard them. The translation from the French into German was done by Mr. Schleif at the Comtext Fremdsprachenservice translation agency in Leipzig. The English translation is by Chris Charlesworth and Kate Walker of Norbert Zänker & Kollegen in Berlin.

2 The Lucklum knight's estate (town of Erkerode, Wolfenbüttel district) was the headquarters of the Saxon commandery until abolition of all commanderies of the Teutonic Order in the French-controlled Rhenish Confederation (1809). The relationship between Prince Franz and the ecclesiastical knightly orders is not known. However, it is worthy of mention that a commandery of the Teutonic Order was located in Buro (Burow) near Klieken on the Elbe, in other words in the vicinity of the Dessau residency.
Daniel Christoph Graf von der (Schulemburg) Schulenburg (1716–1772), former lieutenant in Hanoverian services, lived in Lucklum as Commander from 1757 to 1772. He was considered to be a proponent of the Enlightenment and, in keeping with the spirit of the time, had the park grounds with the large pond by Daniel August Schwarzkopf, as well as older parts of the gardens, rebuilt in the English style.

3 Saltzdalen=Salzdahlum, large Baroque complex including castle and park, built by Duke Anton Ulrich of Brunswick-Wolfenbüttel as a temple of the muses dedicated to Apollo; castle inaugurated in 1694; varied, spectacular park architecture such as grotto of Narcissus, new fountains, mazes and the "Parnassus" with waterworks and a pagoda, the first chinoise structure in German architecture; the buildings gradually fell into disrepair after the middle of the eighteenth century; the important orangerie was torn down in 1797; castle torn down in 1813; there was a "Dutch kitchen" in the castle, probably similar to the one in the Oranienbaum castle, known as the "summer dining room."
The Duchy of Brunswick-Wolffenbüttel was allied with the Principality of Brunswick-Lüneburg (Hanover), England and Prussia in the Seven Years' War against Austria and France. Prince - Ferdinand, son of Duke Charles of Brunswick-Wolfenbüttel and hereditary prince, married Augusta, daughter of the Prince of Wales, in 1764; Ferdinand was one of the most popular army commanders of the Prussian side during the Seven Years' War, as well as a celebrated war hero in England; he died in 1806.

4 The castle and the park, designed in the Dutch style, in Herrenhausen, former village, now a district in Hanover. The work began in 1694 under Elector George Louis (after 1714 George I of Great Britain, personal union with England 1714–1837). The garden of the summer residence of the Guelphs was created from 1696 to 1714 by the French landscape architect Martin Charbonnier, who was strongly influenced by the Dutch style.

5 The "Kunsthaus" in the rebuilt Ottoneum, the first enclosed theatre building in Germany, contained the princely art collection, including a comprehensive collection of models. The "Modell-Haus" was built in 1711 to hold all of the models built since Landgrave Charles, which had previously been kept in the Kunsthaus. According to a record from 1767, the model of the waterworks on the Carlsberg above Weissenstein castle (Wilhelmshöhe after 1798), which was over 100 metres long, was also kept here. The Modell-Haus no longer exists and all models have been lost. See: Die Bau- und Kunstdenkmäler im Reg. bez. Kassel, Vol. VI, Kreis Kassel-Stadt, edited by Alois Holtmeyer, Marburg 1923, p. 534 ff. and p. 542 ff. I am very grateful to Mr. Klaube of the Kassel City Archive for this information.

6 Princess Henriette Amalie of Anhalt-Dessau (born in Dessau 7 December 1720 – died there 5 December 1793), was the daughter of the "Alter Dessauer (Old Man of Dessau)" Prince Leopold I of Anhalt-Dessau; 1745 canoness, 1764 deaconess, 1779 coadjutor of the Stift Herford, 1793 foundress of the Amalienstiftung in Dessau.

7 Paintings by the genre painter Johann Conrad Seekatz (born 1719 in Grünstadt – died 1768 in Darmstadt) and the "landscape painter" Christian Georg Schütz (born 1718 in Flörsheim – died 1791 in Frankfurt am Main) were later displayed in the Luisium castle in Dessau-Waldersee. The so-called "Rhein-Schütz-Zimmer" on the first floor of the castle with its five views of the Rhine recalls these painters from Frankfurt, who were highly regarded by Prince Franz.

8 La Favorite, garden of the Elector of Mainz, built under Elector Lothar Franz of Schönborn (1695–1729) by Maximilian von Welsch (1668–1745) from 1705 to 1720; completely destroyed in 1793 by French troops.

9 The commandery of the Teutonic order, also known as "Deutschhaus", built from 1730 to 1738 under Francis Louis of Palatinate-Neuburg in a more severe form of the French Baroque that was a forerunner of neo-Classicism; the architect was Anselm Ritter zu Grünsteyn (1700–1765). Today it is the provincial state parliament of Rhineland-Palatinate.

10 Schlangenbad in the Taunus (Rheingau mountains) west of Wiesbaden was already a well-known watering place in the eighteenth century; built by Landgrave Charles of Hesse in 1694.

11 Brühl, Augustusburg castle, pleasure and hunting castle of Clemens August, Elector of Cologne from 1723; died 1761. One of the most magnificent works of art of eighteenth century Europe; cornerstone laid in 1725, construction began under J. C. Schlaun of Münster, remodelled under F. Cuvilliées 1728–1740, completed 1754–1770. Baroque style with neo-Classical tendencies, standard design as moated castle.

12 Dusseldorf, gallery; the history of the collection begins with Elector John William of the Palatinate (1658–1716), one of the most important art collectors in Germany; after 1805 the Palatinate-Bavarian collection was transferred to Munich; first catalogue of the collection in 1719.

13 Colonel Clavering = Sir John Clavering (1722–1777), third son of Sir James Clavering of Greencroft in Lanchester, Durham, began his military career in the Coldstream Guards regiment; in 1759, under General Barrington, John Clavering led the English troops in capturing the French island of Guadeloupe: "Clavering is the real hero of Guadeloupe" wrote Horace Walpole in a letter to Horace Mann; he was appointed a royal adjutant the same year and received the rank of "Colonel of Foot"; he was sent to Hesse-Kassel in 1760 to observe the military actions of the Landgrave during the Seven Years' War.

14 Maastricht, capital of the Dutch province of Limburg; beginning in 1621 Maastricht was expanded to one of the strongest fortresses in Europe, intended to cover the southern part of the Netherlands.

15 Amsterdam, Magazine of the Admiralty; "Its general requirements are to provide security on the sea, on the rivers and in the ports, equip war ships and to protect merchant ships against the enemy and pirates. Each of the chambers (total of five, author's note) is responsible for its portion of the fleet and must maintain it, specifically the one in Amsterdam one third and each of the other four one sixth". Quoted by Johann Jacob Volkmann, Neueste Reisen durch die Vereinigten Niederlande, vorzüglich in Absicht auf die Kunstsammlungen, Naturgeschichte, Oekonomie und Manufakturen, Leipzig 1783, p. 109.
Amsterdam, Town Hall, masterpiece of the Classical style in the Netherlands, three-storey building erected from 1648 to 1665 by Jacob van Campen (1595–1657); on the ground floor statues by Artus Quellinus, engravings of it are in Wörlitz, Felseninsel Stein, Villa Hamilton, Green Cabinet, ceiling. Amsterdam, Stock Exchange, located near the Town Hall; construction began in 1608: "An outsider will not fail to visit this place once during business hours, where after millions of transactions are concluded in one hour, people talk about it in undertones and are deafened by the buzzing of several thousand voices and where everyone congregates for one purpose, which is profit and earnings, which each one seeks to achieve in a manner in accordance with his own private interest" (quoted by Volkmann, see above, here p. 304 ff).

16 The painting cabinet of Bramkan ("Braamkamp" in Volkmann, see note 15) was purchased by the Empress of Russia in the 1770's, but the best of the paintings were lost in transit.

17 When Erdmannsdorff saw the "Maison du Bois", Huis Ten Bosch, which was originally built between 1645 and 1648 as a "villa suburbana" (summer house) for Governor Frederick Henry, Prince of Orange and his wife Amalia von Solms and is considered to be the most famous building by the architect Pieter Post, he learned to know and love another important building in the Dutch neo-Classical style.

18 The "cabinet of curiosities" in The Hague, opposite the Residence, belonged to the Hereditary Governor William, Prince of Orange, who inherited it in 1756 from his Mother, Anne of Hanover. It was considered to be unique in Europe and was constantly expanded by items that sailors brought back from their travels. After 1763, under the supervision of Peter Simon Pallas, it could be viewed during regular opening hours.

19 The garden of "Sorgfleet" (Sorgvliet) is certainly intended to refer to that of Count von Bentinck – not Bentheim. The extraordinary appearance of the garden is described – although 20 years later – by J. J. Volkmann (see note 15, here 179 ff): "On the way to Schevelingen one should not fail to see Sorgvliet, the beautiful estate of Count Bentink. Its design is completely different from the usual stiff Dutch gardens and has the advantage that outsiders can always view it, which is usually uncommon in Holland. It is over 1 1/4 hours walk long and half as wide: and in that area nature has been successfully imitated in the English manner and a landscape has been imagined without the fearful assistance of art. It is only about 2,000 paces from the sea and it is only a pity that it does not have a clear view and is rather humid. A maze made of cut hornbeam hedge lies before the entrance. On the north side fields are devoted to fruit and kitchen gardens. The Count's summer house is in a sort of wilderness, surrounded by a meadow, near a moat; however, it is falling into disrepair because it is not inhabited. The same fate awaits a pretty grotto that represents a temple. From there one proceeds northward through undergrowth to a temple with columns on a grassy mound that is paved with gravel".

20 Bergopzoom, county seat of the county of that name, came to Palatinate-Sulzbach through marriage in 1722; known as a particularly strong fortress, it had ten bulwarks, five bastions and many other fortifications; the port was also covered by entrenchments.

21 "Prince Charles" is Charles Alexander, Prince of Lorraine (1712–1780), brother-in-law of Maria Theresa, Austrian Field Marshall, Governor General of the Netherlands; he was defeated by Frederick the Great several times during the Seven Years' War, lost his command of the Imperial Army and returned to Brussels as Governor in 1757.

22 Charles-Philippe-Jean Cobenzl (Karl Graf von Cobenzl) (born 21 Juli 1712 in Laybach [now Slovenia] – died 27 January 1770 in Brussels); due to the high position he inherited (his father was advisor at the Vienna Court and Lord Chamberlain of Emperor Charles VI), he dwelt in the "inner circle" at the court of the Austrian duchy. He carried out several missions on behalf of Empress Maria Theresa, until he entered service in Brussels on May 13, 1753 as "General Minister Plenipotentiary of His Imperial and Royal Majesty of the Netherlands" (in concrete terms the southern Netherlands). He held that position until his death. At that time Prince Charles of Lorraine was Governor in Brussels. In his absence, his authority as Governor was also transferred to Count Cobenzl, due to his great ability. As an art lover and major collector, he played an important role in the establishment of an Art Academy in Gent and had the For de Soignes beech forest extending from the south of Brussels to Waterloo mapped for the first time.

23 Colonel Clavering, see note 13.

24 Johann Jacob Volkmann, Winckelmann's student and the "Baedeker of Goethe's time" (W. Richter, Rostock), see also note 15, describes Chatham in his brilliant publication "Neueste Reisen durch England, vorzüglich in Absicht auf die Kunstsammlungen, Naturgeschichte, Oekonomie, Manufakturen und die Landsitze der Groaen," 4 volumes, Leipzig 1781–82, here volume 1, p. 332: "The arsenal here can be described as one of the most complete in the world. An Englishman who knows that the security and welfare of the nation depend on the strength of its naval power can but view the dockyards in Chatham with satisfaction. The heaviest ships are built here and can be anchored in the Medway due to its great depth". In addition, Fort Sheerness on the Isle of Sheppey at the mouth of the Medway made the route to Chatham the safest port in the world.

25 In spite of the importance of these gardens for the group from Dessau, I was previously unable to find any references to them in the literature. It is not likely that Erdmannsdorff meant "Grays Inn," the small garden within the Inns of Court in the City of London. Instead, he is probably describing a park at Ingress Abbey (Inngress = Inn Grays), as well as the house of the architect Vanbrugh above Greenwich. That "castle" still exists, although the bullwarks and the park do not. I am very grateful to John Harris of London for this information.

26 John Calkraft, Earl of Ormonde, (1726–1772) – Erdmannsdorff incorrectly spelled the name phonetically as "Calkrat" – first went into the "pay office" under the influence of Marquis Gransby. During the Seven Years' War, his later patron Henry Fox, First Lord Holland – paymaster general – appointed him as agent for numerous regiments and negotiated through him with many military commanders. After years of employment as deputy commissary-general of musters, Calkraft retired from government service and advanced to "financial official" for many country estates in England. He had in the meantime purchased several estates, including Rempston, Corfe Castle (in 1757), Wareham (in 1767); as mentioned by Erdmannsdorff, he probably also owned "Inn Grays" (Ingress Abbey), cf. note 25.

27 Greenwich was a residence of the English Kings beginning in the late Middle Ages. Only the west wing of a palace planned in 1660 by John Webb was completed and after 1695 Christopher Wren included it in the Royal Naval Hospital at Greenwich, founded by Queen Anne. Instead of the planned three wings, two opposing blocks (1704) and a chapel (1735) were built after

1699. Colonnades between the two provide a visual link with the Queen's House, which was built in high Palladian style by Inigo Jones from 1616–1637. The Observatory above the park was built by Christopher Wren in 1675.

28 James Radclyffe (Radcliffe), Third Earl of Derwentwater (1689–1716), eldest son of Edward Radclyffe (died 1705) and Lady Mary Tudor, a natural daughter of Charles II, was brought up in the exile court of St. Germain. His disloyalty to the House of Brunswick caused the government to sentence him, along with other rebels, to beheading (1716). After the death of his only son John (1731), part of the extensive Derwentwater properties in Northumberland and Cumberland were transferred to the Greenwich Hospital.

29 James O'Hara, Lord Kilmaine and Second Lord Tyrawley (born 1690) had an extraordinary career; from 1703 Lieutenant in the regiment of his father, whom he succeeded as Lord Tyrawley in 1724, then adjutant of King George II beginning in 1727, special envoy to the Portuguese court until 1741, from 1743–1745 envoy to Russia, became a general in 1761 and in 1762 a member of the Privy Council of George II. He became Field Marshall and Governor of Portsmouth in 1763, the year he met Prince Franz. Lord Tyrawley, who had an estate in Blackheath, died on 14 July 1773 in Twickenham, Middlesex.

30 Members of the upper classes who were not tied to the City of London for professional reasons passed the year on their country estates in their constituencies districts, far from the court and the metropolis, scattered throughout England. They spent only the spring, the "London season", in town. They took advantage of the season to engage in politics, make acquaintances, do business and last but not least, enjoy cultural life in London.

31 Erdmannsdorff is probably referring here to the publication by Beat Ludwig von Muralt, Lettres sur les Anglois et les Francois et sur les voiages, Köln 1725 (edited by Charles Gould, Paris 1933; Bibliothèque de la Revue de la littérature comparée, vol. 86). The patrician Muralt (1665-1749) was not French but was born in Berne in Switzerland. His mother tongue was German and he was educated in French. He came to England in 1694 as an officer in the French army.

32 "Sion Hill" (Syon Hill) was the country seat of Lord Holderness = Robert D'Arcy, 4th Earl of Holderness (1718–1778). He held a number of high offices; for example, in his role as one of the "Lords of the King's bedchamber" (from 1741) he accompanied the king to Hanover in 1743, from 1751 he succeeded John, 4th Duke of Bedford, in his office of one of the "principal secretaries of state" in Henry Pelham's ministry. When George III acceded to the throne he was present along with the Duke of Newcastle at the first meeting of ministers in the "Royal closet". The gardens he had laid out at "Sion Hill" no longer exist.

33 "Sion House" (Syon House), on the north bank of the Thames (Greater London), belonged to Lord Northumberland=Sir Hugh Smithson (he took the name Percy and later became Duke of Northumberland), who was married to Elizabeth Seymour. After the death of the previous owner, the Duke of Somerset, the house, along with Alnwick Castle, went to Sir Hugh Smithson and his wife in 1748. Their extraordinary wealth allowed them to have three of their residences converted by Robert Adam (1728–1792): Alnwick Castle, Northumberland House on Trafalgar Square and Syon House. The latter was converted by Adam between 1762 and 1765, which means that work was in full swing during Prince Franz's trip in mid-September 1763.

34 Hampton Court on the north bank of the Thames was built from 1515 onwards by Thomas Wolsey, Archbishop of York and later cardinal. As royal ambassador he led a lifestyle that was comparable in extravagance only with that of the king. However, when he fell from grace in 1528, he was forced to give Hampton Court to the king, who carried out extensions and modifications. Until

the middle of the 18th century it remained one of the most important residences of the English monarchy. The last king to use it was George II. Under his grandson and successor George III, Hampton Court was converted into apartments for civil servants to the royal households.

35 The portrait and history painter Gottfried Kneller (Kniller) (born in Lübeck in 1646), who studied in Amsterdam, Rome, Naples and Venice and whose name is now almost forgotten, was for a long time considered to be one of the best portrait painters of his generation. As court painter to King James II and William III, he was knighted in 1692. In 1723 he was buried in the garden of Whitton House at Twickenham. In contrast to the general opinion of the 18th century and that of Prince Franz in 1763, Kneller is often undeservedly under-esteemed today.

36 Sir James Thornhill (1675–1734), who studied while travelling in Holland, Belgium and France, worked, apart from at Hampton Court (Queen Anne's Bed-Room), also in the Royal Naval Hospital at Greenwich (Painted Hall). From 1719/20 "serjant painter to the king", he was knighted in the same year. Like Kneller, he too was held in high esteem during his lifetime, unlike today.

37 In 1516 Raphael completed a total of ten cartoons for the tapestries for the Sistine Chapel that were then woven in Brussels and depicted the Acts of Apostles. A special room was created in Hampton Court to house the cartoons bought by Charles I in 1695 (Cartoon Gallery). The originals are now in the Victoria & Albert Museum, London.

38 Woburn Farm in Surrey belonged to Philip Southcot (1698–1758), who from 1734 transformed the original moorland into a so-called "ornamented farm". In other words he enhanced the farmland in a new "natural" style and demonstrated how it is possible to produce a "real" landscape from a naturalistic landscape park by incorporating arable and grazing land: of a total of 130 acres only 35 acres were landscaped (cf. William Shenstone, The Leasowes, Shropshire).

39 Ham Farm near Weybridge in Surrey was the country house of Charles Colyear, 2nd Earl of Portmore – not Protmore (1700–1785). The "rather strange bridge" mentioned here by Erdmannsdorff, that swivels on a pivot to allow ships to pass, may have been the model for the so-called "revolving bridge" that was built in 1782 in Wörlitz Park (today Agnes Bridge).

40 Owners of the park at Oatlands in Surrey were at that time Henry Fiennes Clinton, 9th Earl of Lincoln, 2nd Duke of Newcastle-under-Lyme (not Lyne) (1720–1794). Thanks to the great influence of his uncle, the Prime Minister Henry Pelham, he held numerous important positions in public life. For example, in 1759 he was appointed "High Stewart of Westminster." The landscape garden of Oatlands, which is still in good condition today, was laid out from 1740 by William Kent, Lord Burlington and possibly Southcot; from 1750 Stephen Wright was the architect in charge. Until 1788, the year the duke sold it, it covered 227 hectares.

41 Built in 1750 by Mr. Samuel Decker, a West Indian merchant, with the approval of parliament.

42 Charles Hamilton, youngest son of the 6th Earl of Abercorn (1704–1786), born in Ireland, began in the mid-forties (after his grand tour in 1725) to lay out his famous garden in Cobham (now Painshill) in Surrey. Apart from Henry Hoare (1705–1785), the creator of Stourhead, Hamilton was one of the most important garden creators of his time. Between 1738 and 1773 he landscaped the area which covered some 200 acres. During their visit, the party from Dessau kept exactly to the route prescribed at the time. The smaller buildings at least which, due to lack of funds Hamilton had not built very solidly, seem less significant than the landscape. The "island with grotto" mentioned by Erdmannsdorff (model for the Stein rocky island in Wörlitz Park) was not completed until 1765. For many years it was celebrated as

an imitation of the caves at the Gulf of Naples made famous by Virgil. The "machine" that was also mentioned, a waterwheel with an impressive diameter of twelve meters, was installed by Hamilton in 1750 and was the object most marvelled at by his contemporaries. Due to financial difficulties Hamilton was forced in 1773 to sell his property which had became one of the most famous and most frequently visited landscape gardens in England. "In the Hamilton family" Friedrich Reil, the biographer of Prince Franz, wrote in 1845 "he (Prince Franz, ed.) felt completely at home, their child, their pupil; with them he received his entire education about humanity, (…). Here he was initiated into the sanctity of humanity (…)."

43 Esher Place in Surrey belonged to Henry Pelham (born in 1696), the brother of Thomas Pelham, Earl of Clare, later Duke of Newcastle, creator of Claremont. In 1721 he became Lord of the Treasury, in 1722 Member of Parliament for Sussex County, in 1730 Paymaster of the Forces and from 1743 until his death in 1754 he was Prime Minister.
Two plates in Campbell's "Vitruvius Britannicus" (1739, plates 110/111), of which Prince Franz had a copy in his Wörlitzer Schloßbibliothek (In the handwritten list of the year 1778 the numbers 203–205. Kambel's Vitruvius, 3 Vol.), show the different views of Esher, on the one hand different "riverside-walks, on the other temples and monuments. There is also a design by William Kent for a Chinese building in Esher, probably the earliest example of Chinoise garden architecture in the British Isles. Two decades later, Volkmann (cf. note 22) describes the garden at Esher in more detail: "This country estate, Esher Place, was actually laid out by Cardinal Wolsey. The late Henry Pelham Esquire pulled the building down leaving the two Gothic towers on the front which he incorporated into a new building entirely in the Gothic style which looks quite well; it is just a pity that it is on such low land and is damp due to the Mole which runs past it. On a hill to the left of the entrance is a Pleasure-House, from which you can see for many miles around on both sides of the Thames. The entire place and park are absolutely simple and without artifice, but it may have taken a great deal of artistic talent to create this impression. In one corner, however, there is a wilderness planted with all manner of evergreen trees with alleys running through. It contains a grotto and various seats.

44 Sir John Vanbrugh built the first house – called Claremont – to the south-west of Esher in 1708 for himself. In 1714 he sold it to his friend Thomas Pelham, Earl of Clare, later Duke of Newcastle. Vanbrugh added large wings to the house, which had since been named "Claremont" in honour of its new owner, and from 1716 Charles Bridgeman laid out the Pleasureground and a formal garden (cf. the plan in Campbell's "Vitruvius Britannicus", III vol., 1725). It was not until the death of the duke in 1768 that the estate was sold to Lord Clive who had the house demolished. Lancelot Brown and Henry Holland were commissioned by him to build a neo-Palladian country house. William Kent transformed the formal garden into a landscape garden. Although building work on the house began as early as 1769, the last drawings were not finished until 1771. There is thus no longer any question of Claremont being the model for Wörlitz Palace (1769–1773) that is has to date so often been said to be, since there is evidence that Prince Franz did not visit this place again during his grand tour (1765–1767). The general admiration for this English country house in Wörlitz is nevertheless well expressed in the fact that in the "Blue Chamber" of the Gothic House Prince Franz displayed a copperplate with the view: "Vue de Clair Mount avec des maisons de plaisir du Duc de Newcastle."

45 The royal garden at Richmond(-upon-Thames) in Surrey is today the largest park in Greater London. Queen Caroline, born Princess of Ansbach (died 1737) and wife of King George II (1683–1760), commissioned William Kent (1685–1748) to design it. His plans were implemented by Charles Bridgeman. The famous hermitage (circa 1731–1732), which houses busts of five eminent British scientists, philosophers and theologians (Boyle, Newton, Locke, Wollaston and Clark) and Merlin's Cave (1735) with six statues, including the wizard Merlin, Queen Elisabeth and the goddess Minerva.
As early as 1722, the countryside along the Thames near Richmond and Twickenham was known as the "Frascati of England" due to the number of magnificent country estates. (S. John Macky, A Journey Through England, in: Familiar Letters from a Gentleman Here, To His Friend Abroad, (1722), 4. edition, (o. O.) 1724, p. 62).

46 Prince Frederick August (16.8.1763–5.1.1827), Duke of York, the second son of King George III of Great Britain and his wife Queen Charlotte, born Princess of Mecklenburg-Strelitz, became Bishop of Osnabrück at the age of six months. From 1781 to 1785 he lived in Germany, in 1791 he married Princess Friederike of Prussia, the second daughter of King Frederick William II The Princess Bridge in Wörlitz is named after her: "Princess Friederike of Prussia was the first person to cross this completed bridge and permitted it to be named after her on XX. August MDCCLXXXIIX."

47 Between 1726 and 1729 Richard Boyle, 3rd Earl of Burlington (born 1695), one of the main representatives of Palladianism who enjoyed the title of "Apollo of Arts", designed and built a villa in the Palladian style very close to the country house he already owned (demolished in 1788) in Chiswick, on the Thames to the west of London. William Kent was responsible for the interior design and garden. It is assumed that with his early works of garden architecture (the Orangerie, Casino and Ionian Temple that are no longer extant) and the villa itself, Burlington wanted to create a kind of garden museum in honour of Palladian architecture. Statues of Andrea Palladio and Inigo Jones flanked the entrance to the villa. With Burlington's death in 1753 the property passed via his daughters to the ownership of the Dukes of Devonshire.

48 "Mr. Eliot's house" in Grove not far from Chiswick was possibly Broomfield Lodge in Surrey owned by Edward James Eliot.

49 The Wimbleton (Wimbledon) country estate in Surrey was created by Sarah Churchill, widow of the Duke of Marlborough. She left it to John Spencer (1734–1783), from 1765 Earl of Spencer, the brother of the deceased Duke of Marlborough.

50 Windsor Lodge and the surrounding park in Berkshire was the country seat of William Augustus, Duke of Cumberland (1721–1765), son of King George II and Queen Caroline. The duke's activities in the area of large-scale landscaping are remarkable. For example, he went to great expense to combine a number of small streams into a broad canal suitable for small craft and pleasure boats; a bridge of considerable size spanned it. The grotto mentioned by Erdmannsdorff was destroyed in 1768 by a heavy fall of rain. In the forest adjoining it the duke built a racecourse, reputed to be the finest in England, which the author astonishingly fails to note despite the Dessau prince's love of horses.

51 The motto quoted at the beginning of this essay is the sixteenth and seventeenth line of the descriptive poem "Windsor Forest" by Alexander Pope (1688–1744), which was written in 1704 (part 1) and 1714 (part 2) and which Pope dedicated to the "Right Honourable George, Lord Lansdown." Cf.: The poetical works of Alexander Pope, edited by Adolphus William Ward, London 1879. In the handwritten inventory of the prince's Schloßbibliothek in Wörlitz dating from 1778 there is an entry under number 163–171: "Pope's work's, 9 Tom." (London 1751, Warburton edition).

52 Windsor Castle in Berkshire is of great interest not solely due to the history of how it was built (starting in the 12th century) but

also due to its extensive park which in the Middle Ages included an immense area of forest extending from Guildford to Buckinghamshire. "Windsor Forest" was reserved solely for royal hunting parties. The park as it is today dates from the 17th and 18th century; parts of it are open to the public (Great Park).

53 Antonio Verrio (Lecce 1639–1707 Hampton Court), a painter who studied in cities such as Venice, Naples and Paris, worked in England from about 1676 where he – in the service of Charles II, James II and William III successively – decorated Windsor Castle and Hampton Court Palace and other houses of the aristocracy with allegorical and mythological ceiling and wall paintings.

54 Eton on the north bank of the Thames, still today the largest and most famous private school in England and Oxford and its university, which the travelling companions from Dessauer visited immediately afterwards, are presumed to have been the model for the educational institution known as the "Philantropinum" which was opened in Dessau at the end of 1774. The radically new approach to education stemmed mainly from Johann Bernhard Basedow (1724–1790), who arrived in Dessua from Altona in 1771 and is considered to be one of the main representatives of educational theory of the German Enlightenment (Philantropismus).

55 The reason for visiting Simon Harcourt (1714–1777), 1st Earl Harcourt, in Newnham (Nuneham) probably had something to do with the fact that Prince Franz had met Lord Harcourt in 1761 when following King George III's accession to the throne of Great Britain he was sent as "special ambassador" to Mecklenburg – Strelitz to negotiate the marriage between the king and the Mecklenburg Princess Charlotte. In a description of his tour of England in 1781/1782 J. J. Volkmann writes about this house which was built between 1756 and 1764 by Stiff Leadbetter and James Stuart and extended by Lancelot Brown after 1778: "The rooms are all vaulted because of fire hazard: from them the elevated position affords the most magnificent view over the meandering Thames to Abingdon and Berkshire and to Oxford in the north-west. The late count designed the park and gardens with great taste and had the parish church built in the style of a Roman temple."(Vol. 3, p. 46). Simon Harcourt had busts of Cato and Rousseau and a statue of Hebe erected in the garden and built a temple to Flora.

56 Clarendon Press was founded in 1711. The capital required came from the sale of the "Story of Lord Clarendon", the manuscript of which his sons had donated to the university of Oxford. The vignettes of all books published at this press are on display at the Scheldonean Theatre which was opposite the press.

57 Blenheim Palace in Oxfordshire was built by parliamentary resolution in memory of the Battle of Blenheim in the Spanish War of Accession (1701–1713/14) at which John Churchill, 1st. Duke of Marlborough (1650–1722), as commander-in-chief of the British-Dutch army, defeated the French (allies of Bavaria). The architect who designed the palace was Sir John Vanbrugh. The land was formerly the royal hunting ground of Woodstock and belonged to Woodstock Manor. From 1760 the park was changed into a landscape garden by Lancelot "Capability" Brown (1716–1783) for the fourth duke and included the formal garden.

58 Ditchley/Oxfordshire, the country residence of George Henry Lee, 3rd Earl of Lichfield (1718–1772) – at the time Litchfield, as Erdmannsdorff spells it –, is situated on elevated ground and has a fine view of nearby Blenheim Palace. The design for the country house is by James Gibbs, who is also thought to have been the author of the designs for the triumphal arch and temple in the park (not executed). Around 1750 a menagerie was created in the valley with a Chinese bridge across a fishpond and a grotto. From 1760 onwards, Stiff Leadbetter re-designed some parts to form a landscape garden and built a round temple on the opposite side of the lake. Also worth seeing, apart from the impressive architecture of the main building with its two side wings linked by colonnades, was the magnificent art collection with paintings by Rubens, van Dyck and Holbein. From 1762 Lord Lichfield was Chancellor of the University of Oxford and Vice-President of the Society of Arts.

59 Heythrop in Oxfordshire, not "Heythorps" as Erdmannsdorff writes, was bought in 1697 by Charles Talbot, 12th Earl and first and only Duke of Shrewsbury. After he had visited Italy as part of his grand tour between 1700 and 1705, he commissioned Thomas Archier to built a country house (completed in 1716) inspired by this country. Volkmann (vol. 3, p. 56 describes it as a house with four "fronts" with the gable of the entrance facade resting on four Corinthian columns. "The rooms are in the best of taste and have fine stucco work, marble tables and fireplaces and various good paintings. The stucco work in the library is particularly splendid. The gardens have been laid out with excellent taste; one pleasant scene is succeeded by another. The art is so well concealed that one hardly notices where it has given nature a helping hand."

60 The landscape garden at Rousham (Erdmannsdorff spells it phonetically – Rowsham) House, approximately twenty kilometres to the north of Oxford, is the only garden designed by the famous architect and landscape architect William Kent (1684–1748) that is still preserved almost in its entirety. Originally commissioned by General James Dormer (1679–1741) and his brother Colonel Robert Dormer (died 1737), who were friends of Alexander Pope and Jonathan Swift, after the death of James Dormer the property went to Sir Clement Cottrel. This was probably the first example where Prince Franz and his companions were able to see that the Gothic and Classical styles in a landscape garden are by no means contradictory and that the only important factor is their ability to convey symbolic meaning. This insight probably played a decisive role subsequently in Wörlitz Park, for example when building Wörlitz Palace (1769–1773) and the Gothic House (1773–1813).

61 Work on designing Stowe (Stow) in Buckinghamshire, commissioned by Sir Richard Temple, Viscount Cobham (1669–1749), began in 1715. The history of the garden's creation consists of a total of six phases up to the year 1749. The palace – today a boarding school – and various landscaped garden areas are based on plans by Sir John Vanbrugh and Charles Bridgeman. Principally William Kent (early phase of the garden design) and Lancelot "Capability" Brown (continuation of the garden design) started in the thirties to transform the park into a picturesque landscape garden (at the same time as Rousham, cf. note 60). One of Lord Cobham's nephews, Sir Richard Grenville (1711–1779), from 1750 onwards Lord Cobham, continued the work. Although Stowe is one of the most important landscape gardens in England, Erdmannsdorff thought it "over-ornate". Nevertheless, the prince and his companions visited the park one more time during their second trip to England (1766/1 767) and numerous influences testify to the influence this garden had on Wörlitz. For example, the facade of the Mittelhölzer Wallwachhaus was most probably modelled on the "The Lady's Temple" in Stowe, which no longer exists today.

62 Given Prince Franz's well-known love of horses and riding to hounds, it is understandable that he wanted to go to Newmarket. Traditional horse races took place twice a year in April and October – "the most famous in the land." Twenty years later J. J.Volkmann still mentions English society's special love for this place: "At this time there is an unbelievable confluence of people and commonly a great number of gamblers and bounty-hunters are also present. The aristocracy is also there in equally great numbers and they spend great sums, partly on exaggerated bets on which horse will be victorious and on the cock fighting and

partly on gambling for high stakes. King Charles II used to always attend the horse races and his palace still belongs to the kings who however no longer come here. Many members of the nobility also have their own houses here ." (J. J. Volkmann, Neueste Reisen durch England, 1781–1782, vol. 1, p. 242 f.)

63 The title of Duke of Cumberland was first bestowed by King Charles I of England. Wilhelm August Duke of Cumberland (born 15.4.1721), third son of the British King George II, was not exactly accompanied by great fortune in his military career. As commander-in-chief of the British-Hanoverean army defending the Electorate of Braunschweig-Lüneburg he was defeated by the French during the Seven Years' War at Hastenbeck in 1757. When, in the convention of Kloster Zeven, he conceded the evacuation of Hanover, he was recalled and from then until his death in 1765 he was able to devote himself to his passion – the horse races in Newmarket. The equestrian statue is meant to be in memory of that; it was erected by "Lieutenant General William Strode, in "Gratitude and For his private Kindness, In honour, For his public virtue" on 4. 11. 1770.

64 As Prince Franz had already visited Eton and Oxford, Cambridge with its university was the third stop in the endeavour to become acquainted with the famous English educational institutions which had had a decisive influence on intellectual life in England for centuries. J. W. von Archenholz characterised these English educational institutions in his book about "England and Italy" as follows: "The universities of Oxford and Cambridge are entirely ruled by their own laws and are thus independent of civil authority; they are furthermore free of any external constraints and each send two representatives to parliament…". (Carlsruhe, 2. edition 1791, here part 3., p. 250).

65 As already mentioned at several places in this report, it becomes clear particularly in their visits to the sights in the town of Derby in Derbyshire that Prince Franz and his companions did not undertake their trip to England exclusively to look at sights of art historical interest, but also to get to know and study with great precision the highly developed technology in different fields. This knowledge was consistently implemented in practice in the Principality of Anhalt – Dessau in subsequent years. An example of this is the "Fire-machine from England," which Prince Franz ordered for his Wörlitz Palace.

66 Chatsworth, country residence of the Duke of Devonshire = William (1720–1764), from 1755 4th Duke of Devonshire; he married the daughter of and heiress to Richard Boyles, Earl of Burlington (Chiswick); he was Prime Minister from November 1756 until May 1757. At the time they were built, the palace and park were considered to be amongst the most beautiful formal parks in England – and were thus counted amongst the "Wonders of the Peak District". The Duke commissioned Lancelot "Capability" Brown to re-design parts of the landscape.

67 The thermal baths at Buxton, which the Romans appreciated greatly due to their warm, sulphurous and salty springs, belong to the Duke of Devonshire. " The water tastes good, stimulates the appetite, opens up constipations and is very effective for rheumatic complaints, incidences of scurvy and weak nerves.", writes J. J. Volkmann in his travel journal of 1781/1782 (vol. 3, p. 473).

68 "Devil's arse" and the two other caves near (Castledon) Castleton (Pooles and Elden Caves) also count along with the country house at Chatsworth as "Wonders of the Peak District". Even twenty years later, visitors still used the same simple method to confirm for themselves the fathomless depths of the cave: "…but how deep it is is an unfathomable mystery, although we made all manner of attempts to find out. The sound of large stones dies away gradually, seemingly in the far distance." (J. J. Volkmann, vol. 3, p. 472).

69 These "pretty things" were objects made of fluorspar, so called "Blue John Vessels". Articles of this kind – usually vases or cups –
were extremely popular as decoration in the neo-Classical interiors of English country houses. Prince Franz probably owned about twenty of these vessels and at present two sit on the mantelpiece of his bedroom in Wörlitz Palace. Even now, little is known about how he acquired them. As a list in the Oranienbaum Archives shows, Prince Franz received an offer from the Leipziger art dealer Carl Christian Heinrich Rost (1741–1798) at end of the 18th century. However, this description of his trip of 1763 suggests that it is conceivable that he bought some pieces himself in Castleton during his first trip and transported them in his luggage back to Dessau.

CATALOGUE OF
WORKS ON EXHIBIT

Uwe Quilitzsch
Daniela Clare

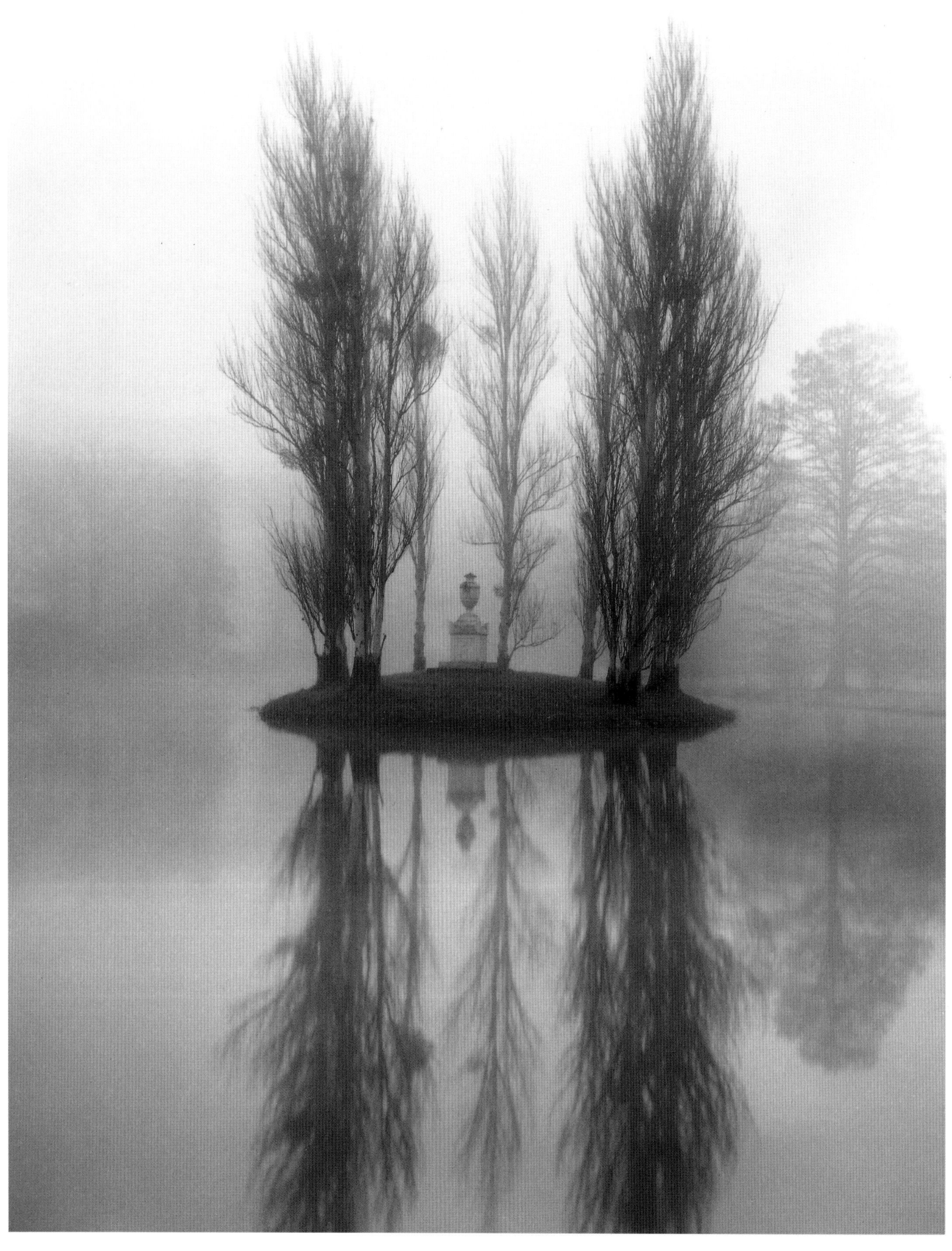

Lutz Winkler, Rousseau Island, Wörlitz (cat. no. 82.9)

"Retour à la nature"

Jean-Jacques Rousseau

INTRODUCTION

The geographical situation

The principality of Anhalt-Dessau, the "garden kingdom" of Prince Leopold III
Friedrich Franz (1740–1817), occupied an area of some 700 square kilometres situated
along the middle stretch of the Elbe and the lower Mulde Rivers – a relatively small
country compared to the other states comprised within the Holy Roman Empire of
German Nations. With its approximately 10,000 inhabitants, about a third of the total
population, the residence city of Dessau was the largest city in the principality. The
historical "garden kingdom" encompassed a number of parks and landscape gardens
which, arranged much like pearls on a string, have been preserved for the most part to
this day.
In the West lies the *Kühnauer Park,* an area covering 77.5 hectares begun in 1805 by
Crown Prince Friedrich von Anhalt-Dessau (1769–1814). The rococo *Mosigkau* park
(5.7 hectares) located to the south – a creation of Anna Wilhelmine von Anhalt-
Dessau (1715–1780), an aunt of Prince Franz – was incorporated into the landscapes
of the garden kingdom. North of the city of Dessau in a low-lying deciduous forest lies
the *Georgium* (188 hectares), a spacious park belonging to the prince's younger
brother Johann Georg (1748–1811), upon which work was begun in 1780. The no
longer existent *Lustgarten* at the Dessauer Stadtschloß and the landscape designs of
the *Tiergarten* marked the eastern boundaries of the courtly city. Leaving the city
towards the East, one first encounters the *Luisium,* a garden (14 hectares) with an
elegant Neoclassical country house which Prince Franz had erected for his wife Luise
(1750–1811) between 1774 and 1778. This house and all of the other Neoclassical
buildings in the garden kingdom were designed by the architect Friedrich Wilhelm
von Erdmannsdorff, a native of Dresden. A few kilometres upstream along the Elbe
a forest garden begun after 1777 known as the *"Waldeinsamkeit"* (Forest Solitude)
covers much of the *Sieglitzer Berg.* An avenue running along a high-water dike
through orchards and past dike watchmen's houses placed at regular intervals ulti-
mately leads to the easternmost park in the principality, the *Wörlitzer Anlagen.* This
earliest German landscape garden, built between 1764 and 1800 and covering an area
of 112.5 hectares, is the grandest of the garden creations of Prince Franz and has been
preserved, virtually unchanged, to this day. Also incorporated into the garden kingdom is the baroque ensemble of *Oranienbaum* (28 hectares), a Dutch-influenced
creation of the prince's great grandmother, Henrietta Catharina von Nassau-Oranien
(1637–1708), located some five kilometres south of Wörlitz. The unique English-
Chinese garden, still present today, was integrated into the baroque park by Prince
Franz between 1792 and 1797.
Stimulated by his travels in England and Italy and by the literature of the Enlightenment, Prince Franz implemented a comprehensive program of reforms. In addition to
his progressive social, economic and educational measures, he also fostered the
aesthetic development of the entire principality through a network of interconnected
gardens, parks and architectures. There is no other "garden kingdom" of comparable
dimensions in all of Europe.

1   Ill. p. 28–29

Johann Conrad Probst
after Michael Seutter
CARTE DES POSTES D'ALLEMAGNE ET DES PAYS VOISINS
MAP OF GERMAN POSTAL ROUTES AND NEIGHBOURING
AREAS
1790
Copper engraving, coloured
52.4 x 64.0 cm
Inscription: lower right "Johann Conrad Probst sculpsit Augsburg 11 April
1790"

Travel in the 18th century was arduous and time-consuming. Travellers were
forced to sacrifice a number of comforts. The best roads were those used as
postal routes. Most people ordinarily rode the mail coaches. Only the
wealthier citizens and aristocrats travelled with private conveyances. It is not
known how Prince Franz made his first journey through Germany and the
Habsburg territories of the Netherlands in 1763. According to the journal kept
by his travel Marshall George Heinrich von Berenhorst, he undertook his
"grand tour" of 1765–1767 in a Landau coach and a heavy "Vaisseau de
Guerre".

2   Ill. p. 8–9

KARTEN DER PREUSSISCHEN URVERMESSUNG
MAPS OF THE ORIGINAL PRUSSIAN LAND SURVEY
1851–1852
Pen and ink, water-colours
Staatsbibliothek zu Berlin Preußischer Kulturbesitz

a) Vol. XI. Sheet 5 (Aken)
44.5 x 45.8 cm
Inscription (translated): "surveyed and drawn in 1852 by Franke"

b) Vol. XI. Sheet 6 (Dessau)
44.3 x 45.8 cm
Inscription (translated): "surveyed and drawn in 1852 by Riese Prem.
Lieutenant in the 39th Inf. Reg."

c) Vol. IX. Sheet 1 (Wörlitz)
44.4 x 45.8 cm
Inscription (translated): "surveyed and drawn Riese Lieut. in the 39th Inf. Reg.
(1851)"

d) Vol. XI. Sheet 2 (Wittenberg)
44.3 x 45.8 cm
Inscription (translated): "surveyed and drawn in 1851 by Schrabisch Pr. Lieut.
in the 2nd Guard Reg. z. F."

e) Vol. XIII. Sheet 5 (Quellendorf)
44.5 x 45.9 cm
Inscription (translated): "surveyed and drawn in 1852 by von Rosenzweig I.
Lieutenant in the 13th Inf. Reg."

f) Vol. XIII. Sheet 6 (Raguhn)
44.2 x 45.9 cm
Inscription (translated): "surveyed and drawn in 1852 by Veith, Prem.
Lieutenant in the 7th Artill. Reg."

g) Vol. XIII. Sheet 1 (Graefenhainichen)
44.5 x 46.0 cm
Inscription (translated): "surveyed and drawn in 1852 by Riese Lieutenant in
the 39th Inf. Reg."

h) Vol. XIII Sheet 2 (Kemberg)
44.4 x 45.8 cm
Inscription (translated): "surveyed and drawn in 1851
von Kamecke, Pr. Lieut. in the Guard Art. Reg.
von Behr, Prem. Lieut. in the 4th Inf. Reg.
von Schrabisch, Pr. Lt. in the 2nd Guard Reg. z. F.
Riese, Lieutenant. in the 39th Inf. Reg.
Drawn in 1851 by von Schrabisch Pr. Lieut. in the 2nd Guard Reg. z. F."

The maps of the Prussian land survey were drawn to the scale of 1:25,000.
Their authentic detail and the density of their data provide excellent sources
of information on the garden kingdom of Dessau-Wörlitz. Completed some
30 years after the death of Prince Franz von Anhalt-Dessau, they depict
both the garden complex and the connecting elements created during the
early period as well as the grounds that originated later under Duke Leopold
Friedrich.

4   Ill. p. 16–17

Johann Christian Püschel (1718-1771)
after von Reck
STAMMBAUM DES HAUSES ANHALT
GENEALOGY OF THE HOUSE OF ANHALT-DESSAU
42.3 x 40.2 cm
in Johann Christoph Beckmann: *ACCESSIONES HISTORIAE
ANHALTINAE. ZERBST* 1716
Inscription: lower left "Püschel sc. L."
Kulturstiftung DessauWörlitz

The copper engraving is dedicated to Prince Carl George Leberecht von
Anhalt-Köthen (1730-1789), who served as Lieutenant Field Marshall of
Cavalry in the army of the Emperor. The family tree was mounted in the
book later. It was originally intended for publication in Samuel Lenz's
Becmannus enucleatus, which appeared in 1757.
Anhalt, united under Prince Joachim Ernst in 1570, was partitioned once
again among his four sons in 1603 following many years of dispute. Three of
the four sovereign lines thus created were eventually extinguished and
returned to the dominion of Dessau: Anhalt-Zerbst in 1793; Anhalt-Köthen in
1847 and Anhalt-Bernburg in 1863. Prince Leopold Friedrich Franz von
Anhalt-Dessau, the Crown Prince, lost both his parents at the age of eleven,
so that Prince Regent Dietrich, brother of the deceased Leopold Maximilian,
assumed the reigns of government until Prince Franz came of age in 1758.
Prince Franz witnessed the death of Prince Friedrich (1769–1814), his only
son, who was married to Christiane Amalie von Hessen-Homburg (1774–1846).
Thus his grandson Leopold Friedrich succeeded him on the throne in 1817.

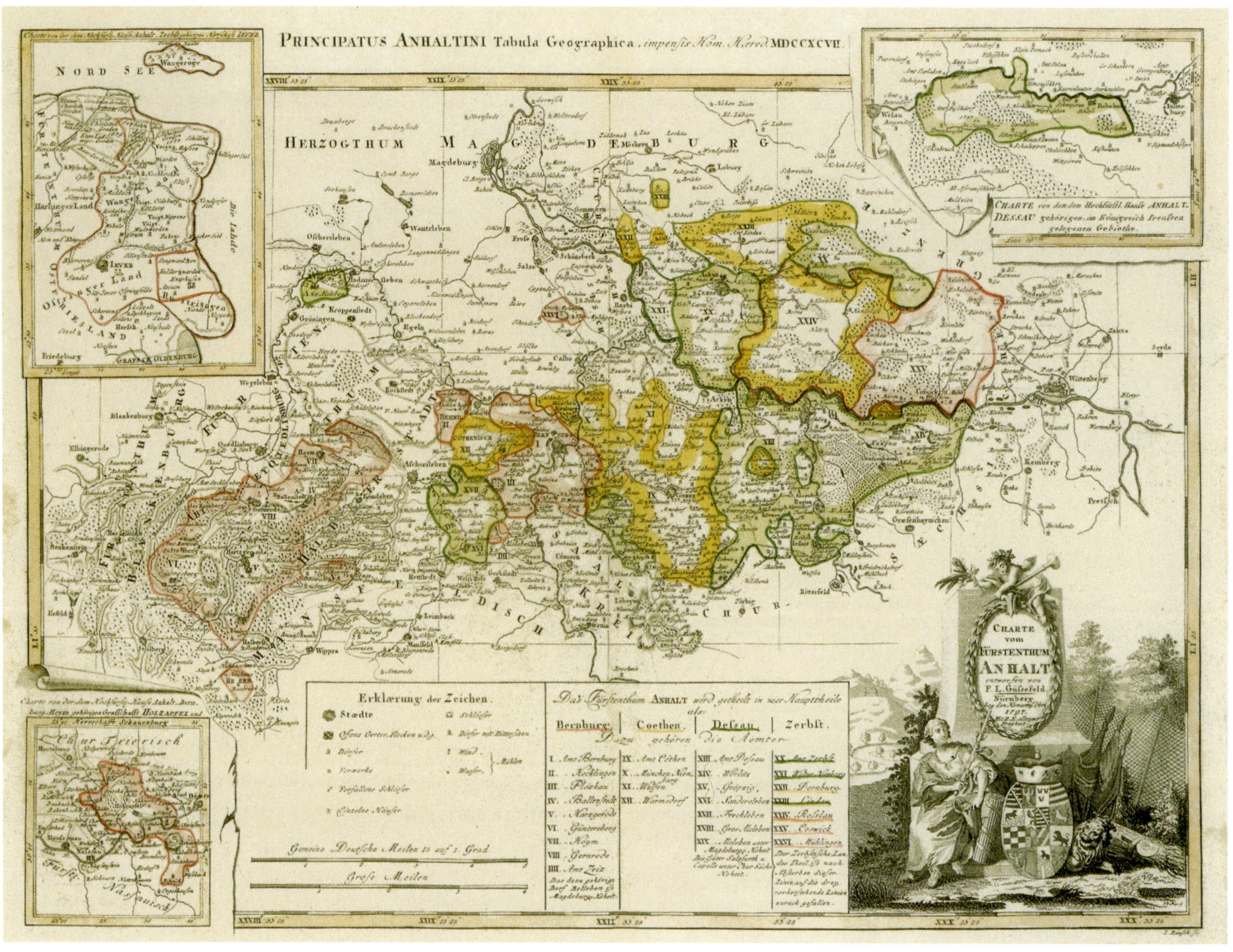

3

I. Rausch (dates of birth and death unknown)

after F. L. Güsselfeld (dates of birth and death unknown)

CHARTE VOM FÜRSTENTHUM ANHALT

MAP OF THE PRINCIPALITY OF ANHALT

1797

Copper engraving, coloured

49.5 x 68.0 cm

Inscribed: lower right "I. Rausch fc."

Kulturstiftung DessauWörlitz

This precise map shows the four sovereign principalities of Anhalt. Particularly interesting is the representation of the land holdings outside the boundaries of the original state.

Of great importance were the "Territories within the Kingdom of Prussia belonging to the High Princely House of Anhalt-Dessau", as considerable income was generated on the leased manor plantations amounting to more than 10,000 hectares.

The princes of Dessau owned a stately castle in Bubainen, which was laid to ruin by Russian troops in the Battle of Großjägersdorf during the Seven Years' War in 1757. Prince Franz later ordered the structure torn down.

Leopold III Friedrich Franz, Prince and Duke (from 1807) of Anhalt-Dessau, assumed rule of his country in 1758, succeeding the regency of his uncle, Prince Dietrich (1702–1769), who had held the reigns of government after the premature death of Franz's parents since 1751. Franz had previously terminated his military career in the Prussian army and declared his country independent during the Seven Years' War (1756–1763), a step that produced profound political consequences. King Friedrich II of Prussia (1712–1786) burdened the land with high demands for contributions of money, grain, horses and recruits.

In the summer of 1763 Franz took his first journey through Germany and the Netherlands to England. Upon his return, he worked to alleviate the effects of the war by declaring a number of tax cuts and economic reforms. Anhalt-Dessau became a breeding ground for Neoclassicism, Gothic Revival and English-style landscape gardening in Germany.

Prince Franz had numerous helpers in his efforts to achieve reform – among them economists, educators, gardeners and artists. Apart from the Prince himself, the most noteworthy personality of the period was Friedrich Wilhelm von Erdmannsdorff (1736–1800), who, although he held no official office, was the most influential of the Prince's friends in practically all matters. After completing his studies in Dresden and Wittenberg, Friedrich Wilhelm Freiherr von Erdmannsdorff, a native of Dresden, was introduced to Crown Prince Franz of Anhalt-Dessau on the occasion of the latter's 16th birthday and served henceforth as his closest confidant and counsellor. His architectural achievements in particular – most of the buildings in the garden kingdom were erected according to his plans – are still very much in evidence today.

Prince Franz married his cousin Luise Henriette Wilhelmine, Princess of Brandenburg-Schwedt (1750–1811) in 1767. The marriage was arranged in accordance with the wishes of the Prussian king, which indicates the degree to which Prussia dominated its neighbour Anhalt. Yet Prince Franz made every effort to preserve the sovereignty of his small country. The duties of the Princess included a number of responsibilities on behalf of the poor and widows of Anhalt-Dessau. Her husband had a small English country house and garden built for her from 1774 to 1778. Both were later given the name *Luisium*. Luise was regarded as a woman of considerable artistic talent. Lavater, Goethe and Alexander von Humboldt were among the prominent figures closest to her. She accompanied her husband on his third trip to England in 1775 and travelled on her own to Italy in 1795 and 1796.

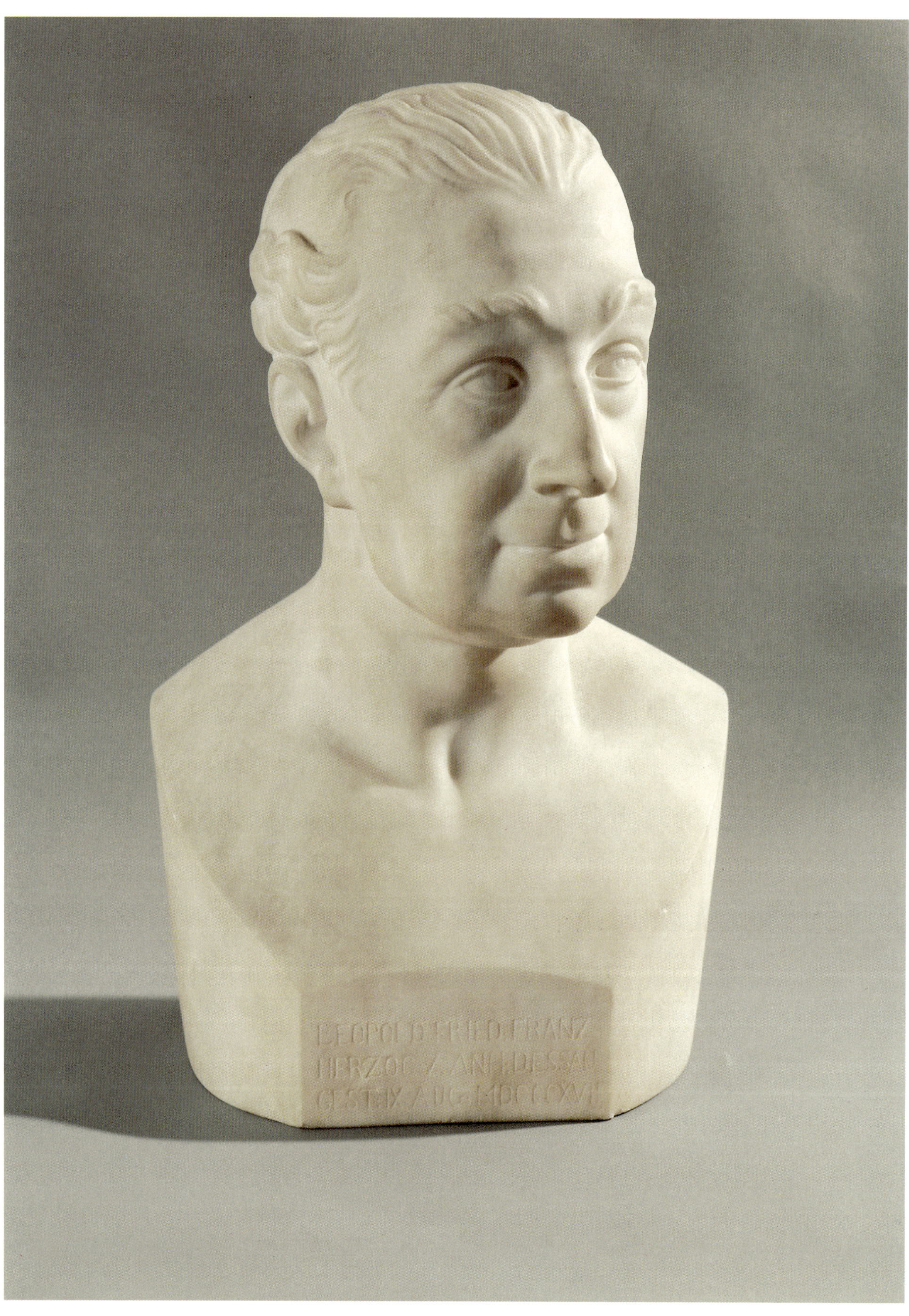
LEOPOLD FRIED. FRANZ
HERZOG Z. ANH. DESSAU
GEST. IX AUG. MDCCCXVII

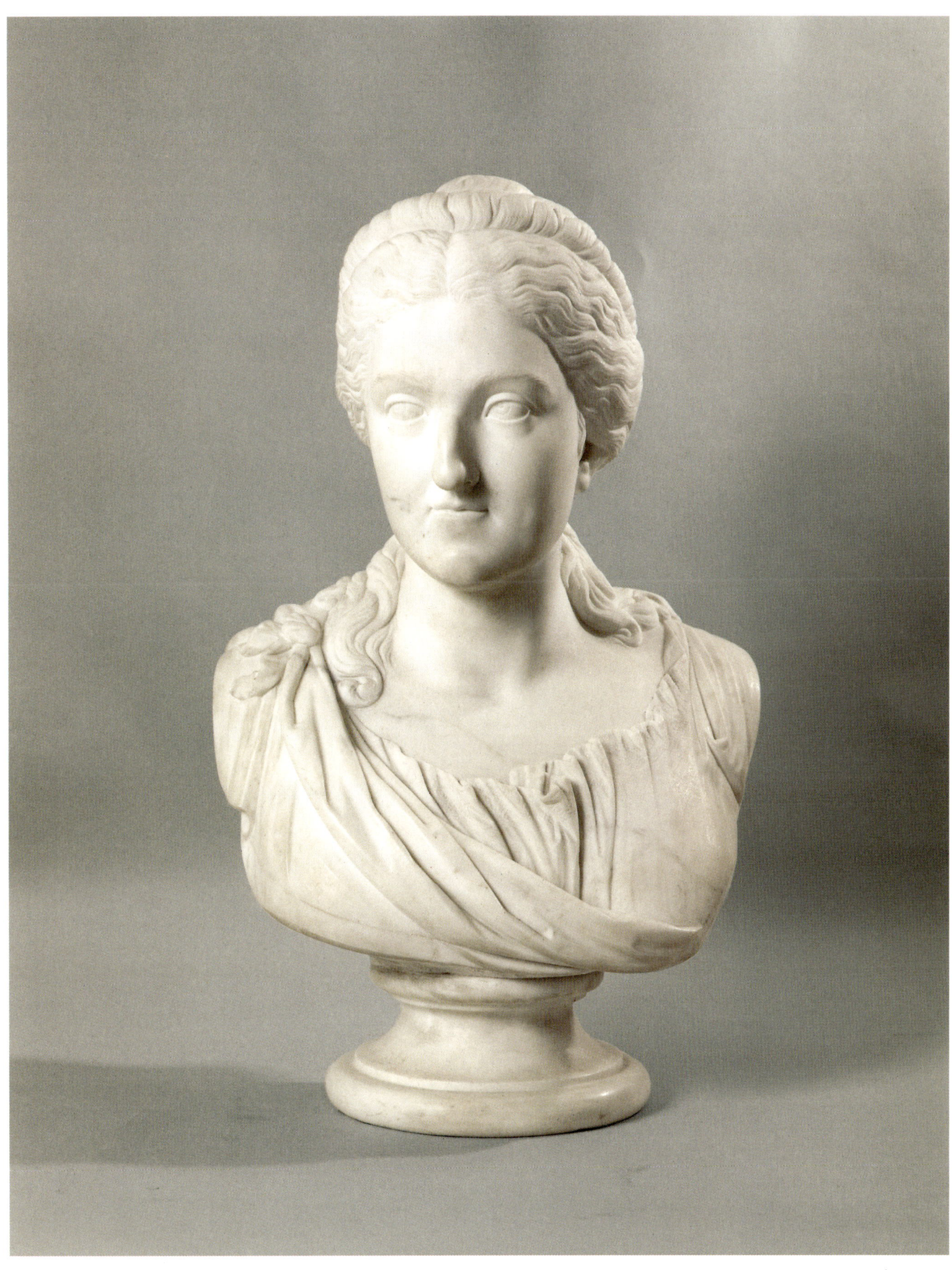

5   Ill. p. 80
Friedemann Hunold (1773–1840)
BÜSTE DES FÜRSTEN LEOPOLD III. FRIEDRICH FRANZ
VON ANHALT-DESSAU
BUST OF PRINCE LEOPOLD III FRIEDRICH FRANZ VON
ANHALT-DESSAU
Circa 1820
White marble
Height: 54.5 cm
Inscription: LEOPOLD FRIED: FRANZ / HERZOG/GEB: X. AUGUST
MDCCXL. / GEST: IX. AUG: MDCCCXVII.
Kulturstiftung DessauWörlitz

The bust of Prince Franz von Anhalt-Dessau was placed after his death in the
so-called *"Monument"* in Wörlitz, a memorial built on order by the Prince
between 1801 and 1805 in the memory of his ancestors. The Dessau poet
Wilhelm Müller (1794–1827) wrote an inscription (translated here) for the
niche in which the bust found its final resting place:
"FOR GOD HE ERECTED CHURCHES, FOR THE POOR COTTA-
GES. / WORTHY TEMPLES FOR THE BOLDEST AND SCIENCES. /
FRIEND AND LOVER OF ALL THAT IS BEAUTIFUL. PROMOTER OF
ALL THAT IS GOOD. / FATHER OF HIS PEOPLE. / SECOND CREA-
TOR OF HIS LAND. FOUNDER OF THIS GARDEN."

6   Ill. p. 81
Friedrich Wilhelm Eugen Doell (1750–1816)
after Bartolomeo Cavaceppi (circa 1716–1799)
BÜSTE DER FÜRSTIN LUISE VON ANHALT-DESSAU
BUST OF PRINCESS LUISE VON ANHALT-DESSAU
1789
White marble
Height: 61.0 cm
Kulturstiftung DessauWörlitz

Henriette Wilhelmine Luise, daughter of Margrave Friedrich Heinrich von
Brandenburg-Schwedt and granddaughter of the *"Alter Dessauer"*, was
married to Franz in 1767 in response to strong influence by the Prussian king
Friedrich II. She was a well-educated, sensitive woman with considerable
artistic talent who enjoyed the company of artists and scholars such as the
painter Angelika Kaufmann (1741–1807), who worked most of her life in
Rome, the poet Friedrich von Matthisson (1761–1831), who read to her and
accompanied her on her journeys, and the Swiss pastor and physiognomist
Johann Kaspar Lavater (1741–1801). Franz himself said of his young wife: "She
is more beautiful than all of the ancient heads, and her character, which is
always the most excellent, surpasses every ideal." The Prince had the *Schloß
und Park Luisium* built for her in Dessau beginning in 1774.

7
Friedemann Hunold (1773–1840)
BÜSTE DES FRIEDRICH WILHELM FREIHERR VON
ERDMANNSDORFF
BUST OF FRIEDRICH WILHELM FREIHERR VON
ERDMANNSDORFF
Circa 1798
Plaster
Height: 50.5 cm
Kulturstiftung DessauWörlitz

Erdmannsdorff was raised at the *Ritterakademie* in his birthplace of Dresden
and studied at the University in Wittenberg. He met the Dessau Crown
Prince in 1756. He took a cavalier's tour of Italy from 1761 to 1763 and later
accompanied the Prince on all of his important journeys. Erdmannsdorff
remained in the service of Prince Franz until his death, although he also
worked in Gotha, Potsdam and Berlin. Goethe ordered the placement of this
bust of Erdmannsdorff in the court library in Weimar in 1798.

8   Ill. p. 85
REISEN DES FÜRSTEN FRANZ
MAP OF EUROPE SHOWING THE ROUTES TAKEN BY
PRINCE FRANZ ON HIS TRAVELS

The travels undertaken by prince Franz served a number of different purposes. From 1763 to 1764 he journeyed through Germany and the Habsburg territories of the Netherlands to England. During this trip, devoted to study, he
met important figures in European politics. His grand tour of 1765-1767 took
him to Italy, France and England. Several stays in Switzerland were devoted
to rest, recreation and education. In 1775 he travelled with his wife and von
Erdmannsdorff to England once again, meeting the naturalist and circum-
navigator of the globe Johann Reinhold Forster and his son George in
London. In Bath the Prince engaged the services of a governess for Crown
Prince Friedrich. A number of inspection tours took him to the land holdings
in East Prussia, other travels included a journey to Silesia on the occasion of
the wedding of the Count of Waldersee and a trip to Carlsbad to restore his
health. The Prince Franz von Anhalt-Dessau, previously elevated to the rank
of Duke, visited the Emperor Napoleon in Paris in 1808 and was received as
the guest of Emperor Franz of Austria in Vienna in 1810.

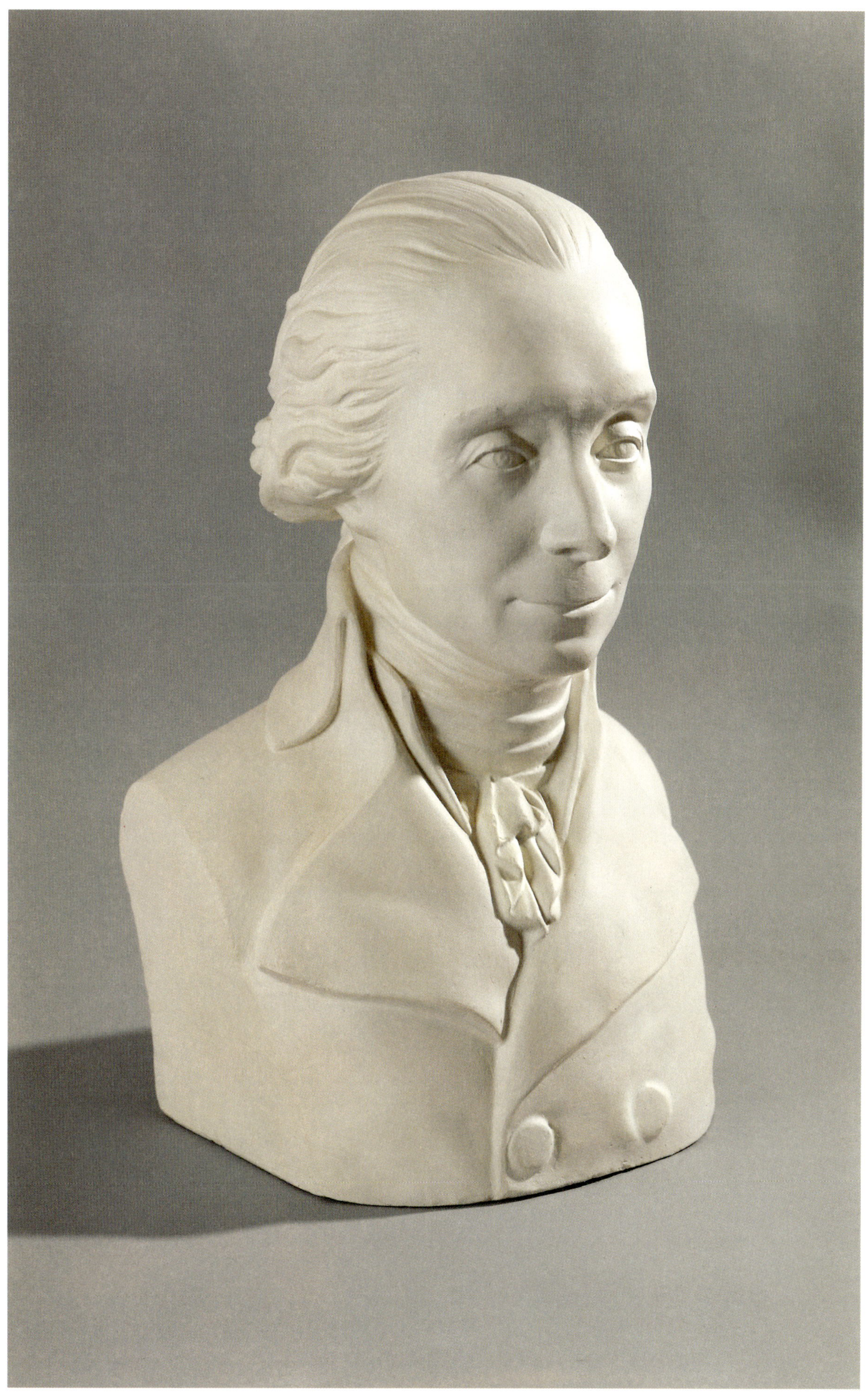

Reason, liberty, the pursuit of happiness – these are the watchwords of the 18th century, the Age of Enlightenment in Europe, a complex phenomenon that may be approached from many different perspectives. Science and art engendered a view of the world liberated from theology. Publications that appeared as journalism grew and expanded communicated new values to a broad public: humanity, independent thought, the stature and dignity of man, the quest for social utility, toleration…

Leopold III Friedrich Franz von Anhalt-Dessau was regarded as an enlightened monarch in an age of absolutism. He was strongly influenced by European enlightenment literature and the personal experiences gathered on his own frequent travels, which took him to England four times. The new world power attracted considerable attention for a number of reasons: its modern system of government; the mobility permitted by its social constitution, which opened a wide range of opportunities to the middle class; the attitude of public spirit evident in its population; its flourishing manufacturing industry; its productive agriculture and not least of all its architecture and accomplishments in landscape gardening.

Following the example set by English landed gentry, Prince Franz, his younger brother Johann Georg (1748–1811), accompanied by his mentor Georg Heinrich von Berenhorst (1733–1814), and Erdmannsdorff undertook a grand tour, whose first destination was Italy. In Rome they were introduced to Johann Joachim Winckelmann, the leading art historian of his time. Guided by Winckelmann, they viewed the collections of Cardinal Albani and visited the most important ancient sites in the Eternal City. Winckelmann also arranged introductions to artists such as Clérisseau, Cavaceppi and Piranesi. The Germans were also interested in works of Italian Renaissance art, especially Raffael's grotesques, which would subsequently influence Erdmannsdorff's interior designs, and the architecture of Palladio in Vicenza and Venice. During their stay in Naples they climbed Mount Vesuvius, visited the excavations of the ancient city of Pompeii and saw the Herculaneum. The travellers made the acquaintance of the diplomat, vulcanologist and art expert Sir William Hamilton (1730–1803). An architectural reproduction of the Gulf of Naples – including a replica of the Villa Hamilton – was later completed in Wörlitz.

The *Gesamtkunstwerk* that is the garden kingdom of Dessau-Wörlitz is an encyclopaedic mirror-image of enlightened 18th-century culture. The models from which its creators drew inspiration were interpreted on the basis of a combination of unique aesthetic views and reformist educational philosophy.

Today, the various influences operating on the principality of Anhalt-Dessau are clearly evident in the landscape gardens and architecture preserved in the garden kingdom.

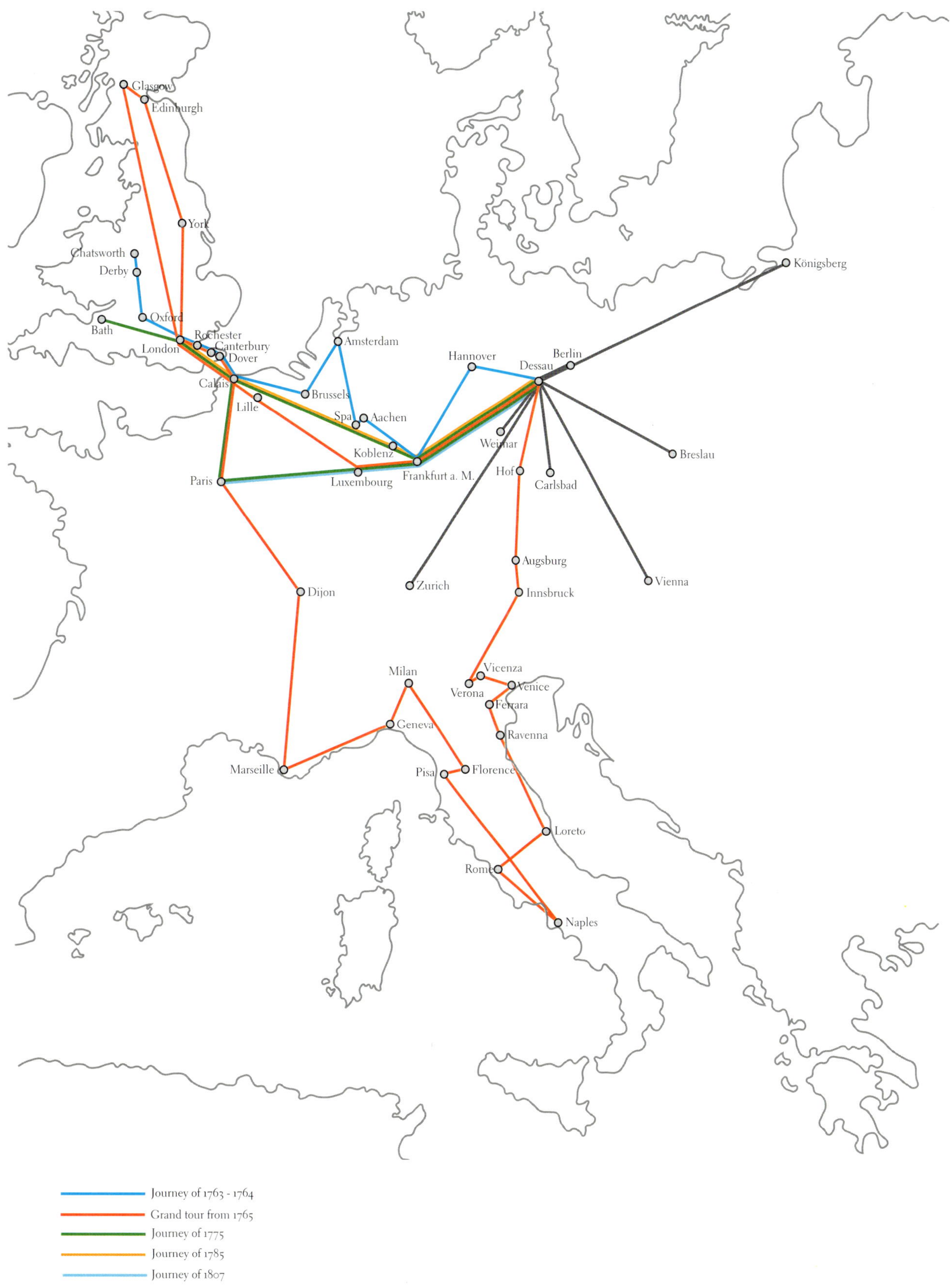

The travels of Prince Franz von Anhalt-Dessau (cat. no. 8)

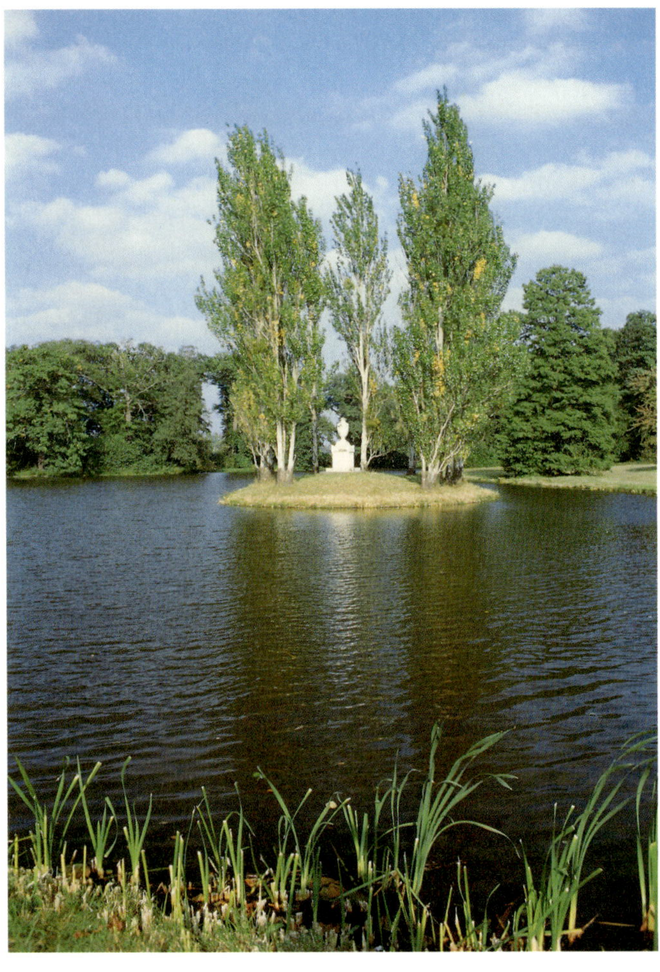

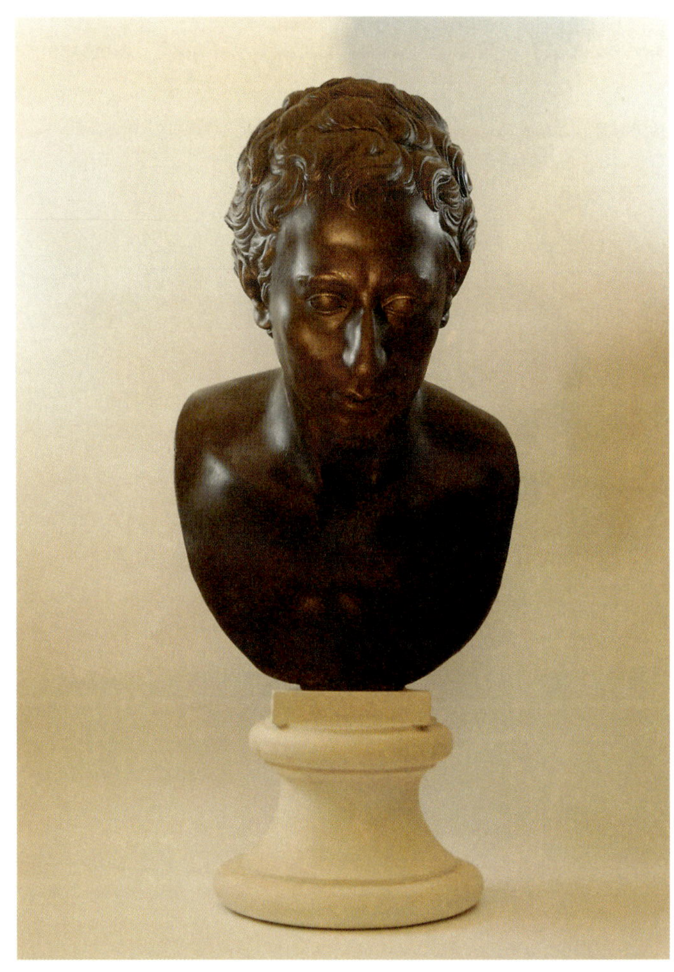

9
ROUSSEAU-DENKMAL AUF DER PAPPELINSEL IN
WÖRLITZ
ROUSSEAU MEMORIAL ON PAPPELINSEL (POPLAR
ISLAND) IN WÖRLITZ
1782
Plastic (cast to scale from the sandstone original)
Height: 300.0 cm
Inscription (translation): IN MEMORY OF J.J. ROUSSEAU / CITIZEN
OF GENEVA / WHO WITH MANLY ELOQUENCE / BROUGHT
FOOLS TO SOUND REASON / GLUTTONS TO TRUE ENJOYMENT /
MISGUIDED ART TO THE UNITY OF NATURE / DOUBTERS TO
THE COMFORT OF THE REVELATION / HE DIED ON II JUL.
MDCCLXXVIII.
Kulturstiftung DessauWörlitz

The sandstone monument surrounded by poplars on a small island in Lake
Wörlitz is a replica of the original version of the gravestone of Jean-Jacques
Rousseau (1712–1778) in Ermenonville near Paris. The ideas of the French
enlightenment philosopher exercised a lasting influence on intellectual and
cultural development in Anhalt-Dessau. In 1775 Prince Franz and Princess
Luise met the philosopher in Paris. The monument, bearing an inscription
authored by the Prince himself, was completed in 1782 on the basis of a
sketch by Erdmannsdorff.

10
Friedrich Wilhelm Eugen Doell (1750–1816)
BÜSTE DES JOHANN JOACHIM WINCKELMANN
BUST OF JOHANN JOACHIM WINCKELMANN
Between 1777 and 1782
Synthetic resin, bronzed, plaster (cast to scale from the bronze original)
Height (with pedestal): 66.0 cm
Kulturstiftung DessauWörlitz

The encounter with Winckelmann in Rome one year after the publication of
his most important work, *Geschichte der Kunst des Altertums* (1764), had a
significant impact upon the aesthetic views of the Dessau Prince and his
architect and advisor Friedrich Wilhelm von Erdmannsdorff. Under Winckelmann's guidance, they studied ancient art in Rome for six months, taking excursions to Tivoli, Frascati and Palestrina as well. Frequent correspondence
and Winckelmann's expressed intention to visit the Prince in Dessau suggest
the growth of a close friendship.

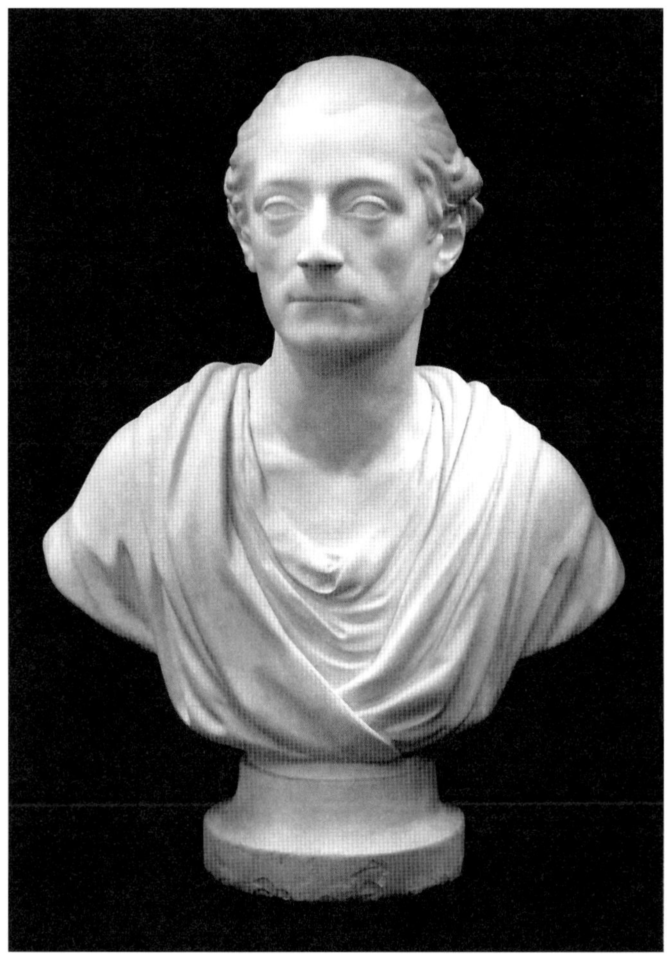

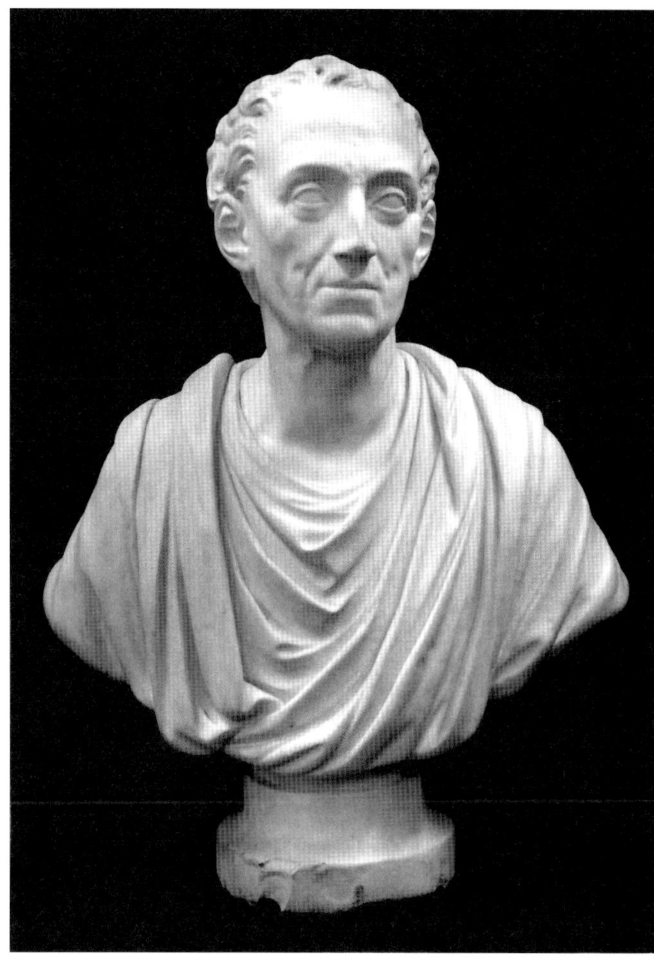

11

BÜSTE DES JOHANN KASPAR LAVATER
BUST OF JOHANN KASPAR LAVATER
1783
Weimar limestone
Height: 70.0 cm
Signature: on the reverse of the bust beneath the draping "Klauer fec. 1783"
Kulturstiftung DessauWörlitz

Lavater (1741–1801) earned widespread respect deriving in particular from his studies in physiognomy. It was he who developed the theory that conclusions could be drawn about an individual's character from the configuration of the lines of the human profile. His major work, *Physiognomische Fragmente zur Beförderung der Menschenkenntnis und Menschenliebe*, was published in 1775–1778 in four volumes. Lavater first approached the Dessau Prince in 1776 with a request to have his portrait for his studies. He enjoyed close contacts with Franz and Luise at certain times, Luise spending several weeks with his family in Zurich in 1783. Lavater's bust was placed in the labyrinth in Neumark's garden in 1784. Another likeness of the scholar appears in a fresco in the library of the *Wörlitzer Schloß*.

12

Martin Gottlieb Klauer (1742–1801)
BÜSTE DES CHRISTIAN FÜRCHTEGOTT GELLERT
BUST OF CHRISTIAN FÜRCHTEGOTT GELLERT
1784
Weimar limestone
Height: 71.0 cm
Kulturstiftung DessauWörlitz

Gellert (1715–1769), a professor of poetics and philosophy in Leipzig, was regarded as the great teacher of ethics in his time. He propagated an enlightened, sentimental ideal of virtue. The grand tour of 1765 began with a visit by the Prince to Gellert in Leipzig. Franz and Luise visited the moral philosopher and poet once again in 1767 for private lectures. The royal couple had Gellert's bust placed in the allegorical section of the labyrinth in Wörlitz.

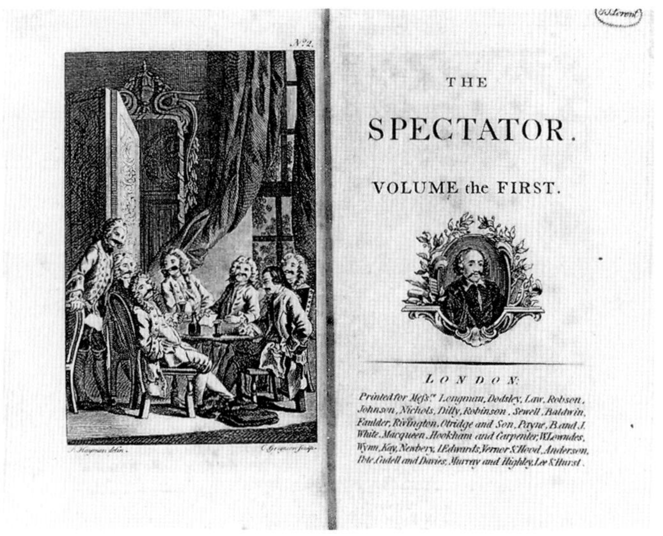

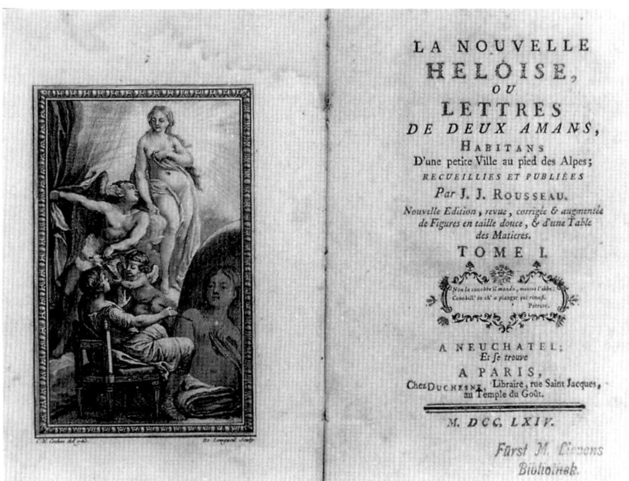

13
Joseph Addison (1672–1719)
and Sir Richard Steele (1672–1729)
THE SPECTATOR (NOS. 1 TO 80)
London: Longman, Dodley et al, n.d.
18.0 x 11.5 cm (closed), 344 pages
Kulturstiftung DessauWörlitz

The Spectator, a collection of moralist essays, appeared daily as a single-sheet
publication from 1711 to 1712 and again in 1714. Distributed in clubs and
coffee houses, it reached an estimated 60,000 readers in Great Britain and
was also made available to a vast circle of readers in numerous book editions.
The essays, most of them written by Addison, addressed moral and philosophical topics, literature and art and also offered instructions for proper social
behaviour. They exercised considerable influence upon public opinion and
the world view of an entire class.

14
Jean-Jacques Rousseau (1712–1778)
*LA NOUVELLE HÉLOISE OU LETTRES DE DEUX AMANS,
HABITANS D'UNE PETITE VILLE AU PIED DES ALPES
THE NEW ELOISE OR LETTERS OF TWO LOVERS LIVING
IN A SMALL TOWN AT THE FOOT OF THE ALPS*
Volume 1, Paris: Duchesne, 1764
18.0 x 12.5 cm (closed), 408 pages
Kulturstiftung DessauWörlitz

Rousseau's immensely popular novel deals with the struggle to overcome sen-
sual passions and the process of purification resulting in intimate friendship.
Nature assumes a significant role in this process as a means of self-discovery.
The novel exercised a strong influence upon continental gardening arts and
promoted the idea of the English landscape garden in France. A copy of the
book is held in the library of the *Wörlitzer Schloß*.

15
Alexander Pope (1688–1744)
*VERSUCH AN DEM MENSCHEN. IN VIER SITTEN BRIEFEN
AN HENRICH ST. JEAN, GRAFEN VON BOLINGBROKE
ÜBER DIE NATUR UND DEN ZUSTAND DES MENSCHEN.
ESSAY ON MAN*
Frankfurt/M.: Frank Varrentrapp, 1741 (German edition)
20.0 x 13.5 cm (closed), 191 pages
Kulturstiftung DessauWörlitz

Pope's philosophical, didactic poem *Essay on Man* was one of the widest-read
and most influential works of poetry of the 18th century. It also contributed
significantly to the dissemination of English philosophy in Germany. The
library of the *Wörlitzer Schloß* holds a copy of the German edition of this
work as well. The deist views of Henry St. John Lord Bolingbroke, to whom
the poem was addressed, exercised a considerable influence on the poetry of
his friend Alexander Pope.

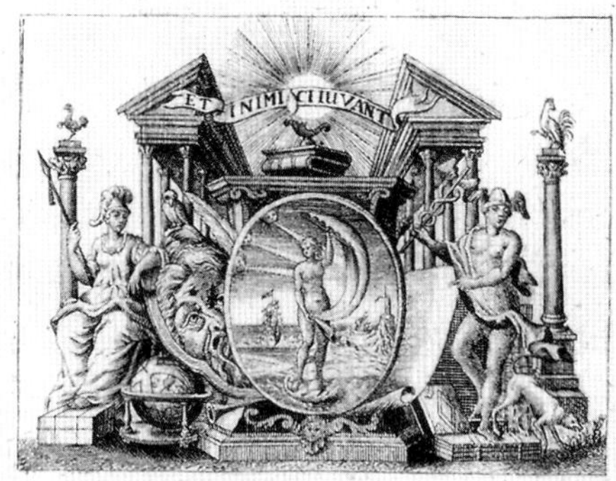

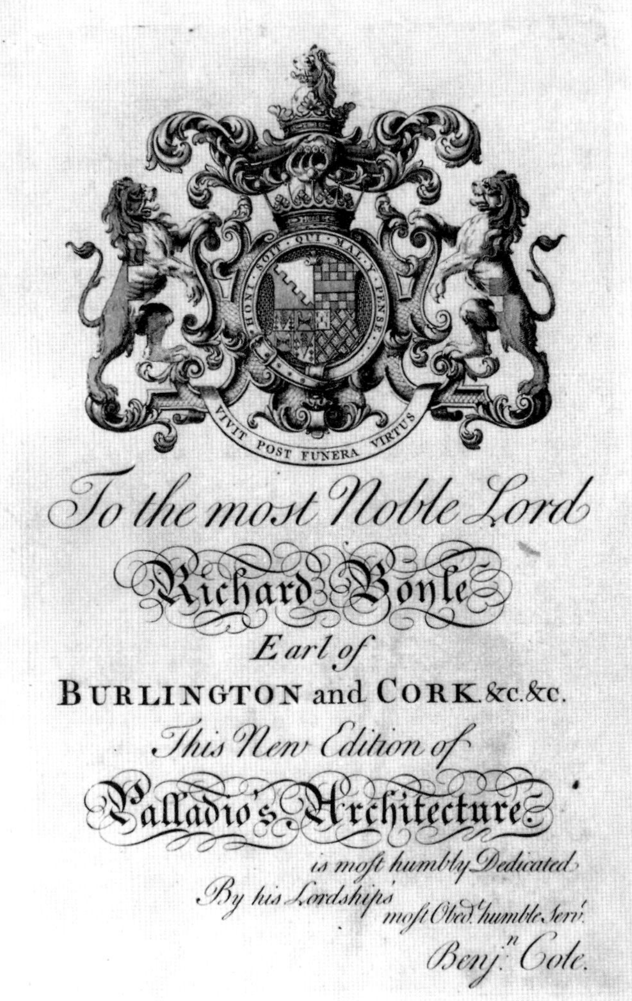

16

Andrea Palladio (1508–1580)

ARCHITECTURE IN FOUR BOOKS. CONTAINING A DISSERTATION ON THE FIVE ORDERS…

London: Cole and Wilcox, 1736

35.5 x 24.5 cm (closed), 121 pages, 61 copper engravings

With a dedication to Lord Burlington

Kulturstiftung DessauWörlitz

The major theoretical treatise by the Italian architect Andrea Palladio, *I quattro libri dell'architettura*, was first published in 1570 and later appeared in a number of new editions and translations. In the course of the following centuries it became the foundation of Neoclassical architecture. This copy bears a dedication to Richard Boyle, third Earl of Burlington, who became a leading advocate of Palladio's teachings in England. Erdmannsdorff's architecture also shows evidence of Palladio's influence. Erdmannsdorff was inspired not only by Palladio's architecture in Italy but by works of the neo-Palladianists in England, particularly the country houses of the English aristocracy built in that style.

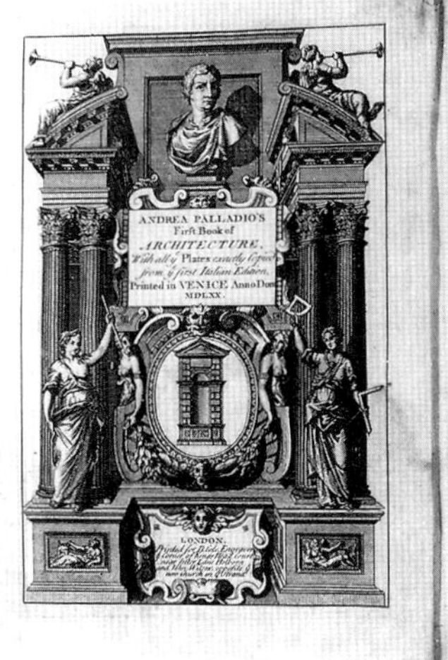

17
Christian Fürchtegott Gellert (1715–1769)
GEISTLICHE ODEN UND LIEDER
SPIRITUAL ODES AND HYMNS
Leipzig: bey M. G. Weidmanns Erben und Reich, 1763
19.9 x 13.3 cm (closed), 160 pages
Private collection

Gellert's bust was placed in the labyrinth of the Wörlitzer Garten, its pedestal
inscribed with a passage from the hymn *"Trost des ewigen Lebens"*: *"Heil
dir! denn du hast mein Leben, Die Seele mir gerettet; du!"* (The Consolation of
Eternal Life: Hail to Thee! For Thou has saved my life, my soul; Thou
alone!).

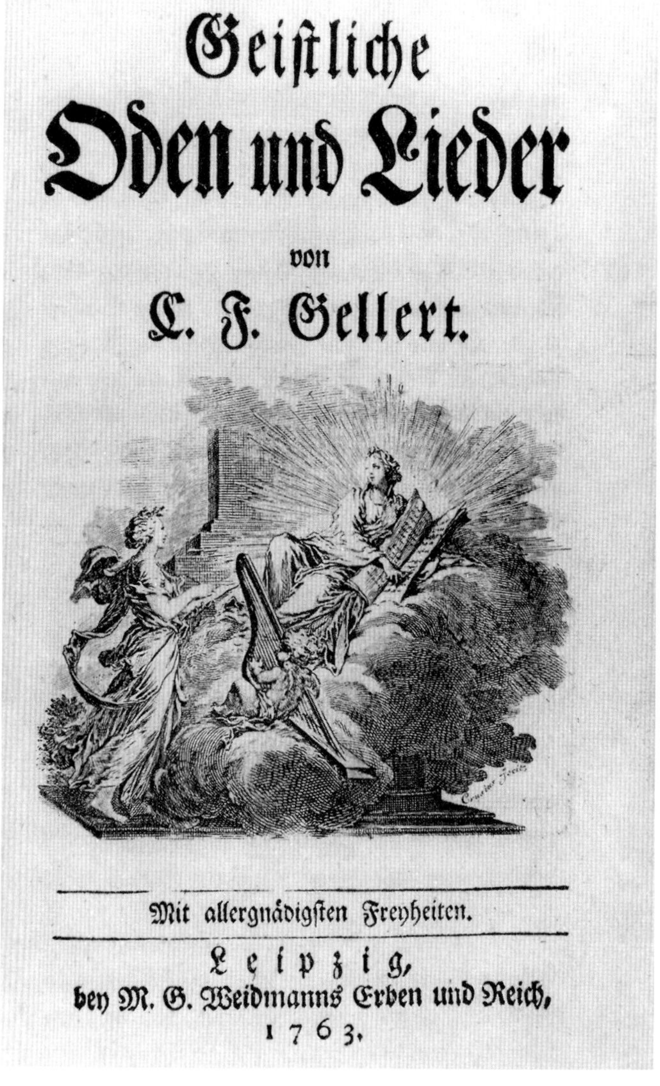

18
François de Salignac de la Mothe Fénelon (1651–1715)
LES AVANTURES DE TÉLÉMAQUE, FILS D'ULYSSE
(GERMAN: DIE BEGEBENHEITEN TELEMACHS, DES
SOHNS DES ULYSSES. EIN HELDENGEDICHT)
THE ADVENTURES OF TELEMACHOS, SON OF ULYSSES
French and German, Ulm: Christian Ulrich Wagner, 1771
18.8 x 12.2 cm (closed), 821 pages, 25 copper engravings
Private collection

Fénelon's portrait on the wall of the library of the *Wörlitzer Schloß* dedicated
to law and ethics. In his *Les Avantures de Telemaque*, Fénelon postulates
models of wisdom and princely education.

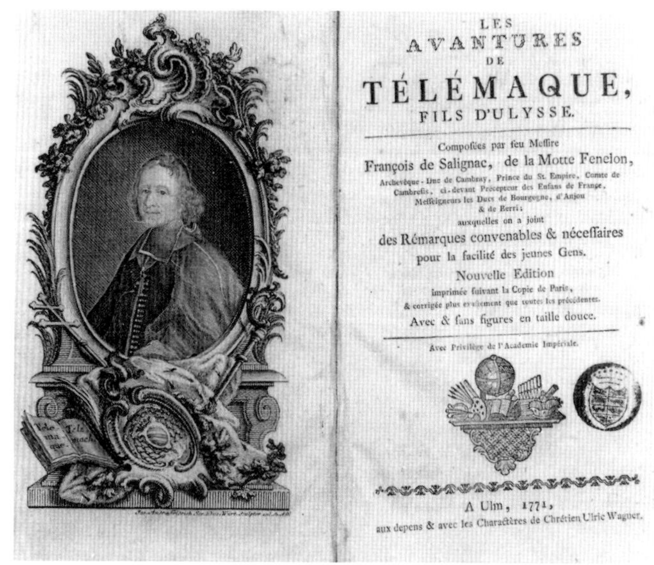

Anhalt became an autonomous principality in 1212 and was ruled by the Askanian dynasty until 1918. Following successive partitions, Anhalt-Dessau, Anhalt-Bernburg, Anhalt-Köthen and Anhalt-Zerbst were established as small, independent states in 1603. Anhalt-Dessau, which grew to fullest flower under the reign of Prince Leopold III Friedrich Franz von Anhalt-Dessau in the 18th century, experienced a significant rise in its fortunes in the middle of the 17th century following the marriage of Johann Georg II to Henriette Catharina von Nassau-Orianien, one of the four daughters of the Crown Prince of the Netherlands. This link with the "Golden Age" of the Netherlands generated both an economic upswing and a process of internal expansion in Anhalt-Dessau. Extensive dike construction by Dutch specialists produced new land and brought protection against floods. With Oranienbaum, Princess Henriette Catharina established the third city of the House of Orange following Oranienburg near Berlin and Oranienstein near Diez an der Lahn. Prince Johann Georg II served from 1657 in the army of the Grand Prince of Brandenburg and thus founded the military tradition of Prussian-Anhalt that reached its zenith under his son Leopold I, the *"Alter Dessauer"*. Of significance to the domestic political situation was Prince Leopold's successful campaign to expel the entire landed nobility from Anhalt-Dessau, thus establishing the economic foundation for his grandson's reform program. Anhalt-Dessau experienced a flourishing of culture under Prince Franz. His rule began under the influence of significant challenges. Caught up in the Seven Years' War that was shaking the foundations of all Europe during that time, little Anhalt-Dessau was brought to the brink of ruin by the contribution obligations imposed by Prussia. The death of Frederick the Great in 1786 made way for a cautious rapprochement with Prussia. Anhalt-Dessau's policy of limited involvement in the wars of coalition against France yielded benefits to the tiny principality in the aftermath of the demise of the Holy Roman Empire of German Nations. During the rule of Napoleon, Prince Franz, now elevated to the status of Duke, pursued an effective policy of diplomacy. Anhalt-Dessau escaped both subjugation under Napoleon and annexation under the edicts of the Congress of Vienna. After 59 years of rule, Duke Franz of Anhalt-Dessau died in 1817. The economic reforms and the educational and aesthetic reorientation he initiated had a significant impact far beyond the borders of Anhalt-Dessau and attracted countless travellers to the little country between the Elbe and the Mulde.

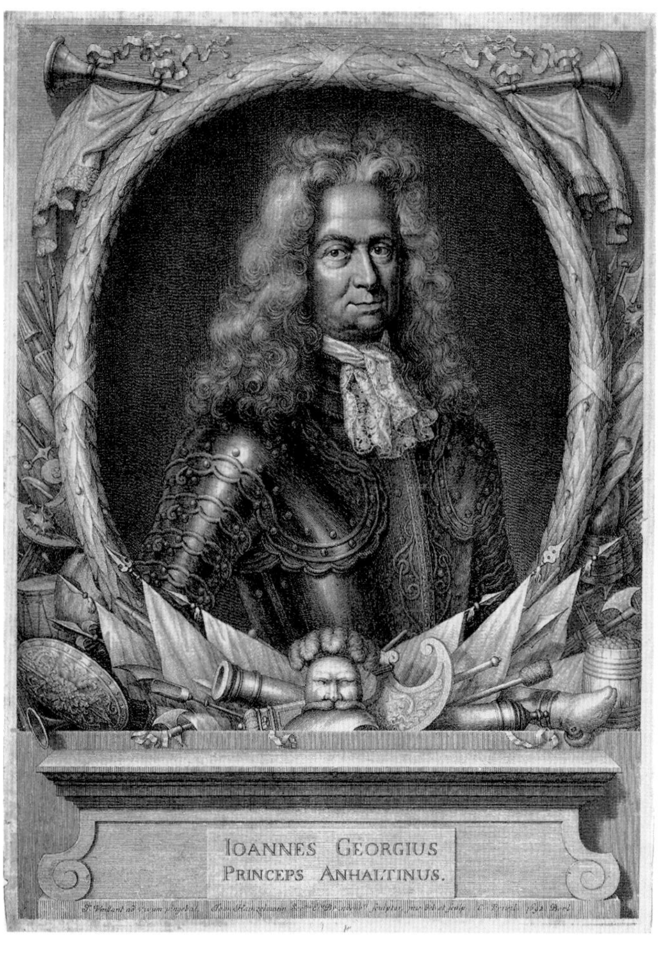

19

Johann Heinzelmann (1641–1693, or 1700)
after Jacques Vaillant (1625–1691)
JOHANN GEORG II. VON ANHALT-DESSAU
JOHANN GEORG II OF ANHALT-DESSAU
Copper engraving (photolithograph copy)
55.5 x 40.5 cm
Inscribed on the lower edge of the painting: "J. Vaillant ad vivum pingeba.
Joan Heizelmann ser.mi El.is Brandenb.ci sculptor, jnv. del. et sculp.
C. Privil. 1692. Berl.", and on the pedestal above: "IOANNES GEORGIUS /
PRINCEPS ANHALTINUS."
Kulturstiftung DessauWörlitz

Johann Georg II, the great-grandfather of Prince Franz, wed Princess Henriette Catharina von Nassau-Oranien in a marriage arranged by the Grand
Prince of Brandenburg in 1659. Shortly after the end of the Thirty Years' War,
considerable financial resources began to flow from the Netherlands into the
ravaged principality of Anhalt-Dessau. Thus the previously insignificant little
state in central Germany came to enjoy the fruits of the Golden Age in
Holland.
As governor of the Kurmark, Prince Johann Georg maintained very close ties
with the court in Berlin. Artists from Brandenburg, including such figures as
Ryckwaert, Vaillant, Hanneman and others, worked in Dessau as well.

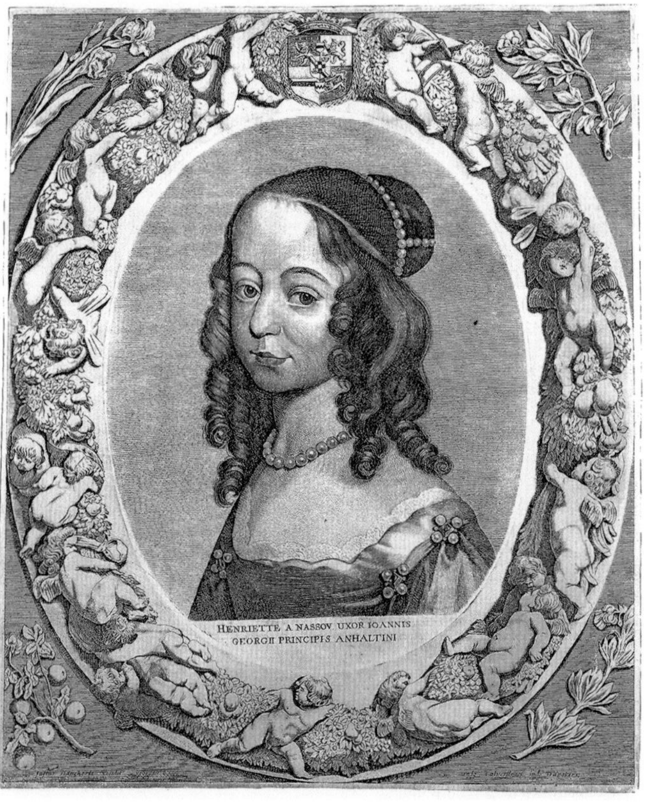

20

Cornelius Vischer (circa 1619–1662)
after Gerhard von Honthorst (1590–1656)
HENRIETTE CATHARINA VON NASSAU-ORANIEN
HENRIETTE CATHARINA OF NASSAU-ORANIEN
1695
Copper engraving (copy, photolithograph)
41.5 x 29.0 cm
Inscription: lower left below the picture "Cornelis Vischer sc."; right "Ger. v.
Honthorst pinx."
Kulturstiftung DessauWörlitz

Henriette Catharina was born the daughter of Friedrich Heinrich, Crown
Prince of the Netherlands, on January 31st, 1637. She married Johann Georg II
von Anhalt-Dessau in 1659. As her sister Luise Henriette had done in
Brandenburg, she brought the Dutch spirit to Anhalt-Dessau. Attributable to
this influence are the recovery of land and the granting of entry to Jews.
Commerce and culture experienced an upswing in Anhalt-Dessau, often in
close association with developments in Brandenburg.

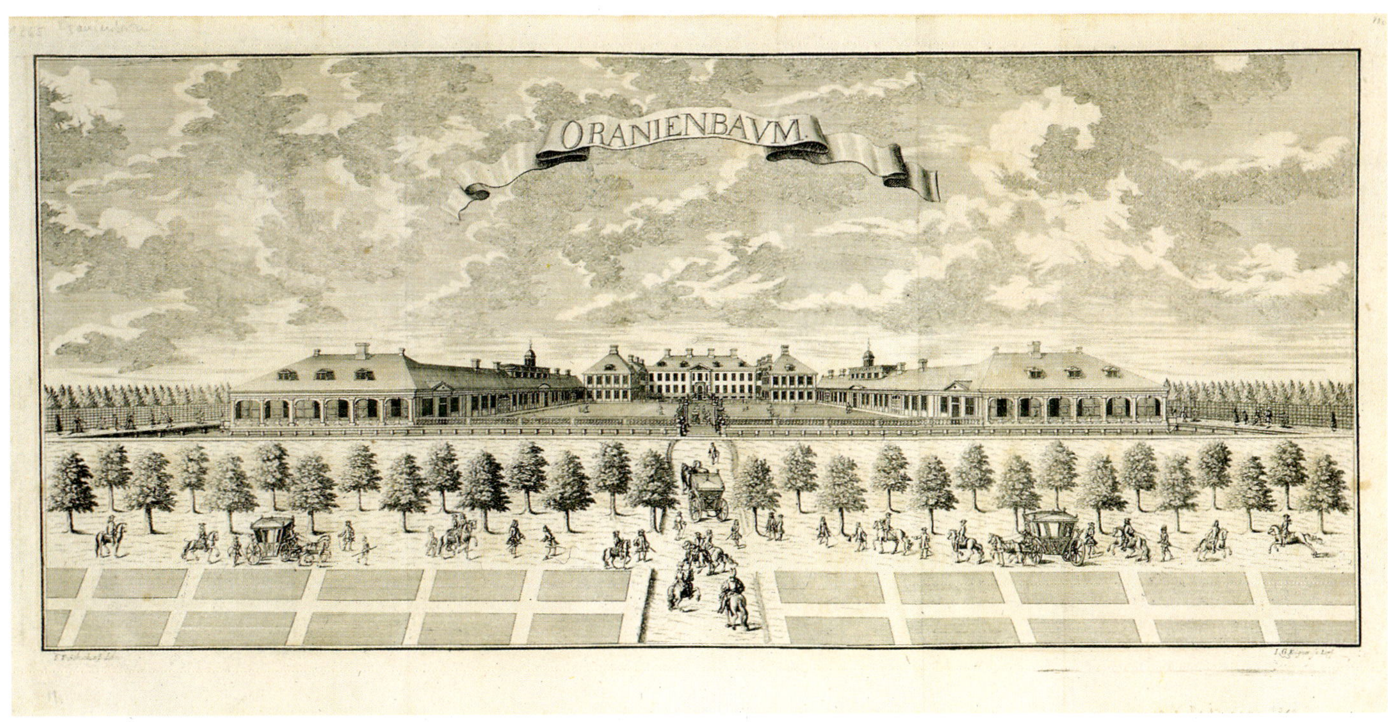

21

Johann Gottfried Krügner (circa 1684?–1769)
after Johann Tobias Schuchart (died 1711)
SCHLOSS ORANIENBAUM
Before 1710
Copper engraving from Johann Christoff Beckmann, *Historia Des Fürsten-
thums Anhalt*, Zerbst: Zimmermann, 1710.
37.0 x 77.6 cm
Inscription: lower left beneath the picture "I.T. Schuchart delin.",
right "I. G. Krügner fc. Lips."
Institut für Auslandsbeziehungen

Henriette Catharina von Nassau-Oranien, the wife of Prince Johann Georg II
von Anhalt-Dessau, received the desolate township of Nischwitz as a wedding
gift in 1660. She promoted the development of the town, first mentioned
under the new name of Oranienbaum in 1673. In 1683 Cornelis Ryckwaert,
an architect of Dutch descent engaged in the service of the Brandenburg
court, began construction of the castle. Related efforts included methodical
development of the city according to a checkerboard grid pattern and the
placement of a large garden area based on the Dutch model. Oranienbaum is
one of the few Dutch-influenced baroque ensembles still remaining in
Germany.

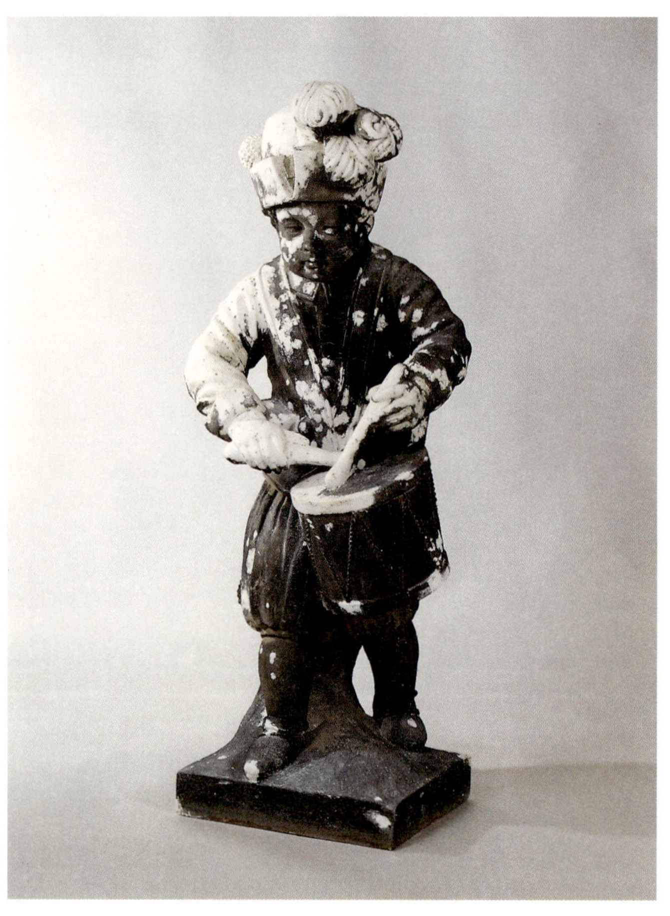

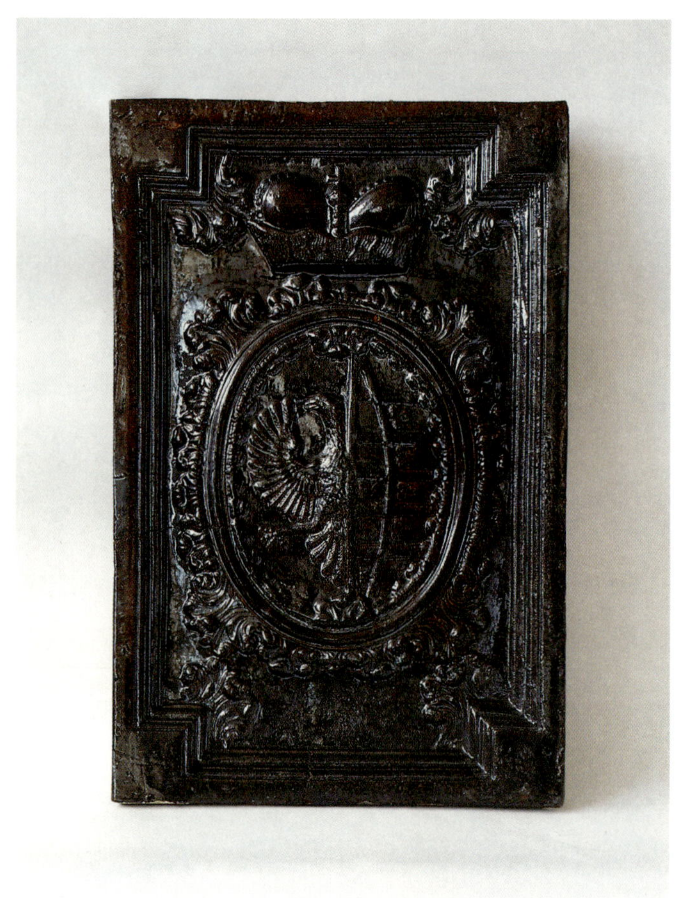

22
PUTTO VOM ALTAN DES SCHLOSSES ORANIENBAUM
STATUE OF PUTTO FROM THE FRONT BALCONY OF
SCHLOSS ORANIENBAUM
Circa 1700
Sandstone
Height: 80.0 cm
Kulturstiftung DessauWörlitz

The gnomelike Putto from the front balcony of the castle in Oranienbaum is
represented as a drummer in the traditional garb of a local militiaman. The
statue is an aesthetic reflection on the events of the Thirty Years' War experienced not long before its creation.

23
OFENKACHEL MIT ANHALTISCHEM WAPPEN
STOVE TILE BEARING AN ANHALT COAT OF ARMS
Circa 1710
Clay, glazed
57.5 x 38.0 cm
Kulturstiftung DessauWörlitz

The motif on the stove tile is the small coat of arms of Dessau, showing the
Brandenburg half eagle and the diamond-shaped shield of Sachsen. In an
allusion to the noble title the coat of arms is crowned by a Prince's hat. Stoves
in Schloß Oranienbaum preserved from the period have tiles bearing both
coats of arms and still lifes of fruit.

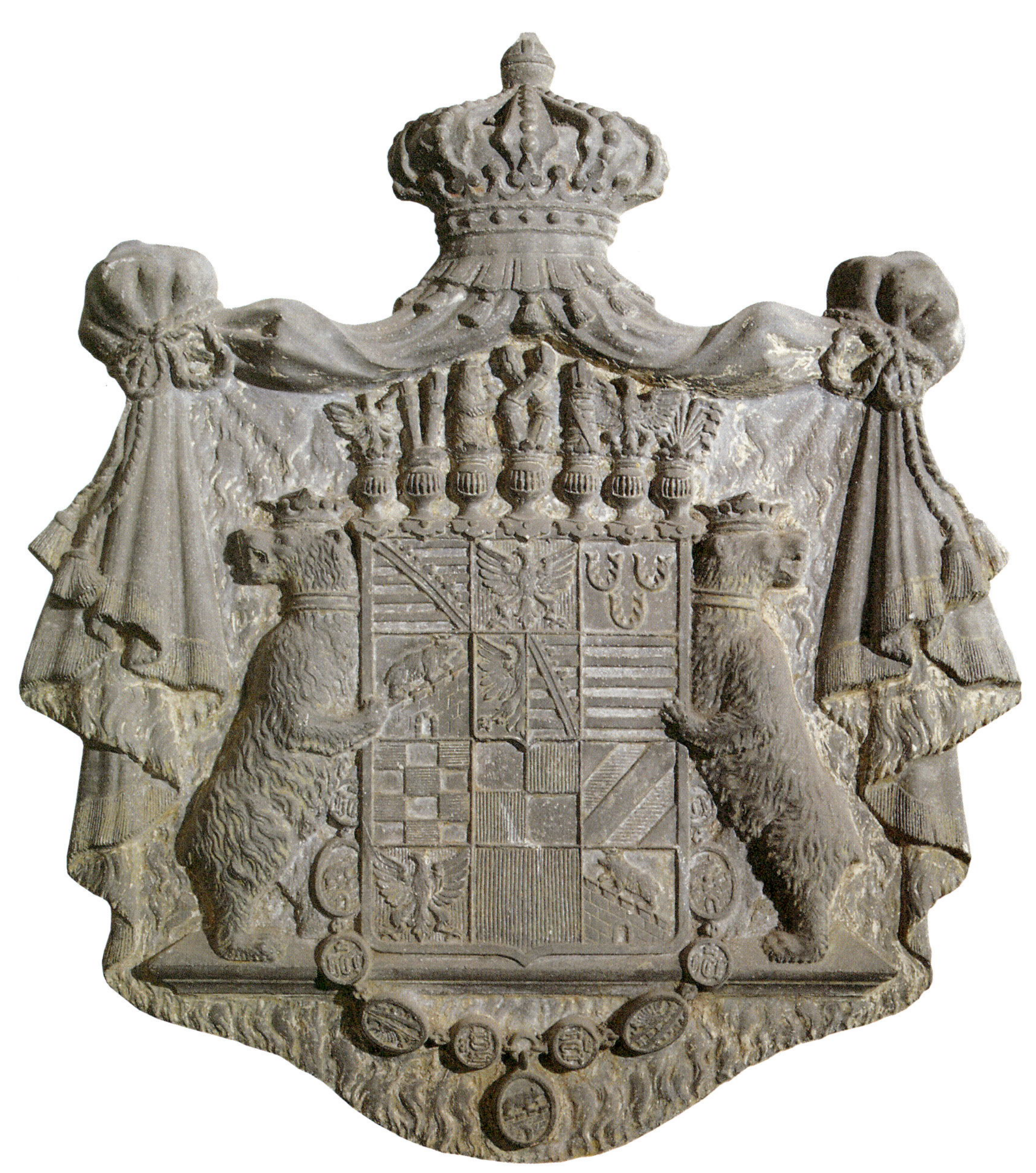

24
ANHALTISCHES WAPPEN
COAT OF ARMS OF ANHALT
After 1836
Zinc cast
76.0 x 68.5 x 7 cm
Kulturstiftung DessauWörlitz

This coat of arms has been in use by the House of Anhalt in the form shown
here since the mid–17th century. The heart-shaped shield, also used as a heral-
dic symbol, derives from the time of Albrecht the Bear (1212–1260), who held
the titles of Duke of Sachsen and Margrave of Nordmark. Both the diamond-
shaped shield of Sachsen and the Brandenburg half red eagle have their
origin in that symbol.
The three coats of arms in the upper row are symbols of claims incorporated
into the main coat of arms by Prince Johann Georg II von Anhalt-Dessau in
1689. They document the claims posed by the House of Anhalt on the medieval duchies of Sachsen, Engern and Westfalen.

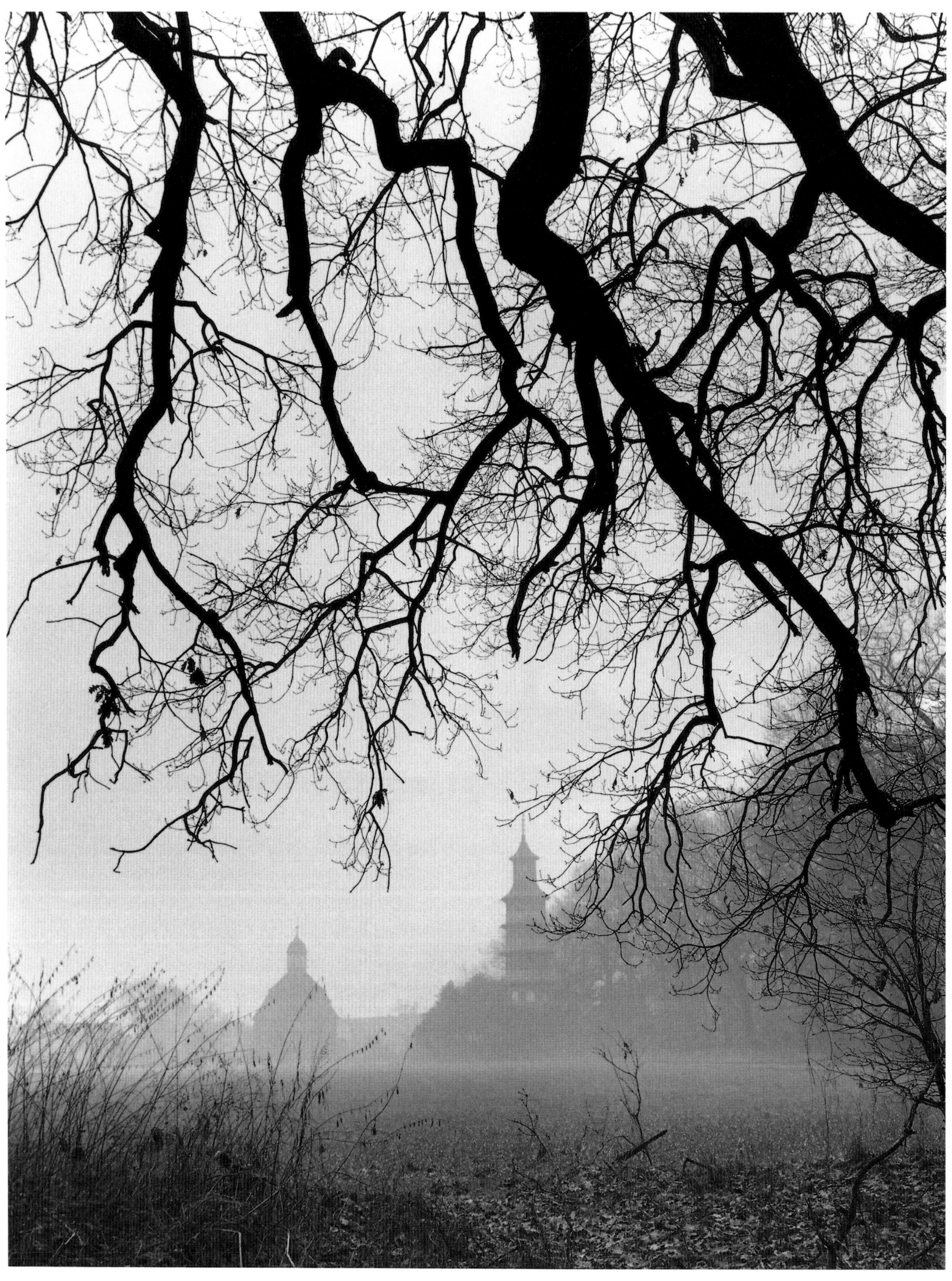

Lutz Winkler, Chinese Garden, Oranienbaum (cat. no. 82.1)

"All Gardening is Landscape Painting"

Alexander Pope

"In lieto aspetto il bel giardin s'aperse:
Acque stagnanti, mobili cristalli,
Fior vari, e varie piante, herbe diverse,
Apriche collinette, ombrose valli,
Selve, e spelunche in una vista offerse.
E quel, che'l bello, e'l caro accresce à l'opre,
L'arte che tutto fa, nulla si scopre."

Torquato Tasso

"Huge forests of oak, with trunks more than a hundred years old cloaked with the thickest abundance of leaves up to their very tops, stretch across the land as far as the eye can see, and interspersed among them are velvet carpets of meadow, on which herbs and flowers of all kinds flourish in copious plenty, filling the air with the most pleasant of smells. The banks of the Elbe are superbly covered on either side with thick, leafy undergrowth that descends like the stands of an amphitheatre into the flowing water. In moderate bends the river slowly winds its way through the landscape at some length, only to disappear suddenly behind a spit of land hidden by thick grasses or behind islands surrounded by reeds or covered by meadow bushes or oaks whose gigantic branches bow into the stream itself; soon it appears again, now rolling forth through ripe fields of grain, now through meadows and fields in meandering curves farther and farther until it finally fades away in the distance…"

This description written in 1795 by Carl Wilhelm Kolbe, a draftsman and engraver who worked in Dessau for many years, gives us an impression of the landscape which formed the basis for the design of the garden kingdom of Dessau-Wörlitz.

Anhalt-Dessau lies in a region shaped by the Ice-Age glaciers which carved the valleys of the Elbe and Mulde Rivers. Broad lowland areas with their stands of oak and elm, open meadowlands with single, solitary trees, whose characteristic appearance was shaped by extensive hog-raising operations in the oak forests from the medieval period into the 18th century, and expansive farmlands dominate the scene and were incorporated by Prince Leopold Friedrich Franz into the man-made park and garden complex. Franz gave considerable attention to flood protection. Following the catastrophic floods of 1770 and 1771, many kilometres of dikes were erected throughout the entire principality, complemented by flood watchmen's houses placed at intervals of roughly four kilometres. Used to store tools and materials needed for repairs, the houses themselves contributed to the aesthetic enhancement of the landscape. Also worthy of note is the integration of the dikes into the artificial landscapes and garden artworks. Visitors walk along elevated paths from which they enjoy an expansive view of the beautified landscape.

The serene, park-like landscape with its highly stylised gardens, which were linked together by tree-lined avenues and vistas, was affected by radical changes during the 19th and 20th centuries. Urban growth and the building of railroads were already taking their toll on the Arcadian landscape scenes in the 19th century. Industrialisation, highway construction and the establishment of the central German chemical and soft-coal industries during the 20th century caused severe damage to the landscape and the works of art it contained. The results of inadequate care and maintenance during and after the two World Wars posed major problems for monument preservation. Today, thanks to extensive restoration and repair efforts, intensified since 1990, much of the garden kingdom can be experienced and enjoyed by visitors once again.

25

Christian Haldenwang (1770–1831)

after Heinrich Theodor **Wehle** (1778–1805)

SIELITZERBERG **AM UFER** DER ELBE

SIELITZERBERG **ON THE BANKS OF THE ELBE**

1800

Aquatint, 25.6 x 33.7 cm

Inscription (translated): lower left below the picture "sig. by Wehle."; right
"etched by **Haldenwang**."; centre "Sielitzerberg / on the banks of the Elbe /
Chalcographische Gesellschaft of Dessau 1800."

Institut für Auslandsbeziehungen

Located in the midst of the landscape of the *Sieglitzer Berg* (Mt. Sieglitz)
between Vockerode and Dessau, regarded by contemporaries as orderly structured nature rather than an artificially designed garden, is a Neoclassical
Doric-style temple known as the *Solitude*. This structure, with its four-col-
umned portico facing the Elbe, was erected according to Erdmannsdorff's
plans between 1777 and 1784. The Prince incorporated natural features such
as ponds, streams and woodlands into the design of the garden in an effort to
beautify by means of "structural" interventions and to avoid creating the
appearance of artificiality. The *Solitude* was destroyed around 1970.

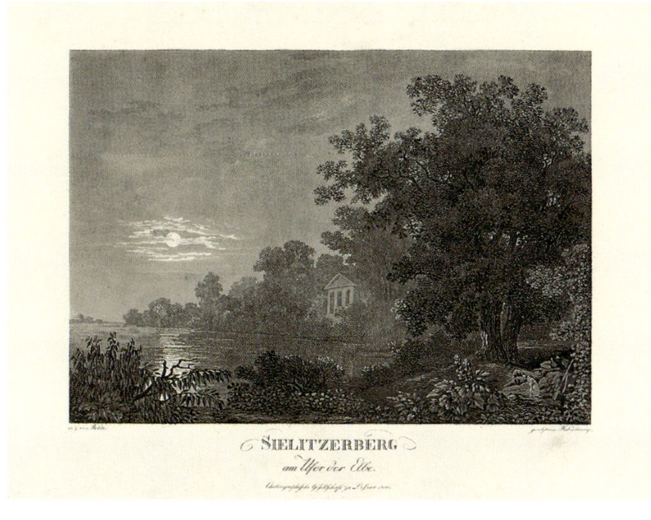

26

Christian Haldenwang (1770–1831)

DIE MULDBRÜCKE UND DAS SCHLOSS ZU DESSAU

THE MULDE BRIDGE AND THE CASTLE OF DESSAU

1799

Aquatint, 25.8 x 33.3 cm

Inscription (translated): lower left below the picture "drawn and [engraved] in
copper"; right "by Haldenwang"; centre "The Mulde Bridge / and the Castle
of Dessau / Chalcographische Gesellschaft of Dessau 1799."

Institut für Auslandsbeziehungen

The engraving shows the Mulde River landscape near Dessau with a view of
the city from the Northeast. Visible are the Mulde Bridge, built by Erdmannsdorff in 1796/97, and behind it the royal mills and the east wing of the
residential *Schloß*, the original Renaissance forms of which were completely
redesigned by the Berlin architect Georg Wenzeslaus von Knobelsdorff
between 1748 and 1753. Today the Mulde Bridge houses gave way to a super-
highway access ramp in 1936, the mills have been torn down and the *Schloß*
was largely destroyed in 1945.

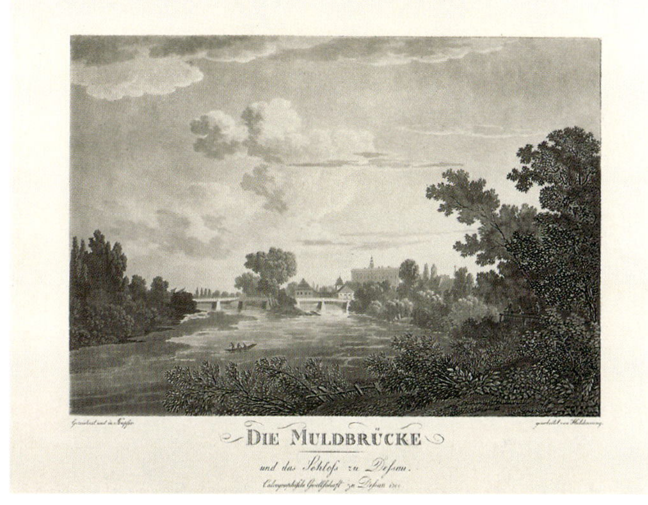

27

Carl Wilhelm Kolbe (1759–1835)

PARKLANDSCHAFT

PARK LANDSCAPE

Circa 1800

Etching, 27.6 x 34.8 cm

Inscription: lower right beneath the picture "C. W. K. f."

Kulturstiftung DessauWörlitz

A number of views of the garden kingdom are attributable to the draftsman
and graphic artist Carl Wilhelm Kolbe, or "Eichenkolbe", as he was called by
contemporaries. The artist placed special emphasis on the oak as a symbol of
the Golden Age of the ancient world. Kolbe enjoyed a close relationship to
Anhalt-Dessau dating from about 1780, as he found its landscape ideally suited
to his creative interests. Kolbe taught French at the *Philanthropin* and worked
after completion of his studies in art in Berlin as a teacher of French and
drawing at the grammar school in Dessau from 1795 until his retirement (1828).

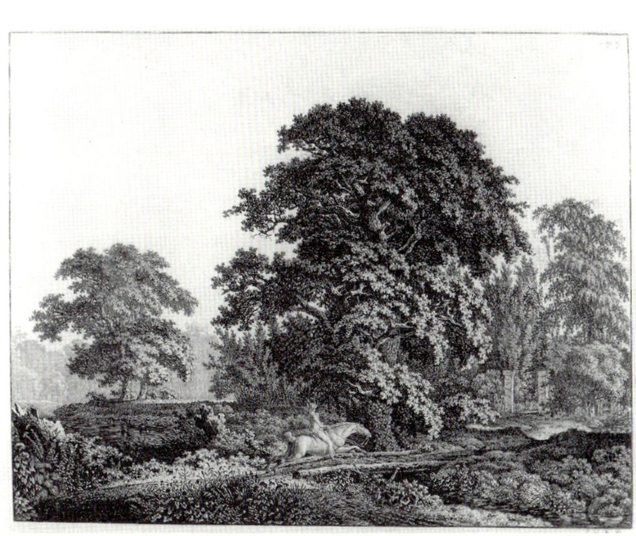

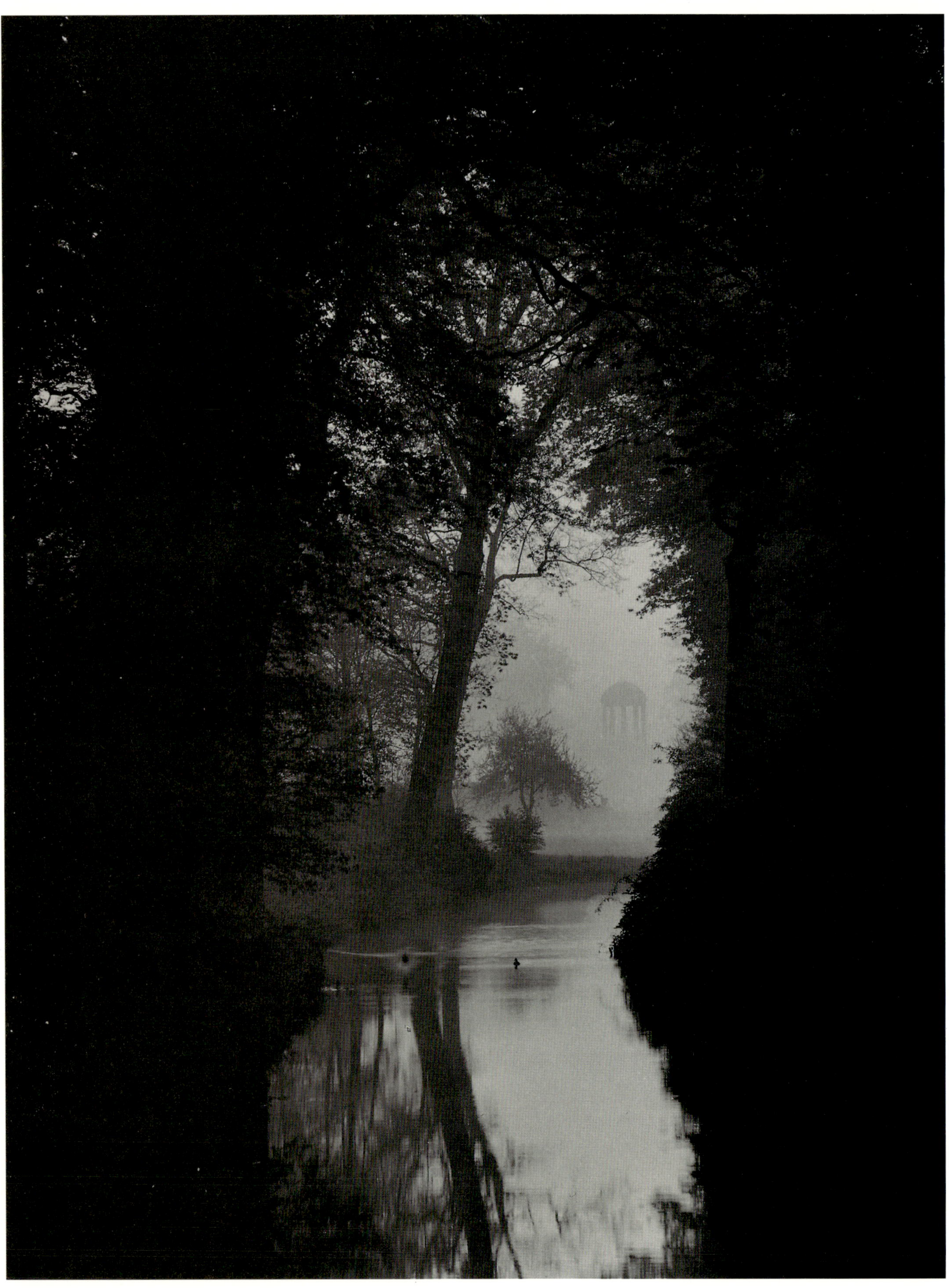

Lutz Winkler, Wolf's Canal, Wörlitz (cat. no. 82.2)

"Hier ist's iezt unendlich schön…
Die Götter haben dem Fürsten erlaubt,
einen Traum um sich zu schaffen…"

Johann Wolfgang von Goethe

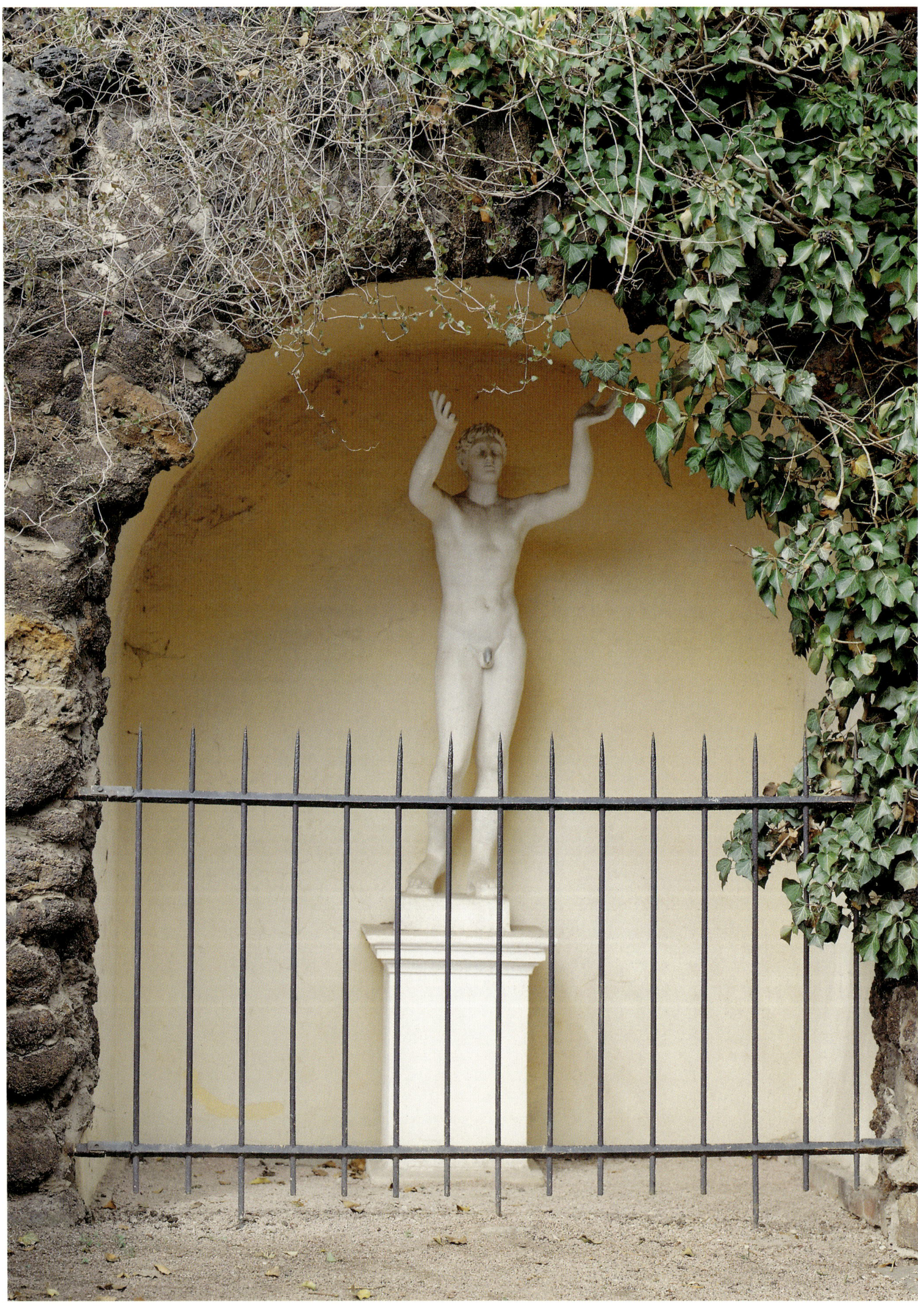

Garden and landscape design

Complex social developments, popular striving for emancipation and stimulus from literature and philosophy combined during the first third of the 18th century to foster the growth of a new ideal in garden design in England that found its most noteworthy expression in the landscape garden.

Characterised by a unity of garden design, architecture and visual art, the garden of Wörlitz became the vanguard of the English style in Germany. Horticultural designers were no longer guided by the ideal of the formal baroque park which bowed to the requirements of architecture. In its place, "true", untouched nature was elevated to the measure of all things in garden culture. Trees were permitted to assume their natural forms, paths to follow irregular courses; the boundaries between artificially shaped nature and the landscape became flexible. The pathways along which visitors wandered led them to deliberately chosen scenes and views. A structured system of vistas radiated from bends in paths, rest spots and bridge crowns. More than 300 such vistas have been identified in the parks and gardens of Wörlitz alone.

After his first journey to England in 1763/64, where he carefully studied the gardens of William Kent and Lancelot Brown, Prince Franz undertook the design of an English-style garden in Wörlitz. Work continued there until about 1800 and was enhanced by experience gained on further travels in England and aided by the study of contemporary literature.

Buildings, sculptures and particularly appealing scenes are the focal points of vistas radiating, often in a fanlike manner, in different directions and linking discreet garden sections with one another. Substantial portions of the garden were put to agricultural use. Evident in this practice and in the policy of incorporating works of art and architecture for the purpose of moulding taste and encouraging imitation is the influence of enlightened, didactic tendencies underlying the design concept for the publicly accessible *Wörlitzer Garten*.

As the point of departure for beautification measures in Anhalt-Dessau, Wörlitz was followed by other English-style landscape gardens which were interconnected by a network of thoughtfully designed avenues and vistas. Older grounds were also integrated into the gradually flourishing "garden kingdom" which drew great praise from contemporaries.

Boy praying, circa 1780
(cat. no. 45)

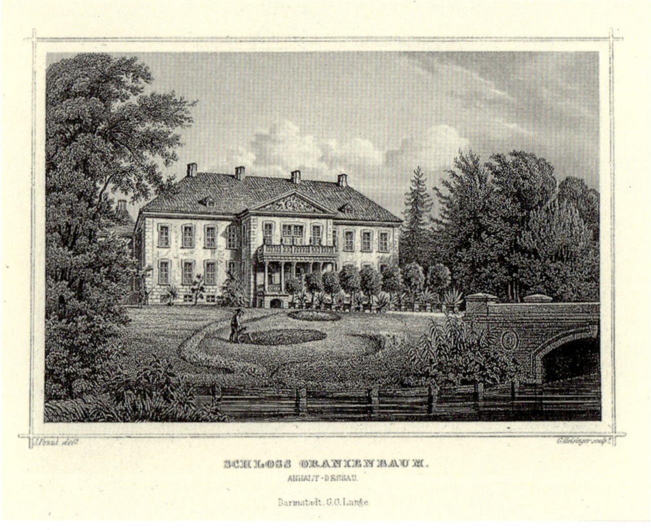

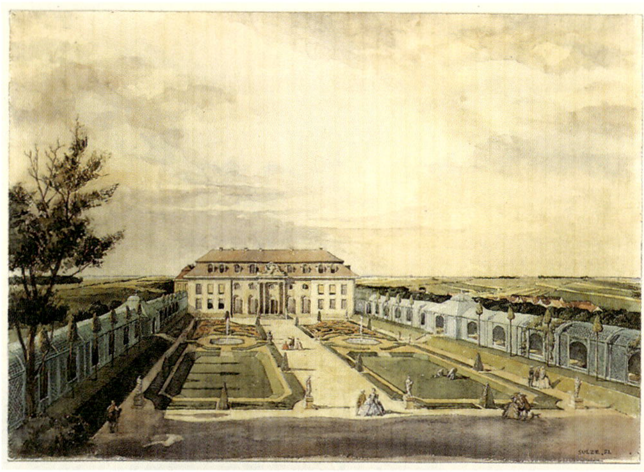

28

G. Heisinger (dates of birth and death unknown)
after Jacobo Pozzi (1814–1897)
SCHLOSS ORANIENBAUM, PARKSEITE
SCHLOSS ORANIENBAUM, PARKSIDE VIEW
1861
Steel engraving
15.2 x 23.8 cm, cropped
Inscription: lower left below the picture "J. Pozzi del.t"; right "G. Heisinger scul.t"; centre "Schloss Oranienbaum. / Anhalt Dessau. / Darmstadt. G. G. Lange"
Kulturstiftung DessauWörlitz

Henriette Catharina von Oranien-Nassau began redesigning Oranienbaum as a summer residence in 1683. The result was the unified baroque ensemble consisting of *Schloß*, park and city structure based upon plans drawn by the architect Cornelis Ryckwaert. Located behind the three-winged castle building was a formal Dutch-style garden very similar to the garden designed by Daniel Marot in Zeist in Holland. The garden was originally subdivided into sections, of which the parterre formed the centrepiece, comprising a pond or island garden, a labyrinth, a zoological garden, a pheasantry and an orange grove. The first modifications were undertaken under the rule of Prince Franz, who had the eastern island garden converted into an English-style *jardin chinois*. The engraving shows the garden parterre with its extensive flower beds and and shrubs.

29

Heinrich Sulze (1888–1958)
SCHLOSS UND PARK MOSIGKAU, SÜDLICHE ANSICHT
MOSIGKAU CASTLE AND PARK, VIEW FROM THE SOUTH
1952
Water-colour (copy)
73.0 x 49.5 cm
Signed on the lower edge of the picture: SULZE, 52
Kulturstiftung DessauWörlitz

The isometric image shows a draft for the reconstruction of the Mosigkau *Schloßgarten* by Heinrich Sulze, the Dresden Professor of garden design. The late baroque grounds of Mosigkau in the western portion of the garden kingdom were put in place beginning in 1752/53 for Anna Wilhelmina, an aunt of Prince Franz's. Parts of the garden of delights featuring a carousel, hedge-lined bowling lanes and a labyrinth were redesigned in the English style beginning in 1777. The three-winged *Schloß* was presumably based upon plans drawn by the Berlin architect Georg Wenzeslaus von Knobelsdorff, who was engaged in the redesign and reconstruction of the residence castle in Dessau at the time. The Mosigkau garden is one of the few extensively preserved rococo ensembles in central Germany.

30

Israel Salomon Probst (worked circa 1784)
after Johann Christian Neumark (1741–1811)
ERKLÄRUNG DES GRUNDRISSES DES GARTENS ZU WÖRLITZ
DESCRIPTION OF THE PLAN OF THE GARDEN AT WÖRLITZ
1784
Copper engraving
53.2 x 46.6 cm
Inscription: lower left below the picture "Neumark f."; right "J. S. Probst. sculp Dessau 1784"
Institut für Auslandsbeziehungen

In 1764 work was begun in Wörlitz on a garden praised as the "ornament and epitome of the 18th century", the first significant example of the English art of landscape gardening in Germany, the cradle of Neoclassicism and late Gothic art and architecture. The first description of the garden, which would soon cover more than 100 hectares of land, was published by August Rode under commission by the Prince in 1788. The second edition of 1798 contains this slightly amended garden plan prepared by the Wörlitz court gardener Johann Christian Neumark in 1784. The relatively simple, schematic, yet highly detailed representation intended for visitors to the grounds shows the state of the garden fifteen years prior to its completion.

Erklärung der Buchstaben.
TAB:1.
Erklärung des Grundrisses des Gartens zu Wörlitz.

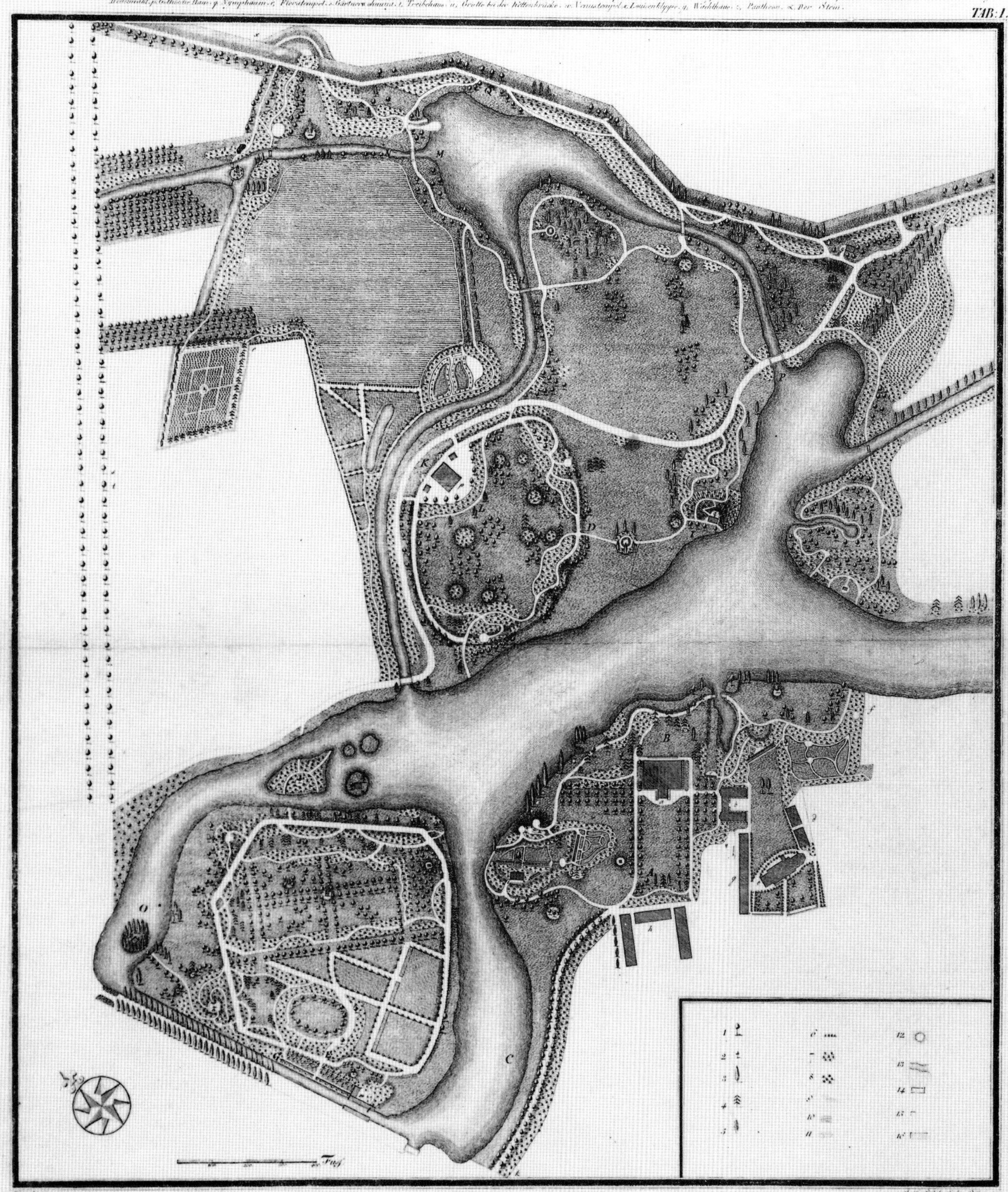

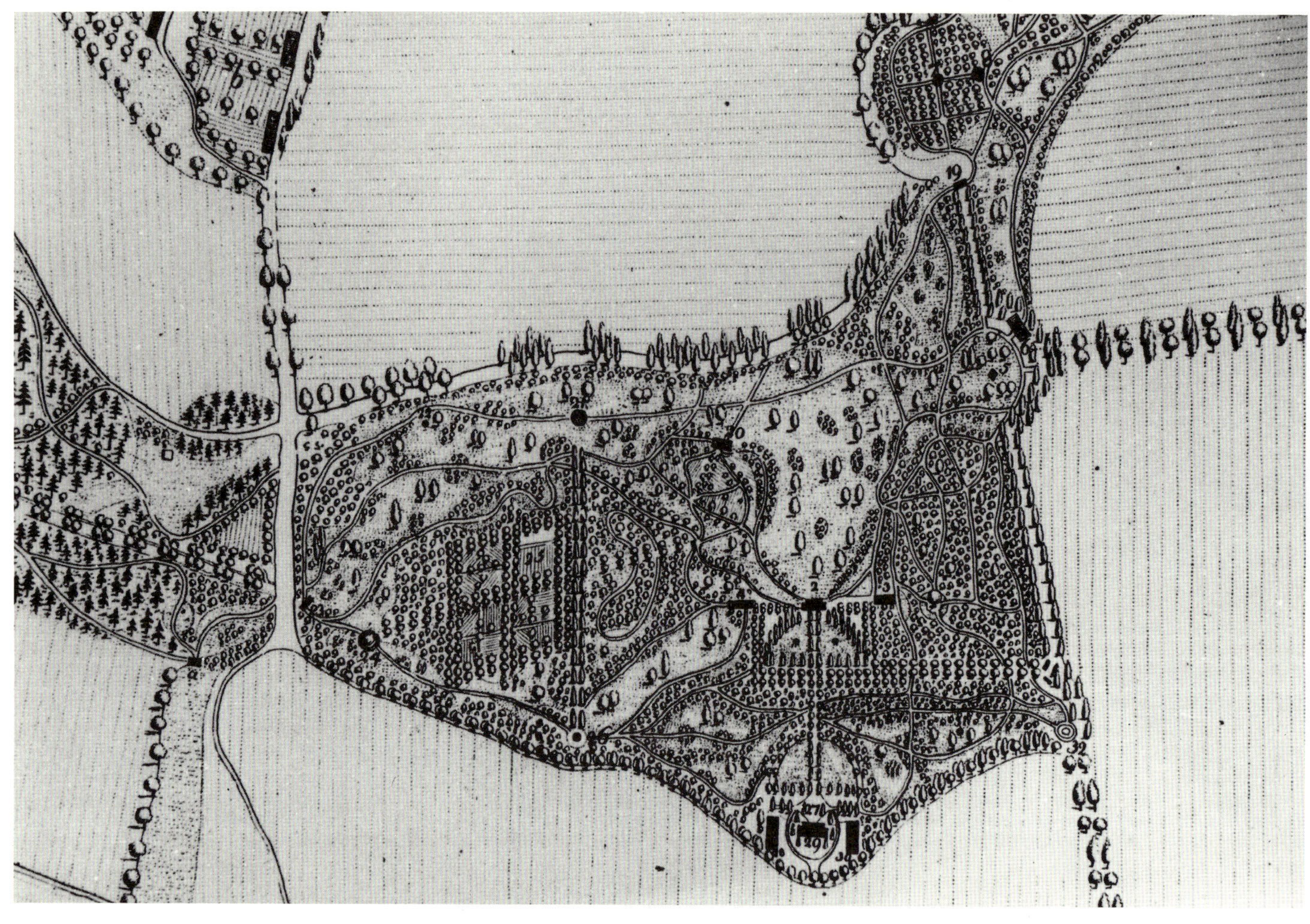

31

Johann Friedrich Rosmaesler (circa 1775–1858)

after Dietrich Klewitz (1767–1840)

GESAMTPLAN DER ANLAGEN DES PRINZEN HANS JÜRGE
(GEORGENGARTEN)

FULL PLAN OF THE GARDENS OF PRINCE HANS JÜRGE
(GEORGENGARTEN)

1796

Copper engraving

91.4 x 59.0 cm

Inscription: lower left below the picture "Dietrich Klewitz del."; right
"Rosmaesler sc."

Kulturstiftung DessauWörlitz

Work on the *Georgengarten*, the summer residence of Prince Hans Jürge,
younger brother of Prince Franz and the jewel of the western portion of the
garden kingdom, was begun in 1780. The young prince commissioned Erdmannsdorff to build a small country house, given the name *Georgium*, for
him in a wooded lowland area north of Dessau. The area around the building
was converted into a spacious English-style garden embellished, like the
grounds in Wörlitz, with Neoclassical park architecture. Garden sculptures
were added to complete the ensemble. Because of its size and natural appearance, the *Georgengarten* was considered by some contemporaries as superior
to its counterpart in Wörlitz.

I. Bäume und Sträucher.

1. Acer Pseudoplatanus.   Gemein weißer Ahorn.
2. Acer Platanoides.   Lenne.
3. Acer campestre.   Der kleine deutsche Ahorn.
4. Acer majus foliis variegatis.   Gemeiner Ahorn mit scheckigen Blättern.
5. Acer striatum.   Nordamerikanisch gestreifter Ahorn.
6. Acer Platanoides foliis variegatis.   Lenne mit gescheckten Blatt.
7. Acer sacharinum.   Zuckerahorn.
8. Acer rubrum. Nordamerikanischer rothblühender Ahorn.
9. Acer tasiocarpos.   Ist eine Abänderung von dem Acer rubrum.
10. Acer Pensylvanicum.   Nordamerikanischer Bergahorn.
11. Acer Monspessulanum.   Der französische Ahorn.
12. Acer Tartaricum.   Tartarischer Ahorn.
13. Acer creticum.   Der kleinblättrige Kretische Ahorn.
14. Acer Negundo.   Virginischer Eschenblättriger Ahorn.
15. Acer Opalus.   Der Italiänische Opalbaum.
16. Acer laciniatum.   Spitzahorn mit tief eingeschnittenen runzlichen Blättern.
17. Acer sempervirens.   Immergrüner Ahorn.
18. Aesculus Hippocastanum.   Gemeine Roßkastanie.

32
Johann Georg Schoch (1758–1826)
VERZEICHNIS DER EIN- UND AUSLÄNDISCHEN BÄUME,
STRÄUCHER, PFLANZEN UND STAUDEN SO IN DEM
HOCHFÜRSTL. WÖRTLITZER GARTEN BEFINDLICH
CATALOGUE OF NATIVE AND IMPORTED TREES, BUSHES,
PLANTS AND SHRUBS IN THE WÖRLITZ GARDEN OF HIS
MAJESTY THE PRINCE
From: August Rode, *Beschreibung des Fürstlichen Anhalt-Dessauischen Land-
hauses und Englischen Gartens zu Wörlitz* (Dessau: 1814)
19.5 x 25.0 cm (each)
Kulturstiftung DessauWörlitz

The index of plants compiled by gardener Johann Georg Schoch lists 462
types of trees and bushes and 644 species of shrubs and exotic flora found
growing in the Wörlitz gardens or raised in the nurseries. The Prince himself
promoted the importation of rare plants and brought back seeds from his own
travels. The nurseries of Wörlitz were soon supplying rare kinds of trees and
bushes for other English-style gardens being created beyond the borders of
Anhalt-Dessau.

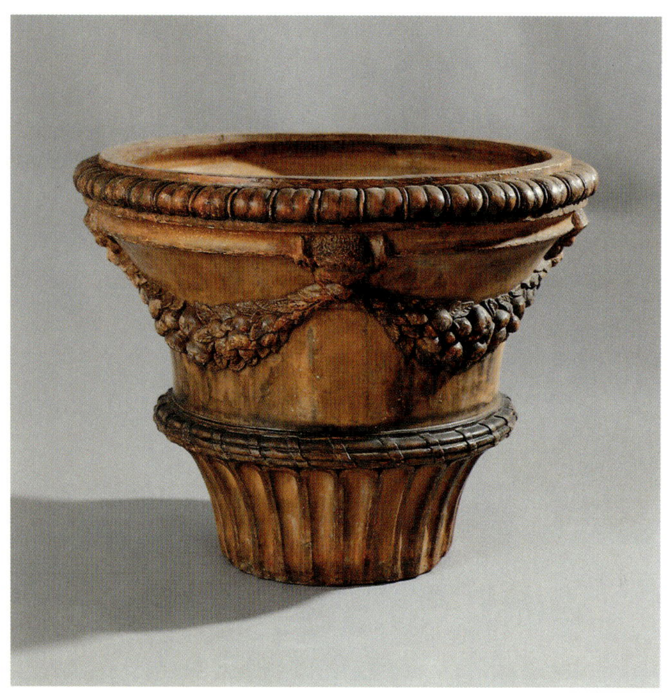 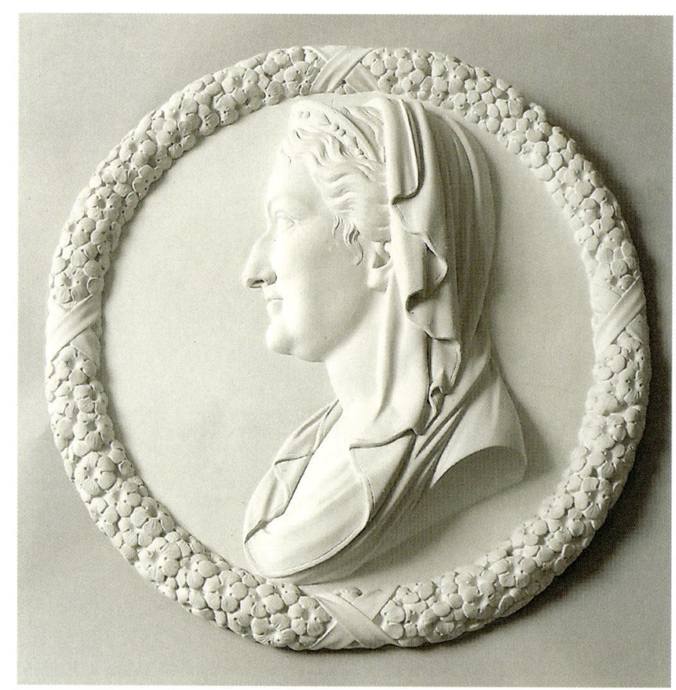

33
Vergile and Carlo Agroste (active circa 1800)
PFLANZGEFÄSS VOM BLUMENTHEATER IM FLORA-
GARTEN
PLANT POT FROM THE THEATRE OF FLOWERS IN THE
FLORAGARTEN
Circa 1800
Terra-cotta
Height: 42.0 cm, diameter: 54.0 cm
Kulturstiftung DessauWörlitz

Prince Franz purchased terra-cotta pots for his "Theatre of Flowers" in the
Wörlitz *Floragarten* in Impruneta. The semi-circular steps of the "Theatre of
Flowers", which call to mind an ancient amphitheatre, provided space onto
which plant-bearing vessels could be placed. Using pots and vases made the
replacement of perishable blooming plants much easier.
Plants, pots and Neoclassical architecture combined to create a unity of
design and were meant to evoke thoughts of Italy, the country of origin.

34
Friedemann Hunold (1773–1840)
PORTRAITRELIEF DER HERZOGIN LUISE VON ANHALT-
DESSAU
RELIEF PORTRAIT OF DUCHESS LUISE VON ANHALT-
DESSAU
1823
Plaster (cast to scale of the marble original in the royal mausoleum in the
tower of the church at Jönitz)
Diameter: 54.0 cm
Kulturstiftung DessauWörlitz

The medallion-shaped relief portrait decorates the front of the sarcophagus
bearing the remains of Luise, which was placed in the mausoleum tower of
the church in Jönitz. Franz himself supervised the initial construction work,
begun in 1816, from the *Luisium* but did not live to see it completed. The
building was completed during the rule of his grandson and successor Leopold
Friedrich and given the following inscription (translated): "Luise Henriette
Wilhelmine/Duchess of Anhalt/born Magravine of Brandenburg Schwedt,
Princess of Pruss./born XXIV September MDCCL. dec. XXI December
MDCCXI./She was of a noble heart and mind. Benefactress of the needy."

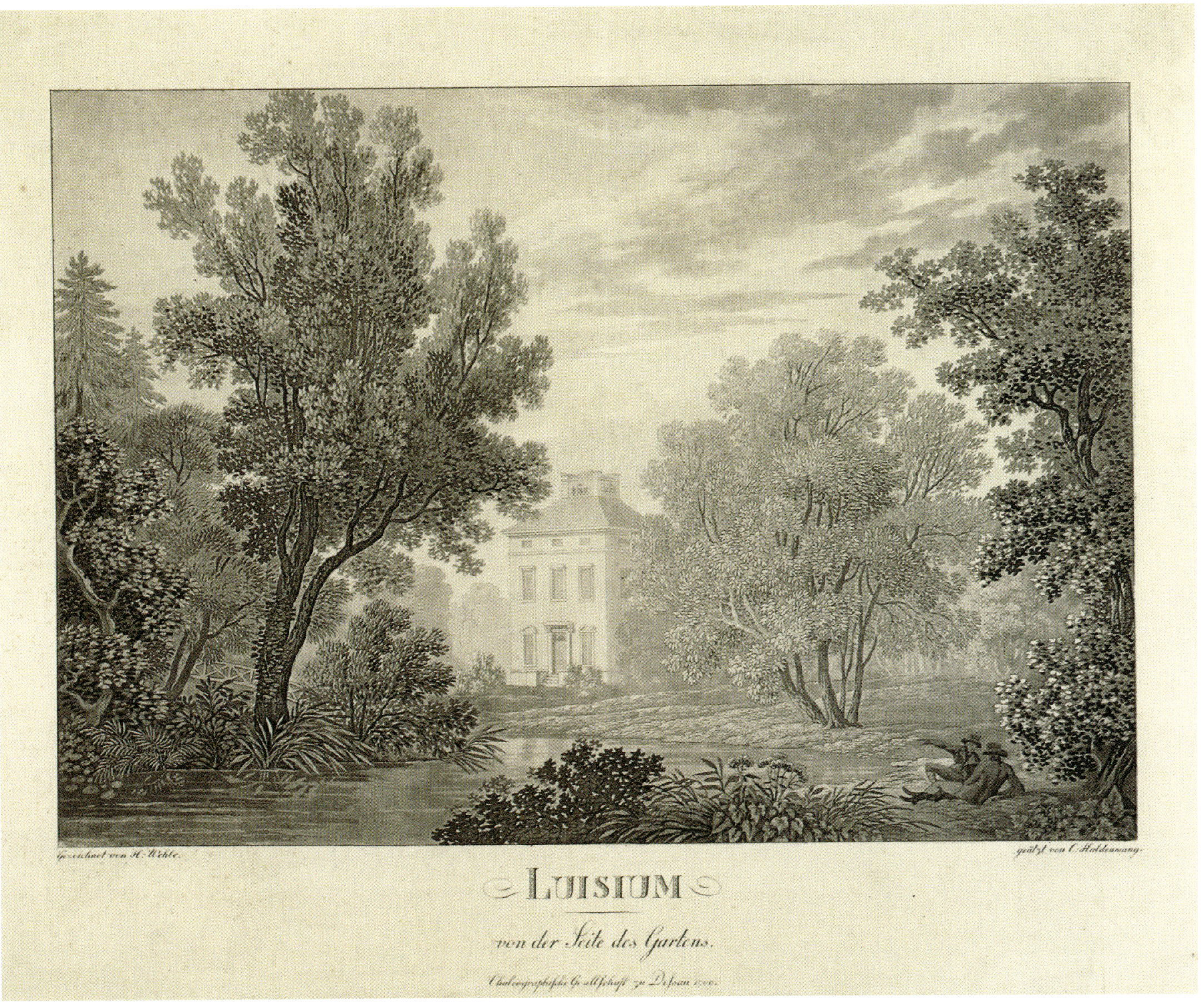

35
Christian Haldenwang (1770–1831)
after Heinrich Theodor Wehle (1778–1805)
LUISIUM VON DER SEITE DES GARTENS
LUISIUM VIEWED FROM THE GARDEN
1799
Aquatint
25.8 x 33.6 cm
Inscription (translated): lower left below the picture "Drawn by H. Wehle";
right "etched by C. Haldenwang."; centre "Luisium/View from the Garden./
Chalcographische Gesellschaft of Dessau 1799."
Institut für Auslandsbeziehungen

Prince Franz had the Neoclassical country house depicted in this etching
built by Erdmannsdorff between 1774 and 1778 as a residence for his wife
Luise, for whom the structure was also named. Visible in the foreground of
the two-storey building is the lake around which the elements comprising the
Luisium are grouped. Prince Franz had spent his youth in the *Vogelherd*, the
building and grounds that had formerly occupied the site. He died in the
house shown here on August 9th, 1817 after suffering a riding accident several
days before.

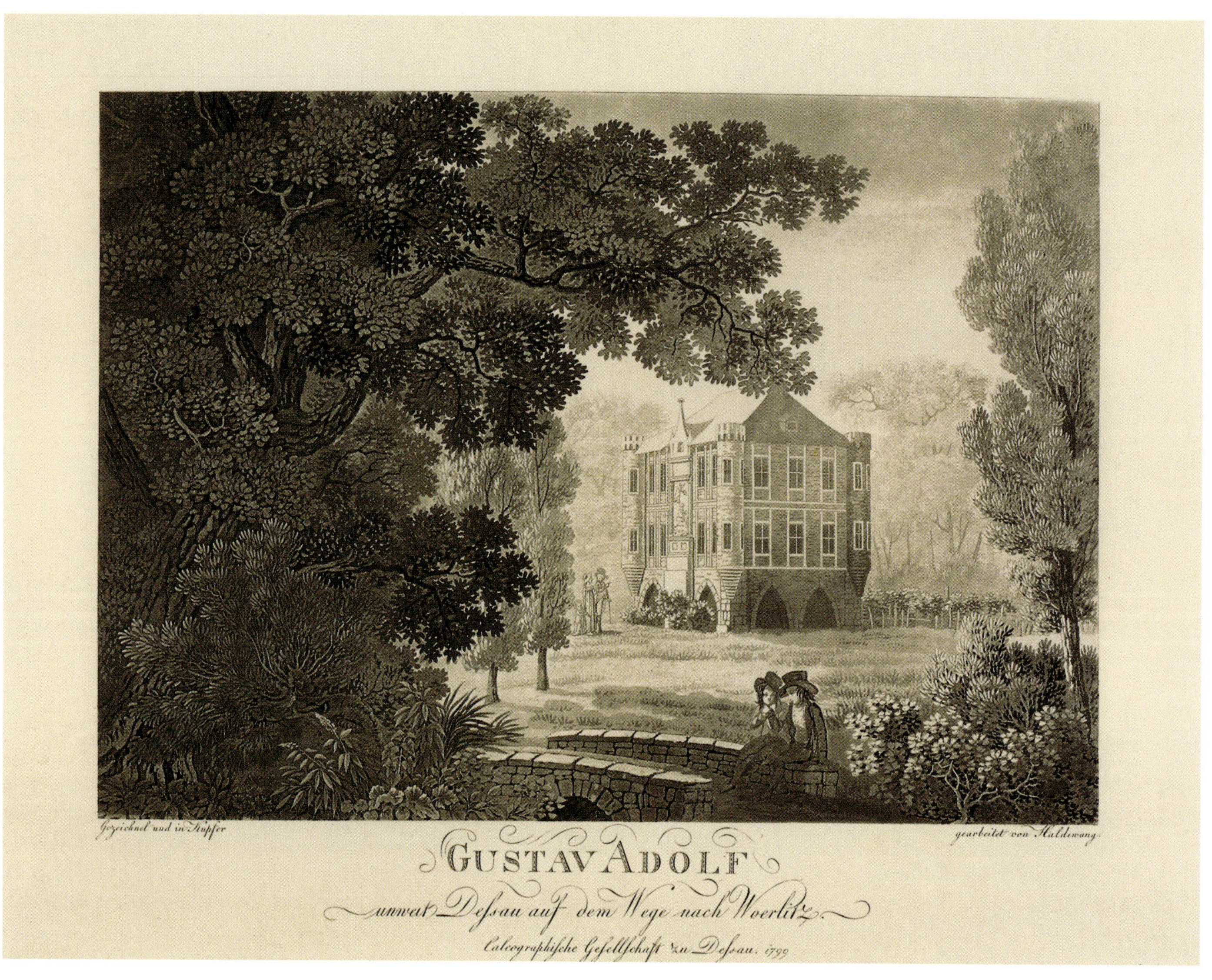

36
Christian Haldenwang (1770–1831)
GUSTAV ADOLF UNWEIT DESSAU AUF DEM WEGE NACH
WOERLITZ
GUSTAV ADOLF NEAR DESSAU ON THE WAY TO WOERLITZ
1799
Aquatint
25.6 x 32.9 cm
Inscription (translated): lower left below the picture "drawn and [engraved] in
copper"; right "by Haldenwang"; centre "Gustav Adolf / near Dessau on his
Way to Woerlitz. / Calcographische Gesellschaft of Dessau 1799"
Institut für Auslandsbeziehungen

The Neogothic building known as the *Gustav Adolf* or the *Schwedenhaus*,
located on the road between Dessau and Wörlitz, was initially built by order
of Prince Franz between 1784 and 1786. It was initially intended to serve as a
dike watchman's house for the purpose of flood protection. Franz later gave it
to the Swedish Baron von Greifenheim as a country residence. Covering the
two upper storeys of the front façade was a decorative sandstone relief depicting the Swedish King Gustav Adolf (1594–1632) on horseback being crowned
by the goddess Victoria. According to legend, Gustav Adolf had concealed
himself from imperial enemy troops nearby during the Thirty Years' War. The
Schwedenhaus was destroyed in 1982.

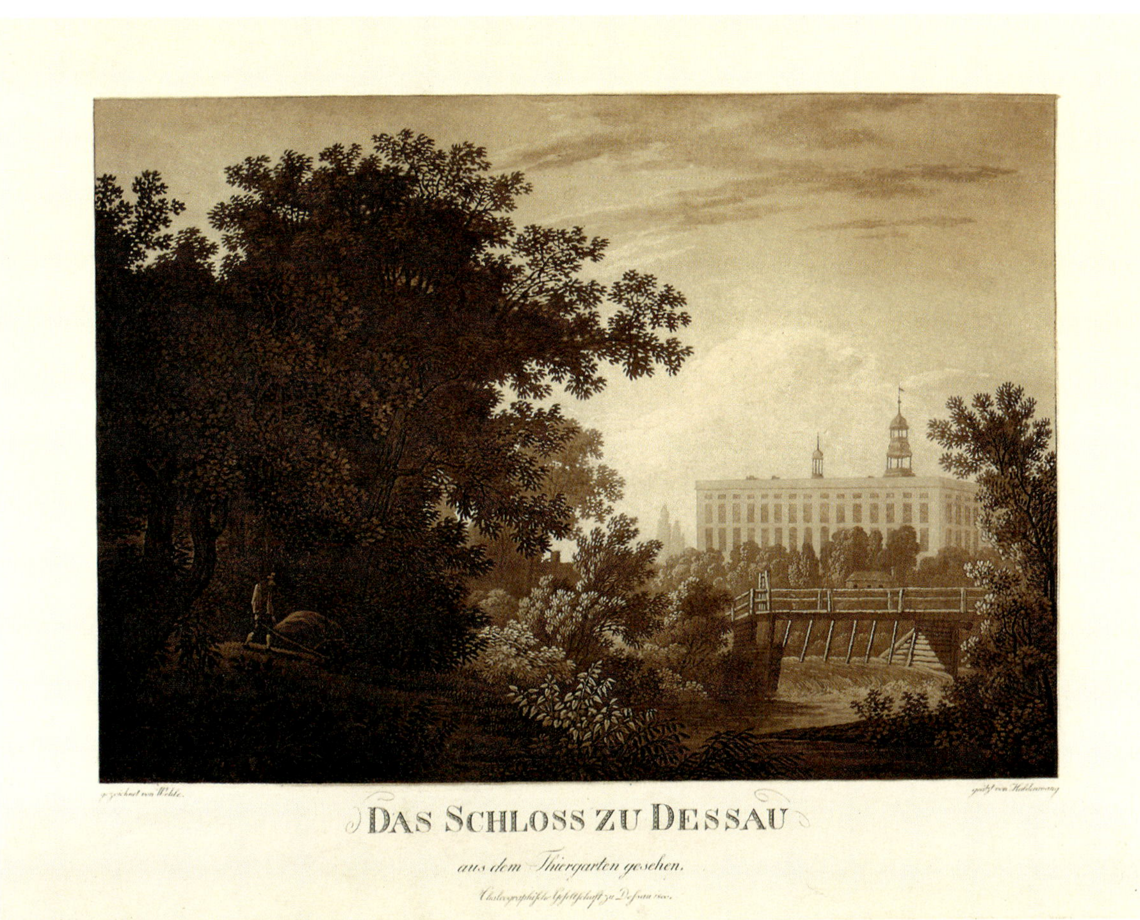

DAS SCHLOSS ZU DESSAU

aus dem Thiergarten gesehen.

Chalcographische Gesellschaft zu Dessau 1800.

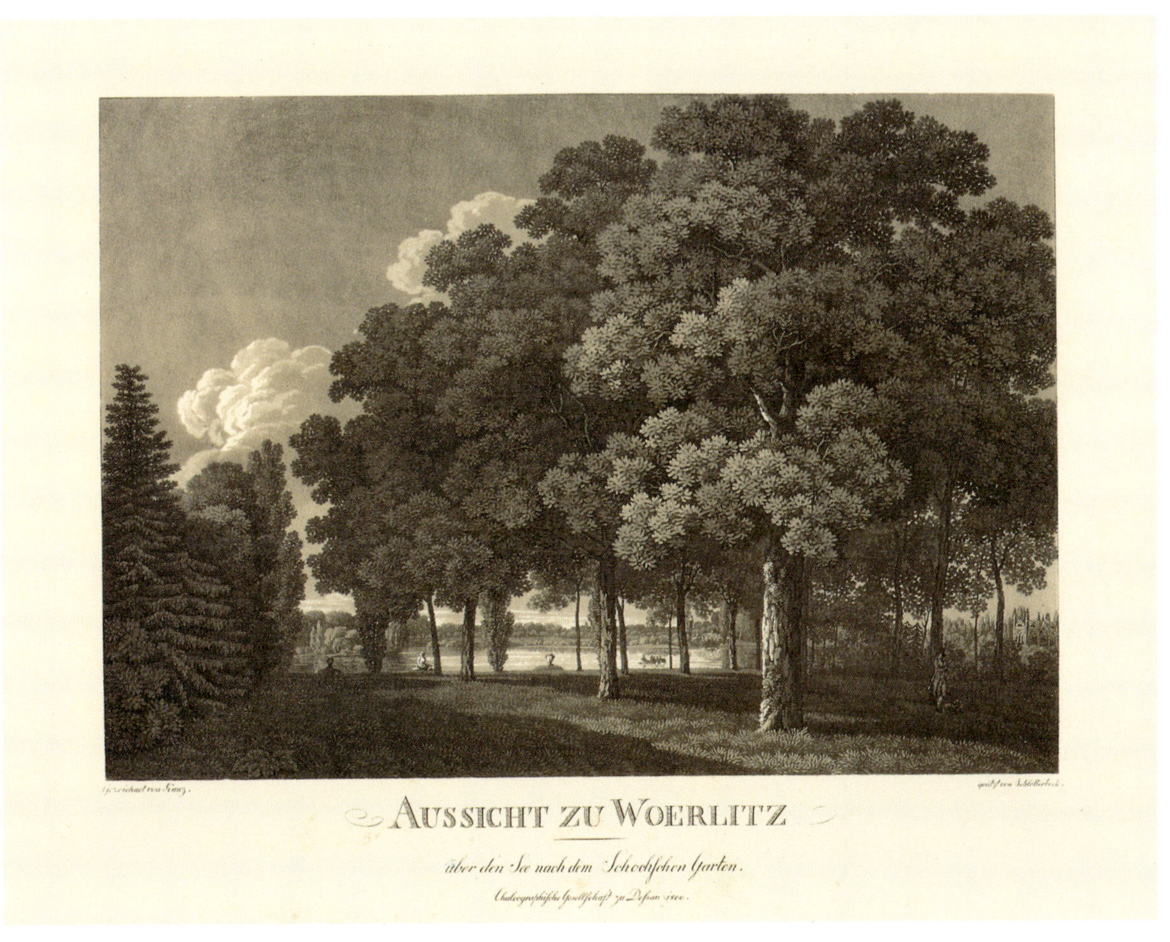

AUSSICHT ZU WOERLITZ

über den See nach dem Schochschen Garten.

Chalcographische Gesellschaft zu Dessau 1800.

37   Ill. p. 111

Christian Haldenwang (1770–1831)

after Heinrich Theodor Wehle (1778–1805)

DAS SCHLOSS ZU DESSAU AUS DEM THIERGARTEN
GESEHEN

THE SCHLOSS IN DESSAU VIEWED FROM THE GAME
PRESERVE

1800

Aquatint

25.5 x 34.2 cm

Inscription (translated): lower left below the picture "Drawn by H. Wehle";
right "etched by C. Haldenwang."; centre "THE SCHLOSS IN DESSAU /
viewed from the game preserve. / Chalcographische Gesellschaft of Dessau
1800."

Kulturstiftung DessauWörlitz

The etching shows a view of the southwest wing of the Dessau *Stadtschloß*
from the *Tiergarten* (game preserve). This wing of the *Schloß* was built by
Georg Wenzeslaus von Knobelsdorff (1699–1753) in 1747, an architect who
worked primarily in Prussia. The old Renaissance garden was converted by
Erdmannsdorff to a garden of delights in the style of an ancient hippodrome
in 1775.

Visible in the foreground is the so-called *Gestänge* (a scaffolded bridge construction) across the Mulde weir, which forms the entryway to the *Tiergarten*.
The *Tiergarten* was originally a royal game reserve enclosed by a fence. First
steps towards redesigning the area, including plantings of new trees and
shrubbery, had already been undertaken in the 17th century. Efforts to beautify
the *Tiergarten*, located along the easternmost boundary of the city of Dessau,
were pursued in earnest during the reign of Prince Franz.

38   Ill. p. 111

Wilhelm Friedrich Schlotterbeck (1770–1819)

after Karl Kuntz (1770–1830)

AUSSICHT ZU WOERLITZ ÜBER DEN SEE NACH DEM
SCHOCHSCHEN GARTEN

VIEW OF WOERLITZ ACROSS THE LAKE TOWARDS THE
SCHOCHSCHER GARTEN

1800

Aquatint

25.7 x 33.2 cm

Inscription (translated): lower left below the picture "Drawn by H. Kunz";
right "etched by Schlotterbeck."; centre "View of Woerlitz / across the lake
towards the Schochscher Garten./ Chalcographische Gesellschaft of Dessau
1800."

Institut für Auslandsbeziehungen

This etching showing the Wörlitz *Schloßgarten* is also part of the series of
scenes from the garden kingdom published by the Calcographische Gesellschaft. The lime trees left over from the earlier baroque garden complex had
formerly been pruned to a box shape but were now allowed to grow naturally,
in keeping with the new view of nature. Visible in the background are the
evocative image of a woman searching for shells, the *Roseninsel* and the landscaped configurations on the opposite bank of the river. The garden-side
façade of the Gothic-style house in the so-called *Schochscher Garten* can be
seen on the right-hand side of the picture.

39

Christian Haldenwang (1770–1831)

after Heinrich Theodor Wehle (1778–1805)

WALLWITZBERG ZU DEN ANLAGEN VOM GEORGEN
GARTEN GEHÖRIG

WALLWITZBERG, BELONGING TO THE GROUNDS OF THE
GEORGEN GARTEN

1800

Aquatint

25.8 x 33.9 cm

Inscription (translated): lower left below the picture "drawn by H. Wehle";
right "etched by C. Haldenwang."; centre "Wallwitzberg / belonging to the
grounds of the Georgen Garten. / Chalcographische Gesellschaft of Dessau
1800."

Institut für Auslandsbeziehungen

The artificial ruins of the *Wallwitzburg* were constructed of Gothic forms in
the northern section of the *Georgengarten* in Dessau near the end of the 18th
century. The ruins stood on a hill some 30 metres above the water-level of the
Elbe and offered superb vantage points from which to view the surrounding
countryside as far into the distance as Zerbst and Wörlitz. The structure lies
in complete ruin today.

40

Wilhelm Friedrich Schlotterbeck (1770–1819)

after Karl Kuntz (1770–1830)

DAS NYMPHEUM IN WOERLITZ

THE NYMPHEUM IN WOERLITZ

1800

Aquatint

26.7 x 34.0 cm

Inscription (translated): lower left below the picture "drawn by Kunz"; right
"etched by Schlotterbeck."; centre "The Nympheum in Woerlitz / Chalcographische Gesellschaft of Dessau 1800."

Institut für Auslandsbeziehungen

The Nympheum, built by Erdmannsdorff in 1767/68, was the first building
erected on the opposite bank of the lake. It was dedicated to the naiads, or
water nymphs, and served as a garden rest spot and outlook for the *Englischer
Sitz* (English Seat) in the *Schloßgarten* on the near side of the water. The
poet Matthisson enjoyed spending time here, which explains the popular
designation of the plane tree depicted in the centre of the picture as the
"Matthison Plane". Visible near the right-hand edge of the picture is the
synagogue built in 1789/90 as a smaller replica of the Vestal Temple on the
bank of the Tiber in Rome.

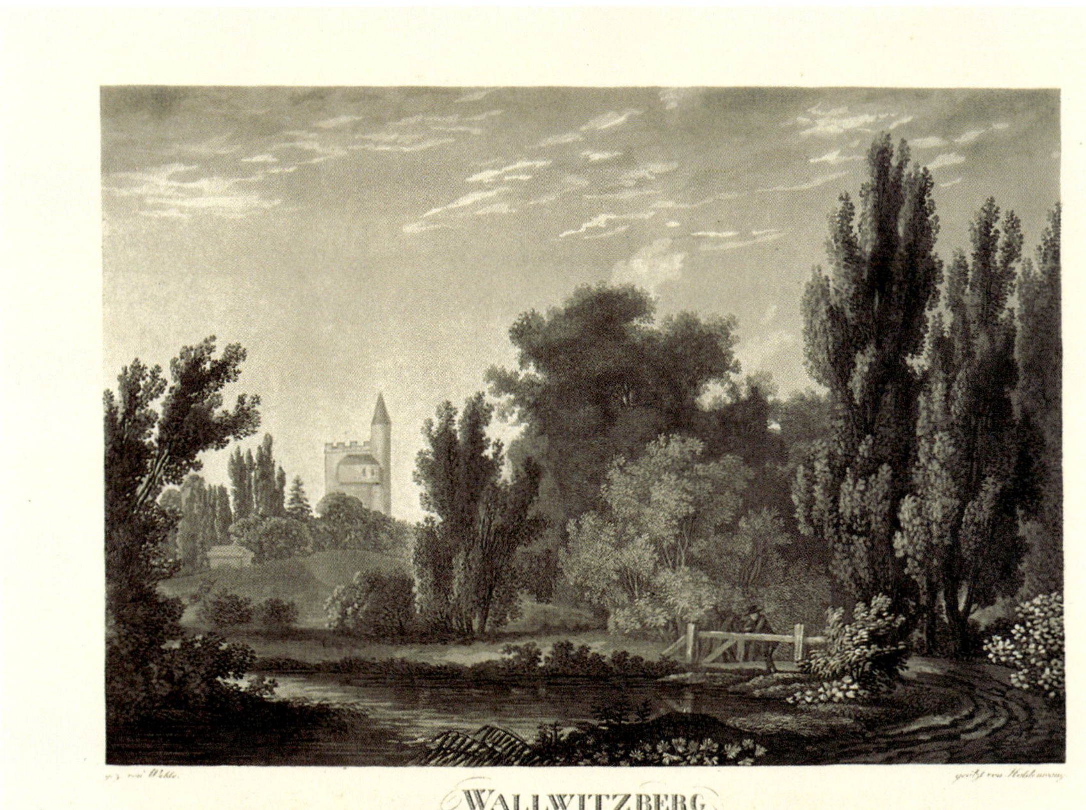

WALLWITZBERG

zu den Anlagen vom Georgen Garten gehörig.

Chalcographische Gesellschaft zu Dessau 1800

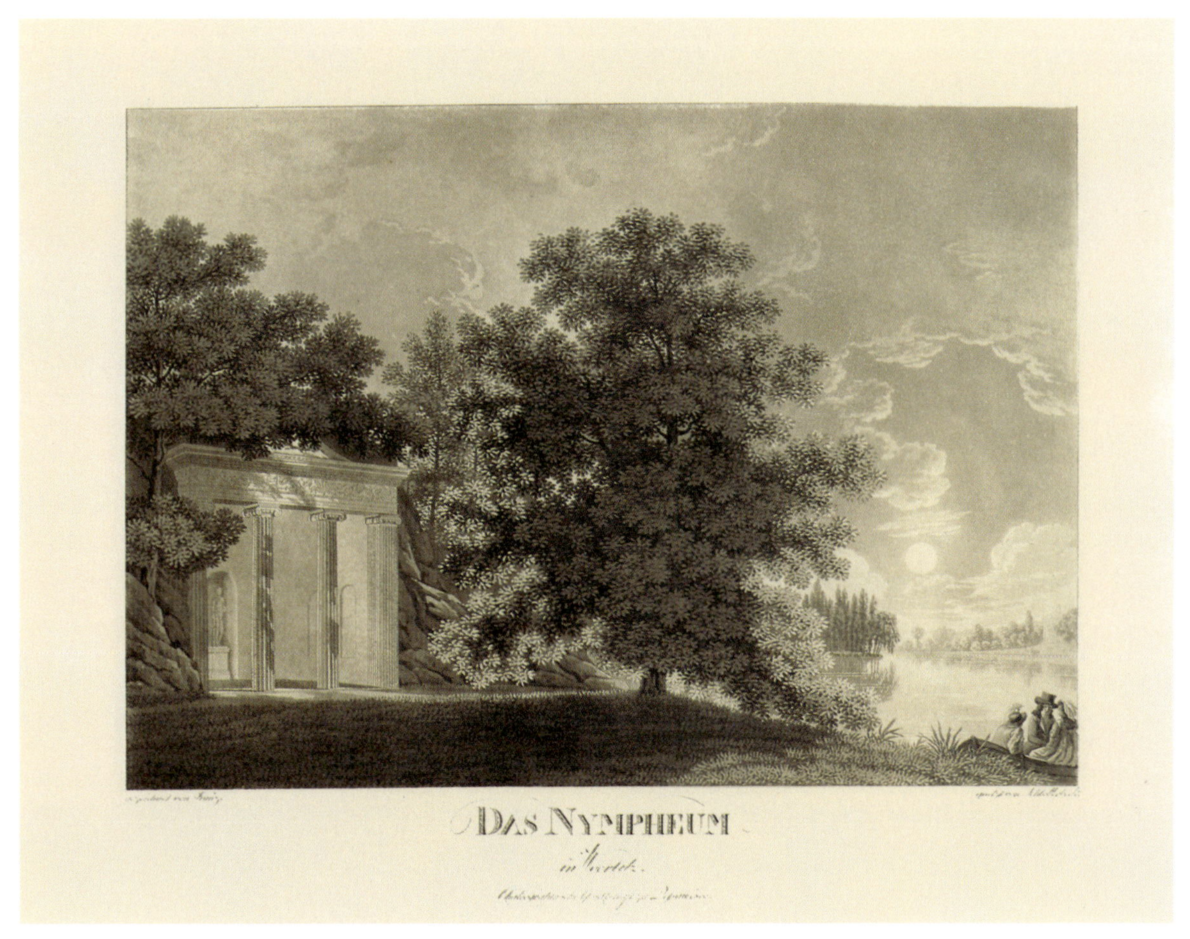

DAS NYMPHEUM

in Wörlitz.

Chalcographische Gesellschaft zu Dessau

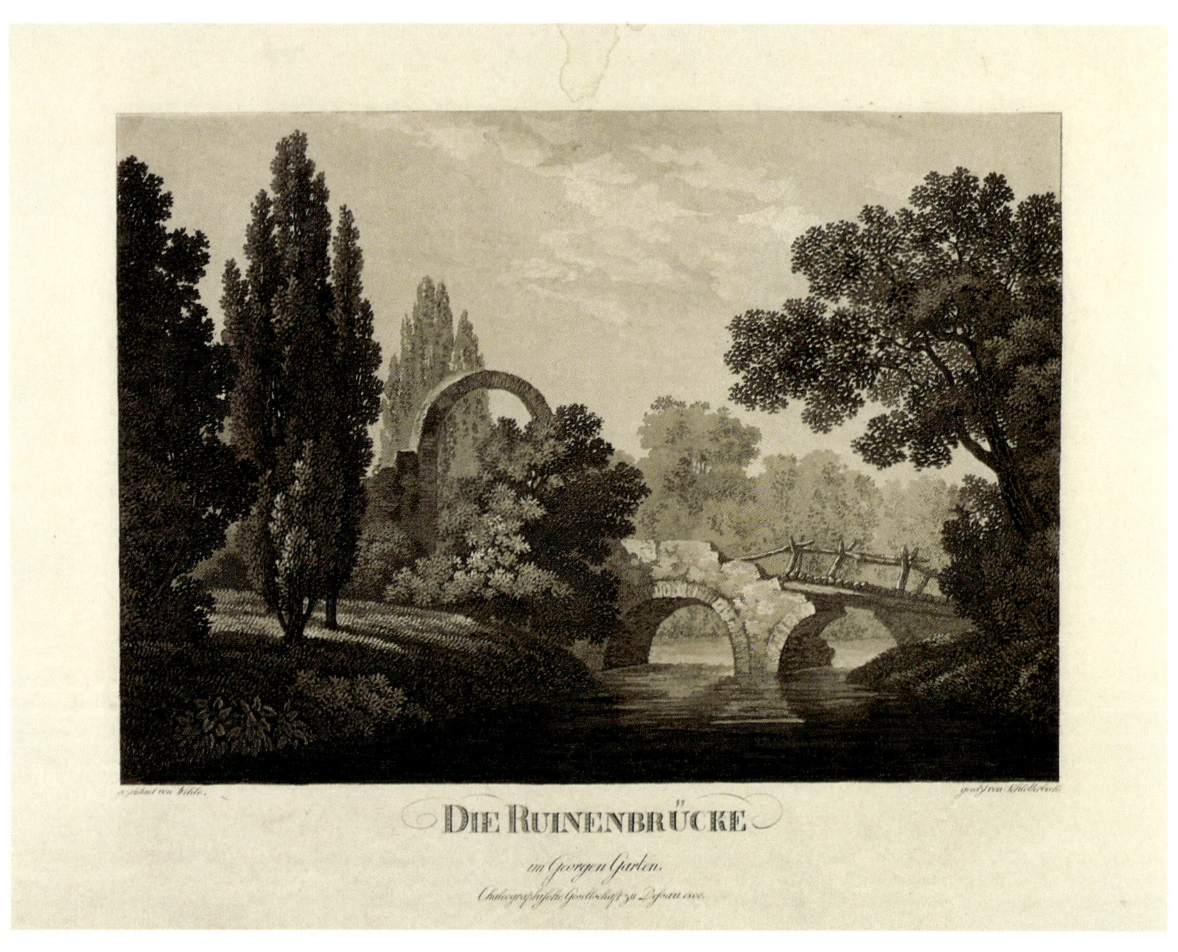

Die Ruinenbrücke

im Georgen Garten.

Chalcographische Gesellschaft zu Dessau 1800.

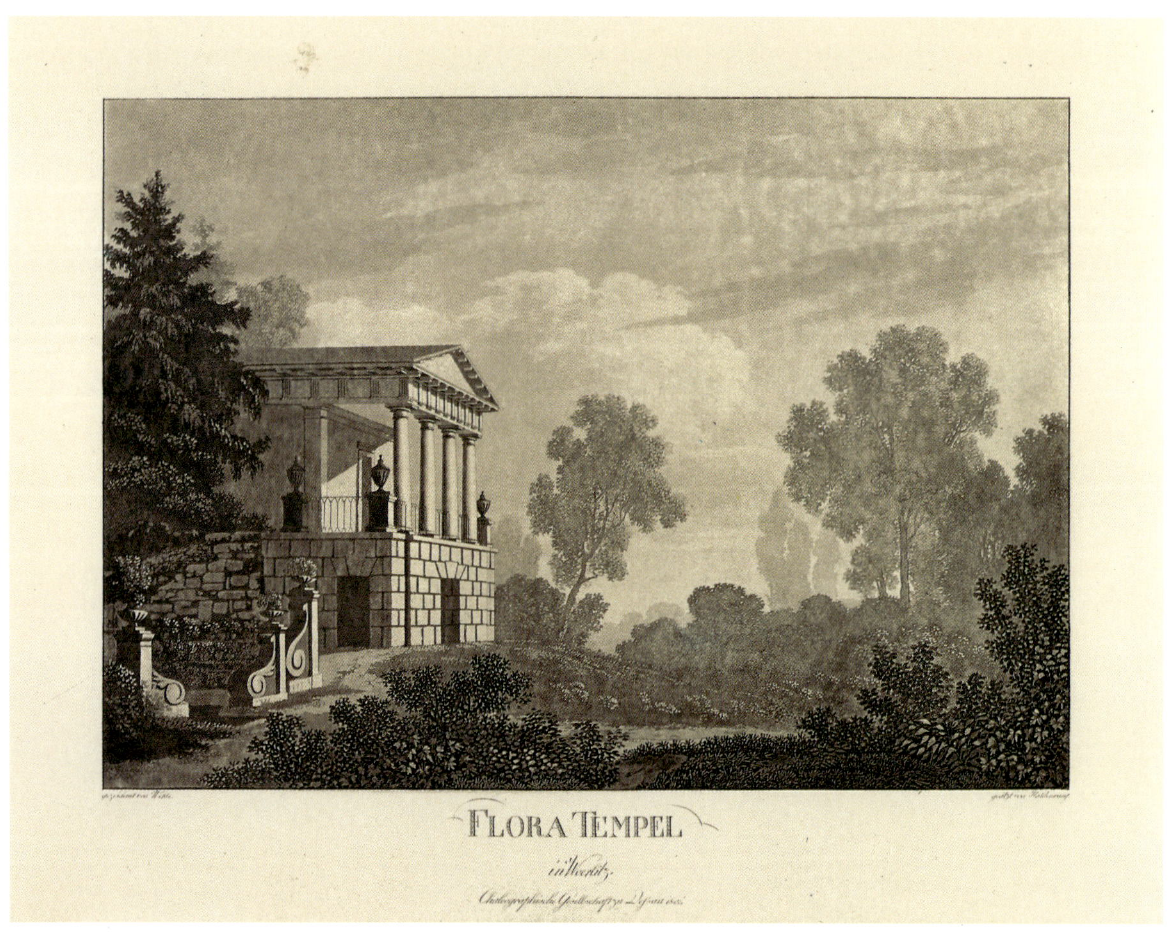

Flora Tempel

in Wörlitz.

Chalcographische Gesellschaft zu Dessau 1800.

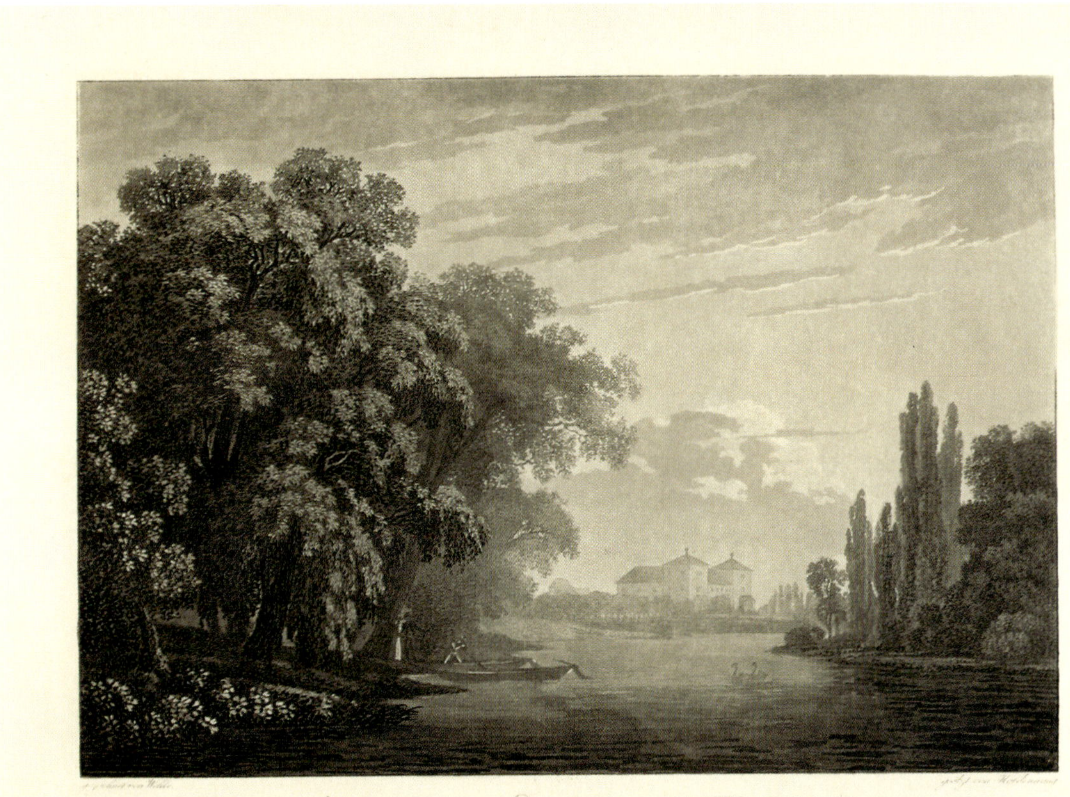

ANSICHT DES GASTHOF'S ZU WOERLITZ

von dem See.

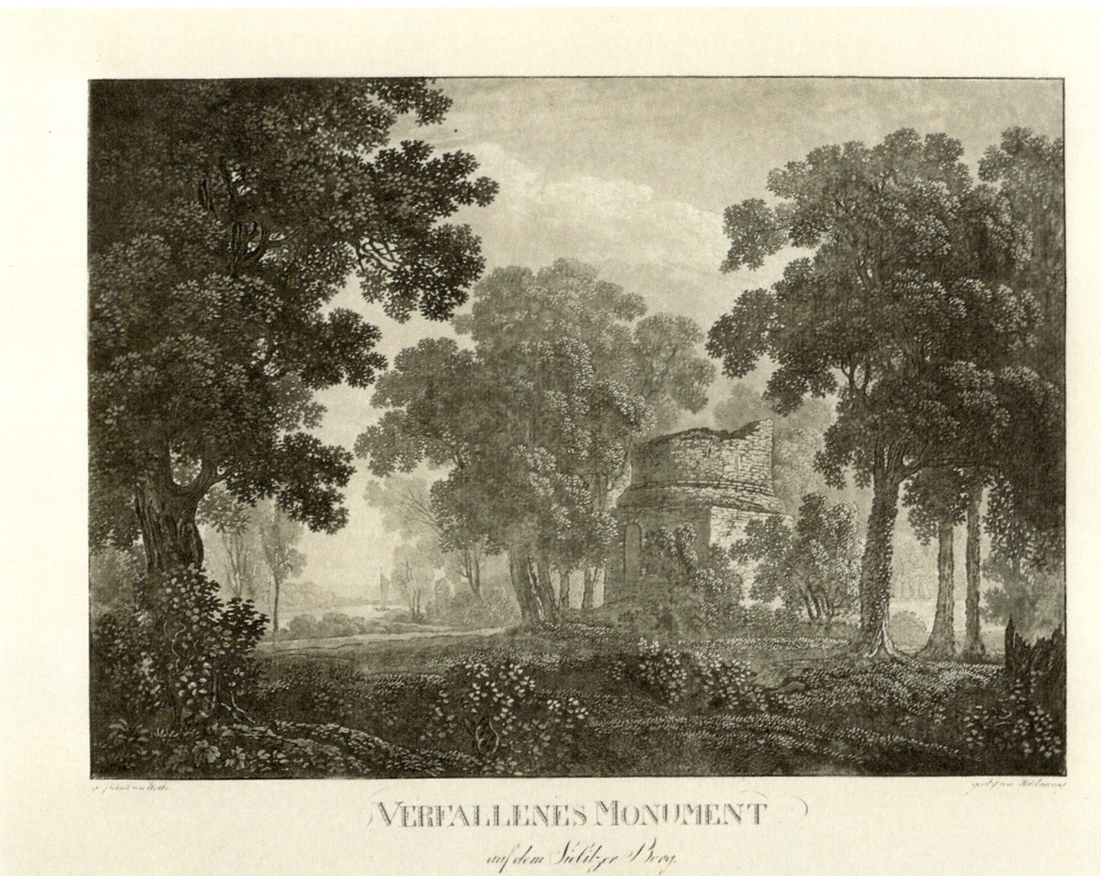

VERFALLENES MONUMENT

auf dem Sieblitzer Berg.

41   Ill. p. 114

Wilhelm Friedrich Schlotterbeck (1770–1819)
after Heinrich Theodor Wehle (1778–1805)
DIE RUINENBRÜCKE IM GEORGEN GARTEN
THE BRIDGE IN RUINS IN THE GEORGEN GARTEN
1800
Aquatint
26.5 x 39.9 cm
Inscription (translated): lower left below the picture "drawn by Wehle"; right
"etched by Schlotterbeck."; centre "The Bridge of Ruins in the Georgen
Garten / Chalcographische Gesellschaft of Dessau 1800."
Institut für Auslandsbeziehungen

The artificial ruins were designed on the basis of an illustration in C. C. L.
Hirschfeld's *Theorie der Gartenkunst.* The bridge, which marks the transition
from the *Georgengarten* proper to the *Beckerbruch,* was described as follows
by August Rode: "The front portions of both arches as well as most of the side
walls have been destroyed. Rough tree trunks laid lengthwise and other, thin-
ner ones placed at right angles to them and covered by boards nailed to them
in makeshift fashion make it possible to traverse the broken arch. The hand-
rails are comprised of defoliated branches."

42   Ill. p. 114

Christian Haldenwang (1770–1831)
after Heinrich Theodor Wehle (1778–1805)
FLORA TEMPEL IN WOERLITZ
THE FLORATEMPEL IN WOERLITZ
1801
Aquatint
26.0 x 33.8 cm
Inscription (translated): lower left below the picture "drawn by Wehle"; right
"etched by C. Haldenwang."; centre "Flora Tempel / in Woerlitz / Chalcographische Gesellschaft of Dessau 1801."
Institut für Auslandsbeziehungen

Built between 1796 and 1798 according to plans drawn by Erdmannsdorff, the
architecture of the *Floratempel* in Woerlitz is modelled on components of the
ancient shrine of Clitumnus near Spoleto, or to be more precise, on Sir William Chambers' reproduction of the shrine in the gardens of Wilton in England. The upper floor designed and furnished as a music room was decorated
with floral motifs painted by Johann Fischer. The ground floor was used to
store tools and equipment for the nearby horticultural nursery. The *Floratempel* and the "Theatre of Flowers" visible on the left-hand side of the picture were part of the *Floragarten,* the only section of the *Wörlitzer Garten* in
which an abundance of flowers was to be found.

43   Ill. p. 115

Christian Haldenwang (1770–1831)
after Heinrich Theodor Wehle (1778–1805)
ANSICHT DES GASTHOFS ZU WOERLITZ VON DEM SEE
VIEW OF THE INN AT WOERLITZ FROM THE LAKE
1801
Aquatint
25.3 x 32.7 cm
Inscription (translated): lower left below the picture "drawn by Wehle";
right "etched by Haldenwang."; centre "View of the Inn at Woerlitz from the
Lake/Chalcographische Gesellschaft of Dessau 1801."
Institut für Auslandsbeziehungen

In clear view across the lake from the *Schochscher Garten* is the "Gasthof
zum Eichenkranz". The building, built between 1785 and 1787 in the form of
a gateway to the city at the entrance to the city, was conceived by Prince
Franz as an inn offering accommodation to the numerous travellers to
Wörlitz. The façade facing the garden shows late Gothic elements, while the
rear face of the building, with its open half-timbered construction, reflects the
architecture typical of residential houses in Wörlitz.

44   Ill. p. 115

Christian Haldenwang (1770–1831)
after Heinrich Theodor Wehle (1778–1805)
VERFALLENES MONUMENT AUF DEM SIELITZER BERG
MONUMENT IN RUINS ON THE SIELITZER BERG
1801
Aquatint
26.1 x 34.0 cm
Inscription (translated): lower left below the picture "drawn by Wehle"; right
"etched by Haldenwang."; centre "Monument in Ruins / on the Sielitzer
Berg / Chalcographische Gesellschaft of Dessau 1801."
Institut für Auslandsbeziehungen

Not far from the little castle *Solitude* on the *Sieglitzer Berg,* a utility building
in the shape of a ruined Roman burial tower was built in 1779/80 based upon
plans prepared by Erdmannsdorff. The original two-storey structure has not
been preserved, however.

45

BETENDER KNABE
BOY PRAYING
Circa 1780
Plaster (cast of the sandstone original)
Height: 140.0 cm
Kulturstiftung DessauWörlitz

The statue of the praying boy is a copy of a bronze figure from the 1st century
BC, which was held in the ancient Greek and Rome collection maintained
by Frederick the Great of Prussia in *Sanssouci*. The figure stands in a niche at
the end of a tree-lined path on the so-called *Eisenhart* in Wörlitz. The idea
for placing the statue here was probably taken from a situation in the lower
garden parterre of the Villa, where a garden sculpture was also set in front of a
niche at the end of a long, covered, tree-lined path.

Ill. p. 102

46

MODELL DES CHINESISCHEN GARTENS IN
ORANIENBAUM
MODEL OF THE CHINESE GARDEN IN ORANIENBAUM
1994
Wood, cardboard, plastic
48.0 x 95.0 cm (scale: 1:500)
Modelbau Firma Stephan Hierl, Neu Egling
Kulturstiftung DessauWörlitz

The grandfather of Prince Franz had ordered an island garden carved out of
the eastern section of the baroque park in Oranienbaum. Prince Franz
redesigned the park grounds, which had been neglected in the meantime,
between 1793 and 1797, having them converted into a unique English-Chinese
(or "bric-a-brac") garden. Twelve islands were created on four hectares of
space. The once level ground was given a gently moulded, irregular topogra-
phy. In addition to a five-storey pagoda and a Chinese House, eight different
bridges grace this outstanding example of 18th-century garden culture.

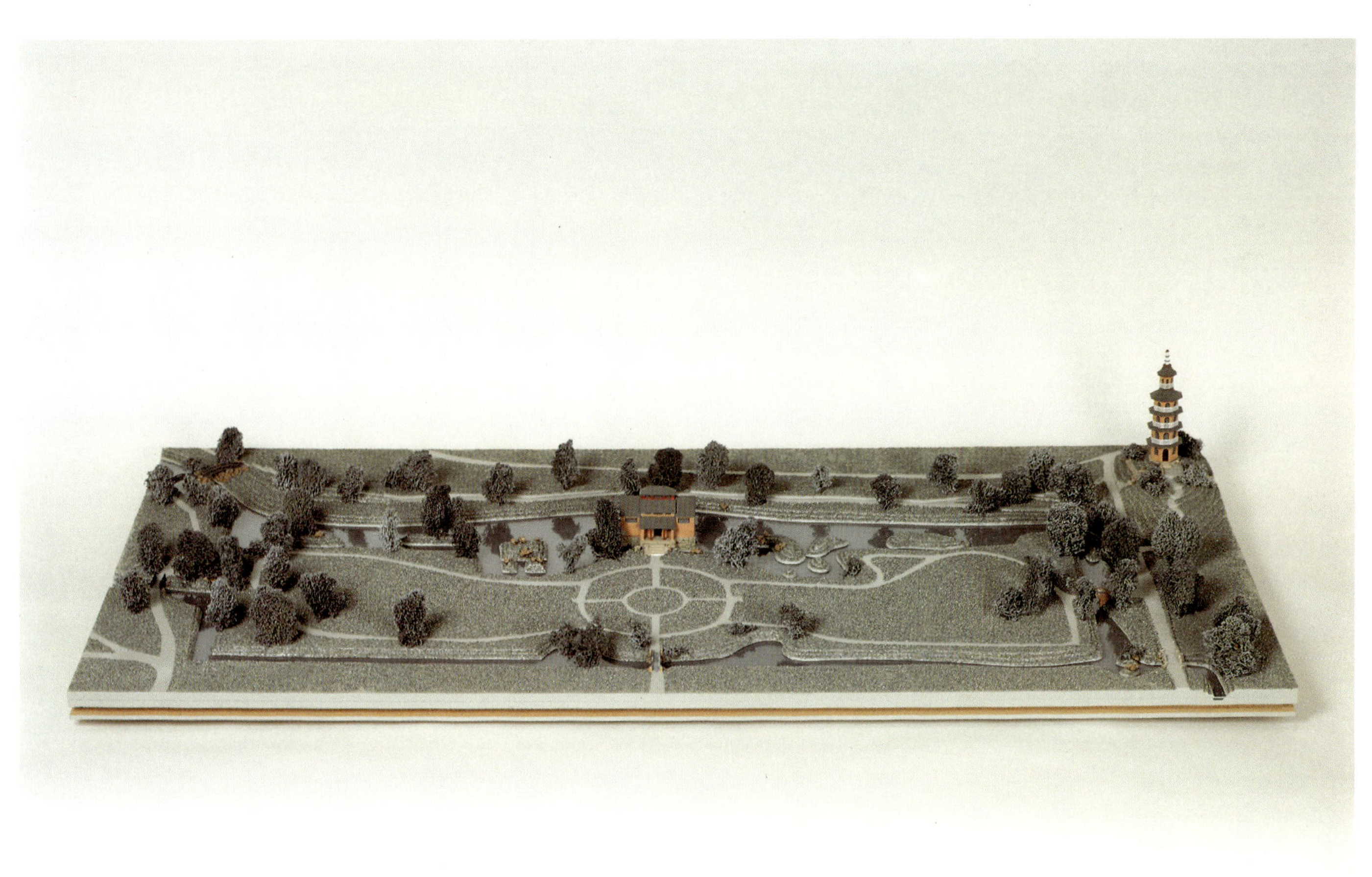

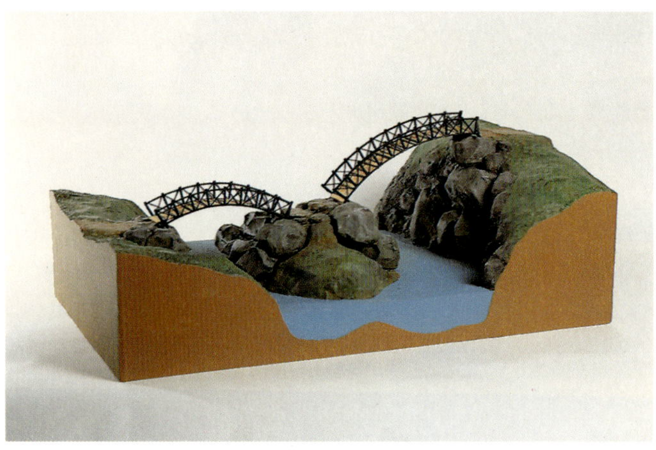

47
MODELL DER CHINESISCHEN DOPPELBRÜCKE IN
ORANIENBAUM
MODEL OF THE CHINESE DOUBLE BRIDGE IN
ORANIENBAUM
1993
Wood, cardboard
25.0 x 59.0 x 36.0
Study project from the Department of Architecture, Institut für Tragwerk-
planung, Seminar conducted by Prof. Berthold Burkhardt, Technische
Universität Braunschweig
Kulturstiftung DessauWörlitz

This iron double bridge is one of eight bridges in the English-Chinese garden
of Oranienbaum. It connects two banks of different heights and a small island
that lies between them. An illustration of this and several other bridges
located in the garden kingdom can be found in Gottfried Grohmann's *Ideenmagazin für Liebhaber von Gärten*.
The original bridge was destroyed in 1910. The reconstructed structure was
completed in 1994 during the restoration of the garden.

William Chambers (1723–1796)
*TRAITÉ DES ÉDIFICES, MEUBLES, HABITS, MACHIES ET
USTENSILES DES CHINOIS, GRAVES SUR LES ORIGINAUX
DESSINÉS A LA CHINE. (BAND V DER DETAILS DES NOU-
VEAUX JARDINS À LA MODE; JARDINS ANGLO-CHINOIS À
LA MODE)
DESIGNS OF CHINESE BUILDINGS...*
Paris: Georges Louis Le Rouge, 1776
29,5 x 22.0 cm (closed), 30 pages, 20 copper engravings
Kulturstiftung DessauWörlitz

Chambers' *Designs of Chinese Buildings* – shown here in one of its most
important translations – was written in 1757 and based upon experience gathered during an extended stay in China in 1748/49. The work is an important
source of information about Chinese architecture, furniture and garden
design in Europe. Prince Franz met the English architect on one of his visits
to England. Chambers' principles of horticulture and his publications exercised a strong influence on architecture and garden design in Anhalt-Dessau.
The structure of the pagoda in Oranienbaum is based upon Chambers'
Designs and his famous pagoda in Kew Gardens, London. Details of the
Chinese House were also borrowed from the *Designs*. The interiors shown in
plates VIII and IX are exact reproductions of the two Chinese rooms in the
Wörlitzer Schloß.

TRAITÉ

DES ÉDIFICES,

MEUBLES, HABITS,

MACHINES ET USTENSILES

DES CHINOIS,

*GRAVÉS SUR LES ORIGINAUX
DESSINÉS A LA CHINE,*

PAR M. CHAMBERS, Architecte Anglois.

*COMPRIS une DESCRIPTION de leurs TEMPLES,
MAISONS, JARDINS, &c.*

A PARIS,

CHEZ le Sieur LE ROUGE, Ingénieur-Géographe du Roi, rue des
Grands Augustins.

M. DCC. LXXVI.

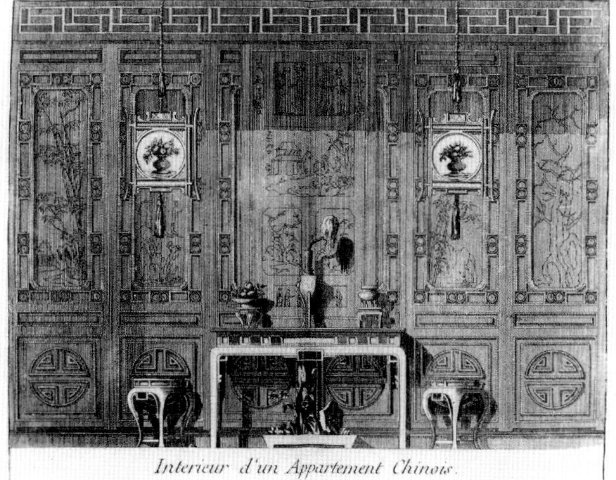

Interieur d'un Appartement Chinois.

IDEENMAGAZIN

für

Liebhaber von Gärten, Englischen Anlagen

und für Besitzer von Landgütern

um

Gärten und ländliche Gegenden, sowohl mit geringem als auch grossem Geldaufwand,

nach den originellsten Englischen, Gothischen, Sinesischen Geschmacksmanieren

zu verschönern und zu veredeln.

Erster Heft

welcher zehn Kupfer mit Französischem und Deutschem Text enthält.

Unter der Aufsicht

von

Johann Gottfried Grohmann

Professor der Philosophie zu Leipzig

herausgegeben.

Leipzig

bei Friedrich Gotthelf Baumgärtner

1796.

50

Johann Gottfried Grohmann (1769–1805)

*IDEENMAGAZIN FÜR LIEBHABER VON GÄRTEN, ENGLI-
SCHEN ANLAGEN UND FÜR BESITZER VON LANDGÜTERN
UM GÄRTEN UND LÄNDLICHE GEGENDEN, SOWOHL MIT
GERINGEM GELDAUFWAND, NACH DEN ORIGINELLSTEN
ENGLISCHEN, GOTHISCHEN, SINESISCHEN
GESCHMACKSMANIEREN ZU VERSCHÖNERN UND ZU
VEREDELN (HEFT 1–6)*
A JOURNAL OF IDEAS FOR LOVERS OF GARDENS AND
ENGLISH LANDSCAPED GROUNDS AND FOR OWNERS OF
COUNTRY MANORS FOR THE PURPOSE OF BEAUTIFYING
AND REFINING GARDENS AND RURAL AREAS WITH
LITTLE EXPENDITURE OF MONEY ACCORDING TO THE
MOST NOVEL ENGLISH, GOTHIC AND CHINESE
MANNERS OF TASTE (ISSUES 1–6)
Leipzig: Friedrich Gotthelf Baumgärtner, 1796
31.0 x 26.0 cm, pages not numbered, 10 copper engravings in each issue
Kulturstiftung DessauWörlitz

Johann Christian Grohmann, a professor at the universities in Wittenberg and
Leipzig, published the *Ideenmagazin für Liebhaber von Gärten…*, a publication highly admired in its time, from 1796 onwards. The journal was the most
extensive compendium of information about garden design available in the
German language. In 60 issues comprising 616 copper engravings with corre-
sponding descriptions, Grohmann introduced his readership to both well-
known garden complexes and horticultural concepts of his own invention,
among them several examples from the garden kingdom of Dessau-Wörlitz.

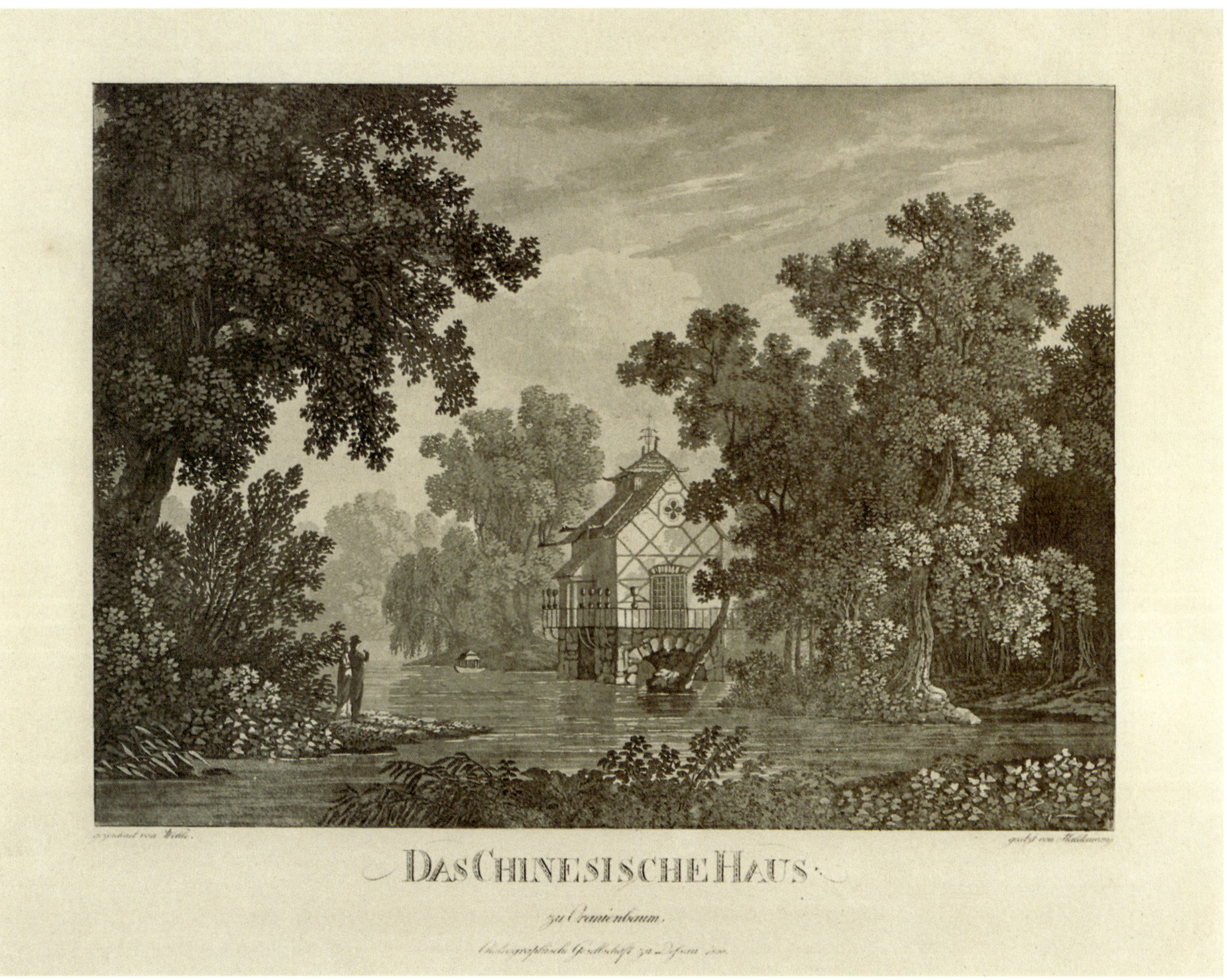

49
Christian Haldenwang (1770–1831)
after Heinrich Theodor Wehle (1778–1805)
DAS CHINESISCHE HAUS ZU ORANIENBAUM
THE CHINESE HOUSE IN ORANIENBAUM
1800
Aquatint
26.0 x 33.7 cm
Inscription (translated): lower left below the picture "drawn by Wehle"; right
"etched by Haldenwang."; centre "The Chinese House / in Oranienbaum. /
Chalcographische Gesellschaft of Dessau 1800."
Institut für Auslandsbeziehungen

Haldenwang's etching gives an impression of the deliberately picturesque
effect of the English-Chinese garden shortly after its completion, although
the plants could not have reached the height depicted by the time the drawing was done. The garden design concept was realised by the Oranienbaum
court gardener Wilhelm Neumark (dates of birth and death unknown), and
construction was supervised by Georg Christoph Hesekiel (1732–1818), the
Prince's Director of Construction.
The house itself, furnished and decorated with Chinese tapestries, two porce-
lain cabinets, papier-mâché figures and precious Chinese furniture, was used
as a tea house.

The architecture of the garden kingdom of Dessau-Wörlitz is closely linked with the name Friedrich Wilhelm von Erdmannsdorff (1736–1800). In addition to the country houses in Wörlitz, the *Luisium* and the *Georgium*, he also erected city buildings and designed numerous smaller structures for the parks and gardens of the principality. Erdmannsdorff is regarded as the founder of German Neoclassicism, an architectural style oriented towards the models of ancient Greece and Rome and their interpretation by the master builders of the Italian Renaissance. In addition to important works by Vitruvius and Andrea Palladio, Erdmannsdorff's library contained copies of the most significant treatises on architectural theory available in his time. His style conformed to the tradition of English Neo-Palladianism, works of which he first encountered in 1763 and 1764. During the grand tour of 1765–1767 he examined Palladio's villas in the Via Veneto and studied the ancient architecture in and around Rome under the guidance of Winckelmann and, in particular, of Clérisseau. His visit to the excavations of Pompeii and the Herculaneum made a vivid and lasting impression on him.

The cornerstone for the *Wörlitzer Landhaus* was laid in 1769. This most modern building of its time on the European continent revolutionised taste with respect to architecture in Germany.

It was not Neoclassical forms alone which shaped the face of architecture in Anhalt-Dessau. One also finds buildings in the Chinese style as well as man-made grottoes. Many of the structures in the garden kingdom are characterised by a pluralism of style in which Neoclassical elements are combined with Neogothic, Romanesque and other historical features. This does not reflect a desire to romanticise the past, as was evident in the subsequent generation, but is indicative instead of an intention to enlighten, to evoke historical associations and to encourage a wide variety of different responses.

The Prince developed a particular preference for Gothic architecture. Here as well, English influences played a significant role. It was its irregular and picturesque qualities that made the Gothic style so appealing. The "naturalness" of Gothic architecture was quite in keeping with Rousseau's call for a return to nature, and thus it became a standard ingredient in English landscape gardens.

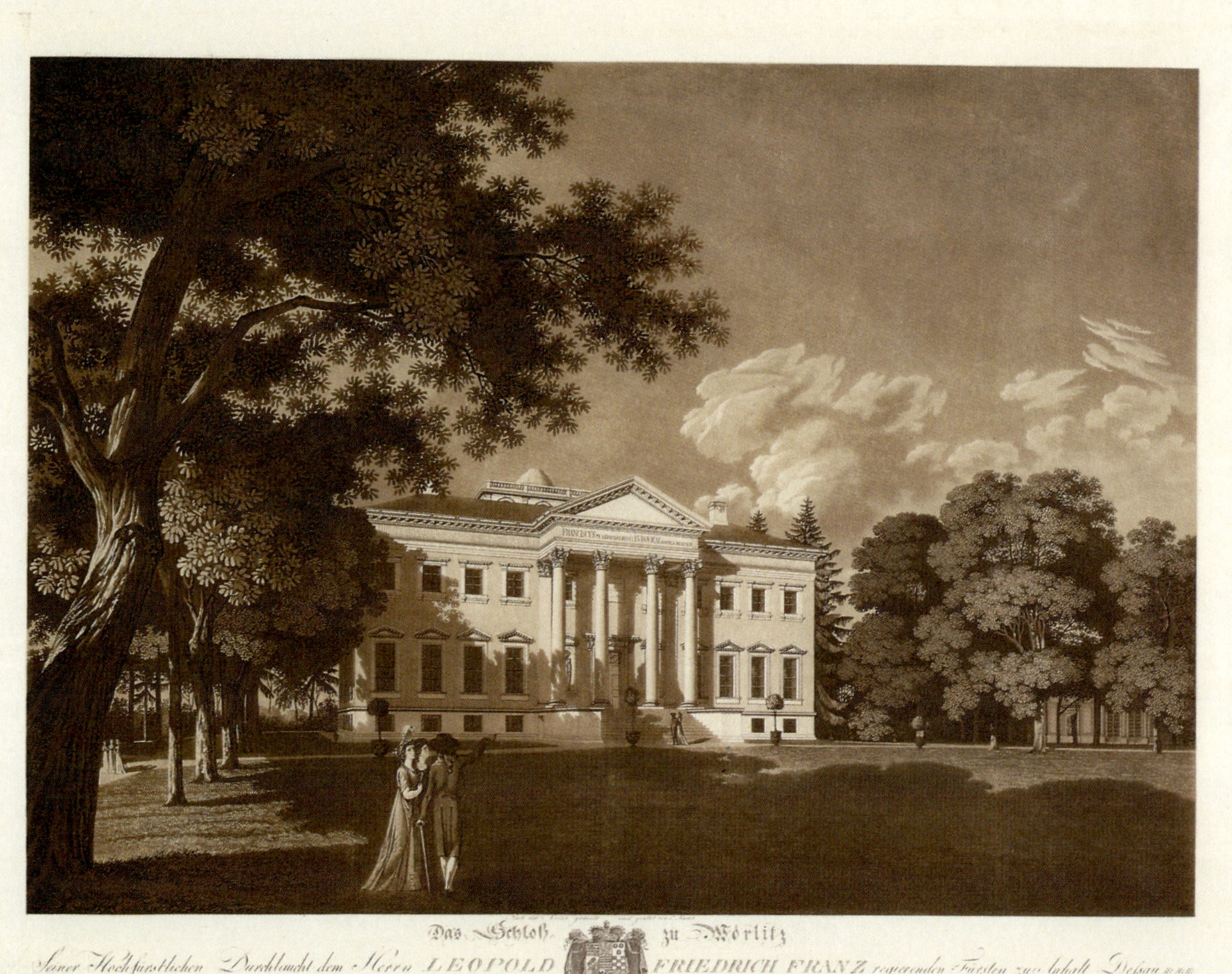

51

Karl Kuntz (1770–1830)
DAS SCHLOSS ZU WÖRLITZ
THE SCHLOSS IN WÖRLITZ
1797
Aquatint
52.0 x 68.0 cm
Inscription (translated): centre, below the picture "Painted from nature and
etched by C. Kuntz / The Schloß in Wörlitz / Dedicated in humble
obedience / To His Highness Prince LEOPOLD FRIEDRICH FRANZ,
Prince and Ruler of Anhalt-Dessau etc. / Issued in Dessau in 1797"
Institut für Auslandsbeziehungen

This etching shows the southern façade of the *Schloß* built by Erdmannsdorff
between 1769 and 1773, the seminal work of Neoclassical architecture in Germany. The building reflects the tradition of Neo-Palladian country houses in
England. Seen rising from the northern roof of the *Schloß* is the belvedere
and its domed lantern, added in 1784. Visible on the right-hand side of the
picture behind the linden trees is the kitchen building with the summer hall
facing the *Schloß*.

52
Johann Wolfgang von Goethe (1749–1832)
SCHLOSS WÖRLITZ
SCHLOSS WÖRLITZ
1778
Pencil, ink, washed (copy)
32.0 x 50.8 cm
Signed at the lower right-hand edge of the picture "Wörliz d. 26. May 78 G."
Kulturstiftung DessauWörlitz

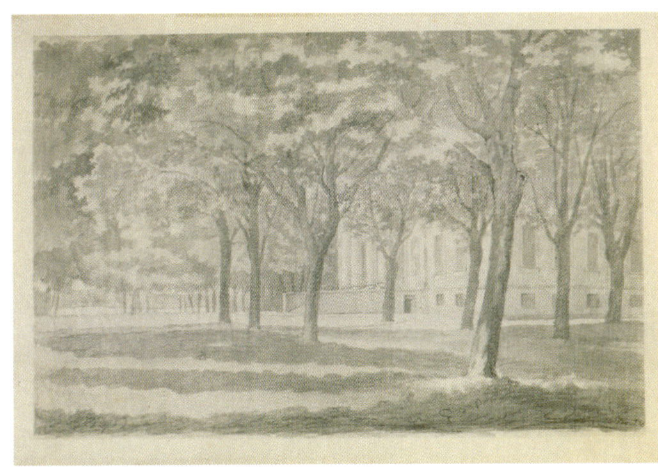

"Like a quiet dream-image passing by" was the impression recorded by
Johann Wolfgang von Goethe in his diary on the occasion of a visit to the castle and grounds in Wörlitz. His drawing of the *Wörlitzer Schloß* shows a view
of it from a southeasterly direction, as seen from the kitchen building.
The famous poet and admirer of Wörlitz – the English-style gardens in
Weimar were designed according to his instructions – provides us in this
quick sketch the first contemporary view of what was then the most modern
building on the European continent. Goethe dedicated his drawing to
Charlotte von Stein.

53
MODELL DES WÖRLITZER SCHLOSSES
MODEL OF THE WÖRLITZER SCHLOSS
1996
Polystyrene, acrylic glass, rendered in colour
31.5 x 72.0 x 49.0 cm (scale: 1:50)
Architektur-Modell-Design Hans Heinz Frickel, Frankfurt am Main
Kulturstiftung Deutsche Bank

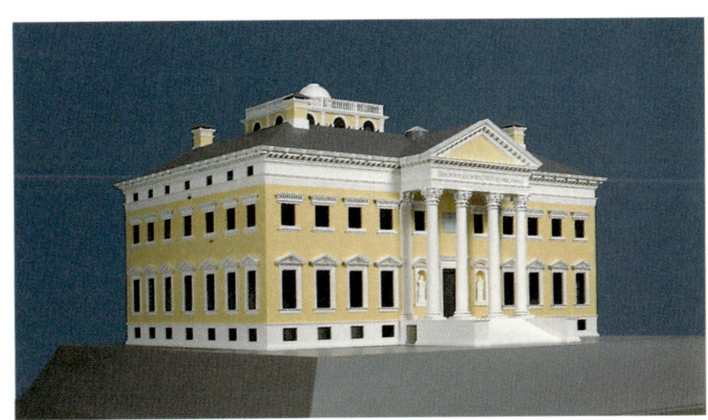

The cubic structure, whose main façade is emphasised only by a dignified
portico, was greatly admired for its functional objectivity. Not intended
to serve the purpose of courtly representation, it was meant instead to symbol-
ise the bourgeois lifestyle the Prince sought to live in his *Landhaus*, or country manor. The design of the house also incorporated a didactic intent: The
publicly accessible rooms were exemplary exhibits of Neoclassical interior
design. The decoration, based upon the style of the brother Adam and Sir
William Chambers, was to contribute to the promotion of good taste. The
noble coloration of the building derives from an evocative combination of the
local alder ochre of the walls and the limestone white of the decorative elements.

54
MODELL DES KÜCHENGEBÄUDES
MODEL OF THE KITCHEN BUILDING
1996
Polystyrene, acrylic glass, rendered in colour
23.5 x 58.0 x 52.0 (scale: 1:50)
Architektur-Modell-Design Hans Heinz Frickel, Frankfurt am Main
Kulturstiftung Deutsche Bank

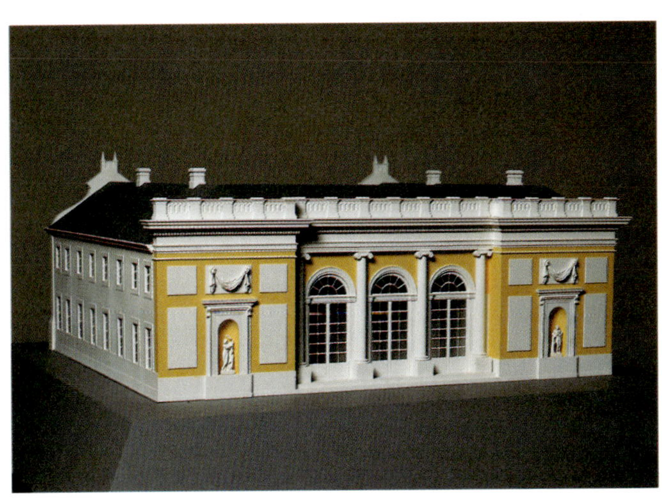

The kitchen building erected in 1770/71 on the grounds east of the *Schloß*
was one of the first functional structures built by Erdmannsdorff. In addition
to the summer dining room, used in winter to house the plants from the
orange grove, the building also contained living quarters for the servants, a
washroom with a cistern and basins, the kitchen itself and a bakery. Worthy of
particular note is the pluralism of style in this building. The side facing the
Schloß is structured along Neoclassical lines, while the façade opposite the
churchyard incorporated the first examples of late Gothic elements typical of
Wörlitz.

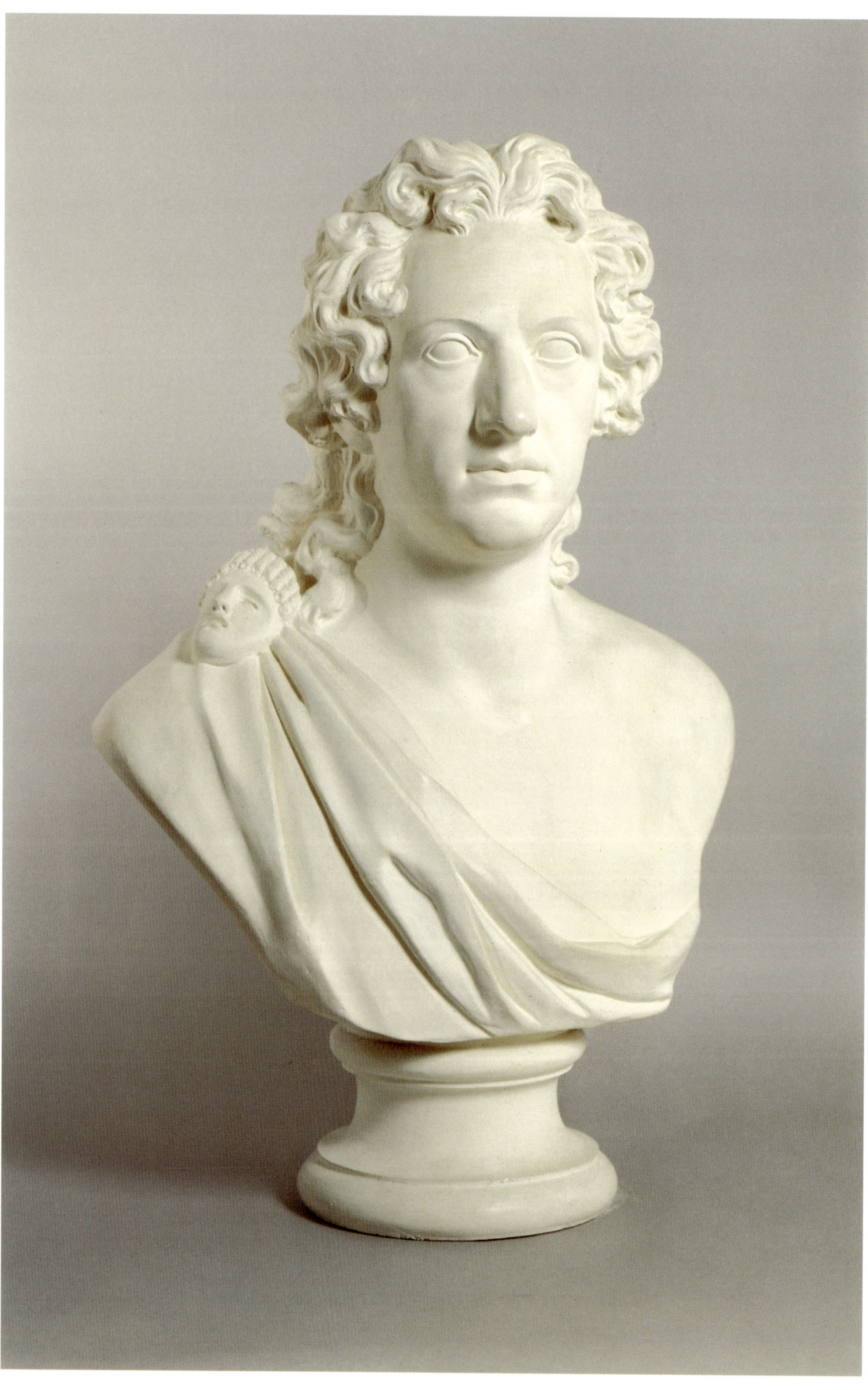

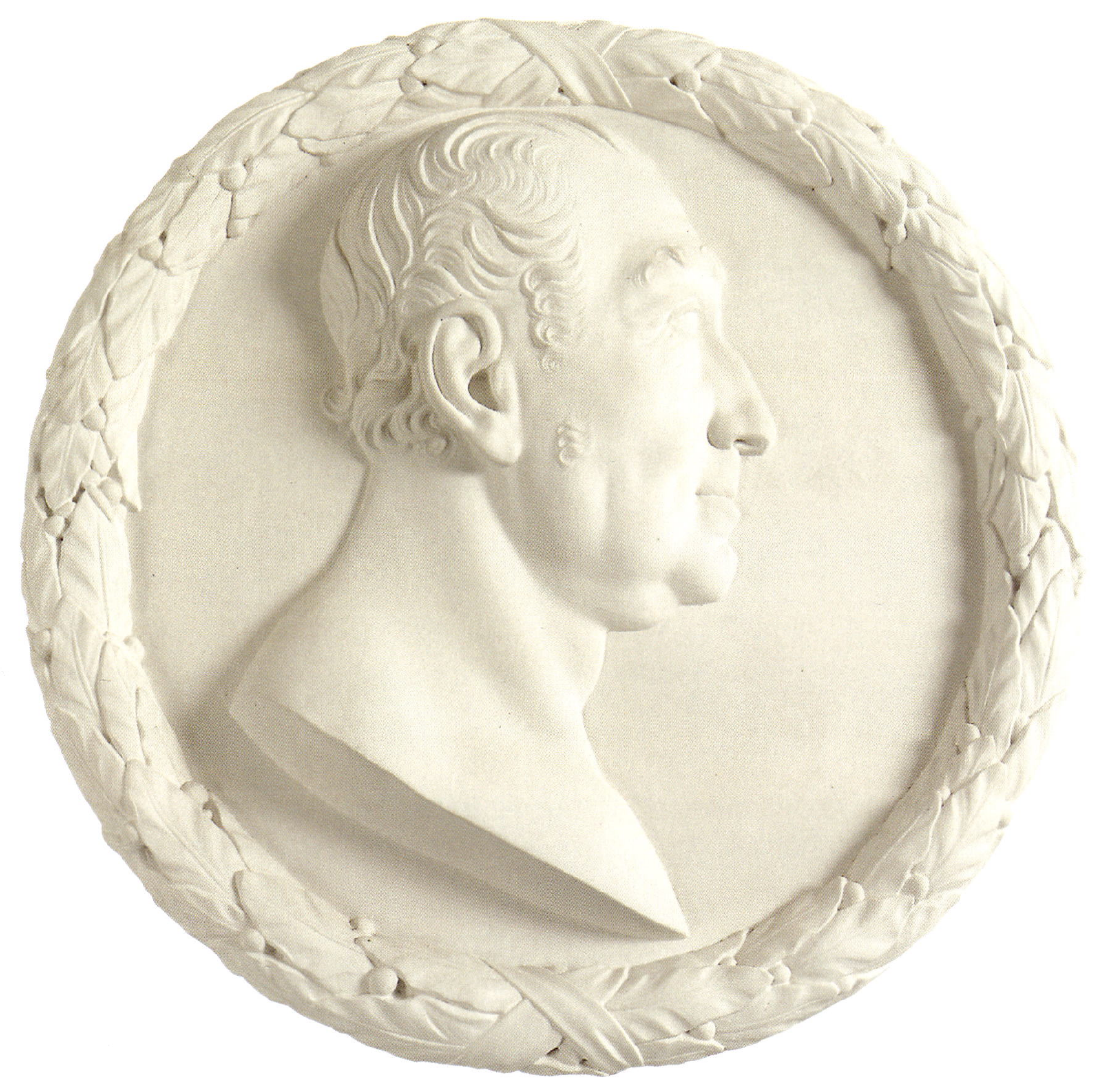

55
Martin Gottlob Klauer (1742–1801)
BÜSTE DES JOHANN WOLFGANG VON GOETHE
BUST OF JOHANN WOLFGANG VON GOETHE
Circa 1790
Plaster
Height: 70.0 cm
Kulturstiftung DessauWörlitz

One of the garden kingdom's most famous visitors, Goethe was frequently
attracted to Wörlitz after his move to Weimar. Alone or in the company of
Duke Carl August von Sachsen-Weimar-Eisenach, he made regular journeys
to the garden kingdom beginning in 1776. Wörlitz served as a stimulus for the
construction of a spacious landscape part on the banks of the Ilm River in
Weimar and for garden projects in nearby Tiefurt, site of the gardens of
Duchess Anna Amalia. In a letter to Charlotte von Stein dated May 14th, 1778
Goethe remarked: "It is now infinitely beautiful here. As we made our way
last evening through the lakes, canals and woods I was touched by the way in
which the gods have permitted the Prince to build such a dream around
himself."

56
Friedemann Hunold (1773–1840)
PORTRAITRELIEF DES HERZOGS FRANZ VON ANHALT-
DESSAU
RELIEF PORTRAIT OF DUKE FRANZ VON ANHALT-DESSAU
1823
Plaster, cast to scale from the marble original at the mausoleum in the tower
of the church in Jönitz
Diameter: 52.0 cm
Kulturstiftung DessauWörlitz

This portrait done by the Dessau court sculptor Hunold decorates the
Prince's mausoleum in the tower of the church in Jönitz.
Work on the mausoleum, initiated by Prince Franz shortly before his death,
was continued by his grandson, Duke Leopold Friedrich, who characterised
his grandfather in the following inscription: "A father to his people. Whose
love and devotion permitted him fifty-nine years of mild and wise rule."

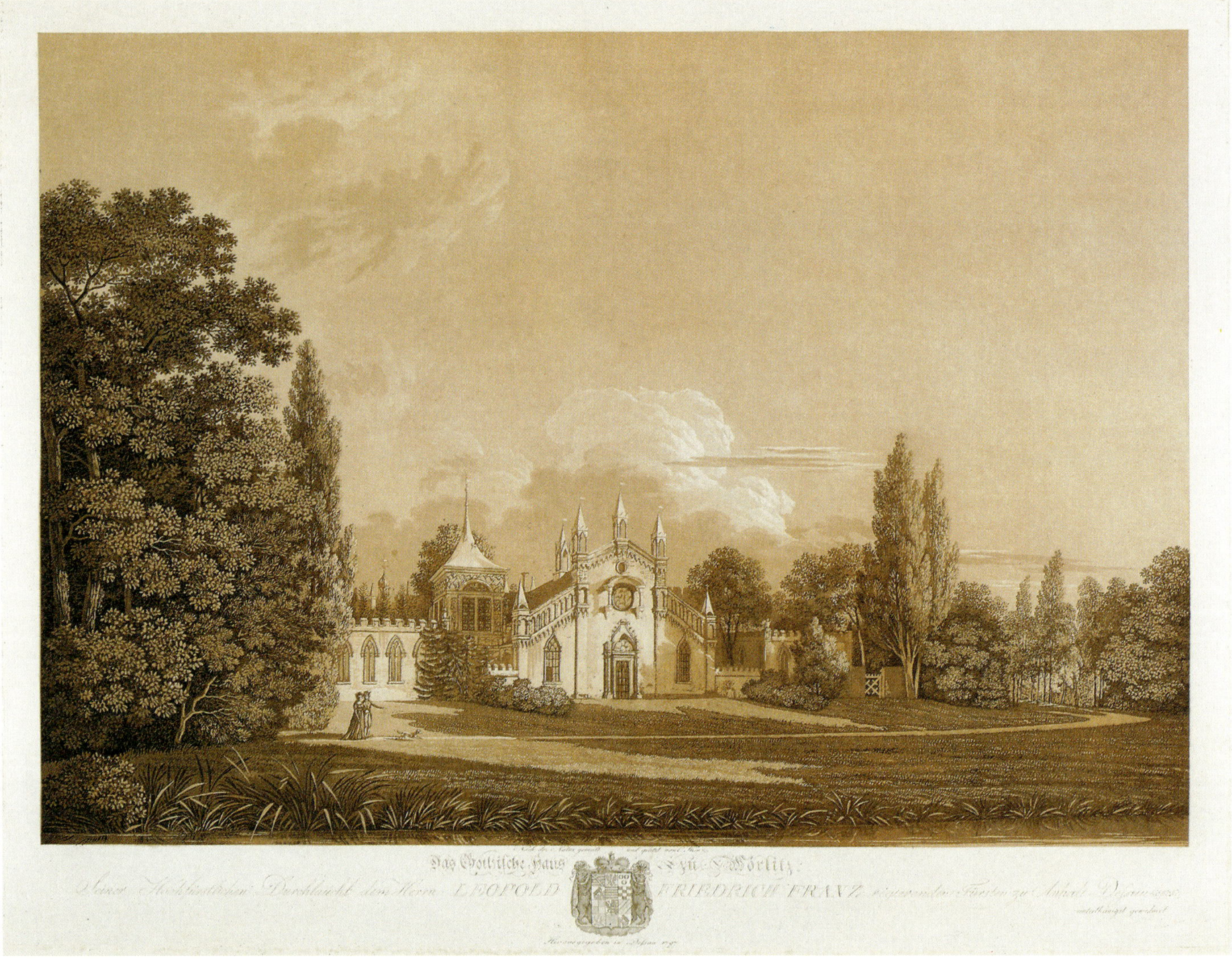

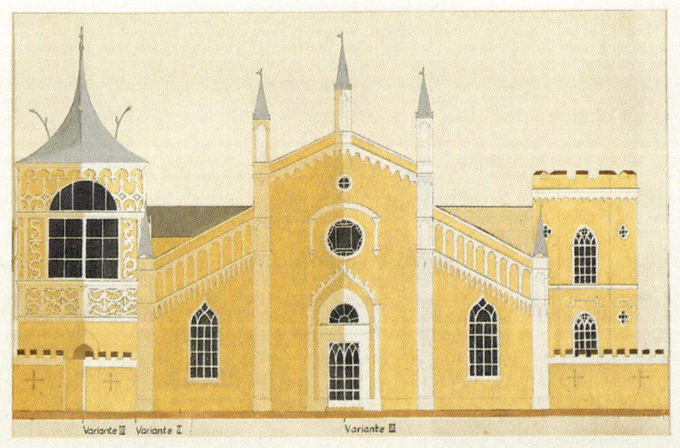

57
Karl Kuntz (1770–1830)
DAS GOTHISCHE HAUS ZU WÖRLITZ
THE GOTHIC HOUSE IN WÖRLITZ
1797
Aquatint, printed in sepia
51.3 x 67.6 cm
Inscription (translated): centre, below the picture "Painted from nature and etched by C. Kunz. / The Gothic House in Wörlitz. / Dedicated in humble obedience / To His Highness Prince LEOPOLD FRIEDRICH FRANZ, Prince and Ruler of Anhalt-Dessau etc. / Issued in Dessau in 1797"
Institut für Auslandsbeziehungen

This etching shows the sides of the Gothic House that faces the canal. It was completed between 1773 and 1776 and modelled on the western façade of the Venetian Church of Madonna dell'Orto. Originally conceived as a gardener's dwelling, the building was enlarged in several stages by 1813. Prince Franz used the house more and more often as a private refuge as the years passed, living there with his mistress amidst his collection of medieval objects, many of which recall the history of the House of Anhalt. Prince Franz chose "Gothic" architectural forms quite deliberately. In doing so, he emphasised his political position as an advocate of the medieval constitution of estates to others of his class. Such restorative views were in complete opposition to the practical politics of the major German powers, Prussia and the Habsburgs.

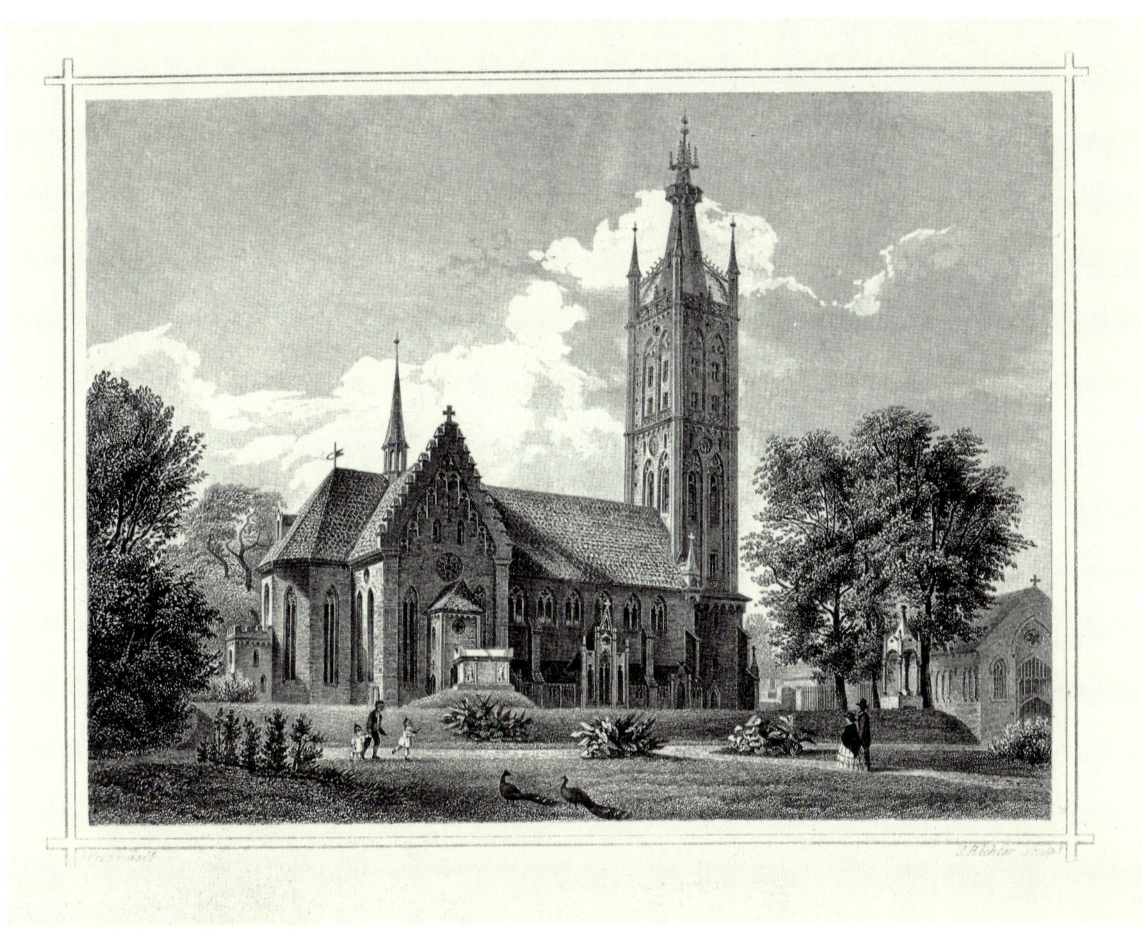

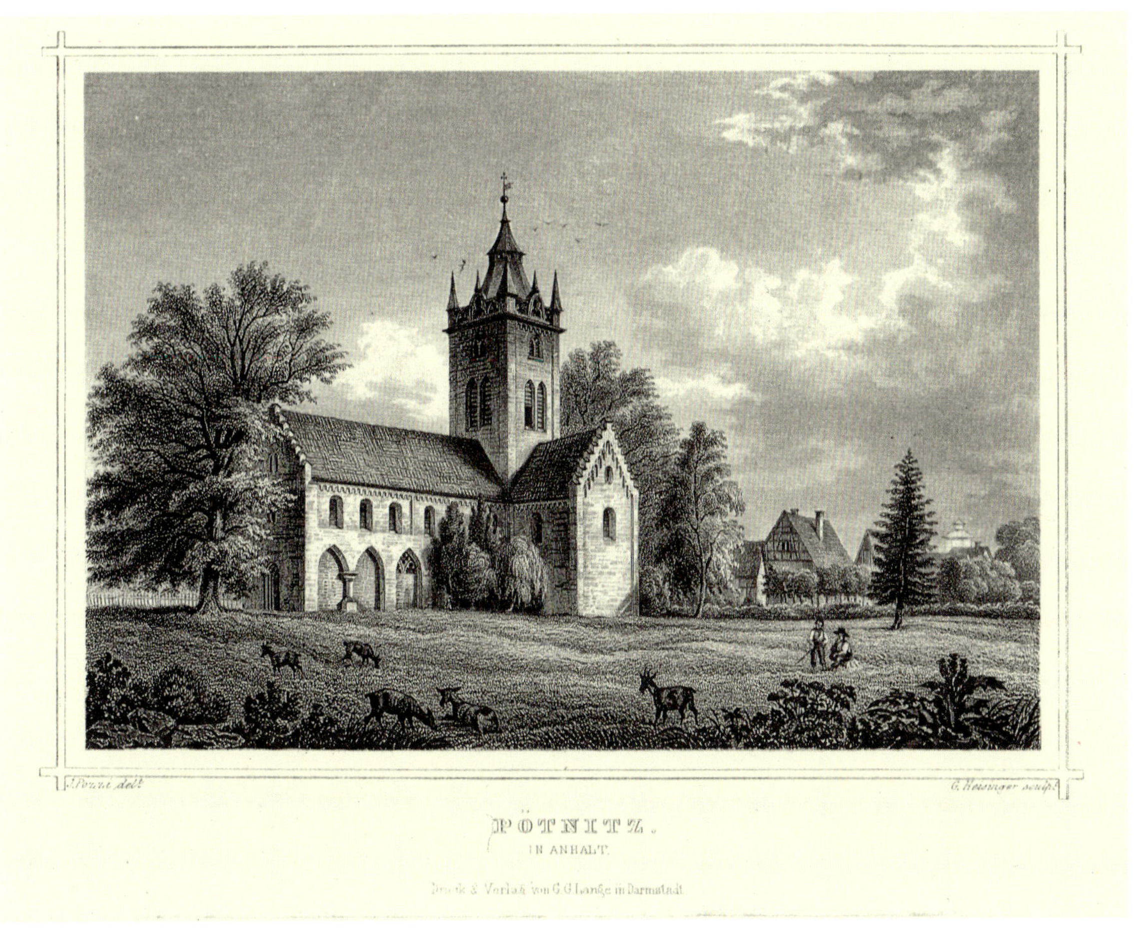

PÖTNITZ.
IN ANHALT.

Druck & Verlag von G. G. Lange in Darmstadt.

58 Ill. p. 126 below
REKONSTRUKTIONSVARIANTEN DER FASSADE DES
GOTISCHEN HAUSES
VARIANT SOLUTIONS FOR THE RECONSTRUCTION OF
THE FAÇADE OF THE GOTHIC HOUSE
1982
Tempera on paper
34.2 x 51.1
Michael Wetzel, Wörlitz
Kulturstiftung DessauWörlitz

The reconstruction of the original polychrome coloration of a building or its
parts is often one of the most difficult problems involved in the care and
maintenance of historic monuments. In the case of the Gothic House, the
problem was to determine precisely which colours were to be used for the
decorative plaster elements on the façade. Neither printed sources nor exist-
ing visual depictions provided definitive clarification, nor did the results of
restorative analysis offer a clear solution. Thus a number of possible variant
solutions were developed and compared with one another. On the basis of
analogies to other comparable structures, conclusions were drawn with
respect to the solution which appeared most probable from a historical point
of view – in this case the white coloration of the decorative elements.

59 Ill. p. 127
J. Richter (dates of birth and death unknown)
after Jacobo Pozzi (1814–1897)
ST. PETRI KIRCHE ZU WÖRLITZ
THE ST. PETRI CHURCH IN WÖRLITZ
1861
Steel engraving, 19.8 x 26.4 cm
Inscription: lower left below the picture "J. Pozzi del.t"; right "J. Richter
sculp.t"
Kulturstiftung DessauWörlitz

The St. Petri Church in Wörlitz, the largest Neogothic church in the garden
kingdom, was erected as a reconstruction of its Romanesque predecessor
undertaken between 1804 and 1808. On viewing the imposing edifice with its
66 metre-high tower, the Russian Prince Putiatin exclaimed with great enthusiasm: "Yes, you are a sign pointing to heaven; a miracle of God and a wonder
of art! Yet we shall remain here: for here it is good, a garden of God!"

60 Ill. p. 127
G. Heisinger (dates of birth and death unknown)
after Jacobo Pozzi (1814–1897)
DIE KIRCHE IN PÖTNITZ
THE CHURCH IN PÖTNITZ
Circa 1840
Steel engraving, 16.2 x 22.0 cm
Inscription: lower left below the picture "J. Pozzi del.t"; right "G. Heisinger
sculp.t"; centre "PÖTNITZ. / IN ANHALT. / Druck und Verlag von G. G.
Lange in Darmstadt."
Private collection

The church in the village of Pötnitz, now Mildensee, was rebuilt in 1805 by
Carlo Ignazio Pozzi (1766–1842), who served as Prince Franz's court architect
following the death of Erdmannsdorff (1800). Prince Franz had the late-
Romanesque convent church restored along late Gothic lines. The structure
alludes to the history of Anhalt during the Middle Ages.

61
MODELL DES GEORGENHAUSES
MODEL OF THE GEORGENHAUS
1986
Plaster, wood, rendered in colour
43.0 x 58.0 x 58.0 cm (scale: 1:50)
Michael Wetzel, Wörlitz
Kulturstiftung DessauWörlitz

The basic form of the "country house" built by Erdmannsdorff for Prince
Johann Georg beginning in about 1780 is already anticipated in *Schloß
Luisium*. The architect constructed a number of such cubic structures with
blunt pyramid roofs and belvederes or central chimneys to serve a variety of
purposes, building them in a different sizes and with façades of varying
design. In addition to the ever-present Palladian influences, Erdmannsdorff
was also stimulated in this case by a conceptual model depicted in Nicolaus
Goldmann's *Zivilbaukunst*, published in 1699.

62
Emanuel Semper (1848–1911)
RELIEFPORTRAIT DES PRINZEN JOHANN GEORG VON
ANHALT-DESSAU
RELIEF PORTRAIT OF PRINCE JOHANN GEORG VON
ANHALT-DESSAU
Circa 1900
Plaster, cast to scale from the copper original
42.3 x 35.0 cm
Kulturstiftung DessauWörlitz

Prince Johann Georg (1748–1811), eight years younger than his brother Prince
Franz, called Hans Jürge by everyone, carried on his family's tradition by
entering the Prussian military, in which he served for many years. The young
Prince was nevertheless just as discerning and fond of art as his brother. He
was a member of the group that undertook the "grand tour" from 1765 to
1767.

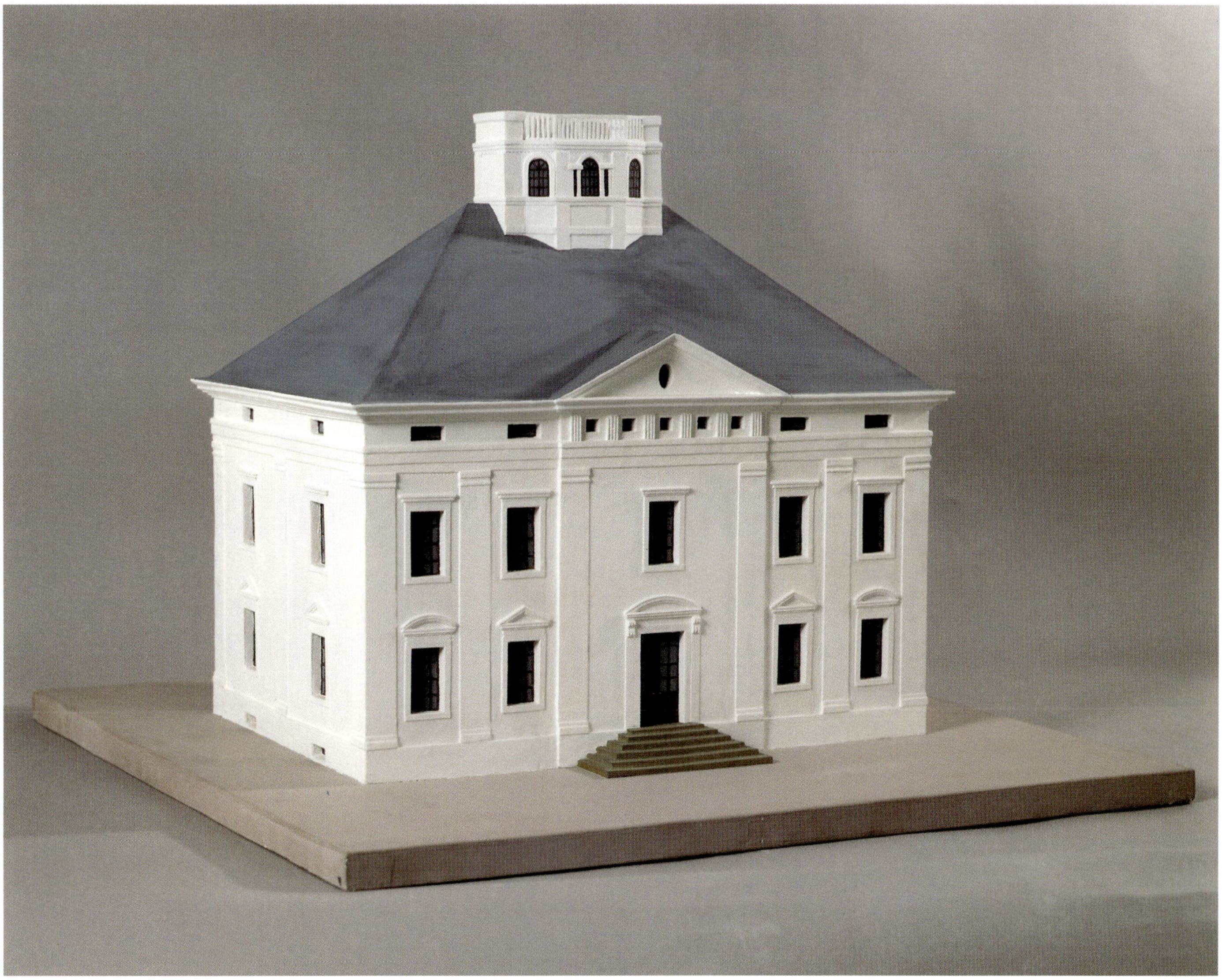

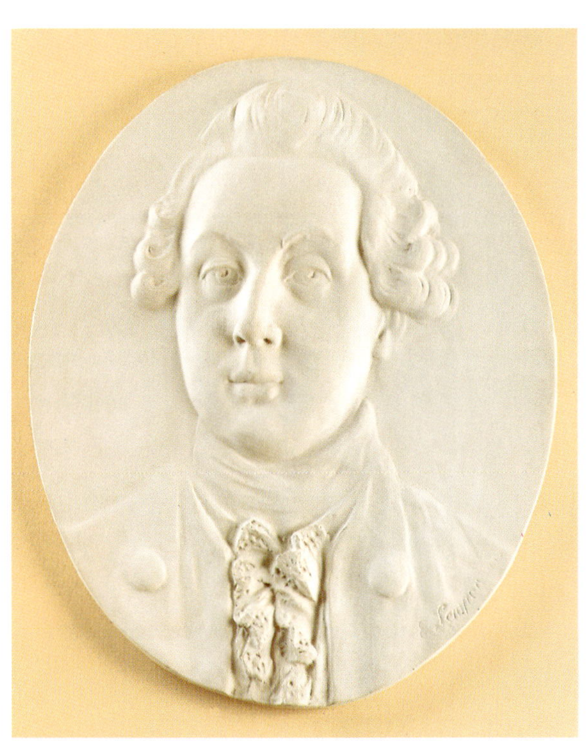

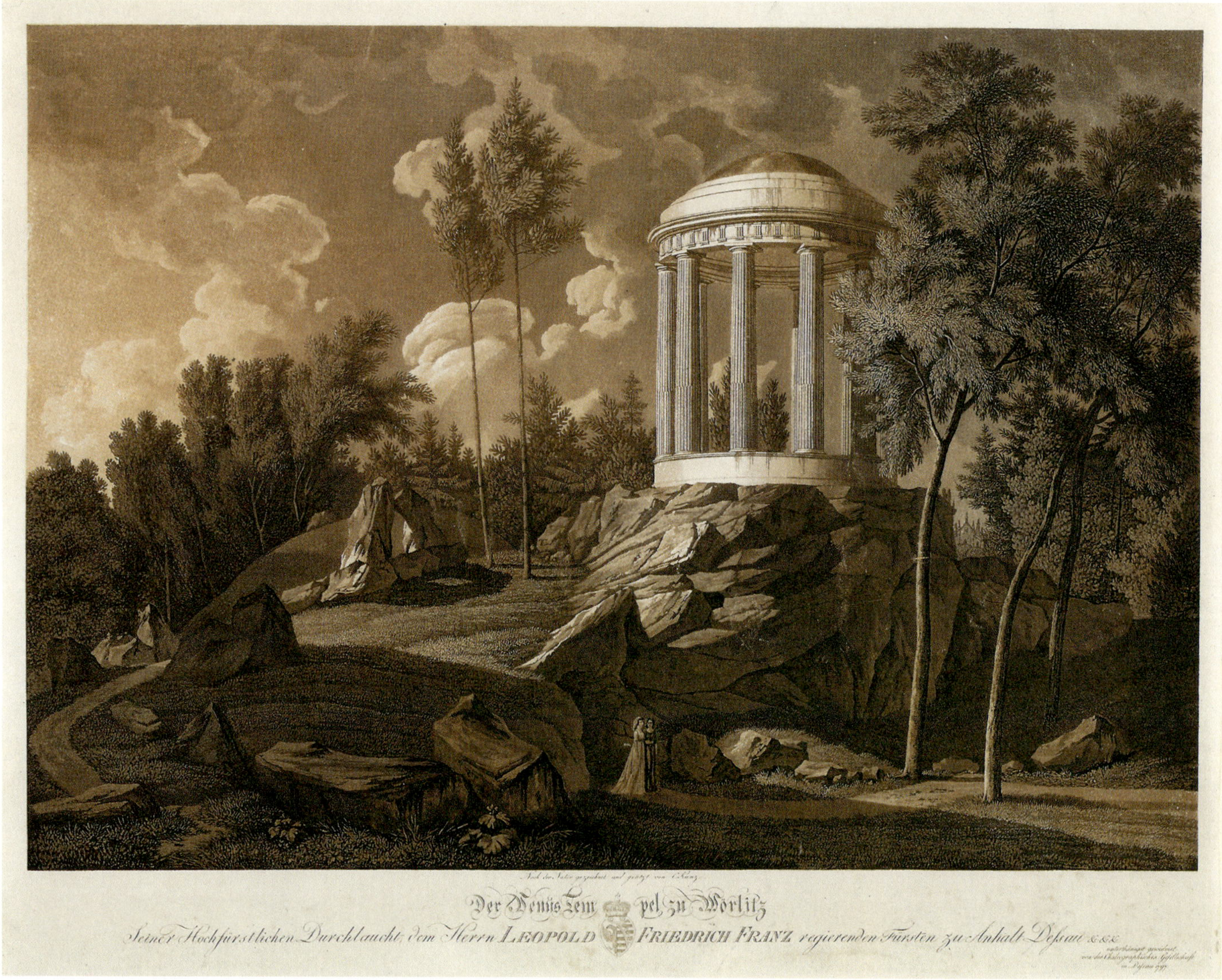

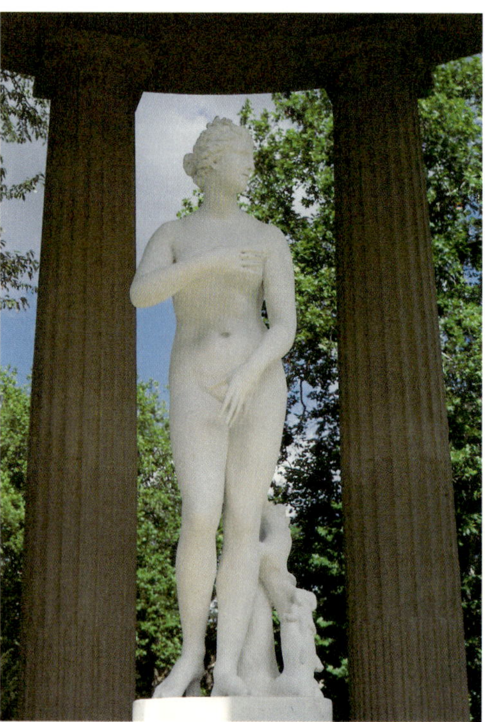

63

Karl Kuntz (1770–1830)

DER VENUSTEMPEL ZU WÖRLITZ
THE TEMPLE OF VENUS IN WÖRLITZ

1797

Aquatint, printed in sepia, 51.0 x 65.9 cm

Inscription (translated): centre, below the picture "Painted from nature and etched by C. Kunz. / The Temple of Venus in Wörlitz. / Dedicated in humble obedience / To His Highness Prince LEOPOLD FRIEDRICH FRANZ, Prince and Ruler of Anhalt-Dessau etc. / by the Chalcographische Gesellschaft in Dessau in 1797"

Institut für Auslandsbeziehungen

The Doric sandstone monopteros built by Erdmannsdorff as a replica of the ancient Temple of the Sybilla in Tivoli in 1794 completes the "mystical" garden segment, pervaded with the masonic symbolism, with its grottoes of Vulcan and Aeolus as symbols of the elements of fire, water and air. The foundations of the temple are integrated into a flood dike. Venus, born of the sea, personifies the element of water. Of particular interest is the interpretation of the presence of a vista towards the Gothic House. Prince Franz had the Neoclassical combined with a Neogothic garden scene, alluding in thematic terms to the fact that Venus, the Goddess of Love, rules in the Gothic House, where the Prince lived with his mistress, the gardener's daughter Luise Schoch.

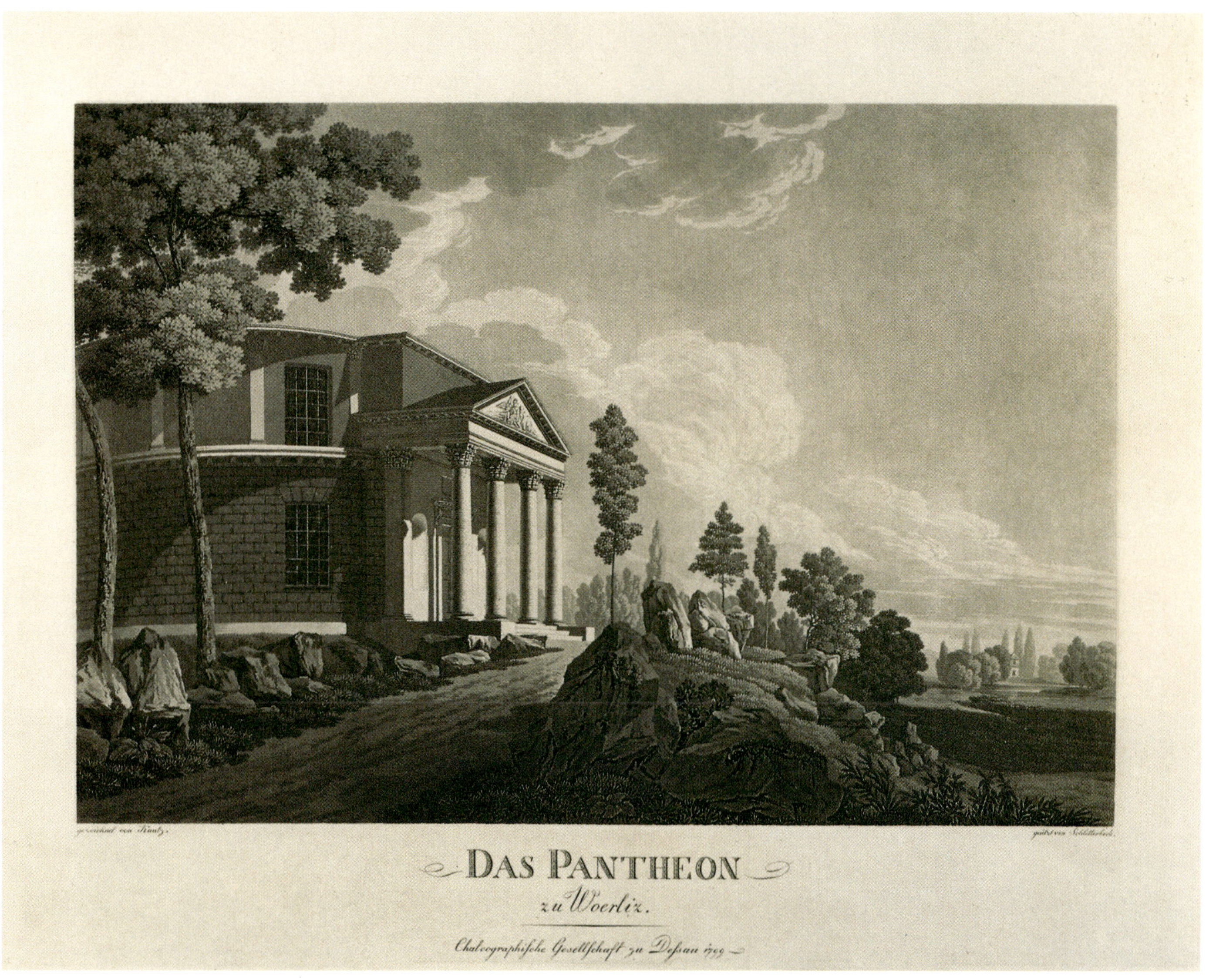

64
VENUS MEDICI
VENUS MEDICI
Circa 1794
Plaster
Height: 160.0 cm
Kulturstiftung DessauWörlitz

A cast of the Venus Medici, one of the most famous and familiar ancient
sculptures of Venus, was selected for placement in the Temple of Venus. The
figure was set on a pedestal of yellow glass in the middle of an open circular
temple. In this way, light was allowed to fall on the Grotto of Vulcan, the husband of Venus according to mythology. Another copy of the Venus Medici
can be found in the front rotunda of the *Wörlitzer Schloß*.

65
Wilhelm Friedrich Schlotterbeck (1770–1819)
after Karl Kuntz (1770–1830)
DAS PANTHEON ZU WOERLIZ
THE PANTHEON IN WÖRLITZ
1799
Aquatint
25.6 x 32.7 cm
Inscription (translated): lower left below the picture "Drawn by Kuntz"; right
"etched by Schlotterbeck."; centre "The Pantheon / in Wörlitz./ Chalcogra-
phische Gesellschaft of Dessau 1799."
Institut für Auslandsbeziehungen

"For the friends of nature and art" is the motto inscribed above the entrance
to the Pantheon. This structure, modelled on similar garden pavilions in England, was originally meant to serve not only as a temple in which to place
ancient sculptures but as a "temple of the muses" as well. The export of sculptures was delayed during the Napoleonic Wars, however, and the statues of
Apollo and the nine muses could not be placed on the upper level of the
Pantheon until 1802. Erdmannsdorff had died in the meantime, and Prince
Franz did not pursue the completion of the project.

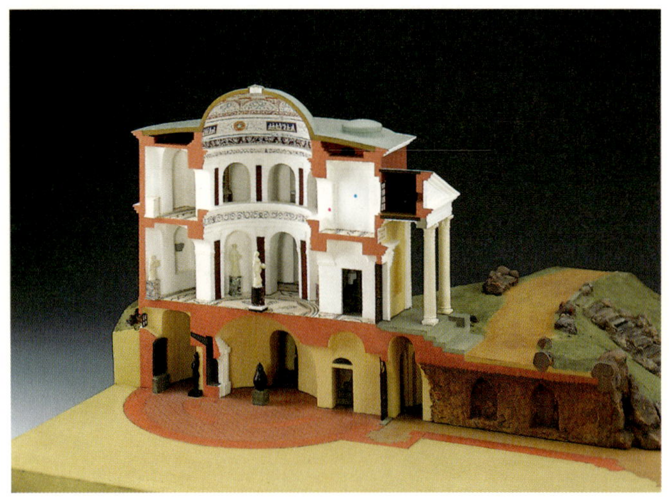

66

SCHNITTMODELL DES PANTHEONS WÖRLITZ
CROSS-SECTIONAL MODEL OF THE WÖRLITZ PANTHEON
1988
Plaster, wood, plastic, rendered in colour
32.0 x 59.0 x 59.0 cm (scale: 1:50)
Michael Wetzel, Wörlitz
Kulturstiftung DessauWörlitz

The cross-sectional model provides an instructive view of the structure of the
Pantheon erected in the eastern part of the Wörlitz garden complex. It is
likely that this version is modelled on Roman principles of monumental
architecture. However, Erdmannsdorff also cited other later English structures, such as those in Chiswick, Stourhead and Stowe.
The basement of the building, built into the Elbe flood dike, contains copies
of Egyptian works of art. This visually embodies the foundation of the two
storeys above ground, which are furnished with Roman antiques.

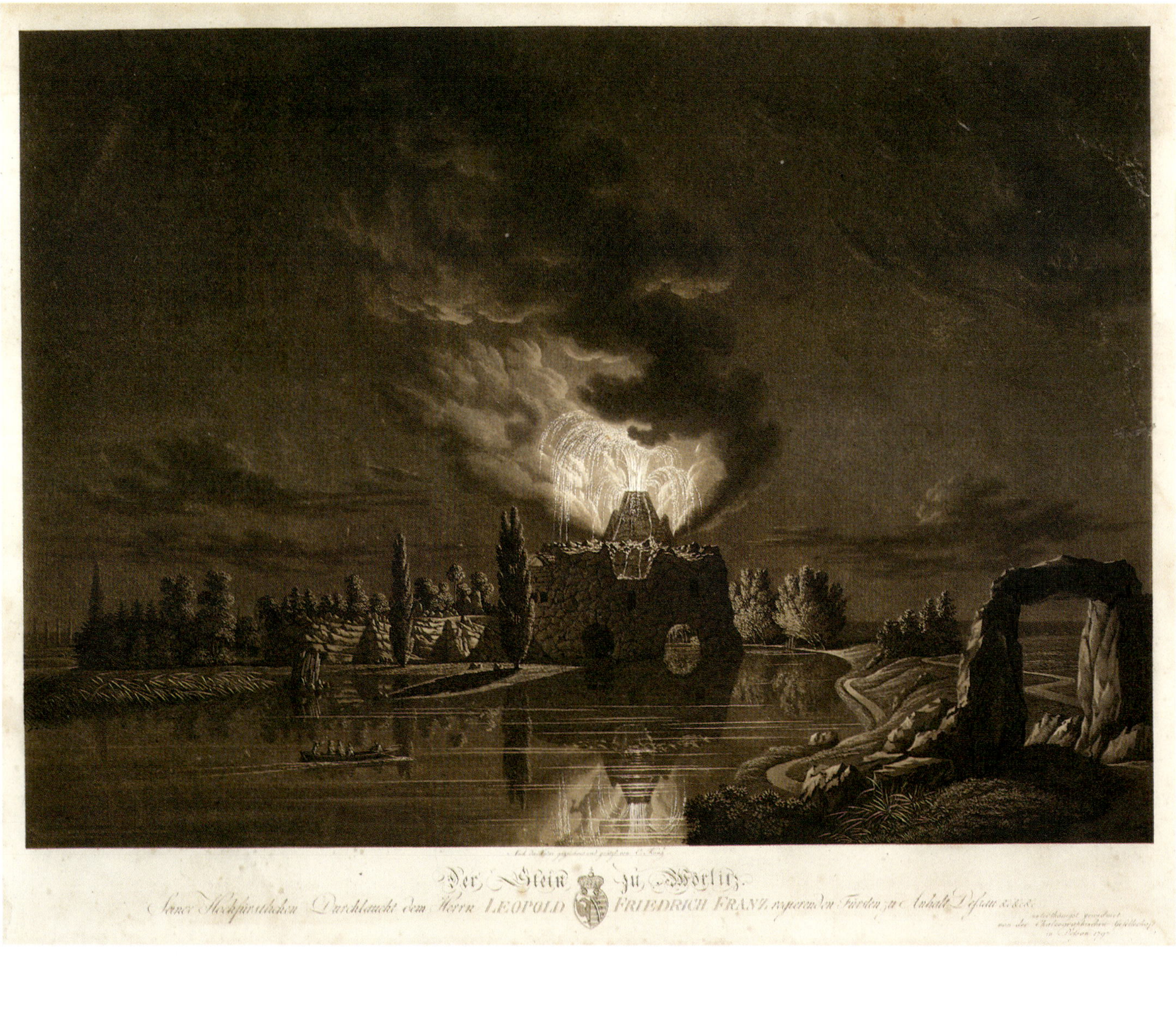

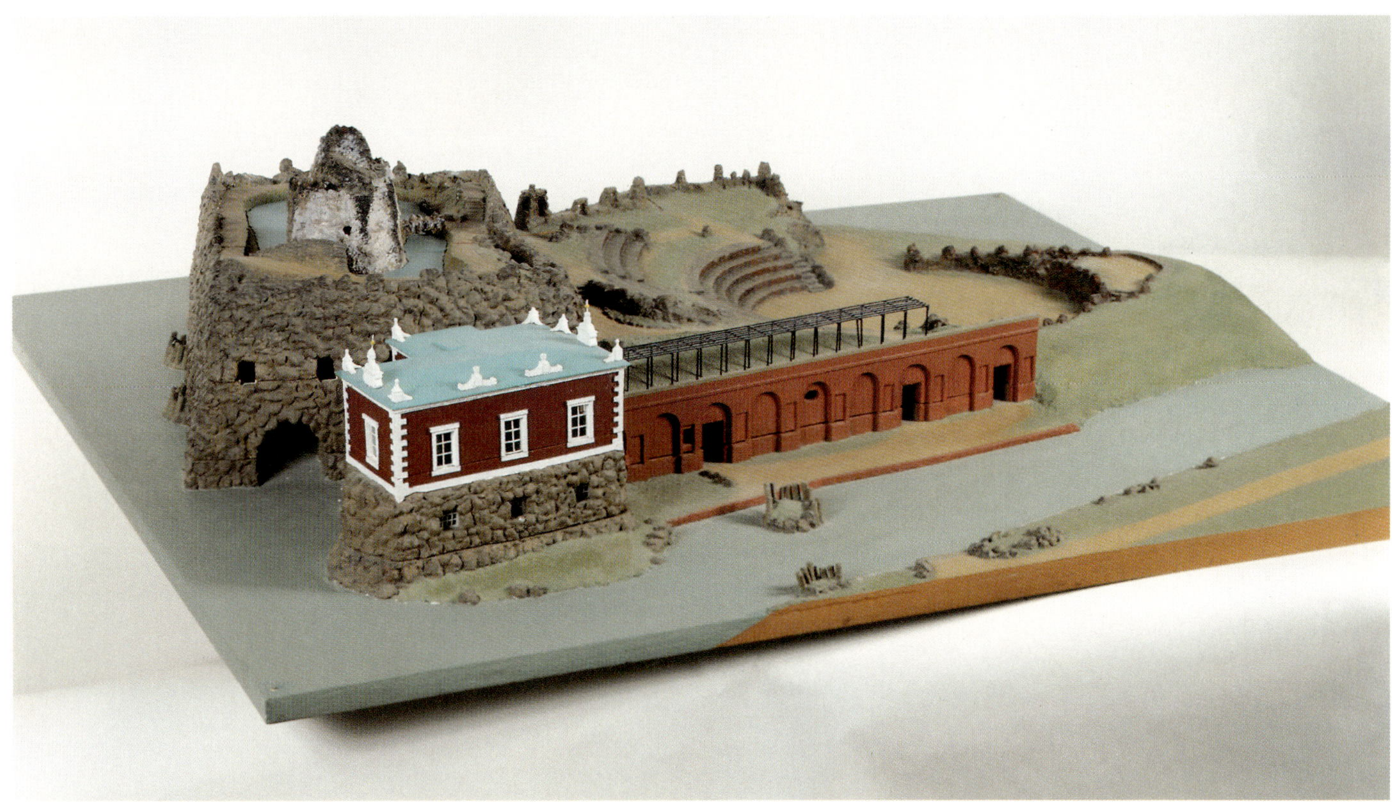

67
Karl Kuntz (1770–1830)
DER STEIN ZU WÖRLITZ
THE "STEIN" OF WÖRLITZ
1797
Aquatint, printed in sepia
50.8 x 66.0 cm
Inscription (translated): centre and right, below the picture "Painted from nature and etched by C. Kunz. / The "Stein" of Wörlitz / Dedicated in humble obedience / To His Highness Prince LEOPOLD FRIEDRICH FRANZ, Prince and Ruler of Anhalt-Dessau etc. / by the Chalcographische Gesellschaft in Dessau in 1797"
Institut für Auslandsbeziehungen

The *Stein* (Stone) was created between 1788 and 1794 as a man-made island containing a number of mementoes of Italy – including architectural citations as well as an accurately detailed replica of the geography of the Gulf of Naples. Towering over the grounds, which are covered with grottoes, is an artificial Mount Vesuvius, which could be made to erupt with the aid of pyrotechnics and clever illumination. The massive stone structure built around a brick core is the most prominent feature of the "Italian landscape" near the garden's east exit. It is fully in keeping with the appeal of the English garden designer William Chambers for sublime garden scenes.

68
SCHNITTMODELL DER FELSENINSEL "STEIN" IN WÖRLITZ
CROSS-SECTIONAL MODEL OF THE ROCK ISLAND "STEIN" IN WÖRLITZ
1992
Plaster, wood, plastic, rendered in colour
24.5 x 100.0 x 85.0 cm (scale: 1:75)
Michael Wetzel, Wörlitz
Kulturstiftung DessauWörlitz

In addition to the reproduction of the grotto-filled, volcanic landscape surrounding Naples, other references to Naples as an artificial landscape were created on the island known as the *Stein*. These included a temple of the day and the night, an amphitheatre, a columbarium and Roman baths. The Villa Hamilton, a small Neoclassical pavilion, rises from an outcropping of rock in the eastern part of the garden complex. It is a replica of the summer house of Sir William Hamilton (1730–1803), the English emissary to Naples, located on the beach of Posillipo. Prince Franz met Sir William during his grand tour.

An essential aspect of the reform program instituted by Prince Franz was the improvement of the local economy, which had been destroyed in the course of the Seven Years' War.

For Anhalt-Dessau, an agricultural region, this called first and foremost for a process of agricultural reform. Based upon English models, an exemplary economy developed during the decades following 1763 which attracted both the attention and the admiration of contemporaries. A significant impulse to development was the introduction of more efficient methods of cultivation. The productive capacity of the three-field system employed in Germany for more than a thousand years, in which a third of the soil was left unplanted for a year, was increased considerably by the shift to the use of formerly fallow fields for the cultivation of feed crops. The planting of clover, previously unheard of in Germany, was propagated in Anhalt-Dessau alongside the newly introduced practice of stall feeding. Prince Franz and Erdmannsdorff brought back large quantities of clover seeds from their first journey to England in 1763/64. The newest methods of cultivation were demonstrated at various model farms, at the *Wörlitzer Domäne* and even in the gardens. The *Domäne* (a demesne), built on the model of Palladio's Villa Emo between 1783 and 1787, united a manor house with stables and servants' quarters.

According to historic sources, Anhalt-Dessau derived thirty per cent of its fiscal income from its orchards. The Prince, regarded by his contemporaries as "a friend and patron of fruit cultivation in Germany", owned a collection of over 200 wax fruits, replicas of most of the varieties of fruit known at the time in their original sizes and colours. The collection was housed in the *"Pomologisches Kabinett"* (a display of fruits) in the Gothic House and was used for purposes of instruction and classification. Trial cultivation of various types of fruit was carried out on the fields and meadows surrounding the Gothic House. The planting of fruit trees along the roads not only brought economic benefits in the form of lease income but contributed to the aesthetic enhancement of the countryside as well. Wherever one looked, utility and beauty were united in a symbiotic partnership. In his treatise on the agricultural system of Anhalt-Dessau, published in 1808, the Dutch farmer Heinrich Friedrich de Bruiningk commented: "…this economy deserves the scrutiny of educated experts in particular. Fields and meadowlands overflow with blessings; … and where one's eye loses sight of the fruits of diligence, the beauty of art extends its hand."

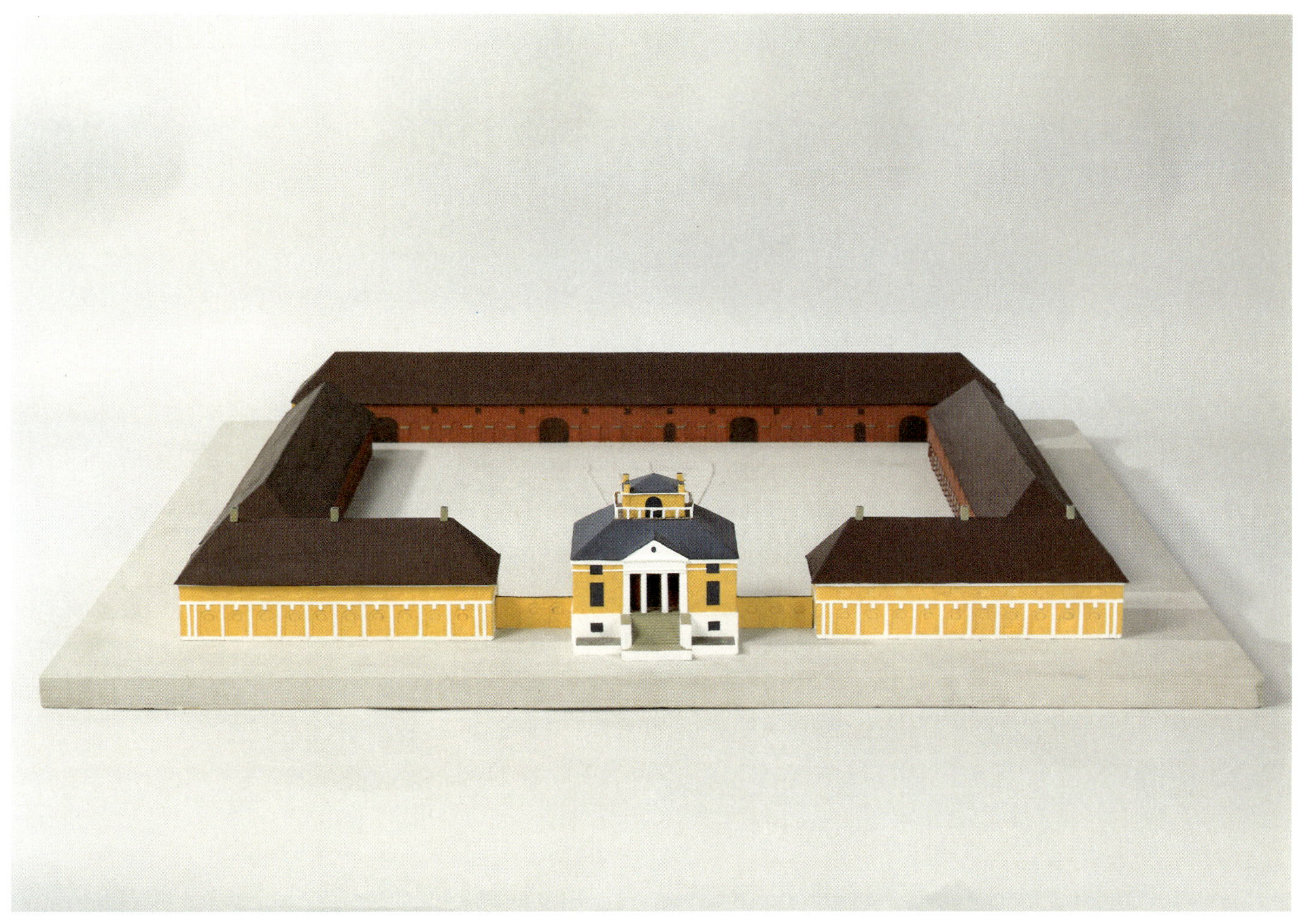

69
MODELL DER WÖRLITZER DOMÄNE
MODEL OF THE WÖRLITZER DOMÄNE
1984
Plaster, wood, rendered in colour
78.0 x 72.0 x 11.0 cm (scale: 1:150)
Michael Wetzel, Wörlitz
Kulturstiftung DessauWörlitz

Modelled on Andrea Palladio's Villa Emo, the *Wörlitzer Domäne* was
designed by Erdmannsdorff and built between 1783 and 1787. It was here that
the Georg Karl von Raumer (1755–1822), Director of the Wörlitz *Ökonomie*,
put into practice the new English-style model agricultural system that generated substantial increases in farming income and attracted numerous interested farmers to Dessau-Wörlitz. The cross-shaped manor complex comprised
the manor house itself as well as stables and servants' quarters. The times
demanded precisely this combination of architectural quality and economic
utility, and Erdmannsdorff responded to that demand in an entirely consistent manner.

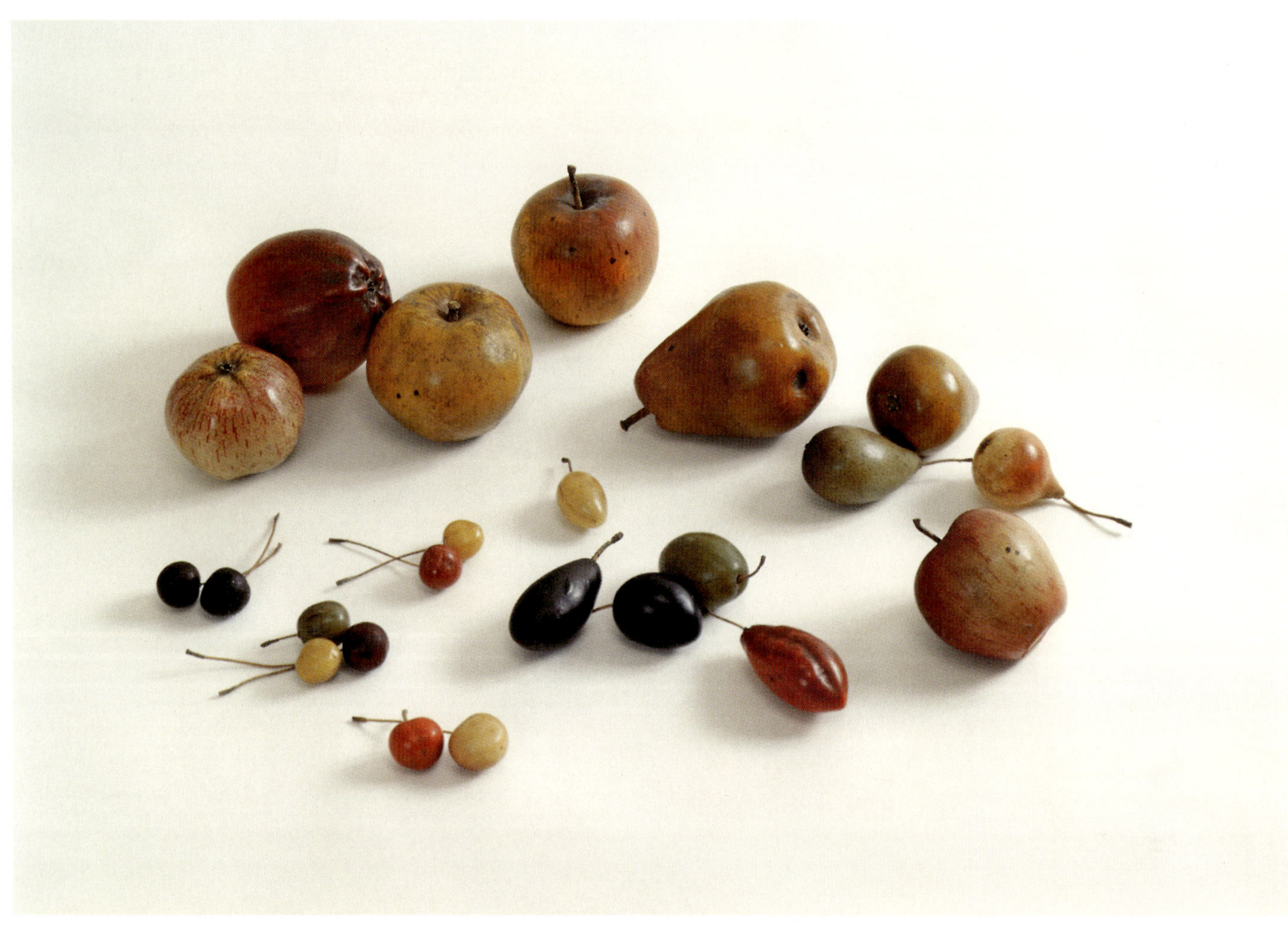

WACHSFRÜCHTE AUS DEM POMOLOGISCHEN KABINETT
WAX FRUITS FROM THE "POMOLOGISCHES KABINETT"
Supplied by Friedrich Justin Bertuch's Landes-Industrie-Comptoir in Weimar
beginning in 1804
Wax, rendered in colour
Imitation fruits in their respective original sizes; largest diameter: 10.0 cm
Kulturstiftung DessauWörlitz

Prince Franz carried out his studies in fruit cultivation in the *Pomologisches
Kabinett* at the Gothic House. This collection of over 200 original-sized wax
fruits represented a three-dimensional version of the many fruit varieties illustrated by the Weimar entrepreneur Friedrich Justin Bertuch (1747–1822) in
the *Allgemeines Teutsches Garten-Magazin*. They facilitated the classification
of fruits on the basis of their external characteristics and were useful as visual
aids in instructional situations.
Intent upon shaping his small principality into a unique garden kingdom,
Prince Franz had trees, mostly fruit-bearing varieties, planted along the paths
and roads that connected the individual gardens and prominent landscape
features, thus improving significantly the aesthetic appearance of the countryside.

71
ALLEGORIE DER LANDWIRTSCHAFT
ALLEGORIE AUF DIE JAGD
AN ALLEGORY ON AGRICULTURE
AN ALLEGORY ON HUNTING
Plaster, cast to scale from reliefs on the Wörlitz Dietrich Monument
Sandstone
75.0 x 63.0 cm each
Kulturstiftung DessauWörlitz

In memory of his uncle and guardian, Prince Dietrich von Anhalt-Dessau
(1702–1769), Franz had an unpretentious monument built in the vicinity of
the *Schloß*. Reliefs depicting allegorical agricultural, hunting and warfare
scenes were added to three sides of the structure's base. Hunting, especially
coursing, was a pastime pursued with great enthusiasm in the game-rich
forests of Anhalt-Dessau.

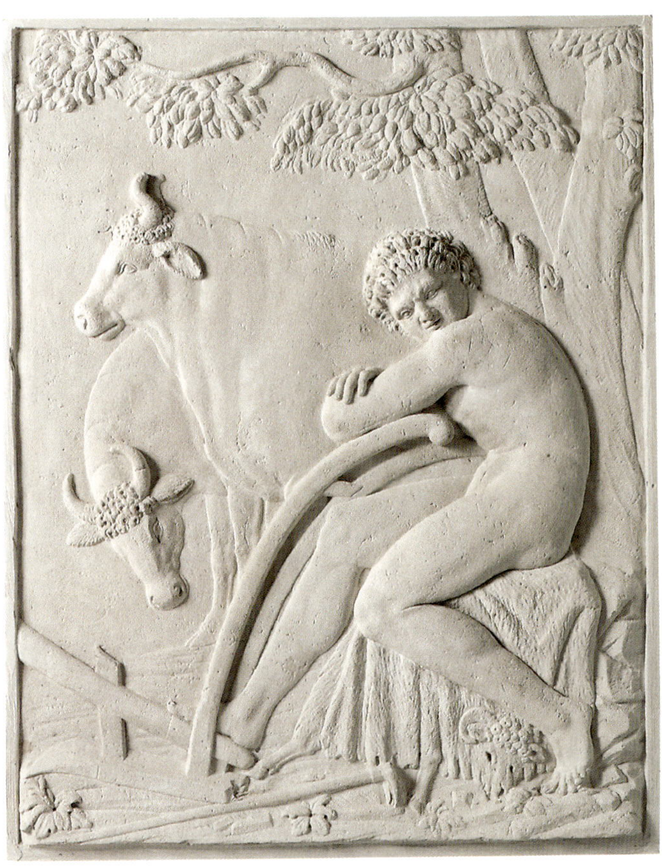

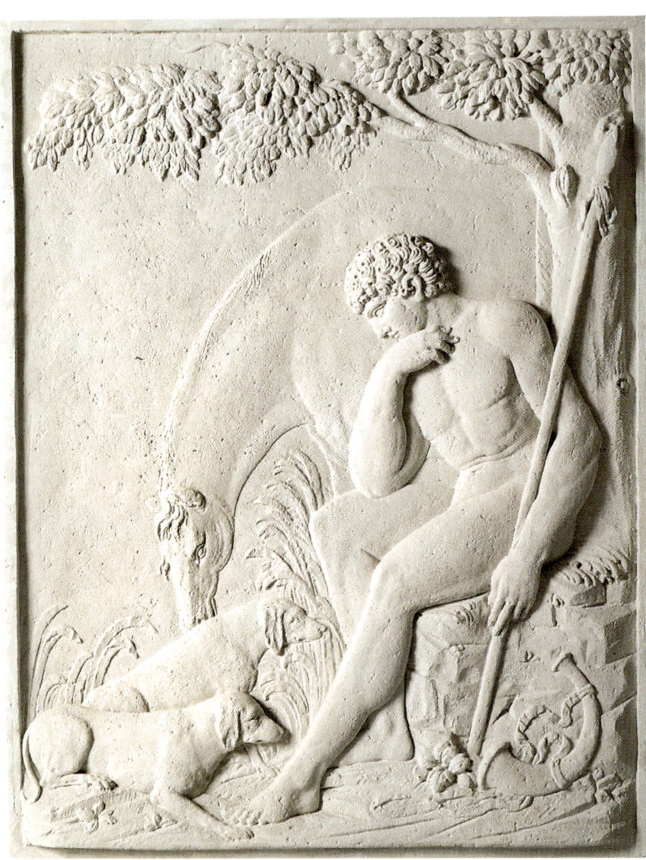

72
Christian Haldenwang (1770–1831)
DIE HEIDEBURG UNWEIT DESSAU AUF DER STRASSE
NACH LEIPZIG
THE HEIDEBURG NEAR DESSAU ON THE ROAD TO
LEIPZIG
1799
Aquatint (reprint)
25.6 x 32.6 cm
Inscription (translated): lower left below the picture "drawn and engraved in
copper"; right "by Haldenwang."; centre "DIE HEIDEBURG / near Dessau
on the Road to Leipzig. / Chalcographisches Gesellschaft of Dessau."
Kulturstiftung DessauWörlitz

Originally located outside Dessau on the road to Leipzig, this Neogothic
brick building was erected by Friedrich Wilhelm von Erdmannsdorff in
1782/83 and modelled to a certain extent upon the Coronation Castle of the
Prussian Kings in Königsberg. The man-made ruin with its five-storey tower
was use for hunting and forestry purposes.

73
Christian Haldenwang (1770–1831)
after Heinrich Theodor Wehle (1778–1805)
STADT DESSAU NOERDLICHER SEITE
THE CITY OF DESSAU, NORTH SIDE
1801
Aquatint (reprint)
25.9 x 33.8 cm
Inscription (translated): lower left below the picture "drawn by Wehle.";
right "etched by Haldenwang."; centre "CITY OF DESSAU / north side /
Chalcographische Gesellschaft of Dessau 1801."
Kulturstiftung DessauWörlitz

The etching shows an expanse of cultivated fields and orchards, much like
those that dominated the landscape everywhere in Anhalt-Dessau, outside the
gates of the city of Dessau. In his description of Anhalt written in 1833, the
ducal librarian Lindner remarked: "At that time, the so-called English form of
agriculture was being introduced and modified to suit the needs of our land
by industrious, perceptive farmers; it was not long before the regions of
Dessau had made outstanding progress in the breeding of horses, cattle and
sheep, in improving fruit yields and in expanding the cultivation of feed
crops.

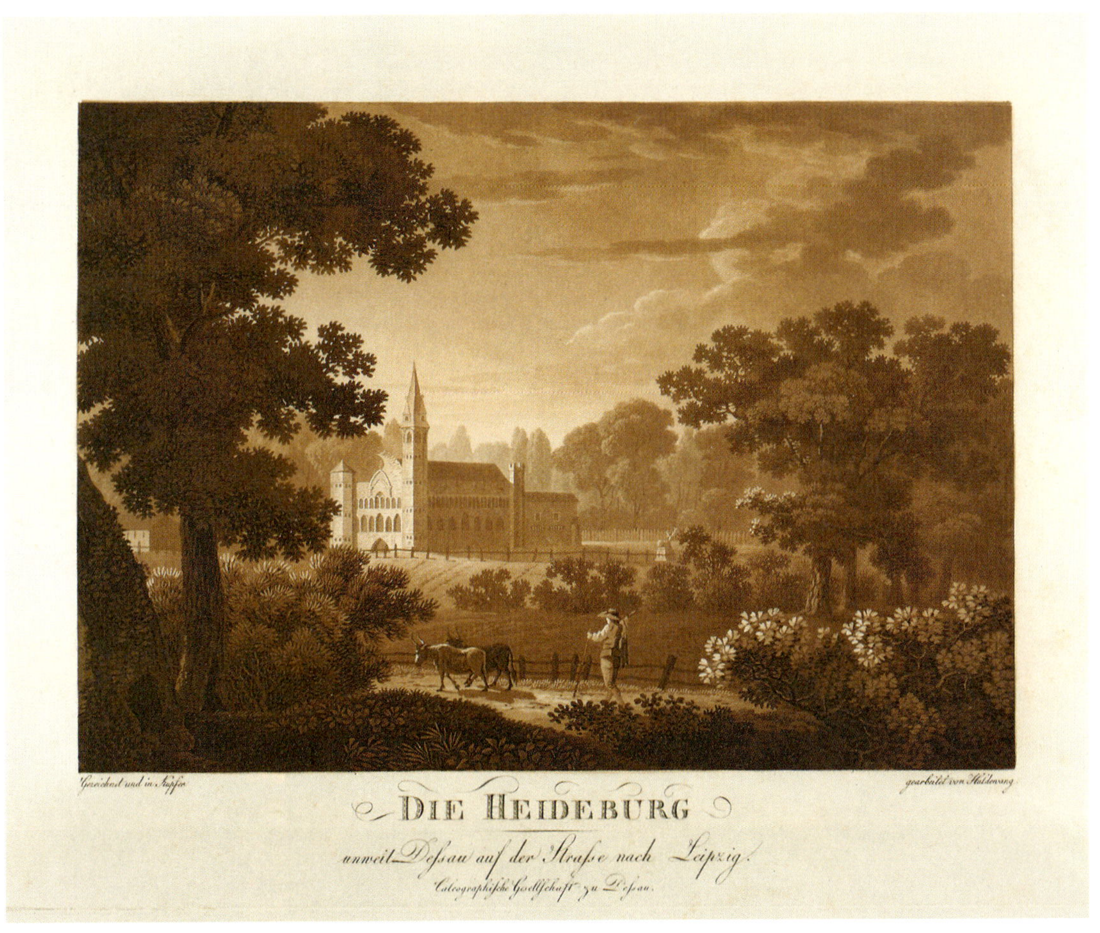

DIE HEIDEBURG

unweit Dessau auf der Straße nach Leipzig.

Calcographische Gesellschaft zu Dessau.

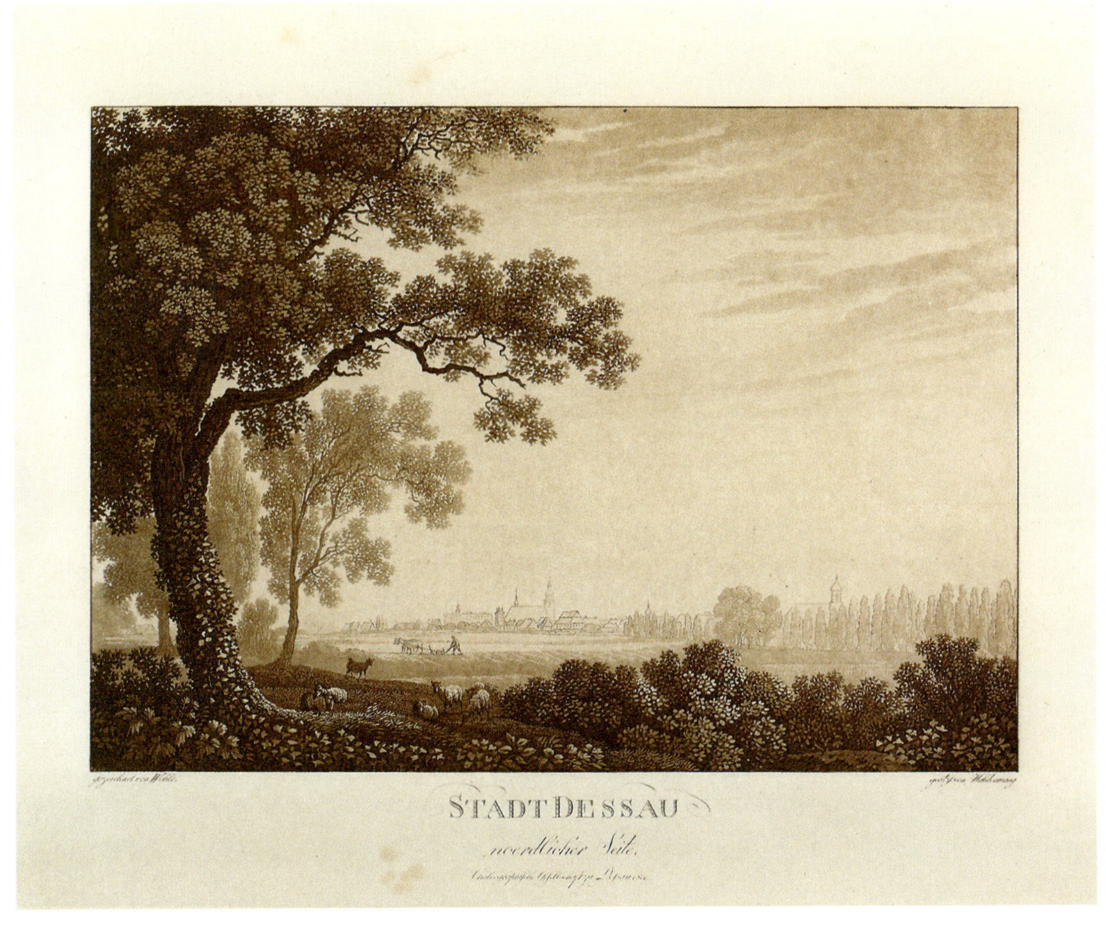

STADT DESSAU

nordliche Seite.

Calcographische Gesellschaft zu Dessau.

Scholarship and education were essential focal points of the German Enlightenment. An important aspect of the comprehensive reform program instituted by Prince Franz, which affected all areas of life, was the restructuring of the school system. For this purpose, in 1771 the Prince called Johann Bernhard Basedow (1724–1790) of Altona to Dessau, a man whose studies of the ideas of Jean-Jacques Rousseau (1712–1778) with respect to humanist scholarship and an approach to education oriented towards the needs of children led him to advocate a "reform of the school system from top to bottom". His *Elementarwerk*, a epoch-making contribution to the development of German educational theory, was published in four volumes in 1774. On December 27th of the same year, the famous *Philanthropin*, a school devoted to humanistic studies, was established as a model educational institution under the direction of Basedow, its first headmaster. Aside from "classical" subjects such as fencing, dancing and foreign languages, other disciplines, including physics, geometry, mechanics, anatomy, horticulture, manual skills and sports were also assumed into the curriculum. In keeping with Enlightenment principles, the intent was to bring forth the ideally educated human being, in whom superior qualities of mind and body were united in harmony. Although the *Philanthropin*, a school catering to the higher classes, made no contribution to the education of the majority of the public, a comprehensive national school reform affecting a broad segment of the population was carried out from 1785 to 1787 by Carl Gottfried Neuendorf (1750–1798). Under the *"Allgemeine Schulordnung für die sämtlichen Stadt- und Landschulen des Fürstentums"* (General Regulations for all Rural and Urban Schools in the Principality) the school system was reformed from the inside out. Above all, the new regulations established the separation of church and school system demanded by the advocates of enlightenment, taking the responsibility for school supervision away from the church and placing it in the hands of a secular directorate. Teachers were given better pay and trained in a national teachers' institute. The newly founded grammar school in Dessau, the only institution at which students could qualify for university studies, was made accessible at no charge to children of the poorer segments of the population.
These efforts towards improving the educational system also found expression in garden design. The public garden in Wörlitz, in particular, took on the character of an educational park intended to promote the development of good taste and to initiate the general public to the innovations that were being demonstrated everywhere.
A first *Beschreibung des Fürstlichen Anhalt-Dessauischen Landhauses und Englischen Gartens zu Wörlitz* (Description of the Royal Country House and English Garden in Wörlitz) was published in 1788.

Seiner

Hochfürstlichen Durchlauchten

Leopold Friedrich

Franz

von Anhalt-Dessau,

Seinem gnädigsten Fürsten

und Herrn,

Für

Beförderung dieses Werks.

Ein Denkmaal der fußfälligen Dankbarkeit

von

Johann Bernhard Basedow.

Des

Elementarwerks
Erster Band.

Ein geordneter Vorrath

aller nöthigen

Erkenntniß.

Zum Unterrichte der Jugend,
von Anfang, bis ins academische Alter,

Zur Belehrung der Eltern,
Schullehrer und Hofmeister,

Zum Nutzen eines jeden Lesers,
die Erkenntniß zu vervollkommnen.

In Verbindung mit einer Sammlung von Kupfer-
stichen, und mit französischer und lateinischer
Uebersetzung dieses Werks.

Mit Chursächsischem gnädigsten Privilegio.

Dessau, 1774.

Bey S. L. Crusius in Leipzig, auch bey dem Verfasser
und seinen Freunden.

74

Johann Bernhard Basedow (1724–1791)

*ELEMENTARY PRINCIPLES, VOL. I. A SYSTEMATIC COMPI-
LATION OF ALL KNOWLEDGE REQUIRED FOR THE
INSTRUCTION OF YOUTH, FROM THE EARLIEST AGE TO
THE ACADEMIC YEARS, FOR THE EDIFICATION OF
PARENTS, SCHOOL TEACHERS AND PRIVATE TUTORS, FOR
THE BENEFIT OF EVERY READER TOWARDS THE PERFEC-
TION OF KNOWLEDGE.*

Dessau and Leipzig: Crucius and Basedow, 1774

17.5 x 11.5 cm (closed), 432 pages

Kulturstiftung DessauWörlitz

The milestone work of 18th-century German educational theory appeared in
four volumes under this title in 1774. In keeping with the new ideas about the
importance of visual aids in instruction, a supplementary volume containing
illustrations relevant to sports, anatomy, natural sciences and a variety of
manual trades was published as an accompaniment to three volumes of text.

75   Ill. p. 142

Wilhelm Friedrich Schlotterbeck (1770–1819)

after Heinrich Theodor Wehle (1778–1805)

DER NEUE BEGRAEBNISPLATZ ZU DESSAU

THE NEW CEMETERY IN DESSAU

1800

Aquatint, 26.5 x 34.0 cm

Inscription (translated): lower left below the picture "drawn by Wehle";
right "etched by Schlotterbeck."; centre "The new Cemetery / in Dessau /
Chalcographische Gesellschaft of Dessau 1800."

Institut für Auslandsbeziehungen

The new cemetery built according to plans by Erdmannsdorff between 1787
and 1789 represents a response to general efforts towards improving general
hygiene in the population, which explains why it was considered necessary to
place it outside the walls of the city. Humanist principles of cemetery design
prescribed burial in rows, without regard to differences in rank or station.
This cemetery became the final resting place of its own architect as well.
Even the combined entrance gateway and integrated mortuary, a classical
triumphal arch was intended to emphasise the humanist character of this
cemetery for the dead of all Christian denominations.

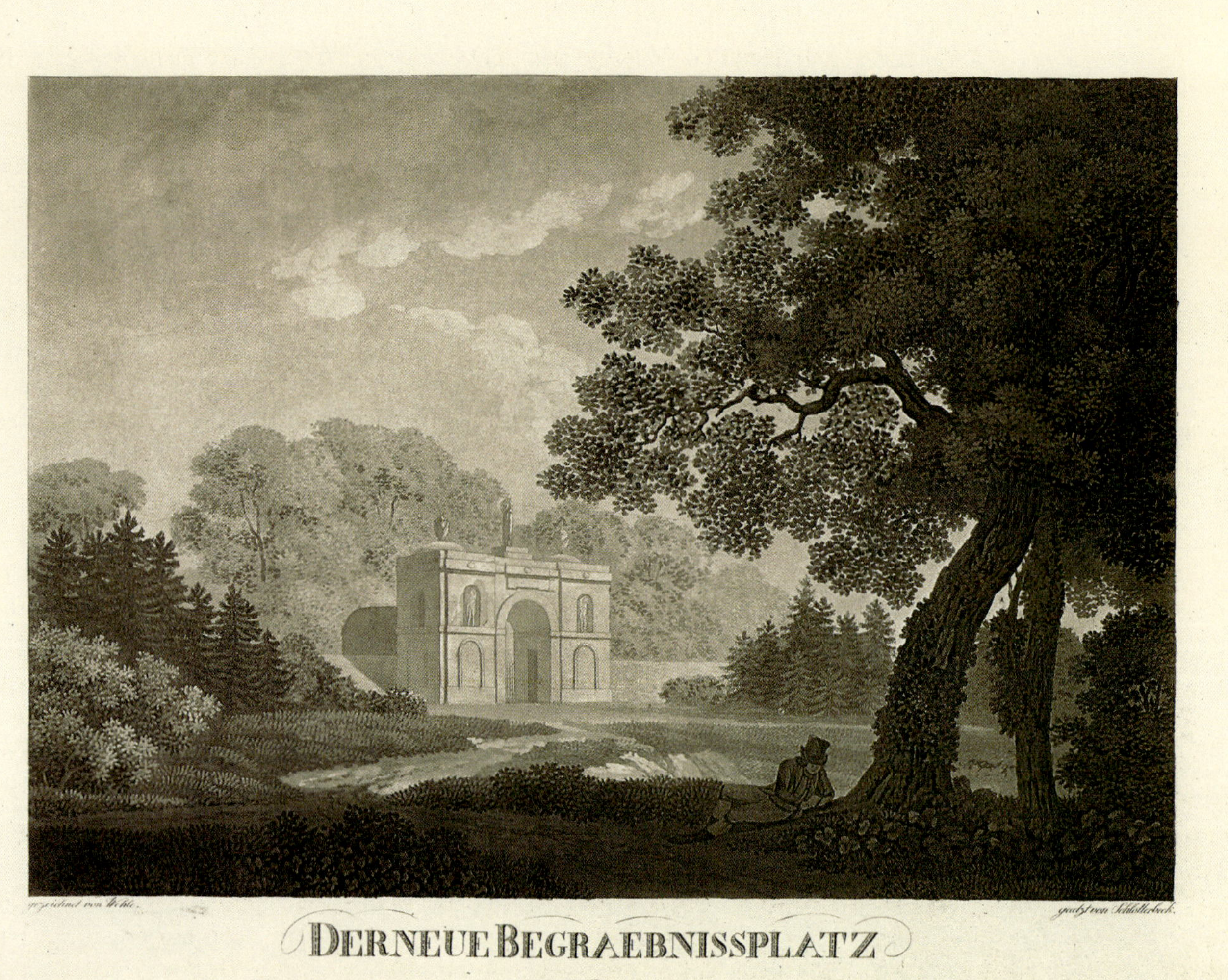

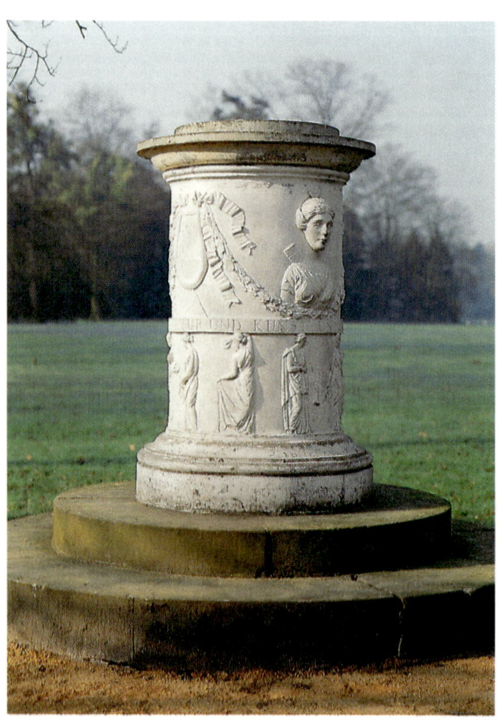

76
DER WARNUNGSALTAR IN WÖRLITZ
THE ALTAR OF WARNING IN WÖRLITZ
1800
Acrylic resin, cast to scale from the sandstone original
Height (altar): 181.0 cm; diameter 100.0 cm; height (base); 4.0 cm; diameter:
130.0 cm
Kulturstiftung DessauWörlitz

The Altar of Warning was erected in the *Schochscher Garten* after the death
of Erdmannsdorff in 1800. The inscription printed around the middle of the
cylindrical base reads as follows (translated): "WANDERER, HEED
NATURE AND ART AND PROTECT THEIR WORKS". Above the
inscription are sculpted reliefs of Diana and Phoebus with images of lyres and
laurel garlands between them. On the lower portion of the monument is a
depiction of the nine muses.

Interest in the cultures of ancient Greece and Rome, reawakened during the Renaissance, grew considerably stronger during the 18th century. Prince Franz's collection efforts were influenced to a significant extent by that interest. Aside from his personal experiences in Italy and his study of the art and architecture of antiquity, recent developments in English culture had the greatest effect on the character of the Prince's collections.

The *Schloß* in Wörlitz, built and furnished in the style of the Neo-Palladian country houses popular among English aristocracy, contains a number of different collections. The development of the collections coincided for the most part with the Prince's travels. In addition to paintings and sculptures, the interior comprises an extensive and highly unique collection of Wedgwood bearing classical motifs, much of which was displayed as hearth decoration. Also used as hearth or mantelpiece ornaments were bronze sculptures by Giacomo Zoffoli (1731–1785).

As an exemplary exhibit of Neoclassical interior design, the publicly accessible *Wörlitzer Schloß* possessed the same didactic significance as the entire complex. Apart from the *Schloß*, the Gothic House, built beginning in 1773, also housed a number of collections within its walls. A total of 385 portraits, countless prints, paraphernalia, furniture and medallions filled its rooms, whose furnishings differed fundamentally from the classical orientation evident in the interiors of the *Schloß*. Many of the objects testify to the Prince's interest in history or are expressive, at the very least, of his concern with the history of his own family. A great number of the paintings and prints refer to English history of the 16th and 17th centuries. Worthy of particular note is a collection of Swiss stained glass from the same period, modelled upon similar collections in English country houses. The purchase of the panes was arranged by the Swiss pastor and physiognomist Johann Kaspar Lavater (1741–1801), who also influenced the development of the extensive portrait collection.

The character of the interior of the Gothic House has changed considerably as a result of losses and damage incurred in the course of two World Wars. The *Schloß* itself, on the other hand, has been preserved for the most part in its original form and is presented today in its authentic historical context.

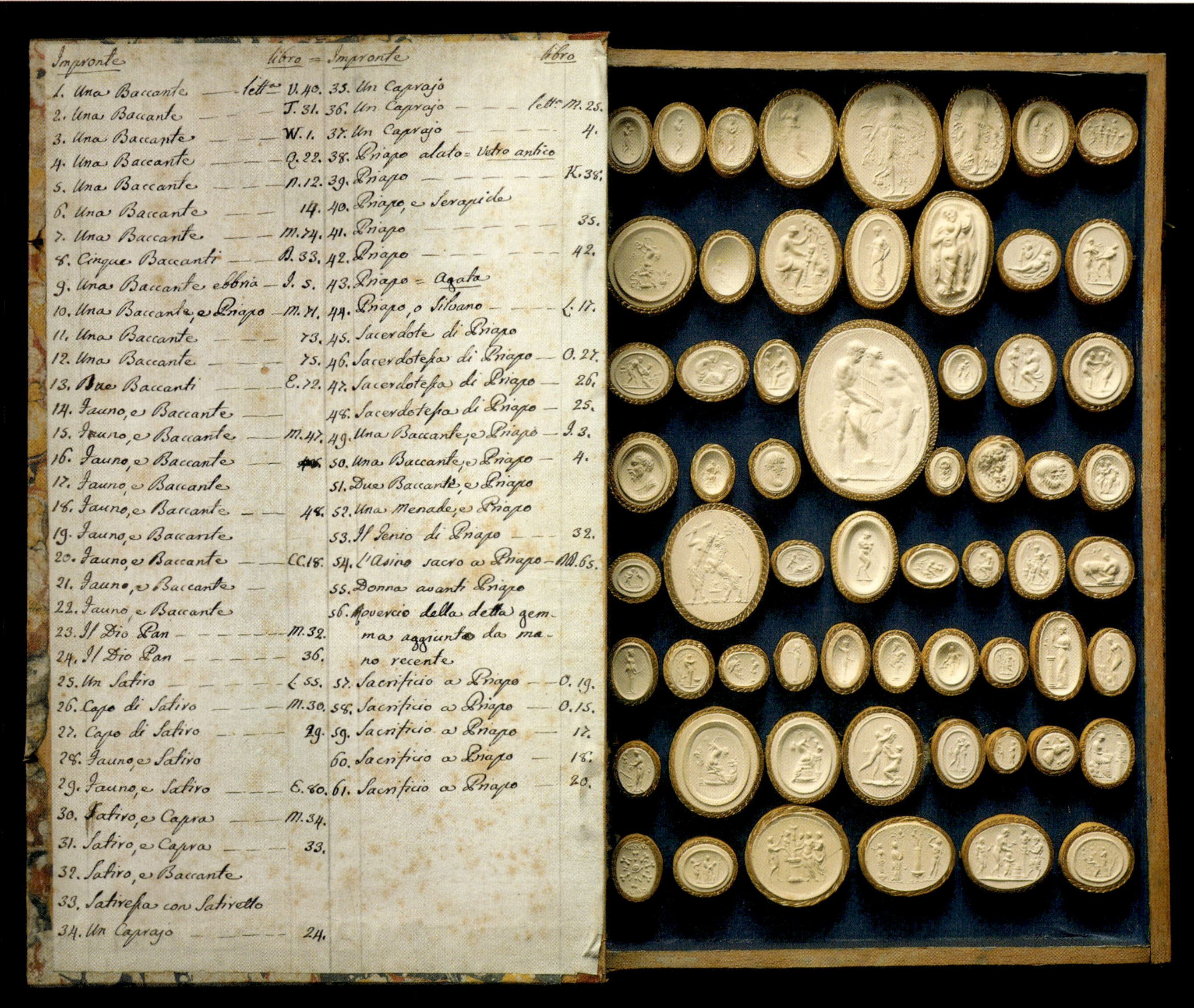

77

Francesco Dolce (dates of birth and death unknown; worked during the first half of the 18th century)

IMPRONTE DIE GEMME BAND XI

INTAGLIO IMPRINTS, VOLUME XI

Circa 1765

Plaster intaglio imprints in cardboard frames with guilt edges, mounted in 29 wooden cases covered with marbled paper; brass mountings; hand-written table of contents on each inside cover

21.5 x 32.5 cm

Kulturstiftung DessauWörlitz

This library of imprints in 29 volumes from the collection of Prince Franz has been preserved in Wörlitz. The plaster impressions of cut stones are mounted individually in guilt-edged cardboard frames. Each volume was carefully and elaborately bound. The enthusiasm for classical Greece and Rome evident in the 18th century was accompanied by a growing interest in cut stones. It is certain that the Wörlitz collection served as a fund of motifs from which Erdmannsdorff drew inspiration for his Neoclassical interior designs.

78

GLASSCHEIBE AUS DEM GOTHISCHEN HAUS IN WÖRLITZ MIT INSCHRIFT JOHANN KASPAR LAVATERS

GLASS PANE FROM THE GOTHIC HOUSE IN WÖRLITZ WITH AN INSCRIPTION BY JOHANN KASPAR LAVATER

1786

Glass copy in the original dimensions

14.5 x 12.0 cm

Inscription (translated): "Thou memorial to ancient art and / Times of trust in God / Admiration, sadness, courage / and hope look to thee / Though art and times gone by / Yet thou showest us in broad views / What pious humanity / Diligence and forthright virtue can do. / Wörlitz, July 15th, 1786 / Johann Casp Lavater."

Kulturstiftung DessauWörlitz

Johann Kaspar Lavater visited Wörlitz and his friends the Prince and Princess in 1786. During his stay he memorialised himself in the Gothic House with an inscription on a pane of glass in the "Geistliches Kabinett" (Religious Exhibit). Although Lavater paid tribute to the character of the collection as a museum, its significance as a political signal escaped the attention of the bourgeois scholar.

Ihr Denkmal' ältrer Kunst und
Gottergebnerer Zeiten.
Erinnerung, Wehmuth, Muth
und Hoffnung ziehn mich an.
Zu der Kunst und Zeiten Sie
Doch zieht Ihr uns in Weiten

Was Schwären Menschheit
Fleiß und reichre Tugend krönt

Wörliz den 15. Jul. 1786
Johañ Casp Lavate[r]

Jacob vermacht die hand mit felen. Bekomt vom Vater so den se[...]
Thut für den Esau sich anstellen. Weil Esau wolt ein wild Erle[...]

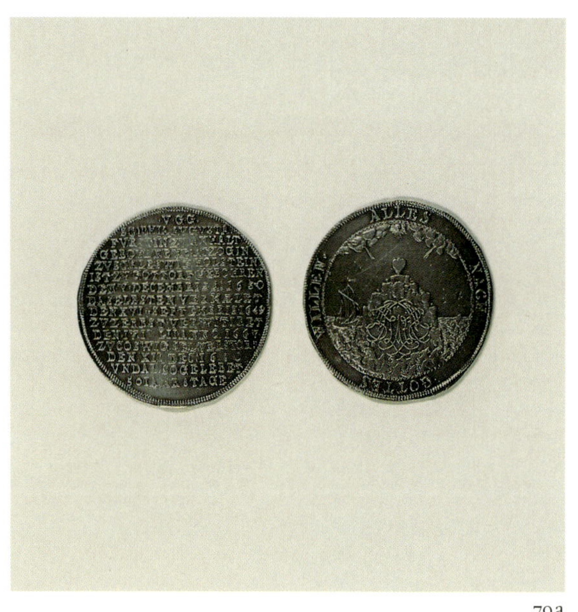

79a

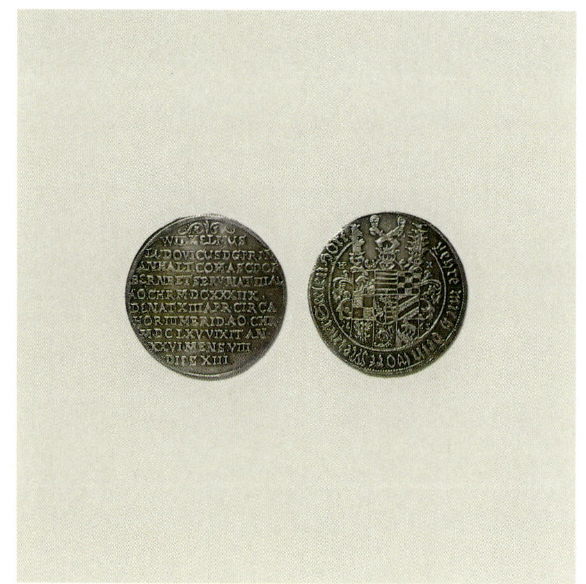

79d

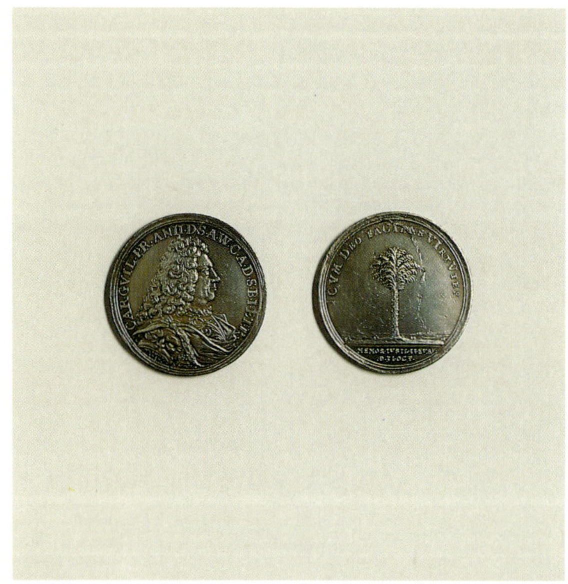

79b

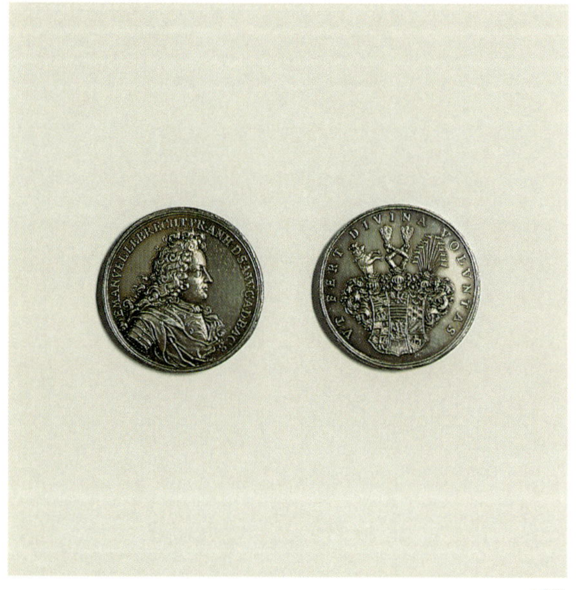

79e

79c

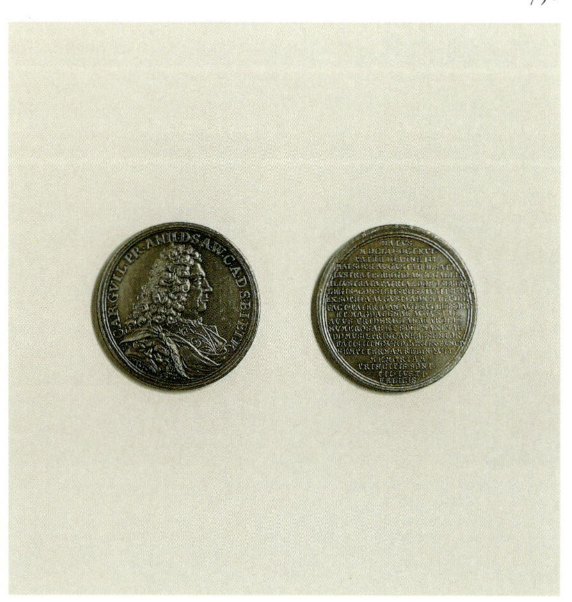

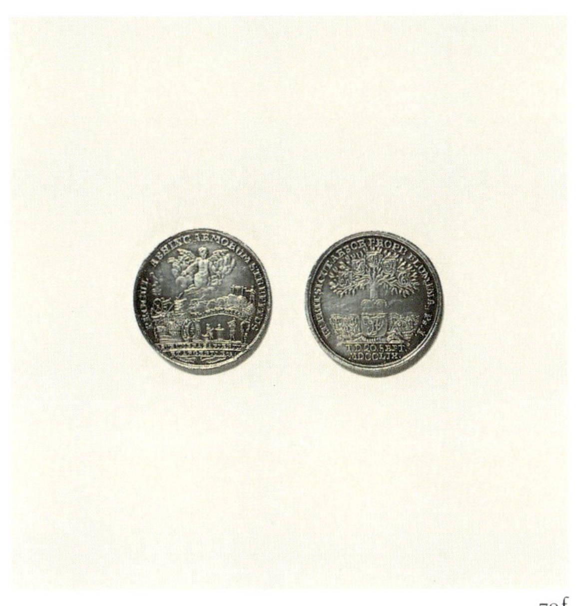

79f

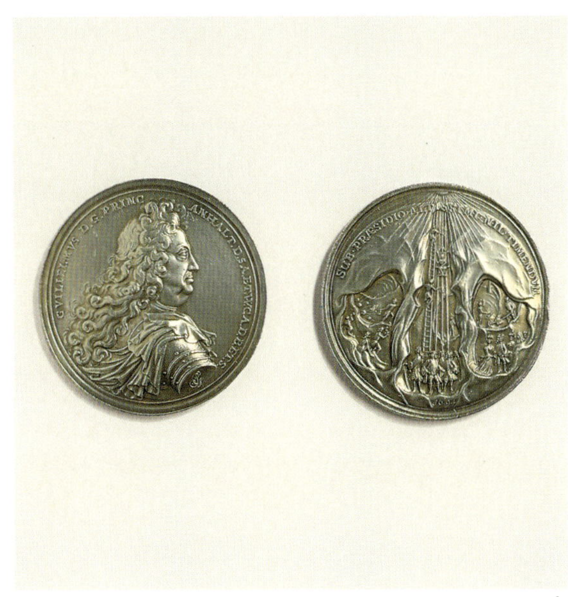

79h

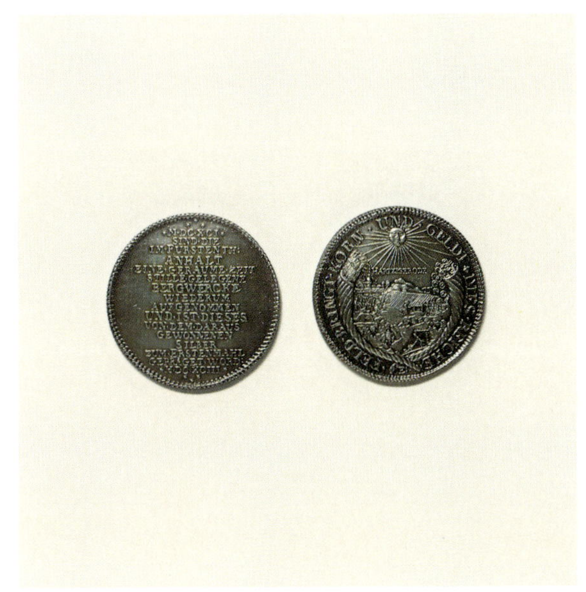

79g

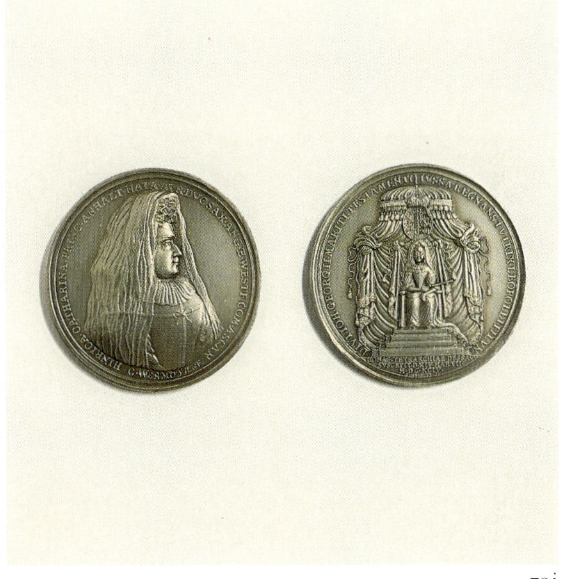

79i

79k

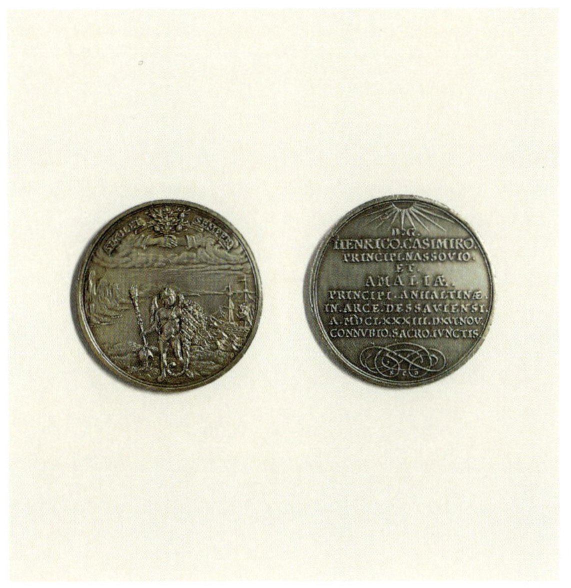

79   Ill. p. 146–147

MÜNZEN

COINS AND MEDALLIONS

Gold-plated brass castings, replicas of coins and medallions from the Gothic
House in Wörlitz

Kulturstiftung DessauWörlitz

Scale of the illustrations: 1:2

a) Medallion issued by Carl Wilhelm von Anhalt-Zerbst commemorating the
death of this mother
1680
Diameter: 5.3 cm

b) Medallion issued by Carl Wilhelm von Anhalt-Zerbst commemorating
the second secular celebration of the Reformation
1717
Diameter: 4.4 cm

c) Medallion issued by Johann August von Anhalt-Zerbst commemorating
the death of his father Carl Wilhelm
1718
Diameter: 4.4 cm

d) Taler. Emanuel von Anhalt-Köthen
1665
Diameter: 4.3 cm

e) Medallion issued by Leopold von Anhalt-Köthen commemorating the
death of this father
1704
Diameter: 4.3 cm

f) Medallion commemorating the 60th birthday of Victor Friedrich von
Anhalt-Köthen
1759
Diameter: 3.7 cm

g) Medallion commemorating the renewal of coal mining operations in
Anhalt
1693
Diameter: 4.6 cm

h) Medallion commemorating the visit of Princess Elisabeth Albertine von
Anhalt-Bernburg to the silver mine
1694
Diameter: 6.2 cm

i) Medallion commemorating the inauguration of Henriette Catharina von
Anhalt-Dessau
1694
Diameter: 5.9 cm

k) Medallion commemorating the marriage of Princess Amalie von Anhalt-
Dessau to Heinrich Casimir von Nassau-Dietz
1683
Diameter: 5.1 cm

A collection of coins was maintained in the Gothic House. Prince Franz
concentrated his collection efforts primarily on coins and medallions of relevance to the history of the House of Anhalt. As August Rode remarked, the
collection of such items was in keeping with the Prince's inclination to "live
himself amongst his renowned ancestors."

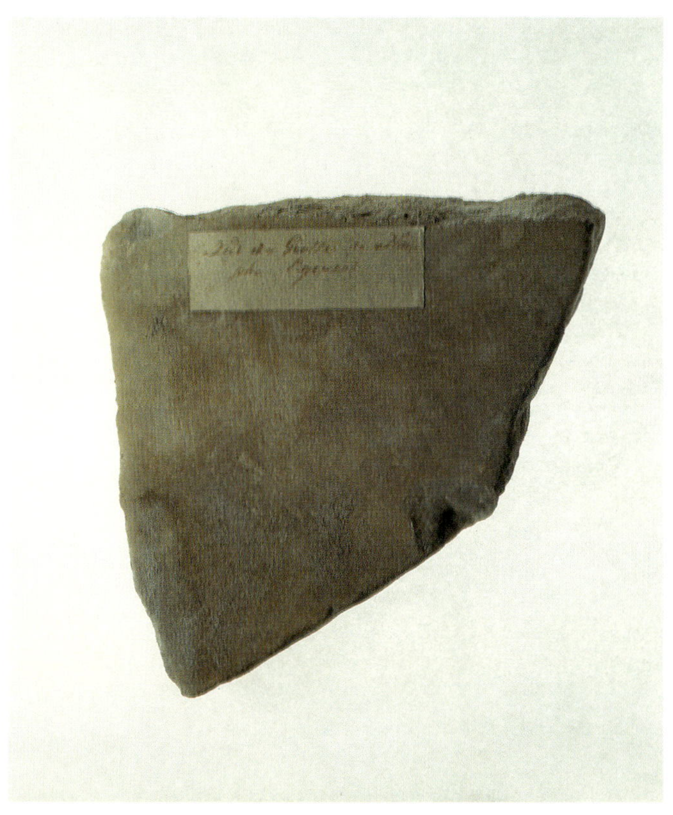

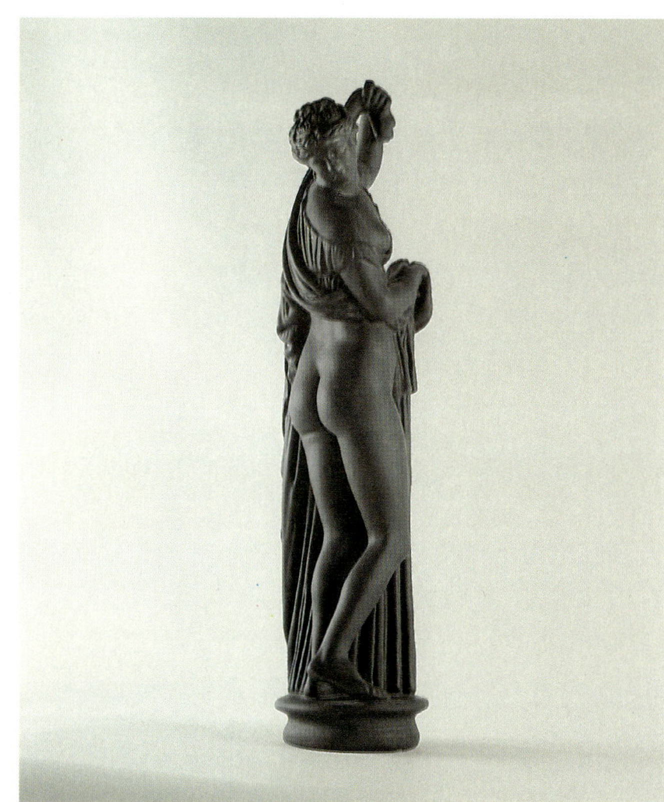

80

PLATTE "AUS DER GROTTE DER NYMPHE EGERIA"
MARBLE SLAB "FROM THE GROTTO OF THE NYMPH
EGERIA"
Marble
15.0 x 14.8 x 2.8 cm (maximum dimensions)
Label affixed (translated): "From the grotto of the nymph Egeria"
Kulturstiftung DessauWörlitz

Numerous smaller, often antique items were kept in the cupboards of the
library of the *Wörlitzer Schloß*. Found among them was this fragment from
the famous structure outside the gates of Rome, brought back by the Prince as
a "souvenir" of his journey to Italy in 1765/66. Prince Franz hat the Grotto of
Egeria built immediately adjacent to the rock island *Stein* beginning in 1790.

81

Giacomo Zoffoli (circa 1731–1785)
VENUS KALLIPYGOS
VENUS KALLIPYGOS
Before 1785
Plaster, cast to scale from the bronze original
Height: 36.0 cm
Kulturstiftung DessauWörlitz

This bronze statue by the roman sculptor and silversmith Giacomo Zoffoli is
a copy of an ancient marble sculpture. Small replicas of classical sculptures,
either in plaster or bronze, were among the most popular souvenirs collected
by foreign tourists in Rome. Zoffoli's pieces were of superb quality and in particular demand among English travellers, who often decorated their hearths
and mantelpieces with them upon their return. Prince Franz did much the
same in furnishing his *Schloß*. His collection of Zoffoli bronzes, originally
numbering 21 pieces, was displayed on the mantelpieces of the Great Hall
and the Prince's bedroom.

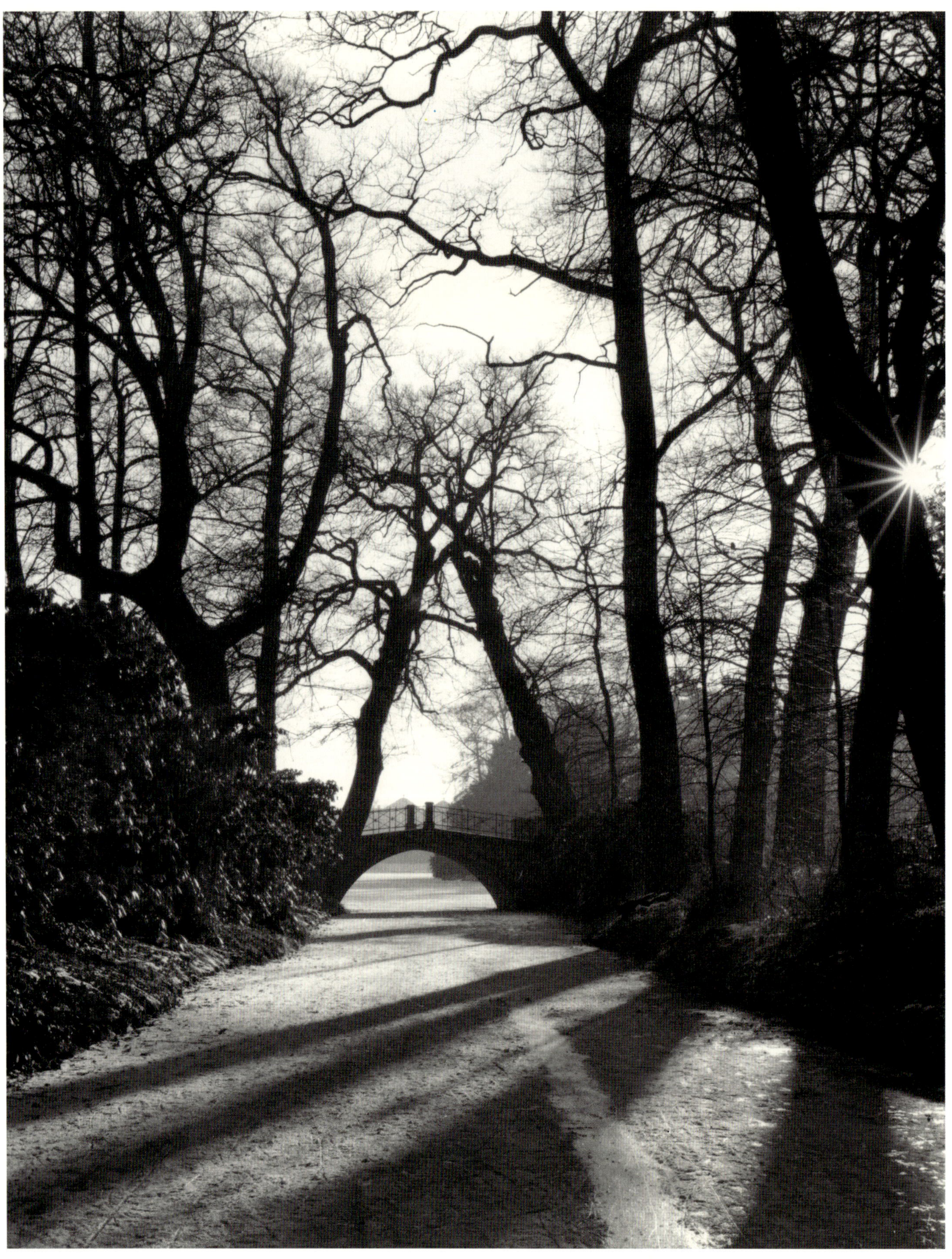

Lutz Winkler, Wolf's Bridge, Wörlitz (cat. no. 82.12)

*"Wörlitz ist keine lokale Größe, Wörlitz ist nicht
einmal eine nur deutsche, es ist eine europäische,
eine Weltangelegenheit."*

Wilhelm van Kempen

"SEASONS IN A CULTIVATED LANDSCAPE"

Lutz Winkler

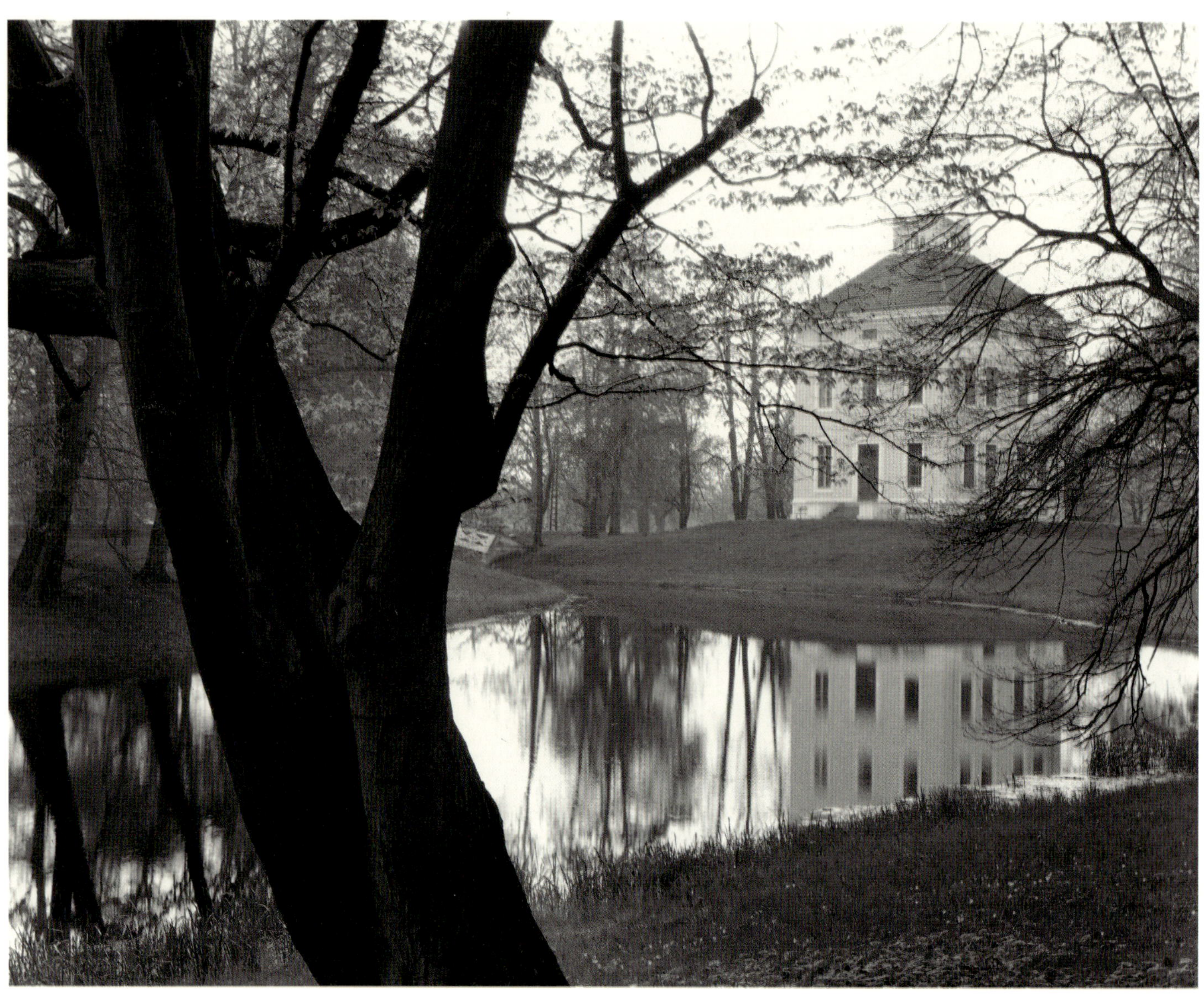

Schloss Luisium, Dessau (cat. no. 82.13)

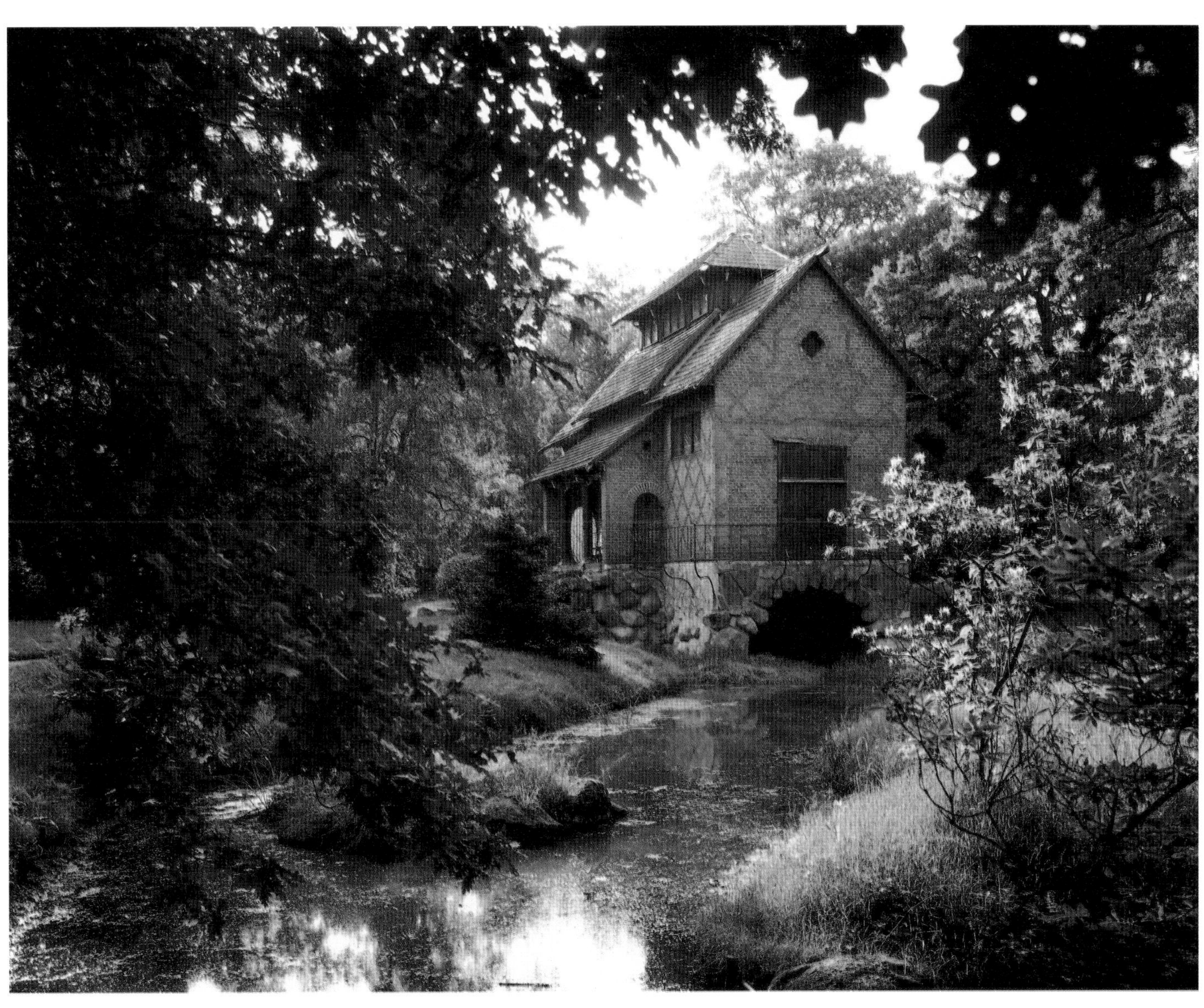

Chinese Teahouse, Oranienbaum (cat. no. 82.7)

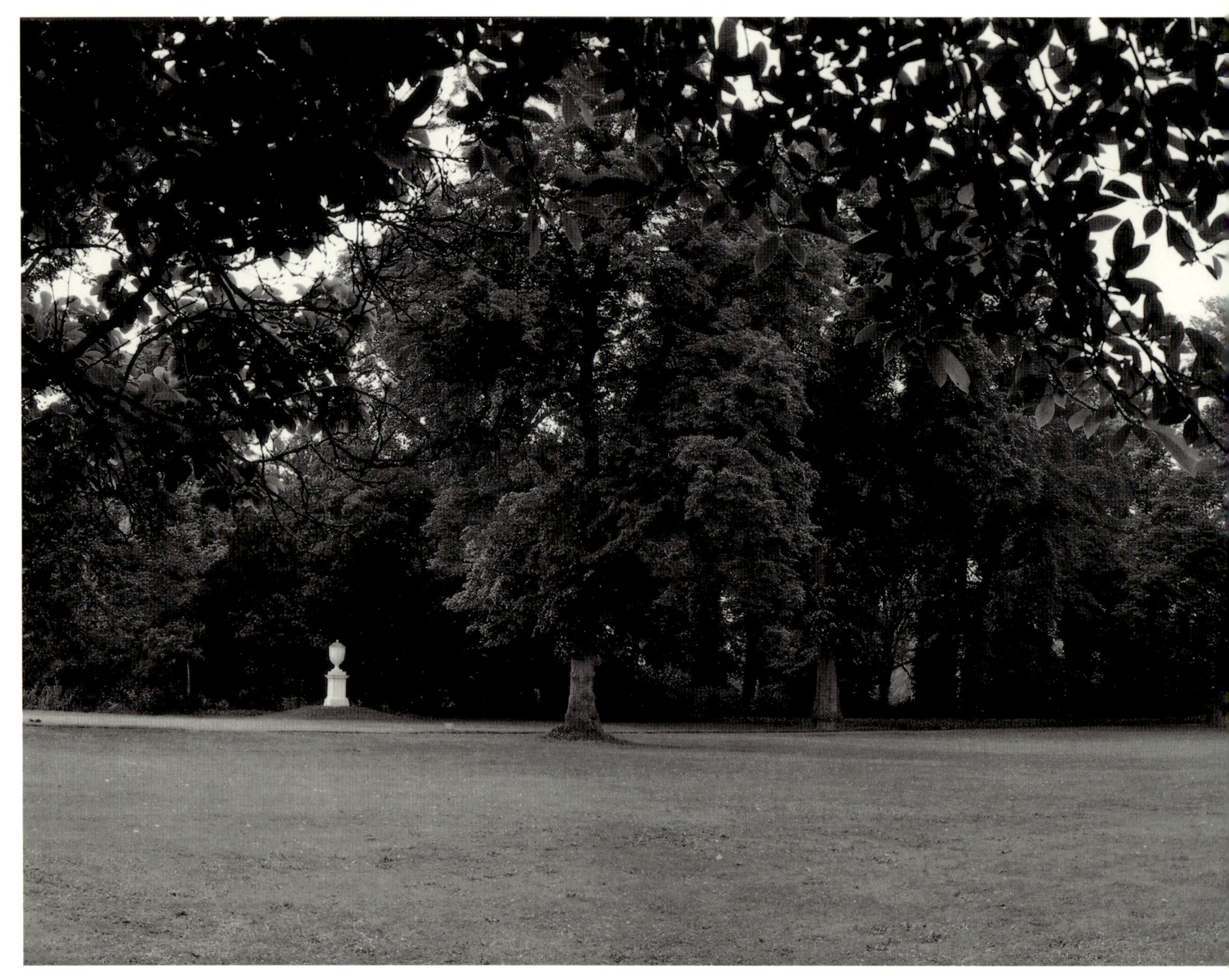

Wörlitz Castle (cat. no. 82.3)

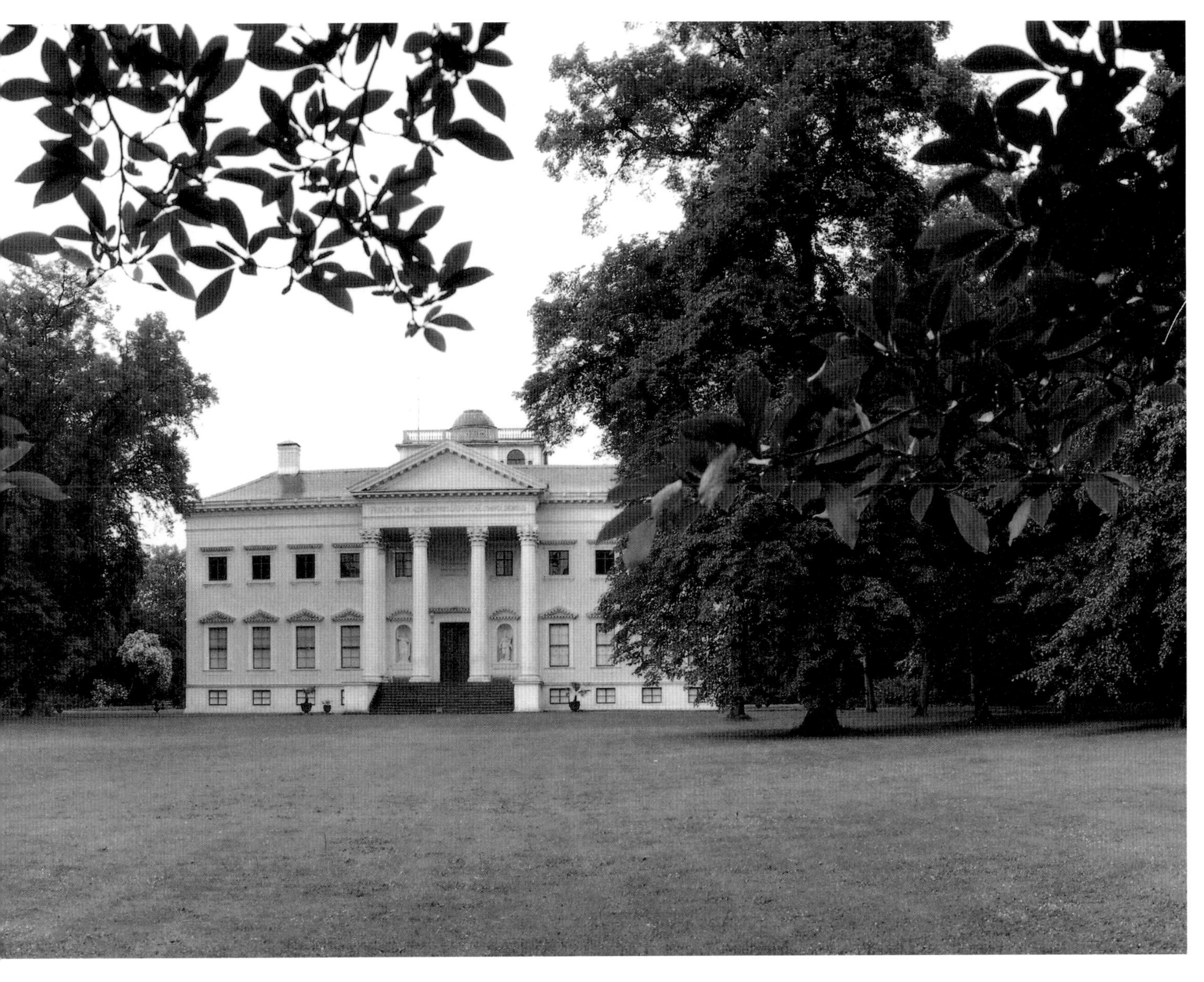

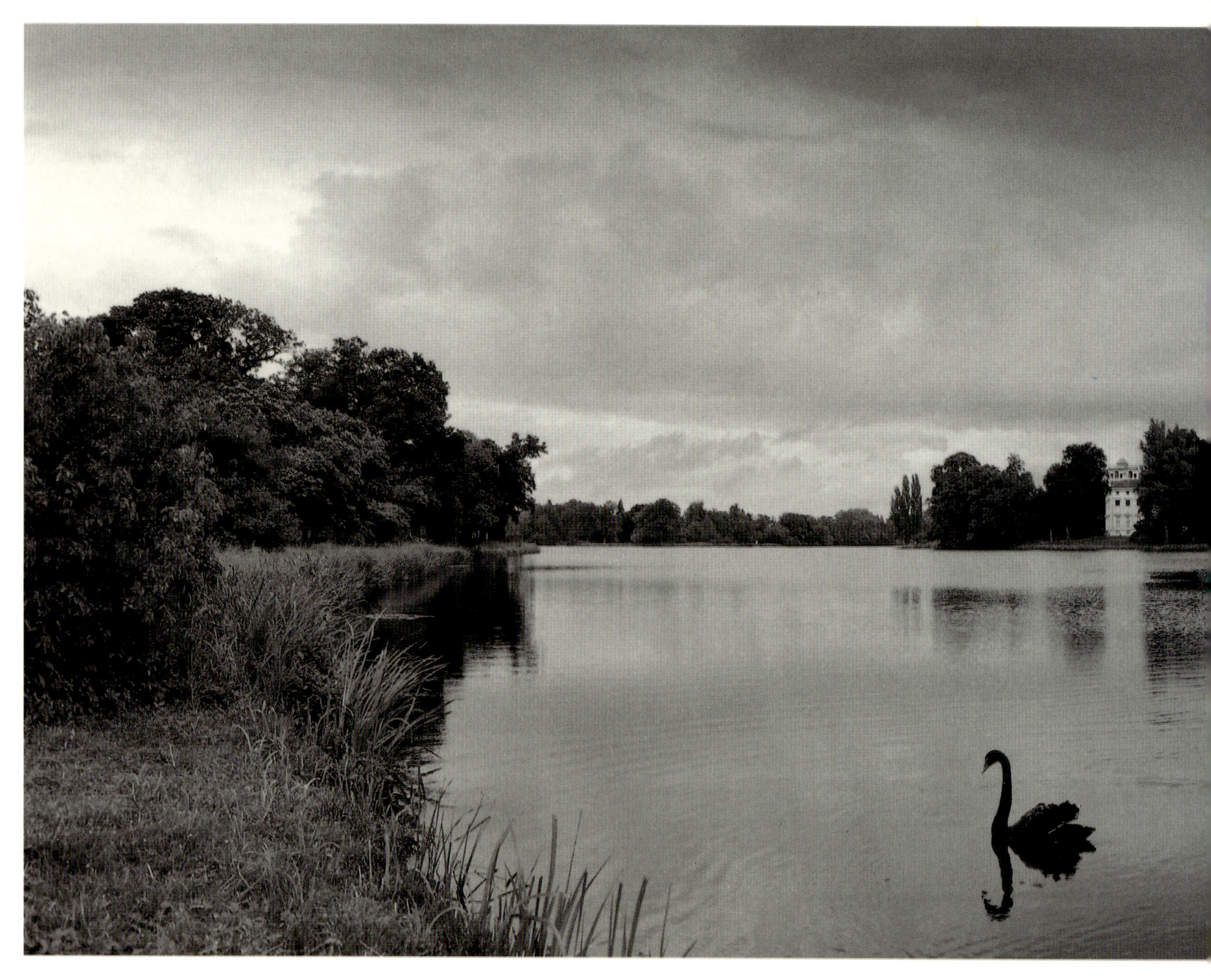

Lake Wörlitz and *Schloss* (cat. no. 82.5)

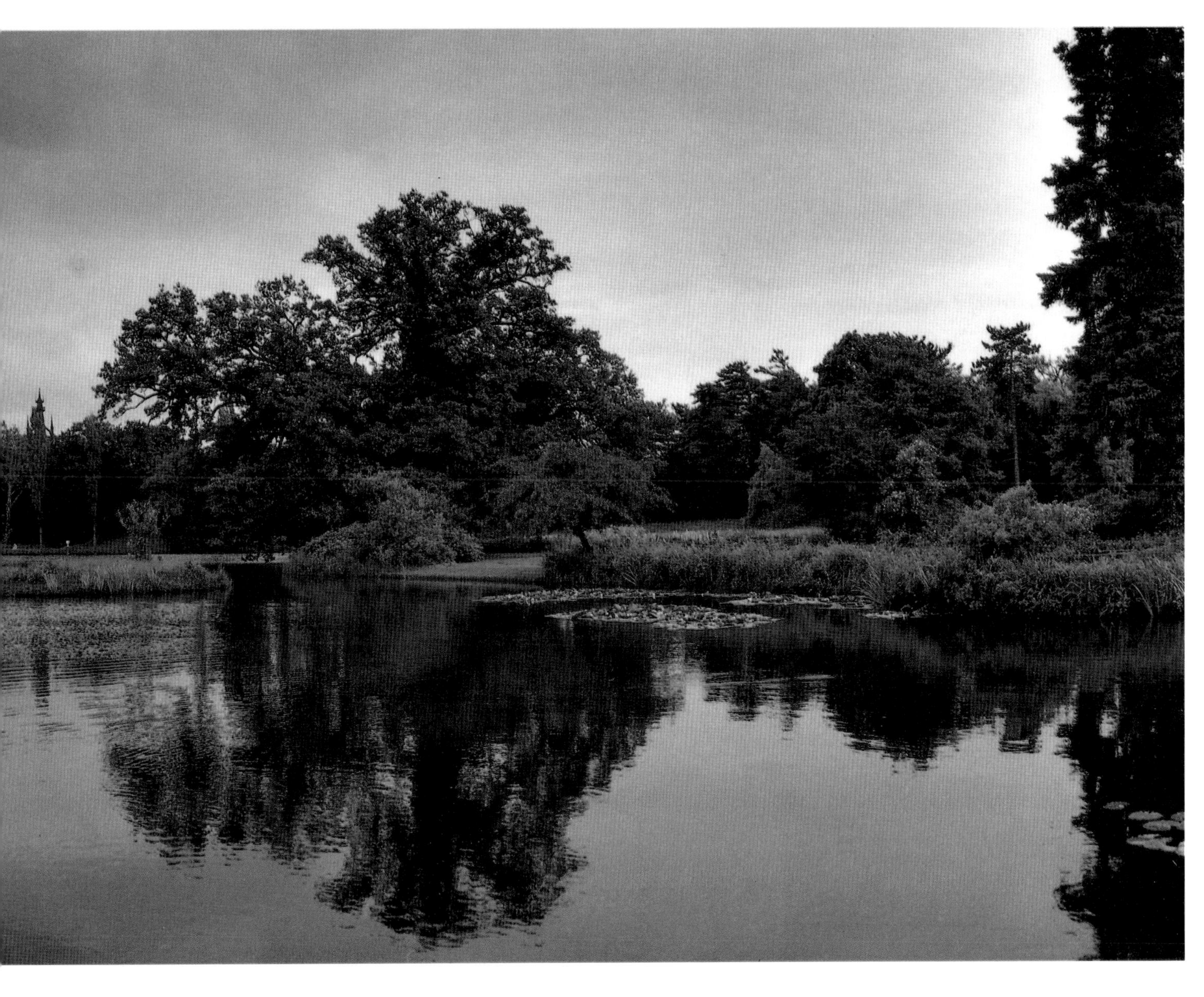

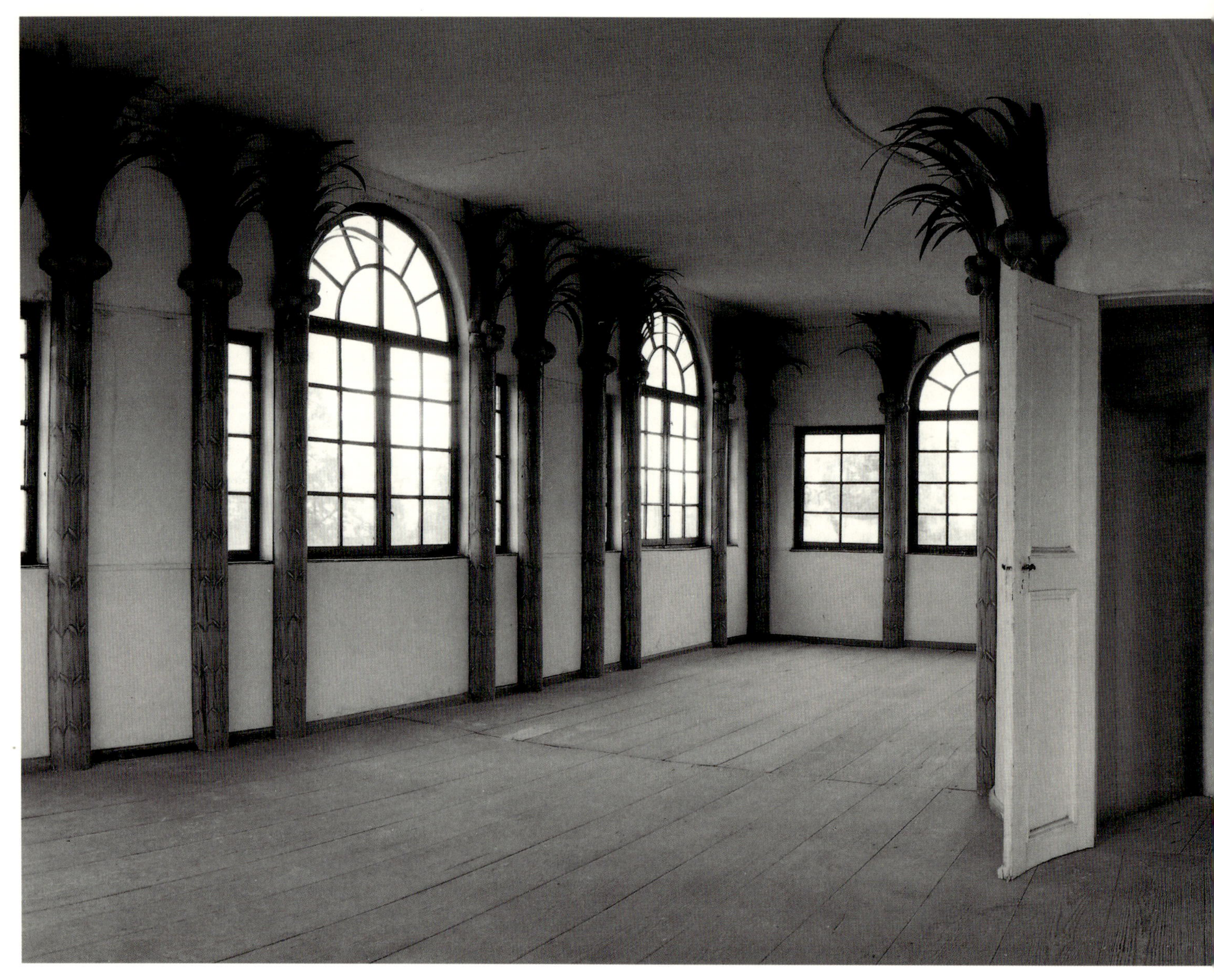

Hall of Palms, Schloss Wörlitz (cat. no. 82.11)

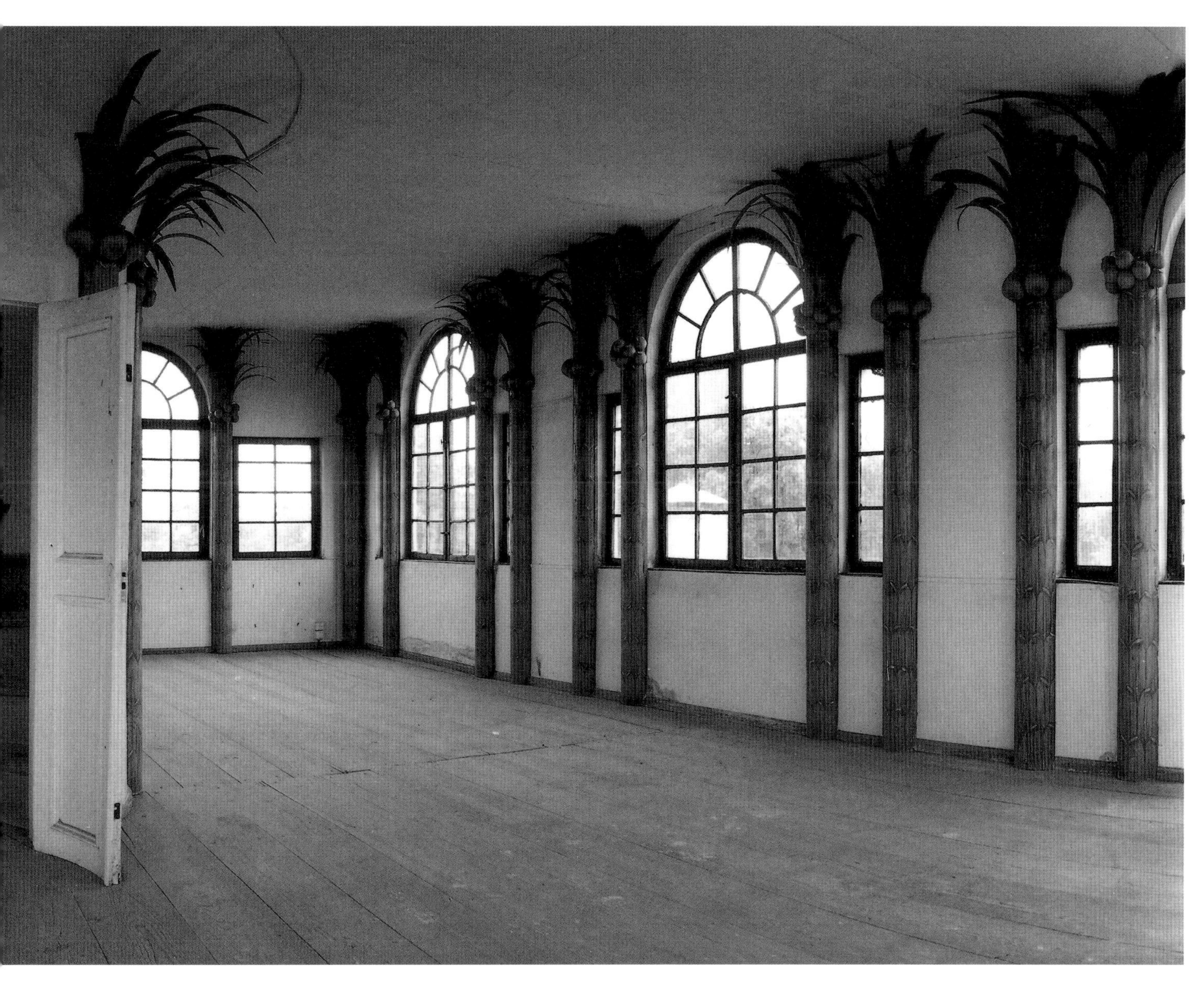

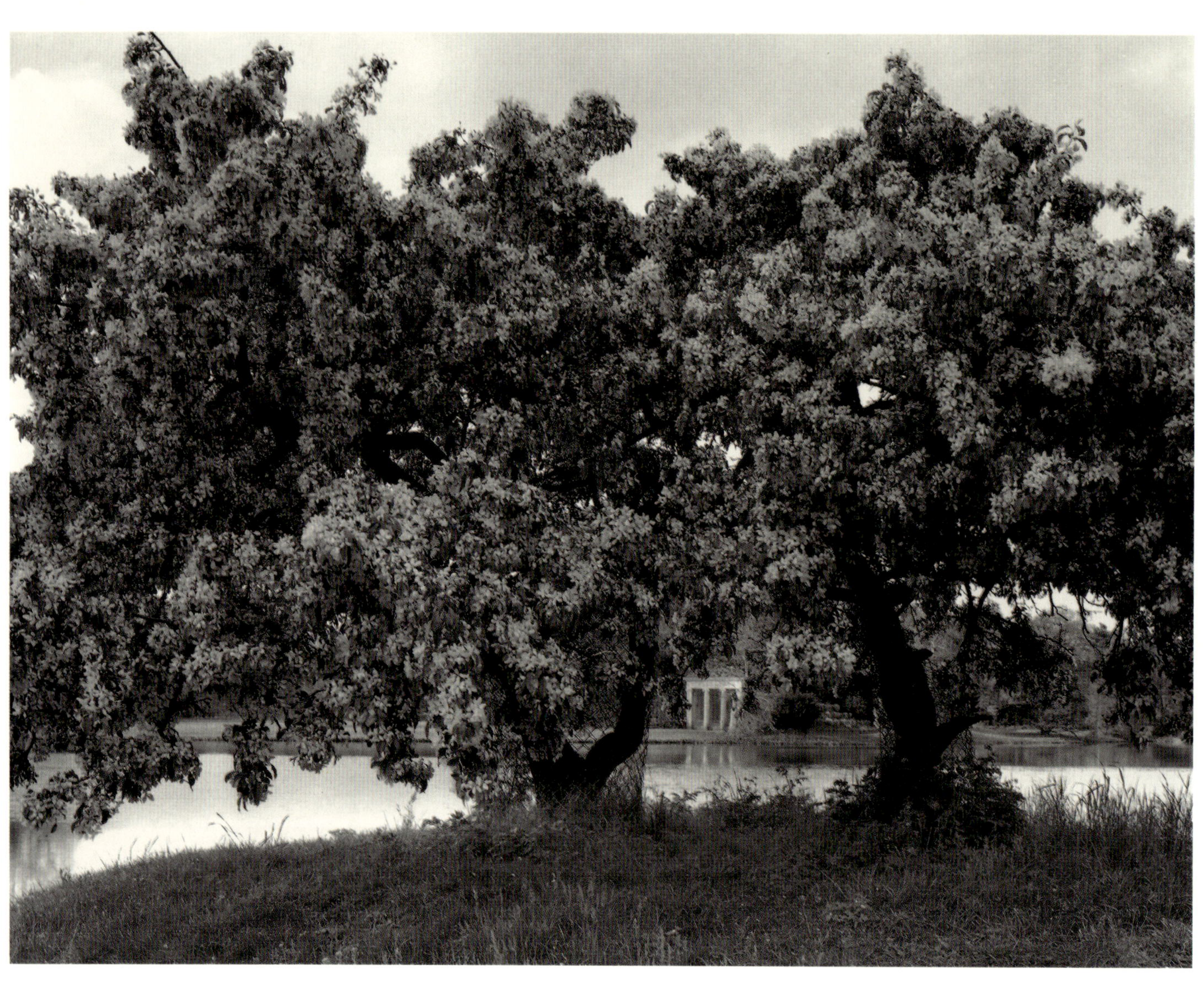

Orchard at the Lake Wörlitz (cat. no. 82.15)

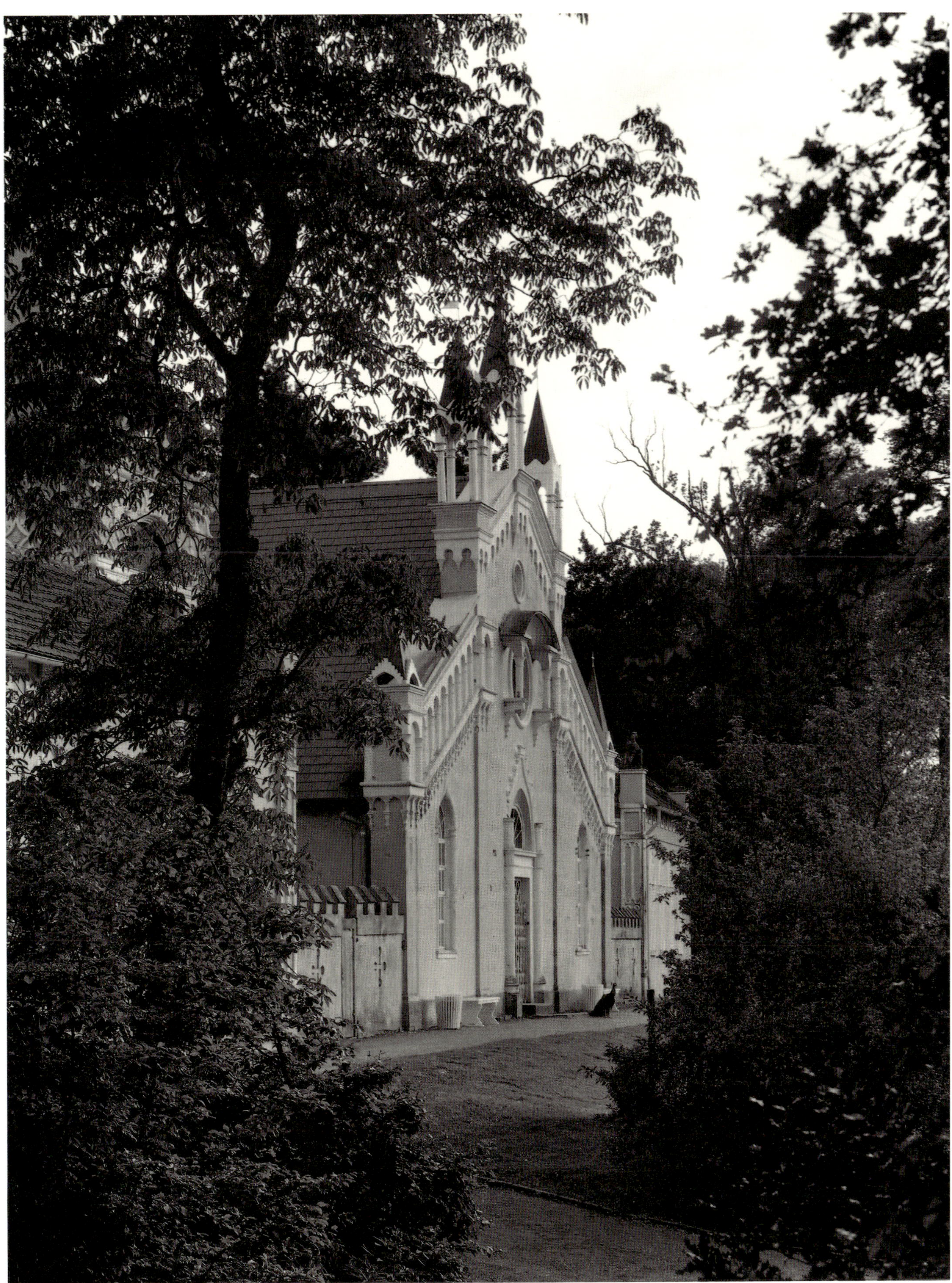

Gothic House / Façade Facing the Canal (cat. no. 82.6)

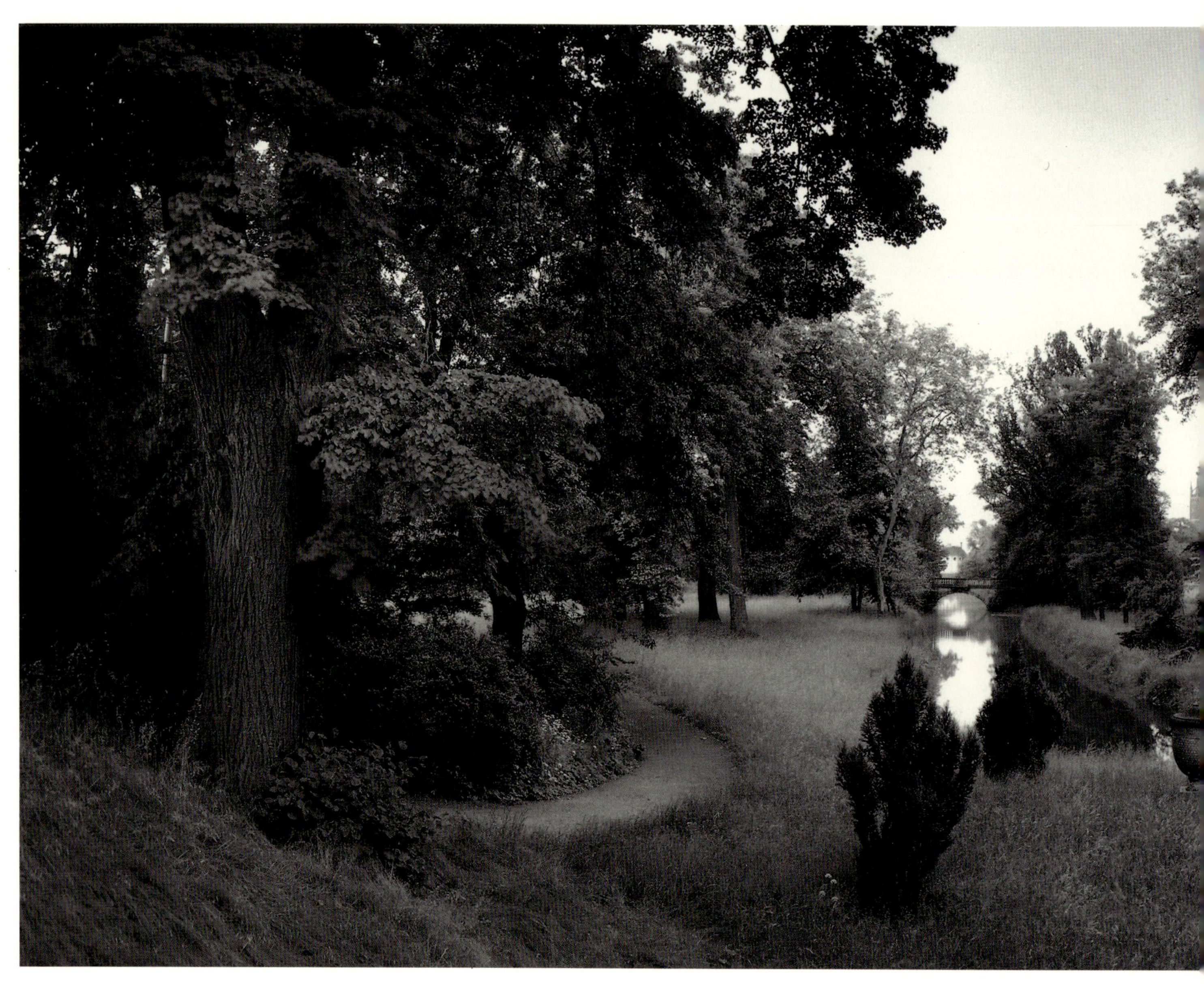

Tolerance Outlook / Golden Urn, Wörlitz (cat. no. 82.4)

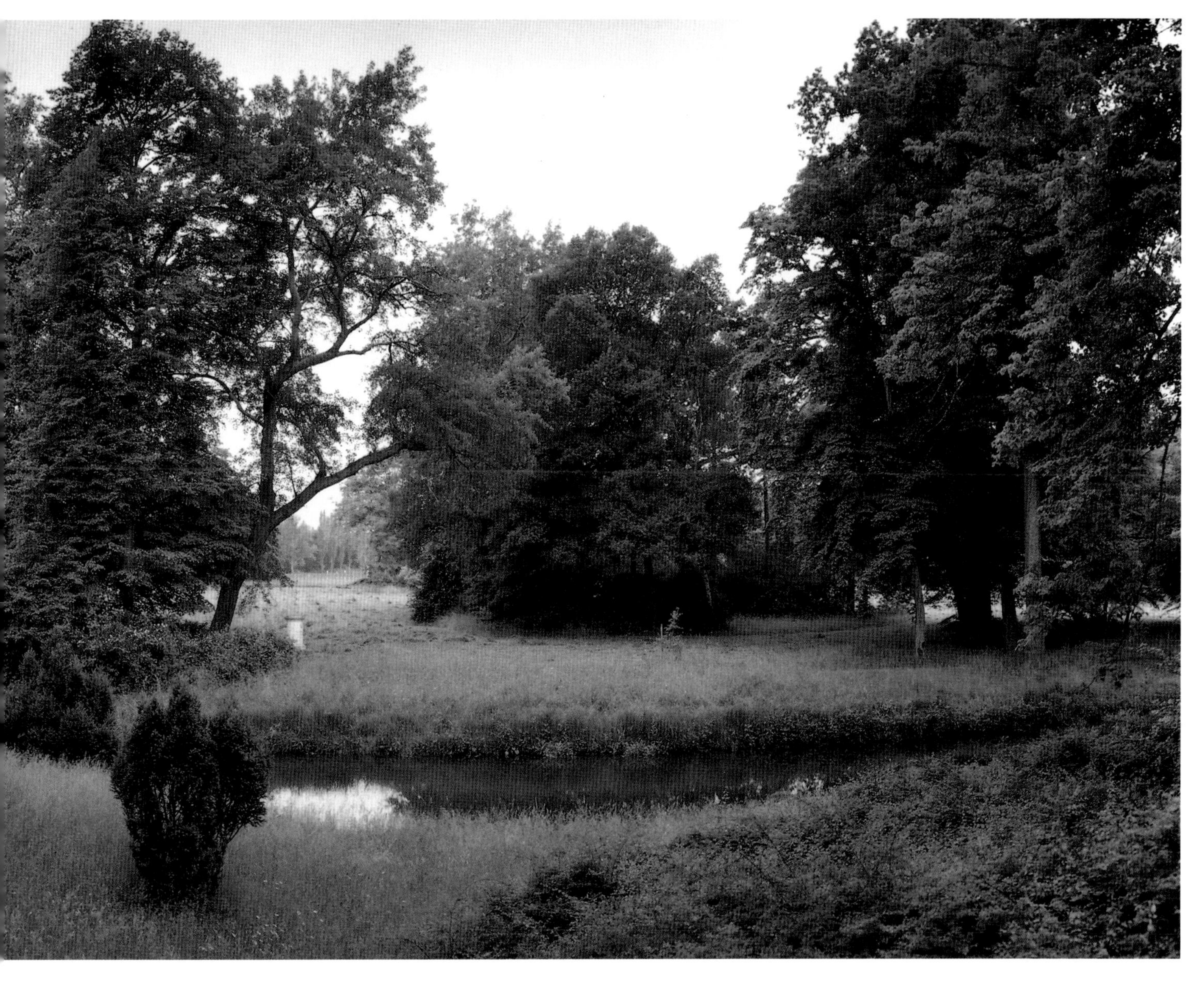

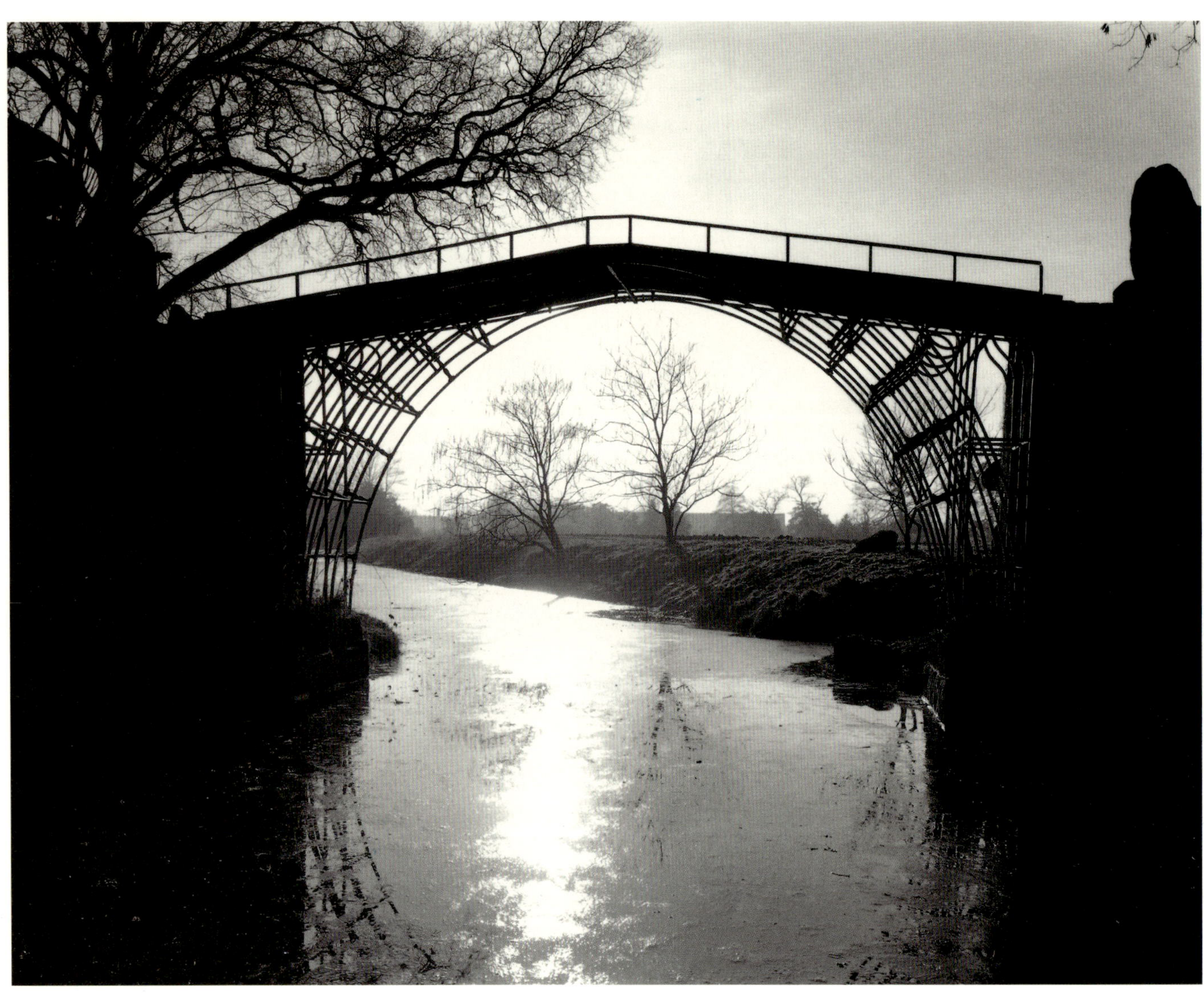

Iron Bridge, Wörlitz (cat. no. 82.10)

Temple of Venus, Wörlitz (cat. no. 82.14)

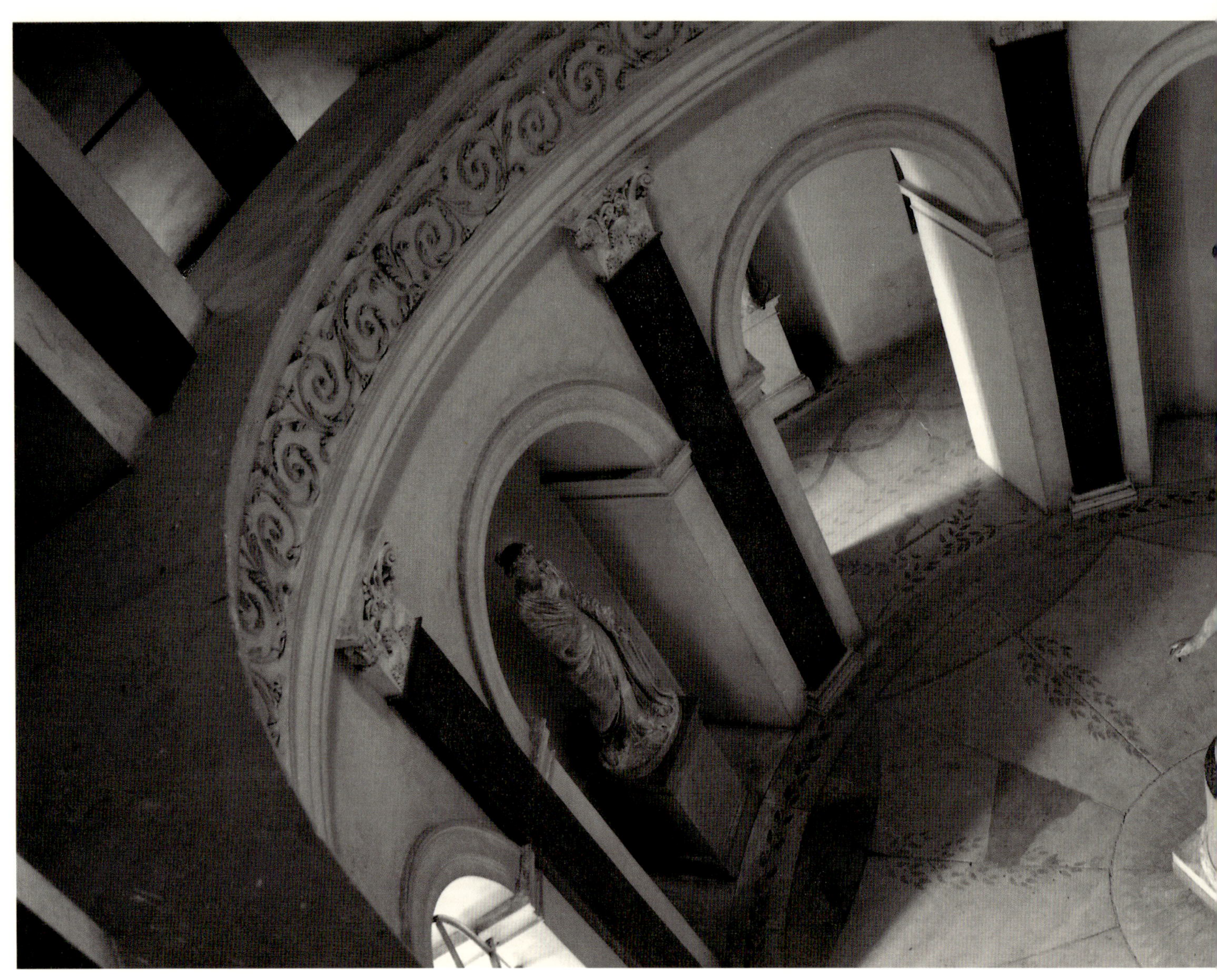

Interior of the Pantheon, Wörlitz (cat. no. 82.8)

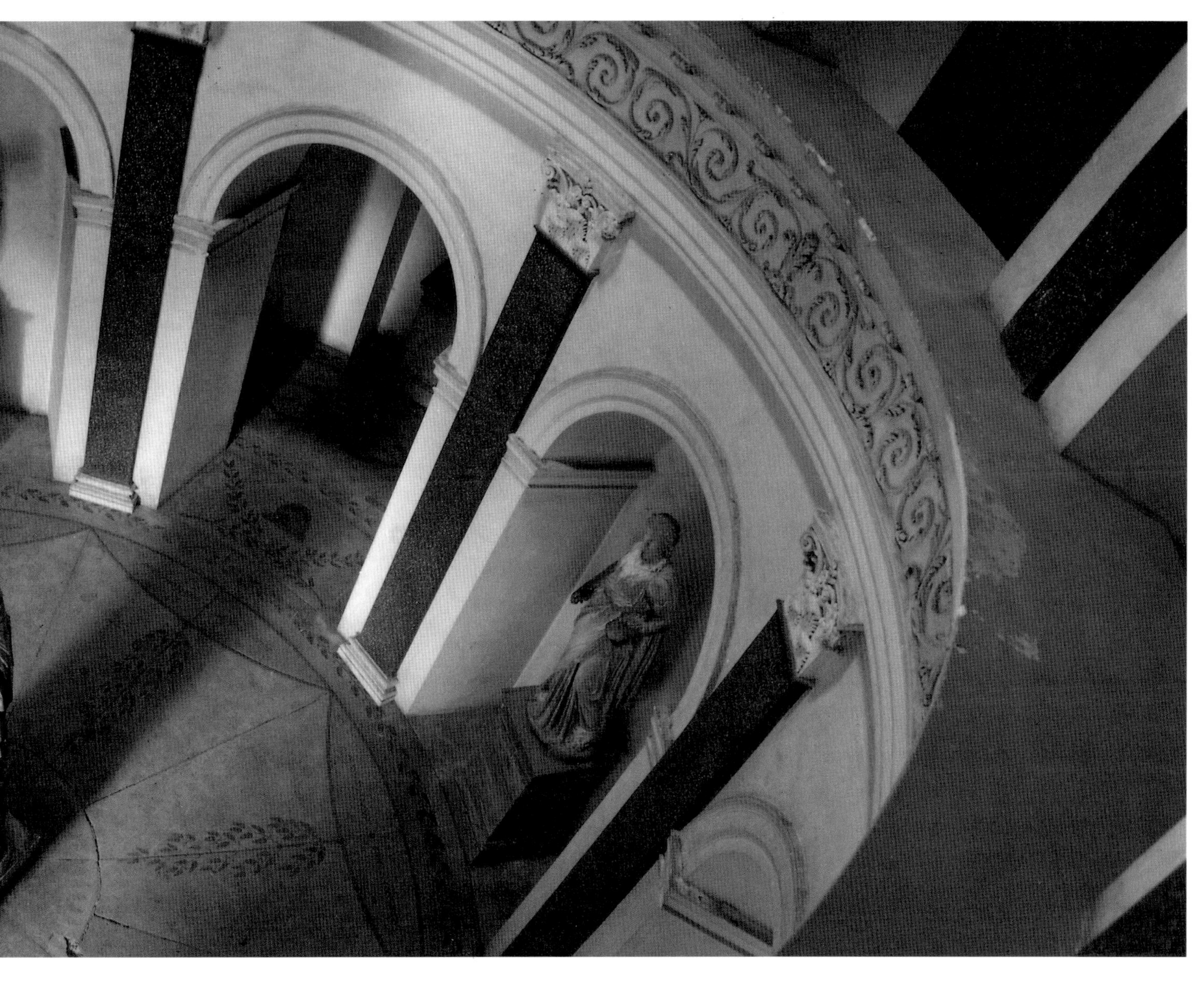

LUTZ WINKLER

1955
Born in Riesa near Dresden
since 1975
intensive work in the medium of photography
September 1984
first photographic projects in Wörlitz and Oranienbaum
since 1990
photojournalist
lives in Leipzig

82.1
CHINESISCHE PARTIE, ORANIENBAUM
CHINESE GARDEN, ORANIENBAUM
November 1987
Baryte print, selenium tint
35.5 x 30.0 cm

82.2
WOLFSKANAL WÖRLITZ
WOLF'S CANAL, WÖRLITZ
October 1989
Baryte print, selenium tint
35.5 x 30.0 cm

82.3
SCHLOSS WÖRLITZ
WÖRLITZ CASTLE
May 1994
Baryte print, selenium tint
23.0 x 57.0 cm

82.4
TOLERANZBLICK / GOLDENE URNE, WÖRLITZ
TOLERANCE OUTLOOK / GOLDEN URN, WÖRLITZ
June 1994
Baryte print, selenium tint
23.0 x 57.0 cm

82.5
WÖRLITZER SEE MIT SCHLOSS
LAKE WÖRLITZ AND SCHLOSS
June 1994
Baryte print, selenium tint
23.0 x 57.0 cm

82.6
GOTISCHES HAUS / KANALFRONT, WÖRLITZ
GOTHIC HOUSE / FAÇADE FACING THE CANAL
May 1995
Baryte print, selenium tint
39.0 x 29.0 cm

82.7
CHINESISCHES TEEHAUS, ORANIENBAUM
CHINESE TEAHOUSE, ORANIENBAUM
May 1995

Baryte print, selenium tint
29.0 x 39.0 cm

82.8
INNENANSICHT PANTHEON, WÖRLITZ
INTERIOR OF THE PANTHEON, WÖRLITZ
September 1995
Baryte print, selenium tint
23.0 x 57.0 cm

82.9
ROUSSEAU-INSEL, WÖRLITZ
ROUSSEAU ISLAND, WÖRLITZ
November 1995
Baryte print, selenium tint
39.0 x 30.0 cm

82.10
EISERNE BRÜCKE, WÖRLITZ
IRON BRIDGE, WÖRLITZ
January 1996
Baryte print, selenium tint
29.0 x 39.0 cm

82.11
PALMENSAAL, SCHLOSS WÖRLITZ
HALL OF PALMS, SCHLOSS WÖRLITZ
September 1996
Baryte print, selenium tint
23.0 x 57.0 cm

82.12
WOLFSBRÜCKE, WÖRLITZ
WOLF'S BRIDGE, WÖRLITZ
January 1997
Baryte print, selenium tint
39.0 x 29.0 cm

82.13
SCHLOSS LUISIUM, DESSAU
April 1997
Baryte print, selenium tint
29.0 x 39.0 cm

82.14
VENUSTEMPEL, WÖRLITZ
TEMPLE OF VENUS, WÖRLITZ
May 1997
Baryte print, selenium tint
29.0 x 39.0 cm

82.15
OBSTGEHÖLZ AM WÖRLITZER SEE
ORCHARD AT LAKE WÖRLITZ
May 1997
Baryte print, selenium tint
29.0 x 39.0 cm

APPENDIX

SELECTED BIBLIOGRAPHY

Albert, Jost.
"Wege und Orte im Dessau-Wörlitzer Gartenreich: Eine Untersuchung zur Entstehungsgeschichte und den Gestaltungsprinzipien einer bedeutenden Kulturlandschaft des ausgehenden 18. Jahrhunderts", in *Die Gartenkunst*, No. 2/1994, pp. 281–319.

Barock und Klassik: Kunstzentren des 18. Jahrhunderts in der Deutschen Demokratischen Republik [exhibition cat.], issued by the Niederösterreichische Landesregierung, Kulturabteilung, catalogues of Niederösterreichisches Landesmuseum, New Series, No. 146 (Vienna: 1984).

Boettiger, Carl August.
Reise nach Wörlitz 1797, from the original manuscript, edited and annotated by Erhard Hirsch, 7th edition, Staatliche Schlösser und Gärten Wörlitz, Oranienbaum, Luisium (Wörlitz: 1988).

Die Chalcographische Gesellschaft Dessau [exhibition cat.], edited by Norbert Michels, Kataloge der Anhaltischen Gemäldegalerie Dessau, Vol. 3 (Weimar: 1996).

Denkmalverzeichnis Sachsen-Anhalt, Vol. 6, *Dessau-Wörlitzer Gartenreich*, issued by the Landesamt für Denkmalpflege Sachsen-Anhalt, prepared by T. Bufe, H. Kleinschmidt, R. Schelenz, W. Steinicke (Halle: 1997).

Der Dessau-Wörlitzer Kulturkreis: Wörlitzer Beiträge zur Geschichte, issued by the Rat der Stadt Wörlitz (Wörlitz: 1965).

Friedrich Wilhelm von Erdmannsdorff 1736–1800: Zum 250. Geburtstag [exhibition cat.], issued by Staatliche Schlösser und Gärten Wörlitz, Oranienbaum, Luisium (Wörlitz: 1986).

Harksen, Marie-Luise.
Die Kunstdenkmale des Landes Anhalt, Bd. 1: Die Stadt Dessau (Burg: 1937).

Harksen, Marie-Luise.
Die Kunstdenkmale des Landes Anhalt, Bd. 2: Der Landkreis Dessau-Köthen außer Wörlitz (Burg: 1943).

Harksen, Marie-Luise.
Die Kunstdenkmale des Landes Anhalt, Bd.2,2: Stadt, Schloß und Park Wörlitz [reprint of the 1939 Burg edition] (Halle: 1998).

Hartmann, Adolf.
Der Wörlitzer Park und seine Kunstschätze (Berlin: 1913).

Heinecke, Wilfried.
"Die Leiden der Fürstin Luise von Anhalt-Dessau. Eine medizinisch-biographische Betrachtung", in *Dessauer Kalender*, 1994–1997, issued by the Stadt Dessau, Stadtarchiv.

Hirsch, Erhard.
Dessau-Wörlitz: Aufklärung und Frühklassik (Leipzig, Munich: 1985).

Hübner, Simone.
Louise von Anhalt-Dessau. Eine aufgeklärte Fürstin – Versuch einer Lebensbeschreibung [thesis] (Berlin: Humboldt Universität, 1993).

Matthisson, Friedrich von.
Erinnerungen, Vols. 3 and 4 (Zürich: 1812/14).

Mitteilungen des Vereins für Anhaltische Geschichte und Altertumskunde, published by Wilhelm Hosäus, 14 vols. (Dessau: 1875–1924).

Paul, Eberhard.
Wörlitzer Antiken: Eine Skulpturensammlung des Klassizismus, 2nd edition (Wörlitz: 1977).

Premio Internazionale Carlo Scarpa per il Giardino, l'ottava edizione, 1997, è dedicata al Dessau-Wörlitzer Gartenreich "regno dei giardini", paesaggio culturale che si svolge in un'area di trecento chilometri quadrati, sulla riva sinistra dell'Elba, nei dintorni della città di Dessau, edited by Domenico Luciani, Fondazione Benetton, Studi Richerche (Treviso: 1997).

Quilitzsch, Uwe.
Wedgwood: Klassizistische Keramik in den Gärten der Aufklärung (Hamburg: 1997).

Recke, Elisa von der.
Tagebücher und Selbstzeugnisse, edited by Christine Träger (Leipzig: 1984).

Reil, Friedrich.
Leopold Friedrich Franz, Herzog und Fürst von Anhalt-Dessau, ältest regierender Fürst von Anhalt, nach seinem Wirken und Wesen [reprint of the original Dessau edition of 1845] (Wörlitz: 1995).

Riesenfeld, E. P.
Erdmannsdorff, der Baumeister des Herzogs Leopold Friedrich Franz von Anhalt-Dessau (Berlin: 1913).

Rode, August von.
Beschreibung des Fürstlichen Anhalt-Dessauischen Landhauses und Englischen Gartens zu Wörlitz [reprint of the original Dessau edition of 1814] (Wörlitz: 1996).

Rode, August.
Leben des Herrn Friedrich Wilhelm von Erdmannsdorff [reprint of the original Dessau edition of 1801] (Wörlitz: 1994).

Das Schöne mit dem Nützlichen: Die Dessau-Wörlitzer Kulturlandschaft. Bemühungen um die Darstellung gartendenkmalpflegerischer Arbeit anhand historischer Ansichten des 18. und 19. Jahrhunderts sowie Fotografien des gegenwärtigen Zustandes [exhibition cat.], issued by Staatliche Schlösser und Gärten Wörlitz, Oranienbaum, Luisium (Wörlitz: 1987).

Sir William Chambers und der Englische-Chinesische Garten in Europa
[published report of the symposium entitled "Sir William Chambers und der
Englisch-Chinesische Garten in Europa" in Oranienbaum, 5–7 October
1995], edited by Thomas Weiss, Kataloge und Schriften der Staatlichen
Schlösser und Gärten Wörlitz, Oranienbaum, Luisium, Vol. 2 (Ostfildern-
Ruit: 1997)

Spieler, Ralf-Torsten.
*Friedrich Wilhelm von Erdmannsdorff: Begründer der klassizistischen Baukunst
in Deutschland* [dissertation in 2 vols.] (Halle/Saale: 1981).

Stürmer, Michael.
Scherben des Glücks: Klassizismus und Revolution (Berlin: 1987).

Trauzettel, Ludwig.
"Das Gartenreich von Dessau und Wörlitz", in *Gärten der Goethezeit*, edited
by Harri Günther (Leipzig: 1993), pp. 44–75.

Verheißungen eines gefährdeten Gartenreiches: Wörlitz [documentation of a
symposium conducted on 10 June 1994], issued by the Förderverein Dessau-
Wörlitzer Anlagen e.V. (Frankfurt am Main: 1995).

Wedgwood 1795–1995: Englische Keramik in Wörlitz [exhibition cat.], edited by
Thomas Weiss, Vol. 1 of the wissenschaftliche Bestandskataloge der Staatlichen Schlösser und Gärten Wörlitz, Oranienbaum, Luisium (Wörlitz: 1995).

Weiss, Thomas.
"'Den Freunden der Natur und Kunst': Das Gartenreich Dessau-Wörlitz und
Andrea Palladio", in *Bauen nach der Natur – Palladio: Die Erben Palladios
in Nordeuropa* [exhibition cat.], edited by Jörgen Bracker (Ostfildern: 1997),
pp. 181–199.

Weltbild Wörlitz: Entwurf einer Kulturlandschaft [exhibition cat.], edited by
Frank-Andreas Bechtoldt and Thomas Weiss, Kataloge und Schriften der
Staatlichen Schlösser und Gärten Wörlitz, Oranienbaum, Luisium 1 (Wörlitz:
1996).

Wörlitz: Ein Garten der Aufklärung [exhibition cat.], edited by Gerd Biegel,
Braunschweigisches Landesmuseum Schloßverwaltung Schwetzingen, Staatliche Schlösser und Gärten Wörlitz, Oranienbaum, Luisium, publications of
the Braunschweigisches Landesmuseum 66 (Braunschweig: 1992).

INDEX OF HISTORICAL NAMES

(Leopold III. Friedrich Franz von Anhalt-Dessau and Friedrich Wilhelm von
Erdmannsdorff were not included in the index of historical names.)

For the Friends of Nature and Art
The Garden Kingdom of Prince Franz von Anhalt-Dessau
in Age of Enlightenment

An Exhibition presented by Institut für Auslandsbeziehungen

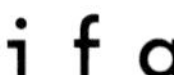 i f a ▮

and the Kulturstiftung DessauWörlitz

Concept and selection: Thomas Weiss, Uwe Quilitzsch
Head Curator: Ursula Zeller
Organisation and Realisation: Bernd Burock
Essays: Ursula Bode, Michael Stürmer, Thomas Weiss
Catalogue of works on exhibit: Uwe Quilitzsch, Daniela Clare

Translations: John Southard
Editing: Maria Platte
Layout: Christine Müller
Printed by: Dr. Cantz'sche Druckerei, Ostfildern bei Stuttgart

© 1997 by Institut für Auslandsbeziehungen, Kulturstiftung DessauWörlitz,
photographers and authors

Published by
Verlag Gerd Hatje, Senefelderstraße 12, 73760 Ostfildern-Ruit
Tel. (0) 711/4 40 50
Fax (0) 711/4 40 52 20

Distribution in the US
DAP, Distributed Art Publishers
155 Avenue of the Americas, Second Floor
New York, N.Y. 10013
T. (001) 212 - 627 19 99
F. (001) 212 - 627 84 94

ISBN 3-7757-0715-8
Printed in Germany

Frontispiece:
Artist unknown, Silhouette of Prince Leopold Friedrich Franz von Anhalt
Dessau, circa 1780, scissor cut, Kulturstiftung DessauWörlitz

Cover illustration:
Lake Wörlitz and Schloss, cat no. 82.5 (Photo: Lutz Winkler)